Agrarian Reform and Farmer Resistance in Punjab

This book examines different dimensions of farmer agitations in Punjab, India. It situates the 2020–2021 farmer resistance movement within the wider context of India's post-independent development trajectory and provides a thorough analysis of various aspects of the farmers' movement in India.

The volume contextualizes Punjab's history of farmer resistance, organization and mobilization strategies, the globalization of the movement, ways of both sustaining the movement and building resilience. While providing a critical understanding of the three farm laws introduced in India in 2020, the book looks at how they may impact farm operations and livelihoods in the post-Green Revolution period and evaluates strategies of inclusive mobilization for gathering support and sustaining the movement both within India and abroad, with special focus on the role of the Sikh diaspora. Essays in this volume also discuss the participation of women in the struggle and how their experience has the potential to transform gender relations both at home and in the public sphere.

Integrated, comprehensive and concisely written by well-known experts, this book will be of interest to those involved with Punjab's social, political and economic history, and students and researchers of food and agriculture in developing countries, peasant and social movements, Indian federalism and role of diasporas as non-state actors.

Shinder Singh Thandi, PhD, is a former Professor who taught in the Global Studies Department at the University of California, Santa Barbara, USA. Previously, he was based at Coventry University, UK, where he was head of Department of Economics, Finance and Accounting from 2009 to 2015. He is founder-editor of the *Journal of Sikh & Punjab Studies*, published since 1994. He has published many journal articles and book chapters on Indian and Punjabi migration and on different dimensions of Sikh diaspora and homeland relations. He co-authored *A South Asian History of Britain: Four Centuries of Peoples from the Indian Sub-Continent* (with Michael Fisher and Shompa Lahiri; 2007) and co-edited *People on the Move: Punjabi Colonial and Post-Colonial Migration* (with Ian Talbot; 2004) and *Punjabi Identity in a Global Context* (with Pritam Singh; 1999).

Agrarian Reform and Farmer Resistance in Punjab

Mobilization and Resilience

Edited by
Shinder Singh Thandi

Routledge
Taylor & Francis Group
LONDON AND NEW YORK

First published 2023
by Routledge
4 Park Square, Milton Park, Abingdon, Oxon OX14 4RN

and by Routledge
605 Third Avenue, New York, NY 10158

Routledge is an imprint of the Taylor & Francis Group, an informa business

British Library Cataloguing-in-Publication Data
A catalogue record for this book is available from the British Library

ISBN: 978-1-032-29189-5 (hbk)
ISBN: 978-1-032-33522-3 (pbk)
ISBN: 978-1-003-32000-5 (ebk)

DOI: 10.4324/9781003320005

Typeset in Sabon
by codeMantra

Dedicated to all the farmers who participated in the 2020–2021 agitation, including those who gave their lives during the struggle

Contents

Contributors

Dr. Sucha S. Gill is a former Director General (2010–2014) of Centre for Research in Rural and Industrial Development (CRRID), Chandigarh, and also worked there as Senior Professor and Research Coordinator (2014–2019). He also served as member of Revenue Commission, Government of Punjab (2019–2022). Earlier, he taught at Punjabi University Patiala (1972–2010) and served as Professor and Head of the Department of Economics (1997–2000), Dean of Social Sciences (2004–2006), Dean of Academic Affairs (2006–2008), Dean of Research (2008–2009) and Director of Centre for North-West Asia (Pakistan and Afghanistan (2006–2010). He has published extensively on Punjab in reputed journals and edited several volumes. Among these include an edited volume *Philosophy of Guru Nanak* (2020); *Chasing High Growth Rate and Tryst with Inclusiveness* (CRRID, 2019); and edited volumes: *Economic and Environment Sustainability in South Asia* with Lakhwinder Singh and Reena Marwah (Routledge, 2010) and *Land Reforms in India: Capitalist Intervention in Punjab and Haryana* (2001). He is at present Vice Chairman of the Indian Association of Social Science Institutions (IASSI).

Dr. Surinder S. Jodhka is a Professor of Sociology at the Jawaharlal Nehru University, New Delhi. He researches on social inequalities, caste in contemporary times, rural/agrarian change and community identities. His recent publications include *India's Villages in the 21st Century: Revisits and Revisions* (ed with Edward Simpson 2019); *Mapping the Elite: Power, Privilege and Inequality* (ed. with Jules Naudet, 2019); *A Handbook of Rural India*. 2018 (ed.); *Contested Hierarchies: Caste and Power in 21st Century* (ed. with James Manor) 2018; *Inequality in Capitalist Societies,* Routledge (with Boike Rehbien and Jesse Souza) 2018; *The Indian Middle-Class*, 2016 (with Aseem Prakash); *Caste in Contemporary India,* Routledge 2015/2018; and *Caste: Oxford India Short Introductions*, 2012.

Dr. Amandeep Kaur is currently Assistant Professor of English at Guru Nanak Dev University, Amritsar. Her research maps the growth of modern Indian poetry from its progressive phase during and after the colonial period, identifying its transformational propensities with a focus on its representation of resistance through the matrices of caste, class, and gender in the post-progressive phase.

Swaroopa Lahiri is a doctoral student in the Global Studies Department of University of California, Santa Barbara. Her research focuses on how female farm operators, who are based in climate vulnerable regions of India that are also characterized by increasing male exit from agriculture, conduct agricultural operations. She earned a Master's degree in International Affairs from Columbia University's School of International and Public Affairs and a Bachelor's degree from Sciences Po Paris. Her work has been featured in the *Journal of South Asian Studies*, *Telegraph India* and *Wire*. ORCID Number: 0000-0002-1848-3333

Dr. Prabhjot Parmar is an Associate Professor of English at the University of the Fraser Valley, Abbotsford, Canada. She earned her PhD degree in English in postcolonial studies at the University of Western Ontario and earned her Master's degrees in English from Queen's University and Panjab University. She is co-editor of *When Your Voice Tastes like Home: Immigrant Women Write* and has published articles on dementia and music, Partition, Bollywood and the history of Punjabi Cinema. Her research and teaching interests include postcolonial literatures with a focus on South Asian literature and cinema, Partition and Indian soldiers in WWI; through these, her work is strongly linked with community work – anti-racism, anti-colonial and decolonial narrative, Indigenization, migration, violence against women and social justice.

Dr. Ronki Ram is currently a Shaheed Bhagat Singh Chair Professor of Political Science at Panjab University (PU), Chandigarh; a Visiting Professor at the University of Wolverhampton (UK) and University of Ladakh (India); and a member of State Higher Education Council, UT Chandigarh. He also served as Dean of Faculty of Arts, PU; member Senate of PU & NIPPER, Mohali; Hon-Director of ICSSR, NWRC, Chandigarh; member of INCCU with UNESCO; and ICCR Chair Professor of India Studies at Leiden University, the Netherlands and Ryukoku University, Kyoto, Japan. He has published extensively on social mobility and identity politics in books and international peer-reviewed journals like *Modern Asian Studies*, *Journal of Asian Studies*, *Asian Survey*, *Contributions to Indian Sociology*, *Journal of Sikh & Punjab Studies* and *South Asian Survey* among others.

Dr Pritam Singh is a Professor Emeritus at Oxford Brookes Business School. He is author of *Federalism, Nationalism and Development: India and the Punjab Economy* (Routledge, London, 2008; 2nd ed., 2019); *Economy, Culture and Human Rights: Turbulence in Punjab, India and Beyond* (Three Essays Collective, Delhi, 2010), *Hindu Bias in Indian*

Constitution (Delhi, 2017), *Institutional Communalism in India* (Delhi, 2019) and a co-editor with S. Thandi of *Punjabi Identity in a Global Context* (OUP, 1999).

In June 2015, he was awarded the Distinguished Achievement Award in Political Economy for the Twenty-First Century by the World Association of Political Economy, and in May 2021, the University of California, Riverside honoured him with 'a Lifetime Achievement Award for his distinguished contribution to the Punjab Research Group in the UK to promote Sikh and Punjab Studies'. He is on the editorial board of *Capitalism Nature Socialism* and has contributed to *Routledge Handbook of Eco-Socialism* (2021). ORCID number: 0000-0001-7706-0915

Dr. Sukhpal Singh is a Professor and former Chairperson of Centre for Management in Agriculture (CMA), IIM, Ahmedabad, a former DG of Centre for Research in Rural and Industrial Development, Chandigarh, and a former Professor and Head of Institute of Economic Growth (IEG), New Delhi.

He is a Fellow of the Indian Society of Agricultural Economics, Mumbai, since 2018 and founding Editor, *Millennial Asia-An International Journal of Asian Studies* published by Sage. He was a visiting fellow at IDS, Sussex, Chulalongkorn University, Bangkok, University of Manchester and Copenhagen Business School.

Besides 140 research articles and book chapters, he has authored/co-authored 14 books/monographs including *Covid-19 Pandemic and Economic Development, 2021* (co-edited) and *Reverse Subsidies in Global Monopsony Capitalism, 2022* (co-authored).

Dr. Sukhdev S. Sohal is a retired Professor from Department of History, Guru Nanak Dev University, Amritsar (Punjab), India. He has to his credit over 100 research papers, articles and book reviews in reputed journals and popular magazines. His areas of interest include social and cultural transformation and political economy of the colonial Punjab. He has authored *The Making of the Middle Classes in the Punjab (1849–1947)* and *Credit, Rural Debt and the Punjab Peasantry (1849–1947)*. He has edited three monographs. He has supervised over a dozen doctoral theses. He headed the Department of History and School of Social Sciences and Chair for the Study of Ghadar Movement at Guru Nanak Dev University, Amritsar. He was editor of the *Journal of Regional History.*

Dr. Virginia Van Dyke is currently an affiliate Assistant Professor of International Studies at the University of Washington. She was formerly an Assistant Professor of Political Science at the University of Wisconsin-Milwaukee. She has published on the topics of religion and politics, state-level politics in India and coalition politics.

Preface and Acknowledgements

Although the agrarian sector in India has been experiencing deteriorating conditions over a long period, rural distress worsened even more over the last decade. Successive governments, with a distinct urban and industrial bias, have been more interested in offering short-term fixes such as 'debt waivers', usually for electoral gain, rather than dealing with the underlying structural problems which perpetuate inequalities and rural distress. Incidences of rising farmer indebtedness, farmer suicides and growing landlessness increased throughout the country due to official indifference. Lack of employment opportunities, whether in the non-farm rural sector or formal sector of urban areas, led to emergence of many social movements where even the so-called 'dominant rural castes' – Jats in Haryana, Patels in Gujarat and Marathas in Maharashtra – felt threatened and began campaigns to demand Other Backward Class (OBC) status to take advantage of jobs reserved in the public sector for this category. Farmer protests also gathered momentum with Delhi witnessing one of the largest farming rallies in the summer of 2017. A policy of 'doubling farmers' incomes by 2022' was floated by the government to appease farmers, but only to be dropped quietly.

The state of Punjab, acknowledged as the 'food bowl' of India, that had witnessed an unwavering and successful implementation of the Green Revolution strategy from the mid-1960s was now also beginning to experience diminishing returns in agriculture coupled with pending environmental crisis. Sustainability of rural livelihoods was threatened because of stagnating productivity, tired and poisoned soil due to massive usage of fertilizers and pesticides, depletion of water table due to intensive wheat-paddy cropping rotation, especially of water-guzzling paddy, growing farmer indebtedness, landlessness and marginalization and farmer suicides. Causes and solutions to this acute agrarian crisis have been widely discussed by academics and policymakers for over a couple of decades but nothing of substance was adopted to alleviate the crisis, with business as usual only worsening the malaise.

The real jolt to the status quo came with an attempt by the BJP government to transform agriculture by imposing neo-liberal solutions that had already taken hold in other sectors of the economy since economic reforms began in the early 1990s. The government, rather hastily and arrogantly, passed three new farm laws which would impact the procurement, storage and distribution of agricultural produce. The Punjabi farmers, fearing end of the Minimum Support Price system and impending land grab by agri-businesses which posed a direct threat to their livelihoods, reacted angrily to the Ordinances and then passing of these new laws and immediately launched a *morcha*, initially in Punjab but later made a call to march towards Delhi. Several protest sites emerged on the borders of Delhi after farmers from other states, particularly from Haryana and Uttar Pradesh, also joined the agitation. Discussions between farmer organizations and government officials failed to resolve the issue and, in fact, the trust gap between them widened over time. With the farm protests on the borders of Delhi approaching their first anniversary, Prime Minister Modi took everyone by surprise by announcing that the new farm laws would be fully withdrawn. They were, in fact, as hastily repealed as they were introduced.

The 2020–2021 farmers' protest movement was the longest and the largest social movement in the history of modern India and Punjab, with the latter itself having over a hundred year history of peasant struggles. The movement demonstrated several achievements, the legacy of which may take some time to disappear from public memory. First, the movement was able to endure and overcome the onslaught leashed upon it by an authoritarian state and a compliant media with its intention of demeaning it. Second, it offered a powerful and successful resistance to the wholesale encroachment into agriculture of a discredited neo-liberal ideology, an ideology, wherever tried, that had failed to protect the weak and vulnerable and only giving primacy to corporate needs. Third, the movement received widespread support, despite provocations, from different sections of the rural population from across different parts of the country, even from some urban areas. Further, the Punjabi diaspora not only fully support the resistance movement but also actively lobbied for wider global support. Finally, the movement succeeded because it displayed remarkable unity among farmer organizations, despite attempts at division and rising death toll among participants. The movement clearly demonstrated that no government could escape or ignore the power of popular protest within a democratic set-up. The success of this resistance movement will provide important lessons, an inspiration and hope to other social movements which are fighting injustice. Unfortunately, what is not clear is whether success of the movement will create conducive conditions in Punjab, leading to implementation of much needed agrarian reforms that would put agriculture towards the path of sustainability. Scholars may want to revisit this important question in subsequent years.

This prolonged farmer protest generated lot of comment and discussion in the print, visual and social media but generally escaped close and more nuanced academic scrutiny, especially of different dimensions of the protest movement. Noting this vacuum in contextualizing and understanding this historic movement, and after discussions with some academic colleagues, as editor of the *Journal of Sikh and Punjab Studies*, I began to approach some renowned experts on the political economy of Punjab and Punjab agriculture, with view to commissioning papers to be published in a special double issue of the journal focused on Farmers' Agitation. This journal had carried many articles on the evolving agrarian crisis in Punjab in previous years and it made sense to devote a whole issue to it. Papers for this issue were originally written in the summer of 2021 when protests were still in full swing with no end in sight, and an issue containing 13 papers was published in early December 2021. Soon after its publication, with an impasse in negotiations and protests on borders of Delhi approaching their first anniversary, Prime Minister Modi made the remarkable announcement on revoking the farm laws. After further discussion with some of the contributors, we agreed to publish a selected number of revised papers which would take into account repeal of the farm laws and ending of this unprecedented farmer protest movement at the close of 2021. This publication provides the first comprehensive assessment by leading academics working on Punjab of Modi government's attempts at agrarian reform and subsequent farmers' protest movement and is expected to leave an important historical record.

In preparing for this publication, a number of individuals helped to define its parameters and advised on the important themes that needed to be incorporated and potential contributors that could be approached. I am highly indebted to Ronki Ram, Amarjit Chandan, Pritam Singh and Gurinder Singh Mann with their help in this regard. I would also like to gratefully acknowledge the permission granted by the *Global Institute of Sikh Studies*, the publisher of the *Journal of Sikh and Punjab Studies*, to reproduce revised versions of papers that were originally published in the Journal in Vol. 29, Nos. 1&2 (Spring–Fall, 2022). As result of the revisions, some of the titles of the papers were also changed to better reflect the revised content and all contributors gave permission for their publication. This permission applies to both print and digital versions of this publication, including any subsequent editions. Finally, I am also grateful to the commissioning and editorial team of Routledge of Taylor & Francis Group, for making this publication possible.

Shinder S. Thandi
June 2022

Introduction to Agrarian Reforms and the 2020–2021 Farmer Resistance

A Momentous *Morcha**

Shinder S. Thandi

During 2020–2021, India witnessed one of the widest, longest, peaceful and most inclusive farmers' *morcha* (protest) with its roots firmly in Punjab and with Punjabi farmers acting as the vanguard of the movement. On November 19, 2021, day of Guru Nanak's *gurpurab*, as thousands of more farmers started converging towards Delhi's borders, to mark the first anniversary, still totally united on their minimal goals of getting the three controversial farm laws revoked and seek legal guarantee on Minimum Support Prices, Prime Minister Modi did a totally unexpected and humiliating U-Turn by announcing the revoking of the three controversial farm laws in the coming winter session of Parliament. However, there was no apology to the farmers or to families of over 700 famers who lost their lives agitating against the laws, but only to the country for his inability to persuade 'a minority of farmers' to trust him for only looking out for their welfare. This announcement demonstrated the power, strength and tenacity of this year-long movement, despite all attempts by the government to demonize the movement and suppress farmers' democratic rights.

In preparing for this edited book, back in February 2021, a number of the most eminent academic experts with extensive research experience on Punjab were approached to write papers on the ongoing farmer protests and almost all of them responded positively and sent their submissions in a timely manner. Most of these papers were written during summer 2021 when there was an impasse in negotiations between the government and farmers. Most of these papers were originally published in a special double issue of the *Journal of Sikh and Punjab Studies* (Vol. 29, Spring-Fall 2022) in late November 2021 just as Prime Minster Modi made his surprising announcement on revoking the three farm laws. After consultation with some of the contributors and discussions with Routledge a decision was taken to bring out a book containing a selection of the papers but thoroughly revised to take into account the end of the agitation towards end of December 2021.

It was the wish of many contributors to personally visit the camp sites and undertake interviews with various actors and stakeholders to enrich their analysis, however, the ongoing public health crisis and travel restrictions

DOI: 10.4324/9781003320005-1

meant only some were able to do so. Despite this limitation, this collection of papers provides multi-disciplinary approaches in understanding and critically examining the historical, sociological, literary, political, economic and diasporic dimensions of the movement. The collection is expected to provide a comprehensive and rich repository of archival material on the 2020–2021 Farmers' Movement for future generation of scholars. The agitation reaffirmed Punjab's long tradition of being the cauldron of resistance – fighting *against* oppression, tyranny and authoritarianism and standing firmly *for* social justice, dignity, freedom and sovereignty.

The Wider Context: Indian Development Trajectory and Rural Distress

Not wishing to dismiss the enduring legacies of British colonialism and the size and demographic complexity of India or to underplay India's great achievements in reducing levels of absolute poverty, it has become clear to many scholars over the past few years that the political economy of development model utilized by Indian policymakers in its 75-year post-independent period has failed to deliver welfare for the majority of its people. This is clearly reflected in India's comparatively low position in leading indices used to measure different dimensions of economic and human development. India is ranked 131 out of 189 countries in UNDP's *Human Development Index* (2021); ranked 101 out of 116 in the *Global Hunger Index* (2021); ranked 62 out of 74 emerging countries in the World Economic Forum's *Inclusive Development Index* (2021); ranked 111 out of 162 in the *Human Freedom Index* (2020); ranked 40 out of 40 in the Center for Global Development's *Commitment to Development Index* (2021); and ranked 168 out of 180 countries in Yale's *Environmental Performance Index* (2020). Further, according to the World Bank, India's per capita income is only US$1,900, much lower than the global average of US$10,909 and of her much loved-and-hated neighbor China at US$10,500 and some 33 times lower than America at $63,543. Any independent observer looking at these statistics would term the Indian experience as that of a failed model in terms of human development.

Yet, this dismal performance has not stopped successive Indian governments from presenting an alternative image to the outside world. In fact, the gap between 'Brand India' that governments like to present to the world, often marketed in terms of Shining India, Incredible India, Global India, Make in India, etc., and 'Reality' as reflected in major socio-economic indicators discussed above, has continued to widen. Whilst there can be no doubt *some sectors and regions* of the economy or parts of it (e.g. IT and Health Services, Trade and Tourism), and *some classes* of people (Middle and Upper) have prospered in India but many sectors, regions and classes have not – just examine the detailed statistics behind the indices. How do we make sense of all this? Whilst there are many explanations, the Urban Bias Thesis, as developed by Michael Lipton in his influential but under-rated book, *Why the Poor Stay Poor* (Temple-Smith: London, 1977),[1] is helpful in providing an overarching framework for understanding the major thrust of Indian development strategies, whether in the form of Nehruvian Socialism and Neo-Liberalism, both in their soft and hard form from the mid-1980s, or the latter's current variant with its strong Corporatist leanings.[2] All the underlying economic growth or development models, whether at aggregated macro level or in dual economy form, are underpinned by notion of Urban Bias, that is, on the understanding that in the process of economic development, resource allocation decisions have to prioritize industrialization and urbanization with the rural sector passively serving the needs of business and urban classes until structural transformation towards a fully developed stage is achieved. In these models, with their strong ethno-centric and euro-centric bias, it is taken for granted that as industrialization and urbanization proceed, employment will be generated, raising urban incomes and creating even more rural to urban migration until most of the surplus labor is absorbed in the urban sector. The accompanying process of *Trickle Down*, working through employment generation, supposedly improves income inequalities and raises living standards and welfare of all. The only critical decision policymakers need to make is on who is to act as *the* agent of development – the State, the Market or some Mix of the two? Indian policymakers started with total belief in the ability of the State to transform India but moved towards a Mix when it became clear Statist policies geared towards comprehensive development planning were not working. The State also introduced a variety of social safety nets to mitigate rapidly rising poverty and hunger. The Green Revolution strategy was introduced in the 1960s to stop 'ship-to-mouth' food imports and focused on incentivizing farmers in already well-developed agrarian regions such as Punjab and Haryana, to produce food surpluses which would then ensure national food security. The Public Distribution System (PDS) that was developed was reliant on procuring foodgrains at guaranteed minimum support prices, from food surplus states such as Punjab and Haryana and distributing them to the poor at subsidized rates in food-deficit states. The PDS became the cornerstone safety net that prevented acute forms of hunger, malnutrition and famine in post-Independent but not totally eradicating them. Undoubtedly, Punjab, as a food surplus state, benefited greatly from this system of having an assured market for its produce and farmers producing foodgrains, increasingly wheat and rice, experienced a relatively higher standard of living than rural people in food deficit states or poor people in urban areas. But as it became abundantly clear some three decades later, this relative economic prosperity was not sustainable as there were serious limitations to this form of rural extraction system. Punjab's agriculture not only began to stagnate but was also becoming unsustainable due to the economic and ecological consequences of the specialized wheat-rice cropping pattern that subsidized agricultural policies produced.

The economic consequences of massive usage of chemical inputs like fertilizers and pesticides had their impact on both fatiguing and polluting the soil, and water-guzzling rice cultivation both disturbed and depleted the water table raising fears of Punjab becoming a desert in time. Whilst the large farmers, who happen to be a minority in Punjab, benefited, the majority, the small and marginal farmers, bore the brunt of adverse terms of trade as produce prices failed to keep up with rising input costs, increasing farmer indebtedness and landlessness. We begin to witness rising incidence of farmer suicides and many small and marginal farmers started to desert farming altogether. This agrarian crisis, when coupled with no significant development in employment-generating large-scale industrialization in the state, is clearly reflected in the continuing downward slide in Punjab's ranking in the league table of Indian states based on per capita income.[3]

The global ideological shift towards Neo-Liberalism, also known as the Washington Consensus because the ideology was aggressively promoted globally by the two Washington-based financial institutions, the IMF and World Bank, from the early 1980s, with its twin beliefs in 'magic of the market' and 'State as the problem, *not* the solution' to development, began to permeate economic policies around the world. India's policymakers also eventually had to succumb and align their policies to the Washington Consensus. In fact, they had no alternative given the severe balance of payments crisis of 1991–1992 and the mandatory conditionality imposed by the IMF and World Bank to access its structural adjustment loans. Over time, almost all sectors of the Indian economy have been subjected to market fundamentalism, with the State *facilitating* through liberalization, privatization, deregulation and opening up to global trade and competition, albeit with only limited degree of success. Although these policies gave an initial boost to economic growth, it could not be sustained and in fact, there was growing evidence of 'jobless growth' with the economy, perhaps, even entering into premature de-industrialization with the services sector leapfrogging manufacturing. Modi government's response to the slowdown in economic growth was to double down on neo-liberal policies despite mounting evidence of increasing income, regional and spatial inequalities, rising unemployment and growing agrarian distress. The more visible symptoms of this rapidly growing rural and agrarian distress, in the form of rising farmer suicides and farmer indebtedness, were either denied or 'resolved' through putting a sticking-plaster of farm loan waivers or slowly raising wages on work guaranteed for only 100 days of the year.[4] This was Urban Bias in action with a vengeance because the agricultural and rural sector was crying out for massive public sector development which was denied. Even several nation-wide mass protests by farmers failed to move the government except for repeating hollow platitudes about doubling farmer incomes.

Although ideas on introducing agrarian reforms had been floated for some time, the agricultural sector had been spared radical reform until

2020, presumably because of its importance in providing national food security and political risk involved given the sheer number of people who could potentially be impacted by such reforms. There are, of course, alternative ways of dealing with the agrarian crisis and reforms, for instance, *either* through massive public sector investment in rural areas, as mentioned above, to cover all aspects of food production, procurement and distribution, crop diversification, incentivizing modernization of agricultural practices and implementing strategies for raising both agricultural employment and non-farm rural employment *or* choosing to open up the sector to market forces with all its intended and unintended consequences. Ruling out the former option or even proposing a policy of gradual reform in consultation with all the stakeholders, the Modi government, indebted to a few powerful corporates who had bank-rolled the RSS-BJP combine into power in two successive Lok Sabha elections[5] and who had signposted their intent on entering the 'protected' agricultural sector and country's food supply chain, hastily and in a callous manner, perhaps calculating that opposition will be muted given the country was undergoing an acute public health crisis created by the COVID pandemic, decided to bypass the usual legislative and democratic norms to radically reform existing arrangements for procuring, storing, distributing and marketing foodgrains. The market-oriented reforms, discussed in detail in this book, would undoubtedly favor a small number of agrifood enterprises at the expense of millions of producers – the farmers. Most of the government's promised income benefits to individual farmers, who would be 'liberated' to sell their produce to anyone and anywhere, were based on pure neo-classical fantasyland economics because buying power of a very small number of Indian or global agrifood corporates would drive down farm prices to a level below production costs of farmers, destroying farmer livelihoods. Overwhelming evidence from around the world confirms this impact and also explains why governments, both in rich and poor countries, continue to have farm price support policies.[6] The manner in which farm laws were introduced was also indicative of Prime Minister Modi's authoritarian style of governance and RSS-BJP combine's larger political project of building Hindutva which necessarily requires greater centralization in decision-making and weakening of federalism, a trend which some have described as moving from 'co-operative federalism' to 'coercive federalism'.

Reflecting on what Galbraith had argued back in 1952 in the context of rise in American agribusiness, unless the farmers quickly develop *effective* counter-vailing power through producer, consumer and citizen organizations, their future would be pretty bleak.[7] The farmers' movements in colonial and post-colonial India were all attempts at building counter-vailing power but unfortunately only had limited or temporary impact. The recent farmer agitation learned from past struggles by strengthening counter-vailing power through building unity in the face of great hostility from the central government, the pro-government media, urban elites whose orientation is focused more towards their global assets and interests than on happenings in their rural hinterlands and urban-based apologist academics and opinion makers who find it difficult to de-colonize their minds from euro-centric ideological thinking. These apologists had nothing better to offer, other than mime colonial tropes about 'irrational peasants' who fail to recognize what was good for them or write patronizing tropes about a pampered '*lakhpati*' and '*crorepati*' rural elite whose only interest was in securing more subsidies.

Thus, although the recent farmers' protests were a direct response to the three farm laws – laws that finally broke the camel's back – we also need to understand them as a sharp *reaction* to decades of urban bias and rural neglect. With hindsight, it is worth reflecting on whether Modi had already set the scene in 2016 for introducing radical farm reforms when he tried to embrace and sweeten farmers by promising to double their incomes by 2022. This ploy became even more apparent after the three farm laws were passed – the entire government case for bringing in new laws was justified in terms of 'saving' and 'enriching' farmers by offering them more 'choices', all helping towards, miraculously, doubling their incomes. But the farmers were not fooled by this yet another Modi *jumla* and began their resistance. Needless to say, any talk of 'doubling farmers' incomes' was quietly dropped during the protests and no longer figures in government policy statements towards agriculture.

Agrarian Protests of 2020–2021

As stated earlier, the undue haste, callousness and sense of total indifference shown by the Modi government in passing the three Farm Acts, generated deep anger amongst farmers and their organizations. In fact, mobilization against the Ordinances, especially in Punjab, started almost instantly after the farmers learned about the nature of these Ordinances and worked out their likely impact on them. Calls for their withdrawal, albeit with support from ineffectual opposition parties in Parliament, fell on deaf ears. The Shiromani Akali Dal (SAD), historically perceiving itself as guardian of farmers' interest and fearing loss of electoral support of farmers in the forthcoming Assembly elections, disassociated itself from the BJP government. Most significantly and perhaps historically for the first time, Harsimrat Kaur Badal, sole SAD MP in the Union Cabinet and Minister for Food Processing, resigned from the government in September 2020, prompting break-up of the long-standing SAD-BJP alliance. But the damage to SAD's integrity seemed to have been already done.

Beginning with targeted protests in Chandigarh, capital of Punjab, and also replicating earlier protests around 'rail *roko*' to protect Punjab, these protests began to cause economic and political havoc, enough to make the Punjab Congress government respond by opposing central laws and bringing its own, albeit toothless, legislation to preserve the status quo as agriculture was considered a state subject under India's federal constitution. A further round of talks among the splintered farmers' organizations led to a unanimous decision by the newly formed *Punjab Kisan Sangharsh Committee*, to take the protest directly to the center of power in New Delhi. This decision and call by the Kisan Committee to '*Dilli Chalo*' lead to the movement of thousands of protesting farmer on their tractor-trolleys towards Delhi via Haryana. The BJP government in Haryana, with help from central agencies, tried everything – water cannons, tear gas, shells, concrete barricades, *lathi*-charges, mass arrests – to stop the march but failed and, if anything, these repressive acts only riled up more farmers in Punjab, Haryana and western UP, Rajasthan and Uttarakhand and join the protest movement. These marchers, unable to proceed further into Delhi due to erection of massive steel and concrete barricades on the main highways, eventually decided to camp at three Delhi borders – Singhu, Tikri and Ghazibad.

The farmer camps grew larger as more and more farmers, encouraged by their organizations in different parts of India, began to join the protest movement. In addition to farmers, other sympathetic individuals, citizen groups and NGOs also joined in, not only socially widening the movement but also prolonging it to the annoyance of central government and its supporters in the print, audio and visual media. All attempts to demonize the protestors and their leaders with various labels, such as Khalistanis, Marxist/Maoists, Urban Naxalites, anti-Nationals, '*tukde-tukde*' gangs, pro-Pakistan agents, Chinese or other foreign agents, did not have much success. This attempt at 'Othering' the movement by Modi government's compliant and lap-dog media (*Godi* media) totally backfired as protestors developed their alternative print and social media channels to present a counter narrative on their grievances and in the process, also succeeding in globalizing the movement.

It is quite remarkable that 32 Punjab-based kisan unions and hundreds of kisan unions from states around the country were able to unite and agree to work under an umbrella body, the *Samyukt Kisan Morcha* (SKM), and be represented by 40 union leaders. The SKM emerged as the lead agency in guiding and organizing the movement and negotiating with the government. There were 11 unsuccessful rounds of talks between the SKM and representatives of the agriculture ministry and the government. Although the government offered concessions on bringing amendments to the three laws and even suspending their implementation, they never agreed to SKM's main demands of withdrawing the three laws and providing a legal guarantee on Minimum Support Prices. In a significant move on January 10, 2021, the government, acting on behalf of business lobbyists, on learning that the SKM had made a call for holding their own alternative march in Delhi to coincide with the Republic Day parade on January 26, approached the Supreme Court (SC) to ban it, citing fear of chaos and disorder. The SC, however, unexpectedly went a step further and suspended implementation of the three farm laws until further orders. With a view to assisting in resolution of the agitation, the Court also set up a committee of 'four eminent persons' to gather further evidence on the farmer agitation and to make recommendations.[8] Although one of the nominated members to the committee decided to recuse himself, the other three allegedly held wide ranging discussions with many stakeholders, gathered evidence and submitted its report in a sealed envelope to the SC on March 19, 2021. It was surprising, however, even though the three laws were repealed and the agitation officially ending soon after that, the SC commissioned report was only put into the public domain recently by one of the committee members, because, as he claimed, despite his repeated requests, the SC failed to release it.[9] Neither did suspension of laws by the SC lead to any urgency on the part of the government to re-start negotiations, with the government just accepting the SC judgment and deciding to suspend implementation of the legislation for 18 months, perhaps hoping this time period would be long enough to divide and weaken the movement. But the movement did not weaken and remained united and Prime Minister Modi was forced to make an unexpected U-turn, a rare occurrence under his period of governance. Speculation still remains on why the Prime Minister decided to make the surprising announcement after months of non-negotiation and at that particular juncture.

Contributors to the Edited Volume

The year-long kisan resistance to the 'black laws' generated much academic and public debate on its causes, its different dimensions and characteristics and reasons for its resilience and sustainability, so it would be impossible to cover them all in a satisfactory way. In this edited book, consisting of this introduction and ten further chapters, the reader is introduced to what eminent scholars of Punjab's economic, political and social history consider as the main issues in the farmers' agitation from their specific area of expertise. The volume is notionally divided into two sections: Section 1 focuses on Historical, Literary and Comparative Perspectives and Section 2 on Dimensions and Dynamics of Reform, Resistance and Resilience. In Section 1, the opening chapter by Ronki Ram provides the longer historical context for understanding the recent farmer agitation. In a comprehensive and detailed analysis, after highlighting the main characteristics of the 2020–2021 agitation, Ram goes on to discuss several farmer agitations in the colonial as well as the post-colonial periods. He draws our attention to the striking parallels and similarities between past struggles and the recent agitation. Complementing the first chapter, the next chapter, written jointly by Prabhjot Parmar and Amandeep Kaur, draws our attention to the long and rich literary lineage associated with farmer protests and resistance movements, starting with the 1907 agitation to the present day. Through a close and contextualized reading of the creative literature produced, in poems, songs and short stories and novels, the authors demonstrate how and why writers record and make social history of defiance, love and solidarity and resilience, which is then made available for popular consumption and left for posterity.

In the third chapter, Sukhdev S. Sohal provides a comparative assessment of, arguably, the two most important farmer struggles witnessed in Punjab, the '*Pagri Sambhal Jatta*' agitation of 1907 and the 2020–2021 struggle. He argues that Punjab's agrarian structure and agrarian character determine power equations both at the local and national levels and why changes in these, especially after a government introduces new legislation relating to agriculture, contribute to building farmer grievance, leading to organized resistance. The fourth chapter by Sucha S. Gill, focuses specifically on the history of farmer organizations since the green revolution period of Punjab, their changing dynamics, different stages in mobilization during the recent movement and their overall achievement. He discusses reasons behind the splintering of Punjab's *Bhartiya Kisan Union* in the 1980s and 1990s and explains why these factions united in 2020 to agitate against the new farm laws. The fifth and final chapter in Section 1 by Virginia Van Dyke complements Gill's chapter and analyses response of farmers' movements to government's embracement of Neo-Liberalism and globalization since the 1980s in the wider north Indian context. She discusses how these processes, in turn, impacted class alliances and ideological shifts among leaders of farmers' unions and how these then changed the form of farmers' engagement with the political party system. Van Dyke argues that contemporary protests opened up space for cross-class, cross-caste and cross-gender struggles of smaller farmers and laborers against a threat to their very livelihood. Van Dyke also examines agrarian movements in western UP, including their main historical and contemporary actors, and how these aligned with agrarian movement in Punjab to offer a united resistance to farm laws.

Section 2 contains a set of papers which offer different perspectives on the dimensions and characteristics of the recent farmer agitation within the Punjab, national and global contexts. The first and sixth chapter in this section by Pritam Singh interrogates the actual functioning of Indian federalism and how the hasty passing of the farm laws by the BJP government, without giving due consideration to views of farmers or states, demonstrates the growing power of the center despite agriculture being a state subject under the Indian constitution. Using a number of examples to illustrate center's role in pro-actively weakening the three main nodes of resistance (farmers, states and regional identities), he provides a strong argument for developing new perspectives in order to strengthen federalism and democracy. He argues this is only possible through greater decentralization, localized small-scale farming, cooperative farming and by building ecological sustainability. The seventh chapter by Surinder S. Jodkha starts by examining reasons behind the surprisingly massive positive response in support of farmers. He then goes on to remind us of the need for a critical engagement with entrenched development ideas about the inevitability of decline of agriculture and demise of associated agrarian cultures. He presents a compelling argument for the need to search for a context specific historical and sociological understanding of agrarian cultures, rather than uncritically accept a pre-scripted teleology that takes the end of agriculture for granted. The eighth chapter by Sukhpal Singh provides a summary and technical details of the three farm laws that were hastily passed in Parliament by the Modi government in 2020, examines their intended objectives and their potential implications for food procurement, storage and distribution across states. Drawing on similar experiments of privatization and deregulation from across the world, as well as in India and Punjab, he points to their potentially negative implications for farmers. He claims that fears raised by farmers, especially by small and marginal farmers, about potential loss of their land due to corporatization, are legitimate and very real. Further, drawing on his vast knowledge of contract farming in Punjab, he highlights the potentially negative implications of the proposed amendment to the Contract Farming Act, although the Act has now been repealed. He contends that actual experience indicates the new Act would not have increased farmer welfare and neither would it have brought benefits to small farmers, aided crop diversification or assisted in offering redress from unequal contractual obligations.

The ninth chapter by Shinder S. Thandi provides a discussion on the multi-faceted but sometimes contentious role of Sikh/Punjabi diaspora in supporting the farmer agitation. After discussing formation of the Sikh diaspora beginning over one and a half centuries ago, he points to the changing nature and degree of diaspora's homeland orientation under globalization, the motives behind diaspora support for farmers and how this support, both financial and material, played an important role in aiding both sustainability and resilience of the movement. Thandi also provides a critical discussion on diaspora's increasing participation in domestic politics of their hostlands and how, along with assistance from gurdwaras, NGOs and advocacy groups, Sikh diaspora communities made extensive use of social media to mobilize support, to organize rallies and raise funding to support farmers back home. He suggests that, unlike during the Khalistan movement of the 1980s, Sikh diaspora community remained united in their mobilization efforts and was able to successfully develop a counter narrative to the government position on farm reforms. The final chapter by Swaroopa Lahiri takes up the issue of gender inclusiveness and gender participation during the farmer movement which gained global attention. She examines the critical and unprecedented role played by women during protest marches: by organizing and joining rallies, by enlisting volunteers to join camp sites and helping with the *seva* there, as well as in sustaining households and farm operations in the absence of men. The author critically examines the motives behind their involvement and also speculates on what the implications of their enhanced visibility may be on future gender relations in deeply patriarchal societies of Punjab and Haryana.

We hope this set of readings will provide readers with interesting and stimulating perspectives that will help our understanding of different dimensions, characteristics and dynamics of the 2020–2021 farmer mobilization and struggle, motives of farmers and their forms of resistance and ways of building resilience. Some of the readings provide new insights into resolving the agrarian crisis and these will require serious consideration by policymakers for the sake of Punjab's future prosperity and sustainability. The Editor is very thankful to the contributors for making this publication possible. Finally, the Editor would also like to acknowledge the assistance of Ronki Ram, Amarjit Chandan, Pritam Singh and Gurinder S. Mann for their encouragement, guidance and advice in putting this edited volume together.

Notes

* This chapter is a revised version of 'Introduction to Special Issue on Farmer Agitation: A Momentous Morcha', first published in *Journal of Sikh and Punjab Studies*, 29(1&2) (Spring–Fall, 2022): 1–10.

1 Michael Lipton's Urban Bias Thesis has been criticized by several scholars for its alleged over-simplification of differences between rural and urban interests and for its universality. Despite these limitations, there are many reasons to believe it still provides a useful framework for critically examining the overall journey of the Indian experience. Lipton explained his thesis as follows:

> The most important class conflict in the poor countries of the world today is not between labour and capital...nor is it between foreign and national interests. It is between the rural classes and urban classes... rural sector contains most of the poverty, and most of the low-cost sources of potential advance; but the urban sector contains most of the articulateness, organization and power. So the urban classes have been able to 'win' most of the rounds of the struggle with the countryside...but in so doing they have made the development process needlessly slow and unfair.
>
> (Lipton, 1977: 62)

2 Given this edited book is concerned with livelihoods of farming communities and sustainability of small-scale farming, it is worth recalling that Chaudhari Charan Singh, a Jat political leader in UP and briefly India's Prime Minister, was a strong advocate for prioritizing agriculture over industry. He offered an alternative model for India based on 'Rural Bias', arguing the country needed policies that would strengthen peasant agriculture and provide jobs in rural areas for the landless. Needless to say Charan Singh's intellectual arguments, very similar and appropriate to debates about agriculture today, did not go far and were forgotten in the pursuit of modernization.

Charan Singh was also the leader of a strong peasant movement in western UP which later gave rise to the BKU and spread to other states. It is interesting that at one of the largest peasant rallies he helped to organize in Delhi in December 1978, government officials and intellectuals painted the protesters as an 'abstraction, not a reality'. Since they represented backwardness, old tradition and uncouthness, they argued, they should be kept out of sight while the nation 'modernizes'. It seems nothing has changed 43 years later. For a critical appreciation of Charan Singh, see Paul R. Brass 'Chaudhuri Charan Singh: An Indian Political Life', *Economic and Political Weekly*, Vol. 28, No.

39 (Sep. 25, 1993), pp. 2087–2090 and Terence J. Byres, 'Charan Singh, 1902-87: An Assessment', *Journal of Peasant Studies*, Vol XV, No 2 (January 1988), pp. 139–189.

3 Punjab's ranking has fallen steadily from number one state in terms of income per capita in the 1980s to about 12 today. This relative decline is attributed to other Indian states experiencing faster rate of economic growth than Punjab. Punjab's growth is still driven largely by the agricultural sector which has been stagnating with no compensatory contribution from other sectors. For recent attempts to explain causes and offer remedies see Lakhwinder Singh and Nirvikar Singh (edited) *Economic Transformation of a Developing Economy: The Experience of Punjab* (Springer, 2016) and Autar S. Dhesi and Gurmail Singh (edited) *Rural Development in Punjab: A Success Story Going Astray* (Routledge, 2008).

4 This relates to the Mahatma Gandhi National Rural Employment Guarantee Act, 2005 (MGNREGA) which was passed in 2005 by the Manmohan Singh government. The purpose of the Act is to provide *at least 100 days of guaranteed wage employment* in a financial year to adult workers of a household who are prepared to do unskilled manual work. What these rural households really need are permanent full-time jobs all year round.

5 Funding for political parties has been a controversial issue in India, as elsewhere, and donations are said to favour the larger parties, undermining democracy and pluralism. Those making political donations were alleged to be dumping their black money or doing so to buy favours. Seen by some as a political masterstroke, in early 2018, the BJP government introduced a new financial instrument called 'electoral bonds', which would allow individuals and businesses to donate to political parties, almost unlimited sums of money through the banking system, in a totally anonymous way. Although it is still possible to gather information on the total value of donations received by each political party, it is no longer possible to identify the names of individual donors or attempt to link donations by rich businessmen with their business fortunes. According to a recent report in *The Economist*, the BJP received three-quarters of the total money, amounting to $500 million plus, donated through these bonds during 2019–2020. The report further goes on to state 'In 2020 the BJP's declared assets of $655m outweighed those of the next 51 political parties combined. More striking, its stash rose by 443% in just five years' (see *The Economist*, 'The Organs of India's Democracy are Decaying', February 12, 2022).
Thus, given the lack of transparency, it is difficult to factually state that big industrialists are buying favours from the BJP government. But given BJP's historical links with trading classes and the massive increase in its income and assets over recent years, it is not unreasonable to assume linkages.

6 First-year economics textbooks tell us perfect markets do not exist in the real world; they are an ideal or aspirational form. In reality, most markets are imperfect and prone to failure as they do not take into account presence of externalities, information failures and existence of monopsonistic buyers, as Indian industrialists Mukesh Ambani and Gautam Adani were feared of emerging in procuring farm produce. These market failures mean state intervention is necessary to deal with them. Agricultural markets are particularly prone to failure as they can suffer from acute price fluctuations as described in various cobweb models and therefore need state intervention to provide price stability.

7 John Kenneth Galbraith in his 1952 book, *American Capitalism*, discussed the importance of having counter-vailing power in a free market economy given its in-built bias in favour of large businesses, making free and fair bargaining impossible. Due to this bias 'counter-vailing' powers emerge in different sectors, including agriculture to offset business's excessive market power.

8 The four members of the Supreme Court-appointed committee were Anil J. Ghanwat, President of Shetkari Sanghatana (Maharashtra's largest farmer union founded by Sharad Joshi), Pramod Kumar Joshi (Director, South Asia international Food Policy), and agriculture-economist and former Chairman of the Commission for Agricultural Costs and Prices (CACP) Ashok Gulati. The fourth member, ex-Bhartiya Kisan Union President and Rajya Sabha member, Bhupinder Singh Mann had recused himself due to conflict of interest.

9 Feeling frustrated, Anil J. Ghanwat decided to release the 92-page report to the press on March 21, 2022. He was reported as saying 'around 85.7 per cent of the farmer organizations, representing over 3.3 crore farmers, supported the laws' and that it would be unfair to suspend or repeal the laws against the wishes of the silent majority. The report was dismissed by leaders of the SKM for being 'fake, plain bogus and trashy'. For details, see Vibha Sharma 'Farmers' bodies dismiss as "fake, plain bogus and trashy" report on farm laws by SC-appointed panel', *Tribune News Service*, March 22, 2022.

Part I

Historical, Literary and Comparative Perspectives

1 Agrarian Resistance in Punjab

Contextualizing Farmer Protests at the Gates of Delhi in a Historical Perspective*

Ronki Ram

Introduction: The Beginning of Grievance

The periphery of Delhi – capital city of India – has earned a unique distinction of being the site of longest ever witnessed farmers' peaceful protest in the history of peasant movements in the world. The protest began in Indian Punjab, (hereafter Punjab) on June 6, 2020, against three ordinances (temporary laws) promulgated by the Central Government of India on June 5, 2020. The first ordinance, the Farmers' Produce Trade and Commerce (Promotion and Facilitation) Ordinance 2020, provided freedom to sell and buy farm produce in the county within the Agricultural Produce Market Committees (APMC) markets or outside them. The central government claimed this ordinance will liberate farmers by giving them the freedom to sell their produce anywhere. The second, the Farmers (Empowerment and Protection) Agreement on Price Assurance and Farm Services Ordinance 2020, dealt with contract farming under which farmers would produce crops as per contracts with corporate investors for a mutually agreed remuneration. The third ordinance, the Essential Commodities (Amendment) Ordinance 2020, regulated the list of essential items whose prices were to be standardized by the government.

The federal government had asserted ad nauseam that the new laws will transform Indian agriculture, attract private investment, revolutionize the lives of the farmers in India and that farmers will have more options to sell their produce and at better prices. This message had been reiterated during all the meetings convened by it with various agitating farmer organizations. As far as Minimum Support Price (MSP) is concerned, the central government reiterated that: 'MSP was, MSP is, and MSP will continue in the future'. It assured farmers that there was no move on its part at all to scrap the MSP, and there was absolutely no reference to it in the new laws. It further asserted that these laws will help the farmers to get connected to big traders and exporters, bringing profit to agriculture (Jha, 2020).

However, as far as farmers were concerned, they had a totally different opinion about the farm laws. A general impression prevailed among them that the three farm laws will dismantle the MSP system and the AMPC.

DOI: 10.4324/9781003320005-3

It was also widely believed that farmers' legal ownership rights on their agricultural land would eventually pass into the hands of the big corporate houses. Deep concern was also shown that in the absence of AMPC, the big corporate houses will acquire monopoly over agriculture markets, fix the price of their produce arbitrarily, and force them to sell their crops at much lower prices than what they would have been getting under the prevailing MSP system. Their common fear was that within the purview of these laws, they would not be able to negotiate effectively with powerful corporate houses who, with the help of big corporate law firms, would bind them to unfavourable contracts with hidden liability clauses that would be beyond the comprehension of many of them, especially the poor and illiterate farmers (Mustafa, 2020). It was further believed that these newly enacted farm laws would dismantle the traditional *arthiyas* system.[1]

The agitating farmers, supported by agricultural labourers, and people from various other directly or indirectly agriculture-related professions, were of unanimous opinion that farm laws will deprive them of their agriculture land and the well-established and long-tested regulated agriculture market set-up. Thus, they wanted their complete rollback; and a legal guarantee for the MSP. Randeep Surjewala, chief spokesperson of the Indian National Congress, while expressing solidarity with the agitating farmers said that his party will fight the Modi government 'tooth and nail' on this issue. He further stated:

> These three draconian ordinances are a death knell for agriculture in India. They will subjugate the farmer at the altar of a handful of crony capitalists, making them labourers to toil on their own land rather than getting a remunerative price for their crop under the system of minimum support price.
>
> (Jha, 2020)

A further apprehension was that once these laws are implemented, the states would not be allowed to levy market fee/cess outside APMC domains. At present, the market fee, rural development fee, and commission of *arhatiyas* (commission agents) are 3 per cent, 3 per cent, and 2.5 per cent, respectively; but in Punjab and Haryana, the epicentre of farmers' protests they were 2 per cent, 2 per cent, and 2.5 per cent, respectively. There was an apprehension that after the implementation of the farm legislation, Punjab and Haryana would lose an estimated Rs 3,500 crore and Rs 1,600 crore each year, respectively (Mustafa, 2020).

Central Government Legislation and Response of Farmers

However, despite farmers' continuous opposition and protests against the farm ordinances in Punjab and Haryana, the central government introduced them as Bills in the Lok Sabha, lower house of the Parliament of

India, on September 14, 2020, and passed them on September 15 and 18, 2020. Subsequently, on September 20 and 22, the same were passed in Rajya Sabha, the upper house of the Parliament of India. And finally on September 27, 2020, the three controversial farm ordinances turned Bills became Acts – the Farmers' Produce Trade and Commerce (Promotion and Facilitation) Act 2020 (FPTC Act), the Farmers (Empowerment and Protection) Agreement on Price Assurance and Farm Services Act 2020 or the Agreement on Price Assurance and Farm Services (APAFS), and the Essential Commodities (Amendment) Act 2020 – after obtaining assent from the President of India. During the entire period of more than three months – from the promulgation of the ordinances to their becoming Acts/laws – hardly a day passed in Punjab and Haryana without protest by farmers who were agitating for their complete rollback. The three controversial agriculture reforms laws (the first two are new, and the third one is a modified version of the Essential Commodities Act 1951), and their vigorous opposition by varied farmer unions has been quietly considered as a long drawn out fight between the people – left alone to fend for themselves since 1991 – and the neo-liberal market economy, supported by international financial institutions like the International Monetary Fund (IMF), World Trade Organization (WTO), and World Bank (The Times of India, 2020; Sharma, 2021b, 2021c). The international financial institutions, as per the Washington Consensus (Naim, 1999), force governments to withdraw all kinds of subsidies from the agriculture sector and let it to be governed via the market logic of demand and supply. Though the three contentious farm laws were passed in 2020, 'the discussion on policy reforms and structural changes in agriculture started around the year 2000. It began with suggestions for changes in market regulation and removal of various restrictions provided under the APMC Act' (Chand, 2020: 6). Since 2020, all the successive central governments made multiple attempts to persuade states to introduce reform in the agriculture sector. However, in finding the state governments were not taking interest in the proposed agricultural reforms, perhaps due to apprehension of farmers' protest, and given the federal angle of the case involved, the current NDA central government took the plunge on June 5, 2020.

On the very next day, June 6, 2020, farmers of Punjab launched an agitation against the three farm ordinances by burning effigies of the NDA in hundreds of villages in the state. Given COVID-19 restrictions, they protested on their rooftops daily for an hour, from June 14 to 30, 2020. Initially, the rooftop protests began in a few villages but soon they spread to over 500 villages in Punjab (Jagga, 2020). Rooftop protests were followed by handing over a memorandum at the offices of sub-divisional magistrates (SDMs) for forwarding to the Prime Minister's Office (PMO). Within a period of one and a half month, 11 major state farmer unions came together to protest against the farm ordinances. On July 20, 2020, they again burnt effigies of the erstwhile SAD-BJP alliance in several villages. On July 27, 2020, these 11 farmer unions collectively organized a massive tractor rally (over 25,000 tractors hit the roads on this particular day) and submitted memorandums to their MPs. One of the tractors was driven by a 17-year-old girl, Baldeep Kaur. She led the march in Bathinda and drove her tractor to submit a memorandum to the former Union Minister Harsimrat Kaur Badal. This massive tractor march became the standard practice of farmers' protest henceforth (Jagga, 2020).

Soon after the July tractor march, farmers of Haryana followed suit and started organizing meetings in protest against the farm ordinances. It was also during this time that the All India Kisan Sangrash Co-ordination Committee (AIKSCC) became active and organized a number of kisan meetings regarding the impact of the farm laws on the life of the farmers. By mid-August 2020, all the 31 Punjab farmer unions, including Khet Mazdoor Union (of Dalit farm labourers), had joined hands to work in co-ordination with the AIKSCC to streamline the protest, giving it a critical thrust and focus. This was followed by *nakabandi* (guarding) of villages against the entry of SAD and BJP leaders, 'jail bharo andolan' (fill the prisons), and sending of memoranda to the PMO (Jagga, 2020).

An inflection point came after the three contentious farm ordinances were introduced as Bills in Parliament on September 14, 2020: Farmers of Punjab and Haryana held *dharnas* (sit-ins), blocked roads, and began 'pakka morcha'[2] outside the residence of Parkash Singh Badal, former Chief Minister of Punjab. On September 23, all 31 Punjab farmer unions announced their joint 'rail roko' (stop the railway trains) agitation from October 1, 2020. They also announced their programme of organizing *dharnas* outside malls, toll plazas, petrol stations of identified corporate houses, as well as outside the residences of BJP leaders. Once these Bills became Acts on September 27, 2020, the farmers of Punjab upped the ante, by blocking railway tracks throughout the length and breadth of their borderland state for about two months. Darshan Pal, former medical doctor, and working group member of AIKSCC, told Raakhi Jagga that:

> We started protests in a phased manner but when we were not heard, we had to come out on roads, block tracks and even roads. People need to know that when governments are deaf, we have to follow these methods, as they did not listen to us, did not talk to us, despite our protests and passed the Bills in Parliament. Many people on social media now ask why we block tracks, roads. So this is our answer to them.
>
> (Jagga, 2020)

It was during the intervening period of the passing of the central farm ordinances and their enactment as Acts/laws, that a strident opposition was gradually built up in Punjab against them by galvanizing varied kisan organizations in the state. The farmers of Punjab established a common platform at Shambu, on the Punjab-Haryana border, and this location almost immediately became the epicentre of the movement. From November 26, 2020, the farmers shifted their protest to the periphery of Delhi in response to *Dilli Chalo* (Let's march to Delhi) call given by the All Indian Kisan Sangharsh (struggle) Co-ordination Committee (The Economic Times, 2020). However, before the call to *Dilli Chalo* was formally put into action, efforts were made to find an amicable solution of the protracted crisis. But the meetings between the Union Agriculture Minister, Narinder Singh Tomar, and representatives from over 32 farmer unions to solve the imbroglio remained inconclusive.

The march was held under the banner of Samyukt Kisan Morcha (SKM) – United Farmers Front. The Rashtriya Kisan Mahasanghathan (apex farmers' organization), various factions of Bharatiya Kisan Union (BKU) – BKU (Ekta-Urgahan), BKU (Rejewal), BKU (Dakaunda), and BKU (Chaduni) – Jan Kisan Andolan, All India Kisan Mazdoor Sabha, Krantikari Kisan Union among others participated in the call to *Dilli Chalo* (The Economic Times, 2020). Despite some initial opposition mounted by the Haryana government to preclude the march from reaching its destination, the agitating farmers from Punjab and Haryana were able to reach the borders of Delhi (Singhu, Tikri, Ghazipur), and after then (November 26, 2020), they camped there with support from various quarters from their respective home states as well as Sikh diaspora till the end of the agitation. Especially worthy of mention is the tremendous and continuing support by the surrounding populace, expressed by way of organized daily deliveries of much-needed material items – mainly various food items and milk, in spite of the logistical hurdles to their daily lives thrown up by this agitation.

Non-Partisan Peaceful Protests

What distinguishes this longest farmers' protest is its thoroughly peaceful nature – though with a blip, motivated by political machinations, surrounding the 26th of January – and the all-inclusive character of its huge gatherings, comprising people across caste, class, creed, gender, region, and professional breakup. It attracted worldwide coverage through its continual addressing of huge gatherings from its historic 'Kisan stage' established at the Singhu border of Delhi and assumed an international character being a non-partisan platform. Meticulously arranged, assiduously managed, and adroitly guarded by the farmers themselves, this unique kisan platform (kisan stage) had attained the lustrous status of a global virtual kisan podium. Leaders of political parties were strictly debarred from sharing the stage or addressing farmers. Kulwant Singh Sandhu, general secretary, Jamhuri (Democratic) Kisan Sabha, Punjab, told *The Print*:

> It was decided that no leader of any political party will be allowed to speak from our stages. Politicians are looking at 2022 (assembly elections) but we are looking at our livelihood. We don't need their support, rather they want to join our protest. But we have strictly banned that.
>
> (Sethi, 2020)

The mainstream national media was also not allowed to cover the protest site for its alleged partisan slant (Suresh, 2020). It was often referred to as 'godi (lap dog) media' by the protesting farmers. The protesting farmers launched their own separate biweekly paper, *Trolley Times*, both in Punjabi and Hindi, to cover their peaceful protest in an undistorted manner (Ramani, 2020).

Another globally talked about aspect of the protesting site of the farmers at Delhi borders was *langa*r (community kitchen). The langar is prepared jointly by the participating farmers – men and women – and managed out of the provisions collected by the farmers from within their community sources as well as those donated by sympathetic philanthropic diasporas. The langar was open not only to farmers but also to all irrespective of caste, colour, and creed. Yet another interesting aspect of this unique farmers' agitation was heavy participation by women, young as well as old. Their participation was not only confined to community kitchen and looking after makeshift staying arrangements at the Delhi borders; they could equally be seen actively participating in various other organizational and managerial activities of the farm unions (Bhattacharya, 2021). A visit to this thoroughly non-violent, non-discriminatory, and non-political site of farmers' protest with copious participation of women was often considered as no less than a pilgrimage (Sura, 2020). Many participating women joined the agitation along with their newly born children in tow, as well as older people, including grand-parents.

The protest at Delhi borders (Singhu, Tikri, and Ghazipur) also gained the support of over 40 farmer organizations from around the country under the SKM. With the passage of time, farmers from Western Uttar Pradesh (UP), Uttarakhand, Rajasthan, and Madhya Pradesh also joined the protests. Apart from the farmers, *arthiyas* (Bhardwaj, 2020; Chaba and Damodaran, 2020), labour unions (Deol, 2021; Kaur, 2021; Toor, 2021); women (Bhowmick, 2021; Gayatri, 2021; Kakhra, 2021; Kaur, 2021; Toor, 2021); students (Iftikhar, 2020); teachers, doctors, and engineers (Butani, 14, 2020); writers (Khanna, 2020); singers (Pandey, 2020); retired soldiers (Singh, 2020); government servants; and various other sections of civil society showed solidarity with the farmers in their struggle for complete annulment of the three agriculture laws since its beginning on November 26, 2020 (Kumar, 2020). Kirti (Workers) Kisan Forum (former IAS, IPS, Army & Civil Service Officers) of Punjab and Haryana were supporting the farmers' agitation by organizing seminars on the three agriculture laws (Kaur, 2021). However, among all the social segments of the agitation, women assumed a special importance by remaining an integral part of the protests against all odds. They even celebrated International Women's Day at the Delhi borders by gathering in their thousands (Kaushal and Kissu, 2021). The *Time* magazine dedicated its cover title to the women agitating against these laws (Bhowmick, 2021).

Though not less than 500 farmers had lost their lives at that time, and 11 rounds of talks were convened between the Government of India and representatives of the agitating farmers, there was no solution in sight as both the sides are adamant regarding their respective positions – farmers wanted total repeal of the three laws and a legal guarantee of the MSP, whereas the Central Government of India continued to repeat its belief in their long-term benefits, and later also began to ask farmers to negotiate amendments in the laws (Sabarwal, 2021; The Tribune, 2021). To end the deadlock in the face of serious health hazards posed by the winter cold and the Corona pandemic, the Supreme Court of India stayed implementation of the three controversial farm laws on January 11 till further orders and formed a committee of experts comprising representatives of the central government and farmers' unions (BusinessToday.in, 2021). It also suggested that agitating farmers should return home to their livelihoods (Rajagopal, 2021). The highest court also appreciated the peaceful conduct of the protests and stated that it did not want to stifle their democratic rights (Rajagopal, 2021).

In a similar vein, on January 20, 2021, the central government also proposed to suspend implementation of the three controversial farm laws for 18 months and set up a joint committee to discuss the laws in detail as well as to find an amicable solution in the interest of the farmers (BusinessToday.in, 2021). In the words of Joginder Singh Ugrahan, president BKU (Ugrahan), 'The government proposed to suspend the farm laws for one and a half years. We rejected the proposal but since it has come from the government, we will meet tomorrow and deliberate over it' (The Times of India, 2021). After consultation among them, the farmers did not accept the Supreme Court suggestion to go back to their homes until their demands to annul the three farm laws and legal guarantee for MSP were met. They also rejected the central government's proposal to put in abeyance the three contentious farm laws for 18 months and reiterated that nothing short of complete rollback of the farm laws is acceptable to them.

Peaceful agitation by farmers and their steadfast determination to get the farm laws rescinded and continued to attract wide supports in favour of their protest from within the country as well as from different quarters of the world. Pop superstar Rihanna of the US, environmental activist Greta Thunberg from Sweden (Aiyar, 2021), and the US Vice President's niece Meena Harris extended support to protesting farmers (Misra, 2021). Whereas, in contrast, Gita Gopinath, the Chief Economist, IMF, and Gerry Rice, Director of Communications at IMF underlined the benefits of the agricultural laws for the farmers (India's Business Standard, 2021; Outlook Web Bureau, 2021). Noam Chomsky, a globally reputed social scientist, philosopher, and linguist, in a conversation with an Indian scientist-turned-filmmaker, Bedabrata Pain, had all praise for the farmers' protest at Delhi borders. When asked for a message to the agitating peasants of India, Chomsky said:

> Because they are doing the right thing with the courage and integrity for the benefit of their own families, for the farmers of India, the people of India and for the entire world who needs this model of struggle to

> carry out the same kinds of actions in their own circumstances which share a lot with the circumstances of the farmers of India and they should be proud of what they are doing and I think this movement is a beacon of light for the world in dark times.
>
> (Pain, 2021)

To keep their spirit high and to underline their demands, the protesting farmers chose to celebrate their struggle at different intervals. On the completion of 100 days of their agitation, on March 6, 2021, thousands of farmers demonstrated wearing black turbans and armbands by peacefully blocking the Kundli-Manesar-Palwal (KMP) and Eastern Peripheral expressways – the two speedways that form a ring around Delhi. Women dressed in black colours – some of them wearing black *dupattas* (long head scarves) – with black flags in their hands – also participated in the blockade (HTC & Agencies, 2021). During the blockade, the farmers raised slogans against the BJP-led government for not accepting their demands. Manjeet Kaur, a woman protester who arrived with a score of women at the protest site of KMP expressway, stated:

> The government wanted to know what was black in three agri bills (sic). Today, we have worn black dresses to show that everything in the laws is black. We will not return home till laws are taken back.
>
> (Times of India, 2021)

The blockade continued for five hours (11 am to 4 pm) and remained peaceful throughout. Vehicles carrying children and women, ambulances, and cranes were not halted. Water, tea, and food were served to those who remained stranded (Times of India, 2021).

Since the beginning of the protest, except for the unfortunate incident of putting up Nishan Sahib and farmer flag on the dome and empty flag post at Red Fort on Republic Day, January 26, 2021 (Kamal, 2021), there has not been even a single incident of violence and sabotage at the site of the agitation. After the temporary setback caused by the unfortunate incident of clashes and confrontation at Red Fort on January 26, 2021, the timely intervention by Rakesh Tikait, UP BKU leader, restored the momentum of the peaceful agitation. His tearful emotional appeal restored, even redoubled, enthusiasm among the farmers (Chaba, 2021; *India Today*, 2021). Commenting on the chaos and violence on Republic Day and the emotive pull of the tears of UP farm leader, Rakesh Tikait, Punjab farmer leader Balbir Singh Rajewal, who heads the BKU (Rajewal), said:

> After the Red Fort incident, the agitation suffered. It (agitation) was hit for a day-and-a half, but picked up after that. Now farmers are again rushing to Delhi borders. We are thankful to Tikait sahib and we will invite him to Punjab and honour him.
>
> (Chaba, 2021)

The Red Fort incident on the R-Day was a conspiracy, argued Rajewal, to scuttle the farmers' peaceful struggle. Rajewal told the *Indian Express* that 'he was aware who was behind it'. He continued:

> We understand that this was done by Centre, BJP, and RSS. They are trying to provoke us that the agitation fizzles out. But I appeal again to the farmers that we do not have to react. We have learnt a lot from the event that unfolded on Republic Day. We have matured. The farmers also realize this that we were more effective when we were peaceful .... We will not indulge in any violence. We are alert to prevent any violence.
>
> (Chaba, 2021)

Tarsem Peter, president, Punjab Pendu Mazdoor (Village Dalit Workers) Union (PMU), was also of the same opinion:

> After the R-Day incident there was a lot of fear among the people that now they will not only lose this battle, but also their image. That fear, he added, has withered away *after the emotive appeal of Tikait.*
>
> (Chaba, 2021, *emphasis added*)

Though the farmers were called names throughout the course of the protests, the intensity of such filthy epithets swelled at once after the Republic Day incident. The protesting farmers were termed as Khalistanis, urban Naxals, and even Maoists by those who supported the farm laws. It was also often heard that those protesting at Delhi borders were not real kisans. The farmers on protest at Delhi borders were also accused of spreading the Coronavirus. Reacting to such accusation, Joginder Singh Ugrahan, president of farm organization BKU (Ekta Ugrahan) said:

> It does not matter much as to how people describe our protest, but the most important is the determination of the farmers who won't settle for anything less than repeal of the laws. For this, we may have to spend many more number of months at borders, away from our homes. We have amply showcased that even though we are away from the homes, yet the crops have been well taken care of and we have even faced the coronavirus pandemic staying in the open.
>
> (Kamal, 2021)

Arguing on the same lines Balbir Singh Rajewal and Darshan Pal – both of the SKM – opined:

> Governments, be it central or Haryana, had always been trying to defame farmers in any way possible. After the central government, now Haryana is calling us super spreaders of Covid but anybody can come and see the record at protest sites as there is no history of protesters

> getting impacted of Covid. It is only a ploy to defame us and deflect attention from the real issue of scrapping farm laws.
>
> (Kamal, 2021)

After celebrating the completion of 100 days of their agitation, the farmers remembered June 5 and 6 (tabling of farm ordinances before the Union Cabinet and the first farmers' protest being held against the ordinances respectively) by burning copies of the farm laws at 250 places in Punjab and also outside the residences of BJP leaders. The protest to mark completion of one year of the introduction of controversial farm laws was organized under the banner of SKM and June 5 was also observed as Sampoorna Kranti Diwas (Total Revolution Day). Relating the eventful account of one year of farmers' struggle to repeal the contentious farm laws, Sukhdev Singh Kokrikalan, general secretary of the BKU (Ugrahan) said:

> Out of 250 places, BKU (Ugrahan) organised protests at 49 places. These included 6 protests outside DC offices in various districts, 26 outside SDM offices and 16 outside BJP leaders' houses. Our cadre organised protests in 12 districts of Punjab. Everywhere, we burnt copies of farm laws. It was on June 5 amid lockdown when ordinances were tabled for the first time. I remember that from June 4 to June 30 last year all our members used to stand on rooftops daily for an hour along with hand written protest charts as there was curfew in Punjab and we were not allowed to assemble. However, slowly we started village-level protests, later tractor march in July, jail bharo aandolan in August. It was followed by village-level five days protest banning entry of SAD-BJP leaders in villages in August. We also organised pakka morchas at Badal and Patiala in September for 5 days, later 'rail roko' in September and finally indefinite dharnas, protests at various sites from October 1. It has been a year and we have not felt tired even for a day.
>
> (Jagga, 2021)

Speaking on the event of the Sampoorna Kranti Diwas, Jagmohan Singh Patiala, general secretary of the BKU (Dakaunda), lamented on the insensitivity of the central government. He said that the government is not bothering 'that we are protesting against their decisions for the past one year. We started our first protest on June 6, 2020, and it is still continuing' (Jagga, June 6, 2021).

Another occasion that farmers chose for highlighting their protest against the controversial three farm laws was to mark the completion of seven months of their protests at the Delhi borders, by holding protest marches towards the Raj Bhawans (Governor Houses) of Punjab and Haryana. A month before, on the completion of six months of their protests at Delhi borders, farmers also observed 'black day' by putting up black flags and burning the effigies of government leaders at Singhu, Tikri, and Ghazipur borders, the central sites of farmers protests. About the June 26 event, the SKM apprised the stakeholders, a day before i.e. June 25, 2021, through a curtain-raiser on its social media platforms (Kamal, 2021). This event also marked 46 years of imposition of emergency by the Indira Gandhi government in 1975. While comparing the current crisis with that of 1975, Balbir Singh Rajewal, president of the BKU (Rajewal) said:

> The situation is similar to 1975 now as the present regime has put an undeclared emergency in place when right to expression is in danger and the dissenting voices are termed as anti-national. The Narendra Modi government is not ready to listen to the pains of the farmers who are sitting at the borders for seven months and the government is branding them as separatists, anti-nationals and urban naxals. Despite all this, farmers will not sit back till their demands of repeal of three laws, enacting law on MSP are not met.
>
> (Kamal, 2021)

As per the plan, the farmers from Haryana and Punjab gathered in large numbers at Gurdwara Nada Sahib in Panchkula and Amb Sahib in Mohali, respectively. In a repeat of November 26, 2020, scenes of farmers braving water cannons and pushing aside barricades with their mighty tractors amidst police *lathi* charge were witnessed when they broke open the Mohali-Chandigarh border on June 26, 2021. However, what distinguished June 26 march from that of November 26 was the restraint observed by protesting farmers in avoiding direct confrontation with the police. Police too, this time, adopted some restraint. To avoid any unruly scenes, farmers from Haryana handed over their memorandum at the Haryana-Chandigarh border (Kamal, 2021). To ensure a peaceful march towards the Raj Bhawans in Chandigarh, the protesting farmers maintained discipline in dissent, restricted the participation by the youngsters, and raised slogans of 'Save Agriculture, Save Democracy' (Jagga, 2021). During his interaction with the *Indian Express*, the general secretary of BKU (Dakaunda), Jagmohan Singh said:

> We never wanted things to go out of hand in excitement. After January 26, we have been very cautious about maintaining discipline while protesting. Every farmer union leader had been assigned certain duties. It was a mix of our young, middle-aged, and elderly farmers who marched towards Chandigarh on Saturday morning.
>
> (Jagga, 2021)

Reiterating their stand on the legitimacy of farmer protests against the farm laws, Rajewal, the senior-most (77) kisan leader and president of BKU (Rajewal), briefed the *Times of India*:

> It is a matter of survival for farmers. These laws are against the interests of farmers, who fear losing their land and whatever MSP they are getting on a few crops (mainly wheat, paddy). We are here to get the laws repealed and make the government bring an act for legal guarantee of MSP on all crops to all farmers. We are not going back before that despite knowing fully well that we may have to face a lot of onslaught.
>
> (Kamal, 2021)

Endorsing the views of Rajewal, Joginder Singh Ugrahan (75), the president of BKU (Ekta Ugrahan) and the second senior-most kisan leader said:

> The BJP is still not tired of testing our patience. After all its tricks failed, it is now resorting to defamation. We will face this as well but will not go away. These laws are against the economy, social life, the soul and spirit of farmers.
>
> (Kamal, 2021)

Almost six months had passed since the last round of talks were held between the representatives of the central governments and farmer leaders on January 22, 2021, and for more than a year, farmers had been shuttling between their agriculture fields/homes and the sites of protests against the three farm laws. Bone chilling cold and scorching heat failed to dampen their enthusiasm at the seamlessly barricaded borders of Delhi. If for the central government, it is a question of prestige, then for farmers of their *hoNd* – existence. That is what sustains their zeal and endurance. 'For the hegemonic agrarian ruling class in Punjab, land is not merely an economic asset, Kumar argued cogently, but has social and cultural value' (Kumar, 2021). There was a general consensus that the deadlock may turn more complicated in view of reports in the national media that farmer organizations were planning to gherao Parliament during the upcoming monsoon session to reinforce pressure on the central government to withdraw the three controversial farm laws. Buta Singh Burjgill, president, BKU (Dakaunda), told the Indian Express:

> On July 17, we will go to houses of leaders belonging to opposition parties and give them a warning letter. It will be our request to either break their silence in the house or leave their seat. Five days later, a large group of people will leave Singhu, reach the Parliament, and tell the Opposition to disrupt proceedings inside. We will sit outside. We will keep repeating it; this is our plan to protest.
>
> (Express New Service, 2021)

Revealing the action plan of farmers for the upcoming monsoon session of Parliament, the SKM issues a statement that:

> five members per organisation and at least 200 protestors per day will protest every day outside the Parliament during the session – between July 19 and August 13.
>
> (Express New Service, 2021)

The SKM had assured that the protest would remain peaceful, and to forestall any untoward incidents such as those instigated by saboteurs on Republic Day a few months earlier, the farmer unions had issued identification badges to those joining the protest outside Parliament. Despite the unfortunate incidents on January 26, 2021, when farmers were denied entry to central city areas, the very fact of the farmers obtaining permission from Delhi police on July 22, 2021, to hold a 'Kisan Sansad' at Jantar Mantar, in parallel to the official Sansad (Parliament) session, strongly indicated the surging support for farmers' opposition to the three farm laws. Commenting on third day of farmers' protest near Parliament, Rakesh Tikait, the spokesperson of BKU, exhorted the farmers 'to save the soul and freedom of India' (HT Correspondent, 2021). Joginder Singh Ugrahan, president of BKU (Ekta-Ugrahan), speaking on the importance of Kisan Sansad, claimed:

> Staying eight months against a formidable opposition was not easy, after January 26 especially, when the protests had reached its weakest point, but the BJP defeat in three states, including West Bengal, gave us a boost and now Kisan Sansad is preparing us to hurt the BJP in Uttar Pradesh elections.
>
> (Kamal, 2021)

Endorsing Joginder Singh Ugrahan's viewpoint, Balbir Singh Rajewal, President BKU (Rajewal) said: 'The BJP understands only the voice of votes. We got the saffron in Bengal and now we'll get them in UP and Uttarakhand' (Kamal, 2021).

The SKM's resolve to remain peaceful was further vindicated on August 28, 2021, when the Haryana Police baton-charged farmers who blocked a highway in Karnal in a protest against a BJP meeting, attended by Chief Minister Manohar Lal Khattar (Malik, 2021). At least ten people were reportedly injured and 'one of them died from a heart attack a day later'. What further aggravated the crisis was a video of an IAS officer of the Haryana administration, ordering policemen to 'smash the heads of farmers' (BBC News, 2021). The video showed him saying:

> We will not let this line be breached at any cost. Just pick up your *lathi* (baton) and hit them hard... It's very clear, there is no need for any

instruction, just thrash them hard. If I see a single protester here, I want to see his head smashed, crack their heads.

(Ghazali, Mohammed (reported) & Swathi Bhasin (edited), 2021; emphasis added)

The standoff between the Haryana administration and protesting farmers continued for more than a week. Though the Haryana government transferred the officer out of Karnal on September 2, 2021, farmers pressed for the suspension of the officer who ordered the baton-charge. This agitation was suspended after the State government agreed to institute a judicial probe into the August 28 incident by a retired judge of the High Court and to 'give jobs to two family members of the deceased farmer Satish Kajal under sanctioned posts at DC rate in Karnal' (The Economic Times, 2021). However, suspension of that agitation did not put an end to the farmers' strategy of protest outside the venue of BJP meetings until the three laws were not fully withdrawn. The August 28 brutal incident acted as a reminder of the heavy police repression unleashed under the British rule during the Anti-*Bandobast* (Land Settlement) agitation of Amritsar in 1938 against the steep rise of land revenue and *Abiana*/canal water charges as we will discuss later.

The Lakhimpur Kheri incident of October 3, 2021, was another example of mind-numbing violence which involved the UP government and farmers protesting against the farm laws. This incident was a reminder of the peaceful muzaras morcha against the Kathorlia jagirdars of tehsil Pathankot, district Gurdaspur (discussed below). The incident at Lakhimpur Kheri witnessed nine people dead at village Tikunia, located on the connecting road to Banbirpur which was occupied by farmers protesting against the visit of UP Deputy Chief Minister, Keshav Prasad Maurya, to Banbirpur, native village of Union Minister of State for Home Affairs and Lakhimpur Kheri's MP, Ajay Misra Teni. The occasion was a prize distribution function organized by the Union Minister at a school in Tikunia to be presided over by the Deputy Chief Minister of UP.

The genesis of the Lakhimpur Kheri standoff can be traced to some alleged remarks made by the Union Minister Ajay Misra during his visit to Lakhimpur Kheri on September 25 at a gathering of farmers in his Lok Sabha constituency. He allegedly warned a group of farmers over their 'unruly' behaviour by showing him black flags during the event. This had provoked the farmers to protest against him on the Tikunia-Banbirpur road in Lakhimpur Kheri during his visit on October 3. It was during the peaceful protest at this site when a vehicle ploughed through the protesting farmers with murderous intent, leaving four of them (Nakshatra Singh, Daljeet Singh, Lavepreet Singh, and Gurvendra Singh) dead. The other four, out of nine found dead, were reportedly of BJP cadre. They were travelling in a cavalcade vehicle and were allegedly dragged out and lynched by the protesters. The ninth death was of Ratan Kashyap, a journalist who was covering the incident of violence for a TV news channel (India Today, 2021).

In yet another incident, reiterating the peaceful nature of the farmers' protest, SKM condemned the barbaric killing of a farm labourer, Lakhbir Singh from Cheema Khurd village in Tarn Taran district of Punjab, on October 15, 2021, by a group of Nihangs (a Sikh order, distinguished by their blue robes and traditional weapons) at a farmers' protest site at Kundli on the Delhi-Haryana border. The SKM disassociated itself from them (Shaurya, 2021). Lakhbir Singh had reached the protest site at the Delhi border a week earlier before the unfortunate incident and was staying with a group of Nihangs who allegedly found him desecrating the *Sarbloh Granth* (sacred scripture) and consequently chopped off his left wrist and a foot, and broke his legs (*Team TOI*, 2021; The Quint, 2021).

Alleging conspiracy behind Lakhbir's killing and packing it in a religious fold, in order to sabotage their movement, the SKM asked for a thorough probe into the matter and demanded that the culprits should be brought to book (Sharma, 2021a; Shaurya, 2021). The SKM also claimed that the farmers' movement was not a religious one and had nothing to do with the killing (Sharma, 2021a). Jagjit Singh Dallewal, a farmer leader of the SKM said: 'We condemn disrespecting of any religion. We also condemn the reaction (killing)' (Sharma, 2021a).

What gave credence to SKM apprehensions was *The Tribune* expose about Nihang Aman Singh meeting BJP ministers in the presence of former police cat Gurmeet Singh Pinki (Singh, 2021a). Taking note of *The Tribune* expose, the Punjab government formed a three-member Special Investigation Team (SIT) to probe 'all angles involving activities of Nihang leader Baba Aman Singh's group, barbaric killing of Lakhbir Singh at the Singhu border, secret meetings between a police cat-turned-murder convict, and to find out the true identity of some Nihang leaders' (Singh, 2021b).

There is a widely shared impression that all the above-mentioned incidents of violence were the handiwork of invisible anti-farmer forces which continuously hatched deep-rooted conspiracies to discredit and thereby sabotage the peaceful kisan movement from within. However, the leadership of SKM displayed exemplary finesse in thwarting all such Machiavellian machinations and successfully maintained momentum of the agitation.

The long-drawn struggle of the SKM, the peaceful nature of its agitation, together with the perseverance and tenacity of its experienced leadership, finally succeeded in forcing the Central government to repeal the three contentious farm laws. The announcement to repeal the laws was made on November 19, 2021, at the auspicious occasion of gurpurab (birth anniversary) of Baba Guru Nanak. Subsequently, on November 29, the laws were formally withdrawn in both houses of parliament without any discussion. It took the Lok Sabha (lower house) less than four minutes to pass the bill to repeal them on the first day of its Winter Session. In the Rajya Sabha too, the repeal Bill was passed without any discussion (DTE, November 29, 2021). After two days, on December 1, 2021, President of India gave his assent to the Farm Laws Repeal Act 2021.

After receiving a formal communication from the Centre in the form of a letter signed by Sanjay Agarwal, secretary to the Union Ministry of Agriculture and Farmers' Welfare, agreeing to other pending demands of the farmers, including withdrawal of police cases against the agitating farmers, the constitution of a committee for legal guarantees on MSP for crops, and discussion of the Electricity (Amendment) Bill 2021 with farmers' groups before it is tabled in Parliament, the SKM vacated their morcha sites on Delhi borders and returned to their homes on December 11, 2021 (Dey, 2021). However, the government letter was silent on SKM's demand for the removal of Union Minister Ajay Mishra relating to the Lakhimpur Kheri incident on October 3 (Dey, 2021). Gurnam Singh Charuni, Haryana farmer leader, said during a press conference:

> We have decided to suspend our agitation. We will hold a review meeting on Jan 15. If the government does not fulfil its promises, we could resume our agitation.
>
> (India TV News Desk, 2021)

Commenting on some of the other pending issues, Yogendra Yadav, one of the most vocal members of the SKM, told reporters:

> In some form or the other, farmers will have to continue their struggle. The issue of MSP is alive, the fear of (increasing) electricity bills is also real, Ajay Mishra still continues to be a member of the Cabinet. All these issues are there. So, we will continue our struggle but for some time we are suspending everything (demonstrations).
>
> (Dey, 2021)

Rakesh Tikait, Bharatiya Kisan Union leader, and one of main members of the SKM, also said that:

> ...there would be a review meeting on 15 January in which all unresolved issues would be assessed – including the unfulfilled demand regarding the removal of Mishra.
>
> (Dey, 2021)

In a conversation with ANI, Manpreet Singh, Executive Member of Bharatiya Kisan Union (BKU) Punjab, said:

> We have won this battle after the struggles of a year-long protest. We are happy that the Central government has agreed to fulfil our pending demands. We are doing packing here and will return to our homes at 9 am on December 11.
>
> (India TV News Desk, 2021)

Like various earlier heroic struggles of Punjab, the longest (more than year-long) peaceful kisan struggle at the borders of Delhi has already entered into the valorous folk space of Punjab, so much so that one of the volunteer farmer activists from Dhakowal village of Hoshiarpur district told *The Wire* that the bricks of the three-room cemented house which he had built at the Singhu border, and which was later converted into an office of the BKU (Doaba) headed by Manjit Singh Rai, would be used to construct a 'Kisan Morcha Memorial' at his village. He further told *The Wire*:

> In fact, many fellow farmers also took the bricks of this house to construct memorials at their villages. But before dismantling it, I handed over the household stuff including fans, coolers, ACs, washing machine, LCD, bed and other things to local people.
>
> (Arora, 2021)

In retrospect, the farmers' protest has carved out a niche not only at the national, but also global level, as well as developing a close rapport with almost every section of society, for instance many heart-rending scenes were witnessed at the protest sites as farmers pulled down their tents. Over the months the farmers had built a close bond among themselves and with local residents, and these emotional connections were very visible, raw, and deeply moving. This phenomenon gives rise to some searching questions about the movement: From where did it draw such strength to persist with the struggle? What motivated farmers to hold dharnas on railway tracks and national highways, and to spend endless days and nights in the open on Delhi's borders? How was it able to commandeer such unswerving grassroots support for its protests? Such questions probe the very spirit of this long-drawn agitation and, in the following section, an attempt has been made to answer them by contextualizing the farmers' protest within the rich heritage of peasant struggles in both pre-partition undivided Punjab, and post-independence Indian Punjab.

Contextualizing Farmers' Protests

Pre-Independence and Pre-Partition Agrarian Movements

Pre-partition Punjab witnessed many peasant struggles, which bequeathed a rich legacy for latter generations of farmers. With agriculture being the mainstay of majority of its populace, and given the unregulated and oppressive system of local moneylending accompanied by heavy land revenues and water taxes, peasant struggles became a routine occurrence during pre-partition Punjab (Barrier, 1966: Chaps 1–3; Barrier, 1967; Darling, 1977 [1925]). After the annexation of Punjab in 1849, British government put its entire land in the state under meticulously devised legal control (Barrier, 1967: 355–358). Another major project undertaken by the British Raj was the canalization of large tracts of barren land, leading to the advent of irrigation and sudden prosperity among the otherwise pauperized peasant communities of the state (Barrier, 1967: 355–357). This canal-based system of arid land irrigation had not only propelled the high-yielding varieties of crops but also gave rise to residential colonies of farmers around the newly dug canals (Barrier, 1967: 356–358). Many farmers also joined the British army, which brought rich opportunities for Sikh soldiers to visit Europe and North America, but also forced them to face their ignoble social status as subjects of the British Empire (Waraich, 1967; Waraich, 1991; Chandan, 2014; Rahi, 2018). This led to social and political awakening among the inhabitants of the newly established canal colonies in Western Punjab – many of them ex-soldiers in the British army – that eventually played a catalytic role in the emergence of peasant movements in the state against agriculture Acts, which offended their *izzat* (honour, prestige, self-respect).

However, preceding these salutary contributions by the peasantry during the massive British Canal projects, there were many inflexion points, such as introduction of the Persian water wheel in this region in the sixteenth century, and establishment of a Sikh Kingdom by Maharaja Ranjit Singh in 1799. The peasants of Punjab fought for freedom and their land, first under the command of Five *Pyare* and 25 Singhs sent by Guru Gobind Singh – along with Baba Banda Bahadur (Alam, 1982: 95–107) – to help establish just rule in Punjab, and later launch guerrilla warfare through various Sikh *Misls* (confederacies). During this long period of checkered history, the valorous peasantry of Punjab was engaged primarily in fighting for the restoration and protection of their land. It was also the peasants who bore the brunt of brutal persecution at the hands of both alien forces, and of the partition of the vast province of Punjab when circumstances conspired against them and they had to forsake their well-groomed canal irrigated agriculture fields in West Punjab, now in Pakistan.

In addition, the sterling contribution made by the farmers of Punjab in the organization and functioning of the historic *Ghadar* movement, 1913–1948 (Sainsara, 1969; Puri, 1983), Gurdwara Reform Movement, 1920–1925 (Singh, 1978), *Babbar Akali* Movement, 1921–1925 (Babbar, 2006; Waraich and Kangniwal, 2015), *Guru ka Bagh Morcha*, 1922, and *Jaito Da Morcha*, 1924–1925 (Walia, 1972: 26–27, 52) adds a further lustre to the rich heritage of farmers' relentless struggle for the safeguard of their land rights and restoration of their civic and religious liberties (Singh, 1978; Fox, 1985). Guru ka Bagh and Jaito Morchas are well-known for their exemplary non-violent struggle. The genesis of the recently concluded agitation, which galvanized farmers across India, can be traced to these pre-independence agrarian agitations in Punjab.

Pagri Sambhal Jatta Movement (1907)

The *Pagri Sambhal Jatta* movement of 1907 is the pioneer peasant movement of Punjab, which provides clues to understanding what sustained the vigour of the recent farmers' protests at the borders of Delhi. This movement was launched primarily to force the British administration to withdraw the Punjab Land Colonisation Act 1906 (introduced in the Punjab Legislative Council on October 25, 1906, and passed in February 1907), which aimed at depriving landowners of their land. This, however, was not the only agriculture law passed by the Punjab Legislative Assembly since the establishment of the Canal Colonies by the British government in the late nineteenth century after the annexation of Punjab in 1849. A good number of agriculture-related Acts – the Land Alienation Act of 1900, the Punjab Limitation Act 1904, the Transfer of Property Act 1904, the Punjab Pre-Emption Act of 1905, the Court of Wards Act of 1905, and the Punjab Land Alienation Act Amendment Bill 1906 – had already been passed by the provincial government without facing any resistance from the landowners. Instead, all these Acts were presented by the British government as, what N. Gerald Barrier called, 'paternal protection of the cultivating land-owners' (Barrier, 1967: 354).

However, what prompted the landowners to rise against the Punjab Land Colonisation Act 1906 was its various stringent clauses that 'forbade transfer of property by will', introduced 'strict primogeniture as interpreted by the Canal Officer'; imposed fresh conditions like planting of trees as well as prior permission for their cutting, sanitary rules, and higher occupancy fee; legalized fines; and debarred the courts from 'interfering with executive orders' (Barrier, 1967: 359–360). The Act also included a clause stating that 'if a new settler died without gaining occupancy rights (generally before five years), the land lapsed to the government' (Barrier, 1967: 359). However, even though before the enactment of this Act, landowners in the Chenab canal colony were subjected to various hardships by the local administration in the form of corruption and arbitrary fines, they did not raise the banner of revolt against British government laws, which the latter considered benevolent. But as soon as their land was targeted, landowners turned hostile. The increase in the *abiana* (water rate) under the Doab Bari Act of 1907 further aggravated the crisis that forced them to unite first under the 'yeoman grantees' of the Bar Zamindar Association and then under the revolutionary leadership of Ajit Singh, uncle of Shaheed Bhagat Singh, who with the support of the *Bharat Mata Sabha*, an underground organization, fought the Punjab Land Colonisation Act 1906 tooth and nail (Barrier, 1967; Mahajan, 1981; Mukherjee, 2004: 26–29). The threat of losing land was articulated as a threat to the very existence of the landowners, and this sentiment was captured in the movement's slogan: *Pagdi Sambhal Jatta* (take care of thy turban [honour] O, Jat). Eventually, the movement itself came to be known by this very slogan (Sidhu, 2020).

The often repeated epitaph of 'the question of *hoNd* (existence of farmer) in the recent farmers' protests reminds us of the above-mentioned slogan during the 1907 movement. The recent farmers' struggle against the three farm laws, like that of the 1907 peasant movement, is being fought to safeguard the *hoNd* (existence) of farmers. Both of these historic farmers' movements (1907 and the recent 2020–2021 one) were launched after thoroughly debating each and every clause (Barrier, 1967: 364–368; Pal, 2009–2010: 453–455). Another striking parallel between the Punjab Land Colonisation Act 1906 and the recent three farms laws is that both were rushed through the legislative process without a proper discussion (Barrier, 1967: 361, 366). Finally, the Punjab Land Colonisation Act 1906 was withdrawn after the Secretary of State vetoed it on May 26, 1907, that is, just after 6 months whereas the recent one continued for over a year.

Nili Bar Morcha (1938)

Nili Bar da Morcha of 1938 in West Punjab – of *Banney Uttey Adho-addh* (50–50 share of the harvested crop) fame – was another historic farmer movement that provides us significant background to contextualize the ongoing farmers' protest. The Nili Bar da Morcha began with the strike by 50,000 *Muzara* (tenant peasants/share-croppers) under the leadership of the Punjab Kisan Sabha formed on March 23, 1937, led by Baba Jawala Singh, its founder president (Kangniwal, November 22, 2020a). Other prominent leaders of this peasant struggle were Ram Singh Ghalamala, Prof. Jalwant Singh, Baba Jalwant Singh Garewal, Takaia Ram, Wadhava Ram, Sharifdeen, Kherdeen Khanowalia, Hazari Ram, Vaid Sant Singh, and Gian Singh. Joginder Singh Bhambar, Ajit Singh Manakpuri, Ataullah Jahania, and Ghandarv Sen also joined the Nili Bar morcha (Bilga, 1989: 237–238). This muzara kisan morcha was launched against the Unionist Government of the Punjab Province for its anti-kisan policies. Sunder Singh Majithia, the Finance Minister, was entrusted with initiating a dialogue with the Muzaras in Multan. He, in turn, deputed M.L. Darling, Financial Commissioner of Punjab,[3] who on May 1937 went to the Ganji Bar which had a huge gathering of 20,000 Muzaras and met their representatives led by Baba Jawala Singh. He accepted in entirety their 22 demands and prominent among them were: muzaras' right to get their share of crops at the rate of half-half in the field itself, end of *begār* (forced labour), provision for animal fodder, reduction in land revenue, canal water tax and loans, etc., to forgo revenue up to Rs 5, and resolution of disputes by village panchayat (Bilga, 1989: 237). The Nili Bar morcha was the beginning of the Kirti Party's movement against feudalism in the state. The movement was spearheaded by the Punjab Kisan Sabha, founded on March 23, 1937. Baba Jawala Singh and B.P.L. Bedi (father of film star Kabir Bedi) were its founder President and General Secretary, respectively. Bedi and his wife Freda Bedi (Whitehead, 2019) stood with the farmers in their struggle against the dictatorial British regime. These powerful precedents, i.e. the 1907 kisan morcha and the non-violent agitation by the Muzaras of Nili Bar, have demonstrated the tenacity and political prowess of organized kisan movements against legislation which they view to be an existential threat, hence a strong sense of *déjà vu* and historical connection pervaded during the recent farmers' agitation.

Charhik Morcha (1938–1939)

Charhik Morcha of 1938, the Korotana conference struggle of 1941, *Harsa Chhina Mogha* (canal water outlet) morchas of 1946, and *Tanda Urmar Muzara Lehar* of 1947 were some other equally historic kisan struggles organized under the leadership of Punjab Kisan Sabha in pre-partition Punjab. These struggles provide further context to aptly place the recent farmers' protest in its proper and lustrous lineage. The Charhik morcha was launched by the *Kirti Kisan Party* on July 29, 1938, against the autocratic rule of the *Kalsia Riyasat* under the leadership of Baba Rurh Singh Chuharhchak, vice president of the Punjab Kisan Sabha, and unopposed elected member of the Punjab Legislative Assembly in 1937 (Bilga, 1989: 260; Walia, 1972: 141). There was a popular saying that if Baba Jawala Singh was the commander of the muzara movement in West Punjab, Rurh Singh was that of East Punjab (Bilga, 1989: 260). Ujagar Singh Bilga, Gulzar Singh Kandekadh, Gurmukh Singh Ambalwi, and Baba Karam Singh Bilga were among others prominent leaders of this morcha (Bilga, 1989: 262). Farmers of villages Charhik, Burj Duna, Manuke, Berr Raoke, Chupkiti/Sandhuan Wala, Budh Singh Wala, and Raoke were reeling under unjustified heavy taxes levied by the rulers of the Riyasat. Since these villages were situated far away from the Riyasat headquarter, they were deprived of basic civic amenities despite the heavy taxes collected. Within three months of its intensive peaceful struggle, the morcha led to thousands of farmers being arrested, such that jails were unable to accommodate more arrested farmers. The participation of women was equally emphatic, for instance, Bibi Raghbir Kaur, a Kirti Party member of the Punjab Assembly, lead a demonstration of 100 women in favour of agitating farmers. Ultimately, the morcha was an overwhelming success, ending with the acceptance of all its demands by the rulers of the Kalsia Riyasat on January 14, 1939 (Kangniwal, 2020c).

Amritsar Morcha (1938)

Anti-*Bandobast* (Land Settlement) agitation of Amritsar of 1938 was another historic peasant struggle against the proposed unjust increase of Rs 4 lakh in land revenue that began July 20, 1938, and came to a successful end on August 9, 1938, after the removal of Clause 144 which prohibited public gatherings and withdrawal of the decision to initiate the process of land settlement (Bilga, 1989: 250–251; Chayn, 1990: 173; Kangniwal, 2020a).

This peaceful agitation of farmers led by Punjab Kisan Sabha, supported by Akali leaders (Udham Singh Nagoke, Darshan Singh Pheruman among others) and other leaders such as Baba Sohan Singh Bhakna, Harnam Singh Kasel, Sohan Singh Josh, Kartar Singh Gill, Gehal Singh Chhajalwadi, Mohinder Singh, Fauja Singh Bhullar, Dalip Singh Johal, Santa Singh Ghandivind, Jaswant Singh Kairon (brother of Partap Singh Kairon), and Bibi Raghbir Kaur, as well as a crowd of at least 5,000–6,000 peasants and several thousand other sympathizers remained non-violent despite heavy repression unleashed by the police on the participating farmers under the instructions of Muhammad Shafi, the city Magistrate of Amritsar (Bilga, 1989: 249–251; Mukherjee, 2004: 154–165). Another dimension of that morcha, which helps us to better understand the unity between the labour unions and farmers in the recent farmers' protest, is that many labour unions also joined hand with the Amritsar Morcha in support of its demands for withdrawing the increased rate of land revenue, including privately digged wells as well as *shamlat* (common land) and barren land. Further, Jayaprakash Narayan, Saifuddin Kitchlew, Swami Sahajnand, and N.G. Ranga and pan-Indian kisan leaders also spoke in favour of the Anti-Bandobast agitation of Amritsar which had elevated its relevance to the national level (Bilga, 1989: 250; Mukherjee, 2004: 159–160).

Lahore Morcha (1938–1939)

Coming in on the heels of the Amritsar success story, the Lahore Morcha of 1938–1939 presents a piece of significant historical background against which the current farmers' protests can be contrasted in order to understand the enthusiasm and persistence with which its participants, including women, the elderly, and children braved the odds across the highways on the borders of Delhi. The Lahore Morcha was launched against the enhancement of land revenue in the last resettlement of Lahore district. A total of 5,000 people, primarily comprising *jathas* of volunteers marching to the Lahore Assembly, were jailed during this six-month agitation (Bilga, 1989: 266). The first demonstration was organized on March 23, 1939, by the District Kisan Committee of Lahore under the leadership of Yog Raj and Tehal Singh Bhangali (Chayn, 1990: 178). The organizers of this inaugural demonstration were not permitted a meeting with the Premier of Punjab, and were compelled to violate Section 144. By the end of the first week, 374 had courted arrest (Bilga, 1989: 264–265; Mukherjee, 2004: 189–190).

The large number of arrests did not shatter the spirit of the morcha. Though the District Kisan Committee of Lahore launched the morcha without the permission of the Punjab Kisan Committee (PKC), the latter came to its rescue by soliciting volunteers from neighbouring districts. This kept the morcha going at a time when farmers were busy during the April wheat harvesting season and 700 had been arrested by the middle of the month. It was at this time that the PKC took over the morcha and appointed a sub-committee consisting of Baba Rurh Singh, Master Gajjan Singh, and Ram Kishan for the purpose. Thus, between April 17 and May 3, the morcha got a new lease of life. During this period, more women than men courted arrest.[4] Momentum continued to build, with volunteers from a large number of districts joining the morcha. Even volunteers who had only recently returned home after spending a nine-month period in prison threw themselves back into the fray by re-enrolling (Mukherjee, 2004: 189–192).

When the government tightened its grip after the middle of June 1939 by pre-emptively arresting both leaders of the morcha and members of *jathas* in their respective home districts, in order to prevent them from reaching Lahore, the PKC adapted by devising a strategy of sending of *jathas* of only five members. The morcha was given a substantial boost due to support extended by the All-India Kisan Sabha (Rasul, 1974), the Labour Federation of Amritsar, trade unions in Jalandhar, members of both the Congress and Akali Dal, and students of Lahore. The current farmers' protest at Delhi borders has also been supported by a large number of students, with some of them even running mobile libraries at the protest sites. Gurinder Singh, an Oxford University alumnus, told *NewsClick*:

> We are here since day one. We felt that youth here, apart from participating in *seva* activities, have very little to do. So, we created this open space for them to get involved in creative activities. We named this library-cum-cultural centre as Sanjhi Sath, which means shared *chaupal* (place for meeting).
>
> (Anwar, 2020)

Emboldened and empowered by such a broad spectrum of support, the morcha not only survived rampant police repression let loose in the home districts of the *Jathas* in August but thrived. Finally, after a continuous agitation of six months, the morcha was unilaterally withdrawn by the PKS in the last week of September 1939. Though few of its demands had been accepted by Sir Sikandar Hayat Khan, Premier of Punjab, the morcha had generated a political awakening among the peasantry, publicity for its cause, greatly boosted its membership, and benefited from gravitation of several district-level congressmen towards the Communist movement (Chayn, 1990: 178; Mukherjee, 2004: 194–196).

Muzara Struggle of Gurdaspur (1939)

The muzaras of tehsil Pathankot, district Gurdaspur, bore the brunt of many of the worst brutalities. These were perpetrated by the *jagirdars* of Kathrol, known as 'Kathorlia jagirdars', who owned 35–40 villages in the tehsil between them. These muzaras lead wretched lives – after every harvest, the Kathrolia jagirdars routinely usurped a lion's share of the crop using various flimsy pretexts (Bilga, 1989: 245–246). Consequently, the muzaras were left with very little and were compelled to sell even their meagre dairy products for routine household needs, to the great detriment of their families' health, surviving as they did on food of very low nutritional value such as dry chapattis, some pickle, chutney, and onions. The dearth of good quality and affordable health facilities meant that many muzaras died of malaria and other treatable diseases, often falling victim to quacks (Bilga, 1989: 245–246).

The victory of the Nili Bar Morcha had ignited a ray of hope among the muzaras of Pathankot tehsil. Under the leadership of Baba Ishar Singh, founder of the Kirti Party in Gurdaspur district, numerous volunteers joined and began organizing the muzaras in Pathankot tehsil. Prominent among these was Vishnu Dutt Sharma,[5] a student in Banga Town near Phagwara, and native of Khatkar Kalan, who had begun staying with Baba Kharak Singh, at Anup Shahar of Nangal. Baba Kharak Singh was a veteran muzara and Kirti activists enjoyed an open invitation to his house. Chanan Singh Tughalwala, Giani Hari Singh, Chanan Singh Chhota, Shiv Kumar Sharda, Thakur Das Kathrol, Mani Ram Gobindsar, and Bibi Shankuntala, all led the Gurdaspur muzara agitation against the oppression of the Kathorlia landlords (Bilga, 1989: 245–246; Chayn, 1990: 173). Their main demand, like that of the Nili Bar Morcha, was a very reasonable one – give half of the harvested crop for its tiller.

Despite the Kathorlia jagirdars ratcheting up their oppression through henchmen, the agitation went from strength to strength with the opening of a new revolutionary centre called Shiv Kumar Sharda's Paniar Ashram. At this centre, Mai Tabbo of Paniar Ashram used to collect provisions from fellow villagers for the common kitchen to serve Kirti party activists. The poet Lahori Ram Pardesi and Inder Singh Murari, before their moving to Kangra district, had also organized conventions of muzaras against the jagirdars (Bilga, 1989: 247). Ram Singh Dutt was a prominent agitation leader who deserves special mention. He had been interned in his village Viram Dutta after returning from Moscow, but the entire functioning of the muzara movement, including all activities of the Kirti Party, took place under the banner of the Congress Party and operated from his village under his tactful leadership. During the period of his village confinement, a huge mazdoor-kisan-muzara conference was organized in his village. So high was Dutt's popularity, all participants prior to reaching the conference venue would meet him at his residence. He had been legally debarred from undertaking any public activity or making political statements (Bilga, 1989: 247). A similar level of commitment and zeal were visible at the borders of Delhi where support has been pouring in from different sections of society from both within the country and abroad, and many Vishnu Dutt Sharmas have been camping alongside protesting farmers of Punjab, Haryana, and UP in solidarity with their cause.

Korotana Struggle (1941)

The pre-partition Korotana struggle was another illustrious milestone in the history of Punjab Kisan agitations. It took place during World War II when the British government had banned all progressive and radical kisan organizations, and many of their leaders were incarcerated in the Deoli Camp jail in Rajasthan and other prisons in the state. It was during such repressive circumstances that the Kirti Kisan Party decided to hold the fourth Delegate *ijlas* (session) of the Punjab Kisan Sabha at village Kotorana, 14 km from the town of Moga in the Malwa region of Punjab. This was a vast left-leaning kisan region, and even in the recent agitation a large number of protesting farmers hailed from there (Kangniwal, 2020a, 2020b). The preparation for the *ijlas* had already been made after selecting delgates through village-level elections of kisan committees and holding ijlas of the Tehsil and district kisan committees (Kangniwal, 2020c). To thwart the ijlas, the government had made preparations including the stationing of heavy contingents of horse-mounted policemen at different intervals along the route to the ijlas. A rumour was also spread in the surrounding villages through a public announcement system that no one should reach Kotorana because of the possibility of firing taking place over there (Kangniwal, 2020c).

Nevertheless, farmers, paying scant heed to police warnings and arrests pre-ijlas, rushed to village Kotorana in thousands with red flags and raising slogans. During their march to the site of ijlas, a total number of nine presidents – Mangal Singh, Baba Dhara Singh, Teja Singh Chuharchak, Lal Singh Kanwar, Muhammad Hayat, Gazhi Badrudeen, and Wadhava Ram – of the kisan organizations, one after another, were arrested by the police (Kangniwal, 2020c). It is apt to note at this juncture that in striking similarity, protesting farmers from Punjab and Haryana, like the kisans of Kotorana struggle, had also reached the borders of Delhi on November 25, 2020, after overcoming various hurdles thrown in their way by the Haryana government. Against all odds, an estimated 40,000–50,000 farmers were able to reach the site of the ijlas, where Gehal Singh Chhajalwaddi, assisted by Jagjit Singh Lyallpuri in the capacity of secretary, officiated. Like the recent agitation at the gate of Delhi, hundreds of women, under the leadership of Sushila Chayn of the Kirti Party, participated in the ijlas at Kotorana that continued uninterrupted for three days (September 20–22, 1941). About 40,000 kisans were present every day during the three days' ijlas. Meticulous *langar* arrangements were made throughout the programme, and on the last day of the congregation, a kisan workers' drama group of Ludhiana entertained the large gathering through real-life-based skits of kisans and the iniquitous treatment meted out to them at the hands of *patwaris*, *nambardars*, and moneylenders (Kangniwal, 2020c). This protest was another grand success and added another feather to the kisan political movement's cap.

Harsa Chhina 'Mogha' Morcha (1946–1947)

Harsa Chhina 'Mogha'[6] morchas[7] of 1946 (henceforth Harsa Chhina morcha) are yet another celebrated struggle by Punjab farmers in the pre-partition period. This was launched on July 20, 1946, against the Provincial government's notorious 'remodelling scheme' of reducing the size of the 100 outlets which released water from the Upper Bari Doab Canal of Lahore that irrigated the agriculture land of a large number of villages falling under the Ajnala tehsil, in the Majitha sub-division of district Amritsar. The size of 40 of the total number of canal outlets was reduced to a level that would allow only *a quarter* of the given water to pass into the fields. Deeply upset by this inexplicable government action, farmers of 15 surrounding villages of Harsa Chhina approached the concerned ministers through the legislator of their constituency, but failed to enlist a positive response. The aggrieved farmers then submitted a memorandum to the government through the Kisan Sabha of district Amritsar, for withdrawal of the 'remodelling scheme' and restoration to the original size of the canal outlets. It was also mentioned in the resolution that if nothing positive was heard from the government, within a span of 15 days, the affected farmers will dismantle the newly installed smaller size outlets (Kangniwal, unpublished paper[a]).

After receiving no response from the coalition of Congress and Akali government formed after the 1946 provincial elections, 10,000 farmers were organized under the leadership of Achhar Singh Chhina, President of Punjab Kisan Sabha, on July 20, 1946, as per the prior communication to the government. On the same day, 25 volunteers, led by Achhar Singh Chhina, held a march from Gurdwara Babe di Kulli to dismantle the outlets. This was followed by similar marches by volunteer groups from different villages under the common forum of 'Harsa Chhina Mogha Morcha for War Council'. The morcha rapidly acquired momentum, especially after morcha leaders began organizing *dharnas* (sit-ins) by the *Jathās* (volunteer groups) in front of offices of the canal department. This action forced the government to stop arresting the protesting farmers. Many women also participated in the morcha. Bibi Raghbir Kaur (former Legislator), Mohinder Kaur Bedi, Bibi Kirtan Ghudae kee Wali, and Parsinoo Kasel, among others, led a large women-only procession shouting *murdabad* (down with or death to) and *Nehri morcha jit ke rahange* (we will not relent till the Nehri morcha has won) towards the office of the canal department and entered its premises after breaking through a human ring formed by the police. The police arrested the protesting women and sent them to Brostal Jail in Lahore. During the morcha, a total number of 1,800 farmers were arrested, and though the morcha was suspended following the eruption of communal clashes on the eve of partition of Punjab, it left an indelible print of determination and endurance by farmers to fight for their land rights – qualities which were reflected in the recent farmers' protest (Kangniwal, unpublished paper [a]).

Tanda Urmar Morcha (1947)

The *Tanda Urmar Muzara Morcha*[8] is, perhaps, the last kisan morcha for restoration of land rights before the partition of Punjab. This morcha was launched by Hindu, Sikh, and Muslim muzaras and shopkeepers against the oppressive verdicts of a Pathan *jagirdar* Shahbaz Khan, who owned the entire 2,400 acres of agricultural land, upon which the shopkeepers, artisans, muzaras, and labourers all paid fixed rents. Muzaras were not allowed to dig wells on the land, and neither did they have any rights over trees standing on their rented land. If anyone sold a house or shop, 20 per cent of the received price was payable to Shahbaz Khan. The muzaras were also expected to give gifts to the jagirdar on varied occasions. In 1946, the jagirdar brought village graveyards and cremation grounds under his control and simultaneously enhanced the rent of the shanties, houses, and shops. This spurred the affected muzaras and shopkeepers to form a common committee under the leadership of Abdul Kadar Khan, a reputed resident of the town, who then led the first *jatha* of muzaras to harvest the crop of the jagirdar. Events then quickly escalated, with the police arresting and imprisoning all jatha members for a period of one year, leading to Ibrahim, a well-known local personality, being nominated to coordinate a morcha and form an Action Committee under the leadership of Abdul Kadar Khan (Kangniwal, unpublished paper [b]).

In January 1947, the Action Committee convened meetings, organized conferences, and took out processions to build public opinion against oppression perpetrated by the goons of the jagirdar. They were looting the houses of muzaras, insulting their women, and beating them mercilessly without any provocation. Munshi Ahmed Din, Tikka Ram Sukhan, Ashraf, Chaudhary Devi Lal of Haryana, Ramanand Mishra, national leader of the Socialist Party from Bihar, and Pandit Mohan Lal Dutt addressed conferences organized by the morcha. On hearing the wide publicity about this morcha, Mahatma Gandhi deputed Sushila Nayyar to Tanda Urmar. The latter appreciated the non-violent conduct of satyagrahis of the morcha despite repressive actions of the jagirdar (Kangniwal, unpublished paper [b]).

The Action Committee prepared a programme to cut trees from land of the jagirdar and harvest crops sown on the graveyard land forcefully occupied by him. On February 17, 1947, the entire Jatha of 50 satyagrahis deputed for this cause under the command of Abdul Kadar Khan was arrested and imprisoned in Hoshiarpur jail for one year, although a few were sent to other jails due to scarcity of space. Baldev Mittr Bijli and Mubarak Sagar, communist leader, were also arrested and jailed, and Hukam Chand Gulshan, a kisan leader, was jailed without any judicial inquiry (Kangniwal, unpublished paper [b]; Bilga, 1989: 248). The morcha received strong support from various other districts, and a total number of 1,300 volunteers, belonging to all religions, were arrested and imprisoned for one year. More than 300 women also participated in the *satyagraha*, seven of whom were arrested and jailed. Among the arrested satyagrahis were 27 Muslims and 4 Hindus. Of the total arrested 31 were teenagers.

This morcha came to an abrupt end on June 30, 1947, due to the sudden eruption of communal riots on the eve of independence of India and Pakistan and the ensuing partition of Punjab. All arrested volunteers were released on November 27, 1947, with Muslims taken to Delhi under high security cover and then sent to Pakistan. Subsequent to partition and the jagirdar leaving for Pakistan, the remaining village inhabitants were relieved of the draconian jagirdari system, and eventually the muzaras were declared owners of the land they were tilling as tenants of the jagirdar, under the Constitutional provisions of independent India (Kangniwal, Unpublished paper [b]).

Post-Independence Agrarian Movements

PEPSU Muzara Movement (1948–1951)

Other than the above-discussed pre-partition kisan morchas, the post-independence Indian Punjab similarly witnessed farmers' struggles for safeguarding of their land rights. Patiala and East Punjab States Union (PEPSU) Muzara movement (henceforth Pepsu Muzara Movement, PMM) of 1948–1951 was the most prominent in this princely state. The other equally important struggles were: *Khush-hasiyati* Tax morcha (anti-betterment levy agitation) of 1959 and the *Mehatpur Beyt muzara* agitation. The PMM, in fact, was the continuation of the muzaras' protracted struggle against the *biswedars* (big landlords/absentee landlords) since the formation of the *biswedari* system in the 1870s, by the Maharaja of Patiala. The biswedars, mostly the relatives and close confidantes of the Maharaja, established their ownership rights on vast tracts of lands, but the hereditary proprietary peasants who had actually developed these lands, with generations of hard labour, were reduced to make the ignoble status of muzaras.[9] A *Hidayat* (princely fiat) issued in 1872 forced muzaras to pay half of their crop to biswedars as *batai* (the share of a crop going to biswedar under the share-cropping system). However, in actual practice, many of the muzaras were left with only a quarter of their hard-produced crops courtesy of the *kankut* system, under which state functionaries assessed the yield of each crop before its actual harvest and often fixed an exaggerated amount to be handed over to the biswedars, essentially a form of rack-renting (Mukherjee, 2004: 246–247). The biswedari system had been further intensified during the Permanent Land Bandobast (1902–1904) and the First Regular Settlement of Patiala (1908–1909) reinforced it formally (Mukherjee, 1979: 216–283; Mukherjee, 2004: 246; Arshi, 2021).

However, the muzaras did not sit idly by. They approached the courts and also the Viceroy at Shimla to reclaim their grabbed lands but to no avail (Arshi, 2021; Singh, 2021). The failure in getting relief from the courts by ancestors of the recently protesting farmers might have impelled them not to be 'impleaded' in the recent case in the Supreme Court. Rajewal, president of BKU (Rajewal), told The Economic Times:

> We have been included in this matter against our wishes. We have told our lawyers to tell the court that we do not want to be impleaded in the case ... We are prepared to go to jail. The Supreme Court should not discuss the law points going ahead as the matter then be delayed for long.
>
> (Sharma, 2021a)

Finding no relief from the courts, muzaras began vehemently opposing biswedars and their henchmen from taking away their hard produced crops. This led to bloody fights between the erstwhile proprietors, now turned muzaras, and the biswedars supported by their musclemen. The muzara struggle got impetus with the formation of the Punjab *Riyasti Praja Mandal* (henceforth Praja Mandal) on July 17, 1928, at Mansa in Patiala state. Though the Praja Mandal was mainly a movement of the Sikh peasantry that evolved out of the long drawn Gurdwara Reform Movement (1921–1925),[10] the varied ideological affiliations (Akalis, Socialists, Communists, and Congress) of its multi-religious membership gave it a secular platform.[11] It instilled new spirit in the muzara movement through its Akali-Praja Mandal Dewans (religio-political congregations).[12] It also enabled extension to its political campaigns to smaller states of East Punjab, especially the state of Nabha, Jind, and Malerkotla, for protection of rights and liberties of the people, for setting up of representative institutions, and for amelioration of hardships of the Muzaras. In 1933, the Mandal started an Urdu Weekly *Ryasti Duniya* (Lahore) edited by Talib Hussain of Malerkotla and a Punjabi journal *Desh Dardi* (Amritsar) edited by Sardara Singh Yuthup of Nabha Riyasat, to provide extensive coverage of its varied activities (Walia, 1972: 82–83; Bilga, 1989: 240). History repeats itself: the recent farmers' struggle is being spearheaded by more than 32 Punjab farmers unions, and over 40 Indian farmers unions, coalesced into *SKM*, having divergent political affiliations.

Another significant development that further strengthened the muzara movement was the formation of the Communist-led kisan committees, which were also working 'under the influence and direction of Praja Mandal leaders ...' (Mukherjee, 2004: 252). In a nutshell, the Praja Mandal leaders, Akalis and the leaders of the Communist-led Kisan Sabhas stood with the muzaras in their tirade against the biswedars, 'who had no legitimate right to the land which had been theirs (proprietor turned Muzaras) for generations ...' (Mukherjee, 2004: 247). Supported by the Praja Mandal movement, Akalis, and Communists and awakened by new political consciousness ignited by the bloody happenings at Jallianwala Bagh (1919) at Amritsar, the Nankana massacre (1921) at Nankana Sahib Gurdwara, now in Pakistan,

Jaito da morcha (1924) and Morcha Guru ka Bagh, the muzaras formed their own 'Muzara Committee' in 1929 and 'Muzara War Council' in 1938–1939. In 1945, a new 21 member Muzara War Council was also formed and this 'unleashed the most militant movement in the East Punjab States' (Walia, 1972: 95–97, 163). The muzaras stopped paying *batai* to biswedars, leading to pitched battles between them at many villages. Prominent among these were at Rajomajra,[13] Bhadaur, and Qila Hakiman, which culminated in at least three dozen killing of muzaras including some women and children (Mukherjee, 2004: 249–266; Arshi, 2021).

Though the Praja Mandal movement (of self-cultivating kisans) and PMM movement (of occupancy tenants') were considered complimentary,[14] one major factor that differentiated them was their level of commitment to achieve their respective goals. For the former, the basic demands were reduction of land revenues and water rates, right to *shamlat* (village common land), amendment of Nazool land laws (laws which regulate inheritance in case there are no direct descendants), relief from indebtedness, abolition of *begār* (forced labour), right of *shikar*/hunting, etc. (Mukherjee, 2004: 244). In the case of the latter, the muzaras' movement aimed at retrieval of hereditary proprietary land rights divested by arbitrary and iniquitous edicts of Maharaja of Patiala's Riyasat and gifted to the biswedars. For the muzaras, the movement was a fight to the finish, whereas for the self-cultivating peasants of the Praja Mandal, the fight was a game of political expediency since their land ownership rights remained intact. There is another strong parallel. The recent farmers' struggle seemed to be a perfect repeat story: in the 1980s, the farmers' movements were precisely, to quote Kumar, for:

> the enhancement of support prices, institutionalised credit system, regular supply of inputs on subsidised rates, etc. Those protests used to threaten to stop the supply of foodgrain to *cities* of other states. Whereas now the crisis is privatisation of agricultural operations and of food grain not finding a market. This protest is for survival.
>
> (Kumar, 2021, *emphasis added*)

Farmers were steadfast in their determination, as can be gauged from their statements reported in the media, to return home only after getting the three controversial farm laws rescinded.

The question of reclaiming hereditary land rights – the question of survival – kept the muzaras' momentum alive despite the brutal repression unleashed by the aristocracy of Patiala. The movement also suffered several setbacks, such as the passing away of Sewa Singh Thikriwala, the legendary kisan leader and founder President of the Punjab Riyasat Praja Mandal, the arrest of Harnam Singh of Dharamgarh, Master Tara Singh's pact with Maharaja Bhupinder Singh, the steep fall in crop prices because of the Great Depression, and the arrest of the Punjab Socialist and Communist leaders during World War II for their opposition to the war effort. The movement got a fillip after the ban on left-wing parties was withdrawn and once again Communist leaders started building up support in favour of the muzara movement. Dharam Singh Fakkar led the Patiala State Kisan Committee, and Ishar Singh Tamkot led the Patiala State Kisan Muzara Committee, along with Harnam Singh Dharamgarh's efforts after his release from jail. He attempted to reactivate his contacts among sympathetic Akalis and this helped significantly in reviving the dampened spirit of the struggling muzaras (Mukherjee, 2004: 277–295). Emboldened by this groundswell support, especially that given by Harnam Singh Dharamgarh, Jagir Singh Joga, Achhar Singh Chhina, Ishar Singh Tamkot, and Ajmer Singh Tamkot, the muzaras of villages Gurbukhshpura, Dasondhasinghwala, Gobindgarh, Dhandoli Khurd in Sunam District, and Bakshiwala confronted the biswedars by their refusal to pay the *batai* share (Mukherjee, 2004: 287–291). The muzara movement of Patiala State compelled the Maharaja to make a Royal Proclamation on March 11, 1947 to the effect of guaranteeing proprietorship rights to tenants, though, only on a portion of the land (Mukherjee, 2004: 292). The tenants did not accept the proclamation, a sign of their growing strength, and remained steadfast in their resolve to realize the return of their hereditary land.

Lal Communist Party (1948) and the PEPSU Muzara Movement

The muzara movement touched new heights with the entry of the Lal Communist Party Hind Union (henceforth Lal Party) in its struggle against the biswedari system in the PEPSU region of the Punjab state. Led by Teja Singh Swatantar,[15] the Lal Party, a militant breakaway group of erstwhile Ghadrites and 'Kirit' Communists of Punjab who differed with the official line of the Communist Party of India (CPI) on the question of partition as well as support to the peasant movement, was founded on January 5, 1948, in Nakodar in Jalandhar District (Mukherjee, 2004:297). In its founding conference (January 5–8, 1948) at Nakodar, the Lal Party elected a Central Committee and a Punjab State Committee. The former consisted of Teja Singh Swatantar (General Secretary), Bhag Singh, PhD, Ram Singh Dutt, Bujha Singh, Wadhawa Ram, Chhajju Mal Vaid, and Gurcharan Singh Sehnsra. The latter, composed of Chayn Singh Chayn (Secretary), Vishnu Dutt Sharma, Harbans Singh Karnana, Giani Santa Singh, Ajmer Singh Bharu, Dharam Singh Fakkar, Paras Ram Kangra, Lal Singh Kanwar (poet), and Chanan Singh Tugalwal. The party published its own fortnightly newspaper, *Lal Jhanda* (Red Flag) in Punjabi, Hindi, and English edited by Teja Singh Swatantar. The current farmers' agitation also founded its four-page bi-weekly newspaper *Trolley Times* in Punjabi and Hindi to provide an unbiased truer picture of the struggle.

The Lal Party appeared on the scene at a time when the muzaras and biswedars were locked in full confrontation, which for the former was a crucial and an existential struggle. This was also the time when the Communist-dominated Muzara War Council (formed in 1945), the Communists, and muzara-sympathetic Praja Mandal were all passing resolutions calling for total abolishment of the oppressive biswedari system. In the face of increasing strength of the muzaras and the support they received from the Communists and the Congress-backed Praja Mandal, the biswedars began organizing armed gangs to defend their illegally occupied lands and to forcefully take *batai* from their muzaras. These new developments further radicalized the muzara movement which soon found itself enmeshed in pitched battles, involving armed resistance, over issues of non-payment of *batai* and forcefully resuming control over their land occupied by the biswedars.

It was at such a crucial juncture, that Teja Singh Swatantar began the process of organizing small bands of armed men after founding the Lal Party in 1948. The sole aim of the 'armed force wing' of the Lal Party was not to wage a war against the state but to save the muzaras from armed assaults of the biswedars unleashed by their well-organized armed gangs (Mukherjee, 2004: 297–299). Subsequently, muzaras of more than 200 villages were able to reclaim their occupied land and divided the same among themselves under the supervision of Baba Harnam Singh Dharmgarh of the Lal Party (Arshi, 2021). Refusal of payment of *batai* became a routine matter. After the inauguration of the union of Patiala, Nabha, Jind, Kalsia, Faridkot, Kapurthala, and Malerkotla (the East Punjab States), which came to be known as PEPSU on July 15, 1948, the muzara-biswedar confrontation, especially given the increasing influence of the Lal Party among the muzaras, spread to all regions of these princely states. Chanan Singh Dhoot, Chaudhary Wasao Dhaliwal, Master Hari Singh Dhoot, Baba Karam Singh Dhoot, and Baba Harnam Singh Kala Sanghian were among the prominent muzara leaders in Kapurthala Riyasat. Chanan Singh Dhoot, Chaudhary Wasao, and Master Hari Singh were also elected to the Punjab Assembly (Bilga, 1989: 241).

The confrontation reached a climax in village Kishangarh of *tehsil* (sub-division) Mansa in Patiala on March 16 and 18, 1949. On March 16, a sub-inspector of the police was killed in the clash. After a gap of one day, the police, reinforced by a contingent of the army with tanks and armoured cars, surrounded Kishangarh. In the exchange of fire at the village, six people were killed, a dozen seriously injured, and 'twenty six Red Guards along with their leader, Dharam Singh Fakkar were taken into police custody and tried for various offences like murder, rioting etcetera' (Walia, 1972: 193–194). A battery of lawyers, who were also well-known leaders of Praja Mandal, defended the detainees pro bono and ultimately all the accused were acquitted (Arshi, 2021).

It is worth mentioning here that muzaras' political awakening and their stellar commitment to the cause of getting their illegally occupied hereditary land back was so intense, even military action failed to deter them. According to Walia 'The tenancy movement continued till various land reform measures were enacted by the Pepsu Assembly after the 1952 General Elections' (Walia, 1972: 194). In fact, the concrete process of land reform measures began taking shape after the formation of a 'purely Congress ministry in 1952...' (Mukherjee, 2004: 302). Under this Congress ministry, continues Mukherjee:

> An Agrarian Reforms Enquiry Committee was set up to make recommendations regarding suitable legislation to solve the tenants' problems and the process of agrarian reforms set in motion. Till such time as the legislation could be enacted, the PEPSU Tenancy (Temporary Provision) Act was promulgated in January 1952 which protected tenants against eviction.
>
> (Mukherjee, 2004: 302)

In the fast succession of changes at the helm of the governing structure between July 1948 and May 1951, Pepsu witnessed four interim ministries (Walia, 1972: 194). Even following the first General Elections in 1952, the situation remained essentially unaltered. The United Front Ministry formed on April 21, 1952, under the leadership of G.S. Rarewala, failed to survive even for a year. However, before its dissolution and the imposition of presidential rule in March 1953, the Rarewala government was able to introduce much expected agrarian legislation in the Assembly (Walia, 1972: 197; Mukherjee, 2004: 302). Since agrarian reforms were already in process, an amicable solution of the muzaras' lingering agitation was chiselled during the ensuing presidential rule. The president issued the PEPSU Occupancy Tenants (Vesting of Proprietary Rights) Act, which authorized the muzaras (occupancy tenants) to 'become owners of their land by paying compensation amounting to 12 times the land revenues. This amount, given the war-time and post-war inflation and the fact that land revenue continued to be assessed at the pre-war rates, was not too burdensome' (Mukherjee, 2004: 303). The PEPSU Tenancy and Agricultural Lands Act, together with the PEPSU Abolition of *Ala Malkiyat* Act, were also issued by the president, and brought the muzara agitation to its successful conclusion with the restoration of their hereditary proprietary land rights (Mann, 1983: 326–327). After the successful completion of the PMM, the Lal Party reunited with its parent organization, the CPI, and a few years later Pepsu was mostly merged into the Punjab state on November 1, 1956, following the States Reorganisation Act.

The PMM was thus one of the most successful agrarian agitations in this region, and the only one able to get land reforms introduced without much bloodshed. The movement retrieved over 16 lakh acres of land from the illegal control of the biswedars, returning it to their hereditary owners, thus elevating them to the higher category of proprietary farmers (Arshi, 2021). At village Kishangarh, the epicentre of muzaras' protests, where four farmers (Ram Singh, Kunda Singh, Kapura Singh, and one unidentified person) were killed in a bloody clash between state armed forces and villagers supported by the Red Guards of the Lal Party in March 1949. An annual commemorative function is held in memory of the martyrs of the PMM on March 19. A memorial gate dedicated to the contribution of the village to the movement has also been constructed at entrance to Kishangarh. Drawing inspiration from the Pepsu muzara movement, the protesting farmers at Delhi borders also organized the annual function at Tikri as well as at other protest sites on March 19, 2021. Paying tribute to the martyrs of Kishangarh Darshan Pal, president of Krantikari Kisan Union and also a member of SKM, felicitated family members of the martyrs and highlighted the contribution of the movement in securing the rights of muzaras (Jagga, 2021). There are striking similarities between the recent farmers' movement and the PMM. They both forged unity between farmer and agricultural worker unions, generated a social and political awakening among farmers and farm workers, blurred caste and gender fault lines, and aimed at strengthening the country's democratic system.

Anti-Betterment Levy Agitation (1959)

After the PMM, post-independence Punjab witnessed another peaceful mass peasant agitation – Anti-Betterment Levy agitation – against a 'major aspect of Government policy' (Surjeet, 1986: 8).[16] This struggle was led by the CPI's front organization *Punjab Kisan Sabha* which had mastered the art of non-violent struggles in the pre-independence period. Though the Anti-Betterment Levy agitation, locally known as *Khush-hasiyati* Tax morcha, was formally launched on January 21, 1959, it actually began in 1952 when, before the completion of Bhakra canal system, the Punjab Government 'armed itself with a legislation to impose betterment levy, with the aim of meeting all the expenditure on canal system through this tax' (Surjeet, 1986: 4). Like the Punjab Land Colonisation Act 1907, this legislation's raison d'être was the collection of substantial funds via tax on farmers on account of 'fifty percent of the increase in price of land due to the Bhakra canal system' (Surjeet, 1986: 4). A major criticism of this legislation was that the Punjab government wanted to collect tax from farmers to the tune of Rs. 123 crore to meet canal's construction expenditure even before its completion and even though only 30 lakh acres of land, out of the total commanded 49 lakh acres under the Bhakra canal project, would be actually irrigated.

The Punjab Kisan Sabha opposed the tax by arguing that the construction costs of the Bhakra canal system 'could be met through the normal course of taxation like the water tax and surcharge which were in operation at that time' (Surjeet, 1986: 4). It was calculated that the Punjab government could receive more than four crore rupees in the form of water tax and surcharge from the 30 lakh acres of land expected to benefit after completion of the Bhakra canal project and that 'would be sufficient to meet the cost of the irrigation part of the components of the project ...' (Surjeet, 1986: 5). It was also argued that, although the Bhakra project was not for profit but a productive venture, the levy would, nevertheless, adversely impact the already highly indebted and heavily tax-burdened peasantry of Punjab and pushing the financially weakest into distress sales of farmland and subsequent penury. Nonetheless, the adamant Punjab government began serving assessment notices to peasants falling within the canal catchment areas spread over nine districts by the end of 1957 and beginning of 1958 (Surjeet, 1986: 4–8). This, no doubt, instigated the peasantry of the state to rise up en masse to fight for their livilihoods.

More than 11,000 affected peasants approached the courts against the draconian assessment notices and expressed their angst through organizing conventions, conferences, signature campaigns, mass representations, memoranda to both the State and Central government, and massive demonstrations involving more than 1 lakh peasants. In retrospect, the recent protest against the 2020 farm laws is a mirror image of what actually transpired during the Anti-Betterment Levy struggle. Like the various farm unions of the recent protests at Delhi borders, the Punjab Kisan Sabha engaged the then Punjab government to discuss very thoroughly each and every clause of the Levy Act and meticulously argued its case while focusing on their serious repercussions for the already debt and tax burdened Punjab peasantry. But the Punjab government did not pay any heed to peasant concerns and 'promulgated an ordinance on January 4, 1959, to realise betterment levy as advance payment' (Surjeet, 1986: 6).

Thus, the Punjab Kisan Sabha, after unsuccessfully campaigning for more than one and half years, was left with no option but to take to the streets in a direct, but peaceful confrontation with the obstinate Congress government of Partap Singh Kairon. The Sabha formed various Action Committees at different levels and started enlisting volunteers. To establish proper co-ordination among its various Committees, the Sabha also constituted a state-level Action Committee consisting of Jagjit Singh Lyallpuri, Harkrishan Singh Surjeet, Dalip Singh Tapiala, Baba Gurmukh Singh, Mohan Singh Jandiala, Master Hari Singh, Gurcharan Singh Randhawa, Satwant Singh – nephew of Master Tara Singh, who later became secretary of the Punjab unit of the CPI (M) – and Avtar Singh Malhotra to work incognito. Ultimately, the Kairon government, having failed to silence the democratic voice of the struggling peasants, was forced to retreat. Sohan Singh Josh, Baba Bhagat Singh Bilga, Harnam Singh Chamak, Hardit Singh Bhattal, Bhag Singh Canadian, Desh Raj Chadha, V.D. Chopra, and Partap Singh Dhanola were among other prominent leaders of the Punjab Kisan Sabha who waged a vehement struggle against the unjust levy. Within less than one month after the promulgation of the ordinance, more than 10,000 volunteers were enrolled to struggle for its retraction (Surjeet, 1986: 6; Sidhu, 2020b).

Despite the mass democratic mobilization, the state regime initially refused to relent, and deployed all repressive and brutal measures at its disposal – firing, tear-gas, lathi charge, third degree torture of non-violent volunteers, and forcibly taking away property items from peasants' houses in the name of executing attachment orders. Within a period of two months – from January 21, 1959, to March 22, 1959 – of the struggle:

> nineteen thousand volunteers offered Satyagraha by obstructing the work of district courts, ten thousand went to jails, three thousand volunteers got badly beaten by police lathis, hundred were tortured in police stations. Eight became martyrs facing the police bullets, including three women (*Mai Chand Kaur and Mai Bachan Kaur of Aitiana village of Ludhiana district and one woman from Narur village of district Kapurthala*); one died in police custody, due to torture; and two more laid down their lives in prison. Apart from the firing at these places, the police and the security forces organised a seige on many villages with machine guns directed against the villages, in order to restrict the movement of the people in strong centres.
>
> (Surjeet, 1986: 2–3; emphasis added. Also see: Sidhu, 2020b)

Ultimately, the Kairon Government, having failed to silence the democratic voice of the struggling peasants, was forced to retreat.

Summing up, this struggle brought together volunteers from across the divides of caste, class (poor, middling, rich landowners, and landless agricultural labourers), gender, age (inter-generational), religion, political party affiliation (with both Congressites, Akalis, and Communists), and both the urban and rural people. Not only peasants and labourers, but hundreds of *numberdars* (revenue collectors), *panchas* (members of village *panchayat* (governing body), and *sarpanchas* (head of *panchayats*) also joined the struggle (Surjeet, 1986: 2). Various *jathas* of volunteers visited canal catchment areas, priming peasants for a long struggle, and were received with warmth at every village. It generated both a solid cohesive social consciousness based on the syncretic heritage of medieval Punjabi culture, while simultaneously dealing a severe blow to Partition-induced communal consciousness. As stated by Surjeet 'Never before in the post-independence period, had Punjab witnessed such a resounding and massive unity of the popular forces' (Surjeet, 1986: 2). Akin to the upsurge of cultural awakening along the borders of Delhi during 2020–2021 protest, the boys and girls enthralled gatherings of protestors with newly composed revolutionary songs decrying the unjust levy tax.

Mehatpur Byet Muzara Movement (1961)

Mehatpur *Byet*[17] Muzara movement[18] was another resounding peasant success, which also provides valuable historical background for contextualizing the recent farmers' protests at Delhi borders. It was not only recently protesting farmers who were called Khalistanis and 'Urban Naxals', such labels were also frequently hurled at peasants of the Mehatpur *Byet* Muzara Movement. They were allegedly supported by Naxalites and consequently subjected to brutal oppression but nevertheless emerged victorious due to their innate strengths. These strengths arose from the gross injustice inherent in the status of being a muzara[19] which created a steely determination in the affected, and due to the non-violent nature of their agitation against which the government's choices of counter actions were limited.

The story of the Mehatpur *Byet* Muzara Movement began in 1961 with Punjab government's decision to set up a potato seed-farm on 10,000 acres of land spread 65 miles along the Satluj River belt in the Doaba region of Punjab. This land had been already sold by the Central government to the Punjab government at a nominal rate of Rs 5 per acre (Chandan 1979: 188). A portion of this land was with the Forest Department, and the rest, on the North of Satluj, was declared uncultivable and was locally called *Jhall* (Sidhu, 2021). It was on this uncultivable *Jhall* on the Doaba side of the river that 1,682 families, mainly of the Rai-Sikh tribe, had settled on approximately 27,000 acres of land after their displacement from Ferozepur district in 1957, following re-demarcation of the Indo-Pak border. They had also been displaced earlier from West Pakistan due to Partition in 1947.

Some of these displaced families had settled on the Malwa side of the river by establishing small villages with thatched huts and had begun cultivating the occupied land in the river bed in the early 1960s (Chandan, 1979: 188). These occupants came to be known as *abadkar*s (settlers), which was certainly an elevation over their earlier lower social status of so-called refugees (returnees of West Punjab). The Mehatpur *Byet* Muzara struggle was waged by the abadkars of Sanghowal (Jalandhar), Matewara and Hedon (Ludhiana) villages. The Matewara and Hedon abadkar agitations (1972–1976) were fought under the leadership of Comrade Puran Singh Narangwal of the Punjab Kisan Sabha against one Banta Singh, who had occupied 450 acres of evacuee land (Chandan, 1979: 188). In Hedon, the abadkars were able to establish their hold on Banta Singh's occupied evacuee land, and christened the reclaimed land and 'the small colony of thatched huts as Swatantra Nagar, named after the Teja Singh Swatanter, a Communist leader of Punjab' (Chandan, 1979: 188–189). The *abadkars* of Matewara were also restored to their allotted land. Both the Matewara and Hedon agitation were won without the use of violence.[20]

However, the main struggle of the *abadkars*, for which the Mehatpur *Byet* Muzara Movement has been known, was fought on the issue of setting up of a seed-farm, with technical assistance from erstwhile Soviet Union, at village Sanghowal in the vicinity of Mehatpur, another well-known village in the Nakodar tehsil of Jalandhar district. Though in official records the seed-farm was called 'Sanghowal Seed Farm', local people knew it by the name 'Russi[an] seed-farm' (Sidhu, 2021). To complete this ambitious project, the Punjab government brought in 12 giant Russian tractors to flatten the uneven river-bed land along with its wild bushes and trees. In this process, on October 23, 1968, these tractors razed the huts of the abadkars, destroyed their standing crops, and dismantled their tube-wells. To make matters worse for *abadkars*, the majority of surrounding landowners – who had been promised high quality seeds at a low price – supported the government on this issue to the extent of fighting the *abadkars* with goons (Sidhu, 2021).

Caught in the teeth of adversity, the abadkars of Sanghowal organized, under the leadership of the CPI(M) controlled Punjab Kisan Sabha, by constituting a 27-member Abadkar Action Committee (ACC) with a CPI(M) activist, Kulwant Singh[21] belonging to a nearby village Mandiala, elected its secretary. Arjun Anjan, Dona Singh, Arjun Gaunswal, and Kartar Singh Raipur were also members of the ACC, among others. Advocate Harbhajan Singh, Dhanpat Rai Nahar, Hakikat Rai, Surjit Singh Guru, and Santokh Singh were among other prominent members of this morcha (Sidhu, 2021). The ACC approached the court, deputations of abadkars met state officials and clashes frequently occurred between the police and agitating abadkars who threw themselves, along with their women, children, and even elderly family members, before government tractors which were destroying their crops. Demonstrations were also organized against the overly repressive measures taken by the Punjab police (Chandan, 1979, 188; Sidhu, 2021).

In mid-1969, the *abadkars*, armed with conventional weapons and even hoes, took out a massive demonstration at Nakodar, and presented a charter of demands to the SDM. Emboldened by the tremendous grassroots support given, the *abadkars* of Sangowal occupied a 150-acre farm owned by Gujjar Singh of village Khaira Fauja Singh Mushtarka, illegally and distributed it among landless Dalit families of Tara Singh and Bhagat Singh from the Ajnala side, thus forcing him to flee to his native town of Khanna (Chandan, 1979, 188; Sidhu, 2021). The *abadkars* were allegedly accused of aligning with the Naxalite movement, which had successfully established cells in rural Punjab, but this was pure fiction concocted by the state in order to let loose police brutality on the protesting *abadkars* and force them to withdraw their agitation. According to Chandan:

> In June 1970, the Punjab police carried out the biggest-ever combing operation in its history from Ropar to Malsian to terrorise the abadkar. Every hut was searched and people were beaten up indiscriminately.
> (Chandan 1979: 189)

However, police action failed to dampen the spirit of the agitating *abadkars*. According to Chandan 'In the same month a joint abadkar-Muzara convention at Ferozepur of the kisan wings of both the CPI and CPI(M) put forward the major demand of giving ownership rights to the abadkars'

(Chandan, 1979: 189). Finally, in August 1970, at the Sanghowal kisan conference, Akali Finance Minister, Balwant Singh, as per his promise during the 1969 assembly elections, announced that every *abadkar* family, whether it had *girdawri* (land records) or not, would be given 4–5 acres of land with proprietary rights (Chandan, 1979, 188; Sidhu, 2021).[22] Thus, the *abadkar*, with the support of ACC and their peaceful struggle, were able to retain their land in the Mehatpur *Byet* area against all odds.

Chandigarh Morcha (1984)

With the formation of the Punjab Khetibari Zimindara Union (KZU) in 1972,[23] and later its transformation into the Punjab unit of BKU in 1980,[24] a major shift occurred in the nature and politics of the farmers' movement in Punjab. Till the mid-1970s, all farmer struggles were waged under the active leadership of the Communists, primarily the CPI but with significant backing and participation of Ghadri Babas.[25] But with the founding of the KZU (later the BKU), the centre of gravity of Punjab farmers' union politics shifted to affluent farmer leaders with no Communist backgrounds. They successfully entrenched themselves in panchayats, block *samities*, and co-operative institutions, and even a cursory glance at the various issues taken up by the Punjab BKU reveals that they represented primarily the wishes of this particular sub-demographic (Gill and Singhal, 1984: 1729).

The BKU leadership has been, since its inception, monopolized by rich farmers, but even small and marginal farmers joined it – though it was agnostic, or at best lukewarm to their interests – for the reason of clan kinship. As Gill and Singhal have argued 'With the resources of the rich farmers, particularly tractor-trollies and participation of the poor peasants, the union is able to demonstrate its strength at various levels' (Gill and Singhal 1984: 1729). The current unity between the farmers and agricultural labourers witnessed at Delhi borders, with the sharing of common facilities, particularly the trollies modified into mobile rooms, is reminiscent of the 1984 Chandigarh agitation.

The first major kisan agitation launched by the BKU started on January 20, 1983, with the non-payment of electricity bills. After a year-long mobilization, the union planned *dharnas* in front of Punjab State Electricity Board (PSEB) offices and had announced a *gherao* of the Punjab Governor at Chandigarh in January 1984. In parallel to the union's preparation for a massive farmers' agitation on the burning issue of electricity bills, the CPI and CPI(M) led Kisan Sabhas, along with the kisan wing of the Akali Dal, were leading a peasant struggle in the Malwa cotton belt for compensation for previous season's damaged cotton crop. Thus, the BKU and Communist-led Kisan Sabhas were concurrently involved in two different, but equally important, farming issues. After the successful conclusion of the Kisan Sabhas' agitation for damaged cotton crop's compensation and their subsequent entry into the agitation for non-payment of electricity bills led by the BKU, the latter began a gherao of the Punjab Raj Bhavan (Governor's residence) on March 12, 1984 (Gill and Singhal, 1984: 1729–1730).

Comparing the Chandigarh 1984 morcha with the 2020–2021 farmers' protest, one can identify several similarities that are helpful in contextualizing the genesis and the operation of the agitation for the withdrawal of the three agriculture laws. A large number of peasants, numbering between 30,000 and 40,000, and responding to a call by the union to gherao the Governor's residence in Chandigarh, the capital of both Punjab and Haryana, had camped on the adjacent lush green lawns of the golf course for a week (Thukral, 1984; cf Gill and Singhal, 1984: 1730; and Shiva, 1991: 183). Farmers camped with their own provisions, set up *langar* (community kitchen), built thatched huts on areas adjacent to the Raj Bhawan, which came to be known as 'Kisan Nagar', and farmers of nearby villages of both Patiala and Ropar districts regularly supplied milk and vegetables (Gill and Singhal, 1984: 1730). Also, akin to the recent farmers' protest at Delhi, farmers from Haryana, UP, Madhya Pradesh, and Maharashtra[26] participated in batches in the Chandigarh morcha,[27] which continued till March 18, 1984, when it was successfully concluded after an agreement between the union and representatives of the Punjab government (Gill and Singhal, 1984: 1729–1730).

The gherao remained peaceful during its entire one week duration. Although when farmers began arriving residents of nearby sectors were wary, they were won over by the thoroughly peaceful conduct of the gherao. Gobind Thukral, who covered the protest for *India Today*, reported:

> The wife of a senior civil servant, who had kept her children indoors the first two days of the blockade, said: 'With Punjab's violence as backdrop, one expected that they would set the city on fire. But one could envy their informal manners and friendly nature. We shall certainly miss them'.
>
> (Thukral, 1984)

Similarly, scores of local residents, organizations, and establishments at protest sites on Delhi borders volunteered their services to protesting farmers in various ways: opening their homes, allowing access to their washrooms, providing local water supply sources, and arranging 'langar seva' (Sunny, 2020). In yet another parallel between these two farmer agitations, which are separated by more than 37 years, no political party was allowed to participate and neither were they allowed to enter farmers' villages.

Farmer unions' hostility to participation by political parties at the protest sites and elsewhere, and baring their entry to villages, was primarily to do with the non-party political character of the majority of the BKU organizations. During its Chandigarh morcha for gherao of Raj Bhawan, BKU declined not only help offered by many Congress (I) and Akali Dal leaders but also that by Devi Lal, a major Jat leader and Janata Party leader from Haryana (Gill and Singhal, 1984: 1730). However, the Punjab Kisan Sabhas, in total contrast to the various Punjab units of the BKU, were overtly political in their orientation since they were effectively the kisan front organizations of the CPI and CPI (M), thus causing the BKU to view these Kisan Sabhas as stalking horses for these communist movements (Gill and Singhal, 1984: 1729). This difference between the BKU and the Kisan Sabhas was further accentuated by a stark difference between their respective membership support bases, with the BKU largely supported by affluent farmers and the latter supported predominantly by the poor peasantry and landless agricultural labourers (Gill and Singhal, 1984: 1732).

To their great credit, the collective leadership of the recent farmers' protests was able to build an impressively cohesive unity between farmers of all economic strata and landless agricultural labourers, creating a formidable coalition of forces. Responding to a question about ideological differences among the various farmers' unions participating in the protest at Delhi borders, Joginder Singh Ugrahan, President BKU (EU) said, '... despite ideological difference, we were able to come together with a common minimum program' (Singh, 2021).

Critical Reflections on the 2020–2021 Protests

Until now, we have delved deep into the sequence of events related to the recent farmers' protest from its beginning on June 6, 2020, to its conclusion on November 19, 2021, and contextualized it by discussing the rich heritage of farmers' struggles both in pre-partition and post-partition independent India. In this final section, an attempt is made to unravel varied interpretations on emergence of the recent farmers' protest movement. Some have interpreted it as a continuation of the proud tradition of peasant revolts, bearing aloft the banner of justice and opposition to semi-feudalism, dictatorship and authoritarianism disguised in many ways, as discussed in detail in the previous section. The central government's arguments for passing the three farm laws received support from some well-known agro-economists as well as public scholars like Ashok Gulati, Gurcharan Das, Swaminathan S Anklesaria Aiyar, and Arvind Panagariya among others. However, anti-laws arguments were also, and rather more boisterously, supported by a larger number of economists and public scholars – Arun Kumar, Sucha Singh Gill, RS Ghuman, Pramod Kumar, Surinder Jodhka, Sukhpal Singh, Gian Singh, D. Narasimha Reddy, Kamal Narayan Kabra, R. Ramakumar, Vikas Rawal, Devinder Sharma, and P. Sainath among others. They questioned the very paradigm within which these laws were framed and finally enacted.

The central government continued to insist given the abundant production of wheat and rice, the APMC and MSP-based system of sale and purchase had become unviable for these two main MSP-based crops of Punjab and Haryana. It further argued that the central government found it difficult to create more storage facilities for the wheat/rice rotation cropping system of north-western India. It had asked farmers to shift to production of pulses and cultivate seeds for making edible oils. Yet another argument raised in support of new agriculture laws was the depletion of groundwater in Punjab and Haryana since rice is a water-guzzling crop (Shiva, 1991: Chap. 4; Ghuman and Sharma, 2016: 1–20).

This strongly implies that farm laws were enacted, not keeping in view, as often claimed, the welfare of farmers but as a countermeasure to the lack of storage capacity as well as to arrest the water depletion process in states of Punjab and Haryana. In other words, the abolition or the weakening of APMC and MSP, would, in the long run, end the system of assured fixed prices for wheat and rice, and thus eventually force farmers to stop the wheat-rice rotational pattern. There was also another fear that since the central government appeared to want to wash its hands off the wheat and rice procurement process, then concomitantly, the current supply of wheat and rice to the poorest sections of the nation under the Public Distribution System (PDS) will also gradually cease to exist as per liberal market logic. In short, the three laws were strongly suspected to be more in response to the three factors mentioned above and farmers' interests seemed not to have any consideration in their enactment.

It is highly relevant to point out that farmers were coaxed by the central government to grow wheat and rice in preference to the large variety of crops that were grown in the pre-Green Revolution (GR) phase in Punjab. This was done to extricate the nation from the then 'ship-to-mouth' reality which kept India vulnerable to demands of grain exporting nations, especially the US. After the end of World War II, the US had retained a vast munitions production industrial base, which was suddenly turned bereft of a market. However, the production capacities of many US munitions companies had a duality of use and could also make pesticides and fertilizers, e.g. the company IG Farben's explosives facility could be, and were, re-purposed for making nitrogen fertilizers. Native crops were inimical to chemicals (fertilizers and pesticides); therefore, US companies, especially DuPont, had made efforts to genetically engineer crops to suit their chemicals in order to create a captive market out of thin air. These dwarf varieties – misleadingly called 'high-yielding' varieties – were a marketing masterstroke, as they not only needed chemicals for similar crop production to indigenous varieties but also ten times the amount of water to do so.

In 1965, India suffered from a drought and, to build buffer stocks, had solicited the US for grain. The US, however, insisted on the use of its dwarf varieties as a pre-condition for starting the GR, but this failed to find favours with the then Indian Prime Minister, Lal Bahadur Shastri (Shiva, 1991: 32). Some leading economists, as well as agricultural scientists, also questioned the American agricultural strategy on economic grounds and potential risk of disease and displacement of small farmers. The only group that supported the strategy was the young agricultural scientists 'trained over the past decade in the American paradigm of agriculture' (Shiva, 1991: 31).

Subsequent to Shastri's death, the GR pushed for by US corporate interests took hold in India, especially in Punjab (Shiva, 1991: 30–32). The World Bank made loans to India, conditional on implementation of the GR in all its aspects, including building dams and canals, etc. In turn, the Indian Government made loans to farmers conditional on proof of usage of chemicals. The upshot of the GR in Punjab was a calamitous depletion of the water table, widespread indebtedness and health issues emanating from entry of agricultural chemicals into the food supply chain, especially drinking water (Ghuman, 1983: 213–238). Increased crop yields and hence production were attributed by many to increased irrigation, and not to the foreign seed varieties as boasted by US corporates.

In India as a whole, this has led to literally hundreds of thousands of farmer suicides – a pandemic which still remains largely unaddressed by the Indian government. The 1984 political crisis in Punjab was birthed largely by the disastrous consequences of the GR as well as the inherent inequitable pricing mechanism for crops which hugely disadvantaged farmers, reducing most to little more than serfs on their own land, working for a pittance as per the heavily tilted pricing system. This unrest bifurcated into a militant movement, on the one hand, and a Kisan agitation, on the other hand. Farmer unions in Punjab had planned a blockade of trains and grain to Delhi in June 1984 to protest against their oppressive circumstances, but since the vast majority were Sikhs, it was relatively easy for the central government to deflect this by conflating their legitimate demands with those of the militant groups (Shiva, 1991: 183–193). The same sleight of hand had been repeatedly deployed in Machiavellian attempts to defame and discredit the recent farmers' protests.

However, the underlying injustices remained and by 1991 it is estimated that 30 per cent of the $90bn national debt of India, which brought it to the brink of bankruptcy and forced it to approach the IMF and subsequently implement structural reforms, was attributable to financial inputs which were requisites of the continuing GR. Despite all this, the rapacity of corporates and the gross imbalance in the 'inputs-to-output price realization' ratio for farmers – designed and presided over by both the state and central government – went largely unnoticed and uncommented upon. With the passage of time, the rotational wheat-rice cropping system became the mainstay of both the Punjab and Haryana agrarian economies. It was only after the threat of food scarcity subsided, did depletion of groundwater in Punjab and Haryana and the disastrous impact of pesticides and insecticides on health of the soil and on crops produced, began to elicit concerns by the central government. Moreover, overproduction of wheat and rice did not occur overnight and efforts should have been made much earlier to manage and work out the national annual requirement of food grains and total area to be brought under wheat-rice cultivation. There was a dearth of regulatory mechanisms for promoting diversification and optimal use of areas under cultivation, for instance for crops like pulses and seeds for edible oils. Farmers in Punjab and Haryana have proven to be very forthcoming in adapting to new agriculture skills. If they could convert their farms into a 'national food bowl', then the same energies could have been channelized towards the production of pulses and other crops as per the food requirements of the country. But that was not done for reasons best known only to national agriculture policy makers.

The two key issues – fallout of the GR and disadvantageous crop pricing mechanism – nonetheless remain hugely relevant to the present plight of farmers across India, and the recent farmer protest, though focused on the three much vilified farmer laws, also acted as a channel for expressing a deep angst by them. It can therefore be surmised that, observed in a broader context, though farmer laws were the immediate trigger for the protests, the deeper underlying vectors need to be urgently addressed in order to fully deliver justice to this key sector of the economy. Such an approach would involve a complete paradigm shift that would affect approximately two-thirds of the population and change the trajectory of the entire country. Unfortunately, such a vision seems beyond grasp of the present dispensation, intent as it is on following the failing neoliberalism model of the West, without a thought to its own specific national characteristics. This is perhaps the greatest irony for a government, which proclaims 'Swadeshi' as a foundational concept in its ideology.

In light of the above discussion, it will be both an injustice and sheer opportunism to force farmers to abandon the wheat rice rotation crop system in the guise of freedom to sell their produce anywhere in the country and to whomever they deem fit. What must not be forgotten is that the liberal market logic is based on profit. Profit follows the logic of accumulation of wealth at one end of society and proliferation of poverty at the other end, while also outsourcing environmental degradation to local communities as well as to the globe as a whole. Since the farmers did not themselves choose the rotation crop system, they should not be so crassly abandoned to fend for themselves at this crucial moment when they are already enmeshed in a downward economic spiral directly attributable to the cultivation of these two cash crops.

Through the enactment and implementation of alternative or more suitable agriculture-related laws, the government needs to take responsibility in facilitating and generally smoothening the gargantuan reorientation from what over time has become a generational cropping pattern, to a much more diversified agrarian economy. This reorientation scenario would otherwise be completely alien to today's generation of farmers, especially the great majority who are firmly locked into the wheat-rice crop rotation pattern. Further, during the transitional period, farmers' minimum living standard needs to be vouchsafed during their shift to new crops and cropping patterns. Such a scheme should, other than imparting training and market knowledge, also provide adequate financial help to tide over the anticipated farmer losses due to abandonment of the wheat/rice crop cycle.

Moreover, the recent protest was the outcome of a one-sided decision taken by the central government in enacting the three laws and key stakeholders were not taken into confidence, other than some eyewash meetings for gaining favourable publicity. This gross neglect is not without precedent in so far as farmers are concerned – neither were they taken into confidence during the launch of the GR project in the late 1960s. Had farmers been made fully aware of likely depletion of groundwater, and mindless use of pesticides and insecticides detrimental to health of the soil, livestock, and humans, they would have certainly sought a more viable alternative for overcoming the challenge of providing national food security.

This time, given farmers were keenly aware of the likely negative fallouts of the newly enacted legislation and thoroughly opposed to its implementation, the government was forced to repeal the legislation for its own interest rather than of the country. Going forward, the government must confer with all stakeholders with the objective of crafting a comprehensive and sustainable solution to agrarian issues discussed above. It also needs to map out workable mechanisms for viable agricultural markets for desired levels of production, in alignment with the long-term ecological sustainability of such trajectories.

Of paramount importance is giving legitimacy and centrality to *hyit* (interest) of *kisans* and landless agricultural labourers. This must not be viewed as onerous and should be recognized, respected, and upheld in future discussion. This sentiment was conspicuously absent in government's recent approach and was widely perceived to be both unduly corporate-friendly and highly authoritarian. What is most worrying at the current juncture is that although the three farm laws are rescinded, the questions relating to the wider agricultural crisis, comprising of land fragmentation, depletion of underground water, indebtedness, crop diversification, and creeping pauperization of farmers, are still in danger of remaining both unaddressed and vulnerable to predations of Big Business operating in an environment of crony capitalism.

[Acknowledgements: This is a revised and enlarged version of the article prepared for the *Journal of Sikh and Punjab Studies*, Vol. 29, Numbers 1 & 2, Spring-Fall 2022 (GISS, New York). I am grateful to Amarjit Chandan for inspiring me to write on this exemplary farmers' struggle. He also helped me in locating relevant literature relating to both pre and post-partition Punjab's historic *Punjab Kisan Sabha* led peasant agitations and for providing valuable insights and suggestions. I am also thankful to Gurinder Singh Mann and Shinder Thandi for their motivation and academic inputs. Most of the primary data is drawn, in gratitude, from the classic work of Bhagat Singh Bilga (1907–2009), one of the Kirti Kisan leaders who led many agitations in Punjab during pre-1947 eventful years. My thanks to Charanji Lal Kangniwal for sharing his unpublished papers on some of the most important but hitherto neglected peasant struggles of pre-partition Punjab. I am also acutely aware of my intellectual debt to the original works of Ramesh Walia, Mridula Mukherjee, and Vandana Shiva, and my deep gratitude on this count. Dhilpreet Gill deserves my special thanks for not only reading multiple drafts of this longish essay, but also sprucing its contents and language. Last but not least, my thanks to Seema, Sahaj, and Daksh for affording me conducive home space and freedom to do justice to this work. However, I am alone responsible for the views articulated in this study.]

Notes

* This chapter is a revised version of 'Agrarian Resistance in Punjab: Contextualizing Farmer Protests at the Gates of Delhi in a Historical Perspective', first published in *Journal of Sikh and Punjab Studies*, 29(1&2) (Spring–Fall, 2022): 11–68.

1 'The *arhtiyas* (commission agents) and farmers enjoy a friendship and bonding that goes back decades. On average, at least 50–100 farmers are attached with each *arhtiya*, who takes care of farmers' financial loans and ensures timely procurement and adequate prices for their crop. Farmers believe the new laws will end their relationship with these agents and corporates will not be as sympathetic towards them in times of need' (Bhatia, 2021).

2 Agitation, campaign, continuous protests/struggle for some time.

3 M.L. Darling is also known for his seminal books on the Punjab peasantry, the most widely cited among them being *The Punjab Peasant in Prosperity and Debt* (Darling, 1977).

4 Bibi Tej Kaur, Mrs Tehal Singh, and Mrs Yog Raj were among the 107 women who offered themselves for arrest in the morcha between April 17 and May 3, 1939 (Mukherjee, 2004: 192).

5 Vishnu Dutt Sharma (1921–1993) later became the Punjab secretary of the Lal Communist Party of Hind Union. He migrated to the UK in 1957 and became an activist of the Indian Workers Association. He was elected to the National Executive Committee of the Communist Party of Great Britain in 1971. For details see: http://banmarchive.org.uk/collections/mt/pdf/12_79_18.pdf (accessed on July 28, 2021).

6 Canal outlets for releasing water for irrigation of agricultural land.

7 My account of the Harsa Chinna 'Mogha' Morcha is based on the following: Charanji Lal Kangniwal, 'Harsa Chhina Mogha Morcha,' unpublished paper [a]. Incidentally, Margaret Bourke-White, an American photographer, happened to be in Punjab during 1946–1947 and she took many pictures of the Morcha which are now available in the LIFE Photo Collection.

8 My account of the Tanda Urmar Muzara Morcha is based on the following: Charanji Lal Kangniwal, 'Tanda Urmar Muzara Lehar,' unpublished paper [b].

9 Hereditary proprietary peasants turned occupancy tenants.

10 Sewa Singh Thikriwala (Living Martyr), its founder President, and Bhagwan Singh Longowalia, its first General Secretary, were prominent Akali leaders who remained at the forefront of the movement for reform of Sikh shrines (Walia, 1972: 47–55).

11 Prominent leaders of the Praja Mandal movement were Sewa Singh Thikriwala, Bhagwan Singh Longowalia, Jagir Singh Joga, Dharam Singh Fakkar, Jagir Singh Phaguwalia, Harnam Singh Chamak, Harnam Singh Dharmgarh, Harchand Singh Jeji (Panth Dardi – a well-wisher of the Panth), Shamsher Singh Nagri, Wazir Singh Daftriwala, Sadhu Singh Daler, Pritam Singh Gujjran, Ajmer Singh Tamkot, Ishar Singh Tamkot Giani Sardara Singh Yuthap, Master Hari Singh, Giani Bachan Singh, Ujagar Singh Bhaura, Santa Singh Chakarian,

Ujagar Singh Kirti, Narain Singh Bhadaur, Chand Singh Bhadaur, and Hardit Singh Bhattal. They provided solid base to the muzara movement. Saiffudin Kichlu, Sheikh Mohammad Abdullah, P.N. Kaul, Talib Hussain, Sant Ram Vakil, and Labhu Ram were among the earlier Hindu and Muslim members of the Praja Mandal that underlined its secular character and wider reach beyond the PEPSU region.

12 The term *dewan* refers to a religious congregation held in gurdwaras. It was also used for designating Akali Movement meetings, which had a religious-cum-political character. The Praja Mandalists adopted this term for naming their political meetings in order to dodge the stringent clauses of the Royal Hadayat of 1932 (Mukherjee, 2004: 250–251). Popularly known as Hidayat 88, because it was signed on 5th Poh 1988 Bikrami calendar, it was promulgated in Patiala through a special *Firman-i-Shahi* (the Royal Decree) on January 14, 1932 (Walia, 1972: 115).

13 A village near Dhuri was owned by Gurnam Singh, father-in-law of Bhupinder Singh of Patiala state (Walia, 1972: 96).

14 Since both the Muzara and Praja Mandal movements had their main support base among the Sikh peasantry, they had many common leaders (Mukherjee, 2004: 245). Another interesting aspect of both the movements was that though their leadership had multiple political and religious affiliations, all of them were agreed on the question of reclaiming grabbed land from the *Biswedars*.

15 Teja Singh Swatantar (1901–1973), the legendary revolutionary lived a remarkable life which is worth discussing in some detail. He led the tenants' movement in PEPSU. A close associate of the Ghadarites, he cut his political teeth in the Gurdwara Reform movement. He formed his own Jatha named 'Swatantar Jatha' (lit. Free Band) to liberate Gurdwaras from the control of corrupt Mahants patronized by the British administration. In 1921, his Jatha liberated Gurdawara Teja Weela, in village Teja of Gurdaspur district, from the control of its deceitful Mahants, and subsequently liberated many more Gurdwaras. His leading role in eviction of the Mahants from Gurdawara Teja Weela earned him his first name 'Teja, after name of the same Gurdwara and his last name 'Swatantar' originated from name of his Jatha – 'Swatantar Jatha' although his original name was Sumund Singh. He also supported the Babbar Akali movement. In 1922, he became the youngest and most educated executive member of the Shiromani Gurdwara Prabandhak Committee. His leading role in organising agitation against the bloody episode of Jallianwala Bagh, forced him to quit Khalsa College, Amritsar. He later completed his graduation in Arts from the University of Panjab (now Punjab), Lahore during his confinement in Campbellpore jail. In early 1923, he went to Kabul as a Sikh missionary and whilst there he came in contact with Ghadarites who persuaded him to acquire military training. On his return from Kabul, he was arrested and taken to Peshawar, from where he escaped at the first available opportunity. He returned to Kabul in 1923 along with Udham Singh Kasel, Gurmukh Singh, Rattan Singh, and Santokh Singh, then moved to Turkey in 1925, as Azad Beg, from where he acquired Turkish citizenship, graduated in military studies, and eventually received a commission in the army. Five years later, he moved to Berlin and travelled across Europe, where it is believed, he met Ajit Singh of the Pagri Sambhal Jatta fame and who allegedly told him that 'Desh (country) cannot be liberated, just by liberating Gurdwaras', something which, it is said, to have influenced him deeply, convincing him of the necessity of revolution. He eventually reached North America, where it is also believed, and he met Lala Lajpat Rai and Maharaja Mahendra Partap Singh. In January 1932, he left North America and visited Panama, Mexico, Cuba, Chile, Argentina, Uruguay, and Brazil in succession. In Panama, he organized a protest, mainly by Punjabi Sikh immigrants, on March 23, 1931, the day Bhagat Singh was hanged.

From Panama he went to Argentina, where he met Bhagat Singh Bilga. He then reached Brazil and met Ajit Singh, after which both of them went to Europe, travelling to Portugal, Spain, France, Turkey, Berlin in Germany, and finally reaching Moscow in Russia. In Moscow, Teja Singh, joined KUTV – the Communist University of the Toilers of the East. He returned to India via Kenya in December 1934 and reached Punjab in 1935, soon becoming a prominent leader of the Punjab Kirti group and mobilising resistance against British Rule. He was arrested, along with other Communist leaders, on January 16, 1936, and his popularity at that time can be gauged from the fact that while in jail, he was elected unopposed to the Punjab Legislative Assembly in May 1937. He was secretary of the Punjab Communist Party from 1944 to 1947 and remained a prominent leader of the Kisan Sabha. In 1948, during the armed struggle of the Lal Communist Party, reward warrants totalling 1 lakh rupees (a 100,000 rupees) were issued for his arrest, forcing him to go underground. These warrants were withdrawn on January 5, 1963, after a delegation of Gadharite led by Baba Sohan Singh Bhakna met the then Prime Minister, Jawaharlal Nehru, in early 1963. Subsequently, Partap Singh Kairon, as Chief Minister of Punjab, withdrew the warrants and Teja Singh resurfaced after 16 years of an incognito existence. He became a member of the Punjab Legislative Council from 1964 to 1969, and in 1971 was elected a Member of Parliament from the Sangrur Lok Sabha constituency on a CPI ticket. He then became president of the All India Kisan Sabha in 1968 and remained in this capacity until he took his last breath on April 12, 1973, dying from a heart attack in the Central Hall of Parliament. Indira Gandhi, Prime Minister of India at the time, announced his passing and paid tribute to him in the house.

16 My account of the Anti-Betterment Levy agitation is largely based on Surjeet, 1986.

17 Land along the river bank.

18 My information of the Mehatpur *Byet* Muzara movement is taken from Chandan (1979) and Sidhu (2021). Apart from these two field-based studies, despite my best efforts, no other written material could be traced.

19 For a detailed account on the low social status of muzaras, see Mukherjee (2004, pp. 247–248).

20 Based on author's conversation with Comrade Puran Singh Narangwal, Chandigarh, August 14, 2021.

21 Sukhdev Sidhu's 2021 article is also based on information provided by Kulwant Singh Mandiala. He left the UK and returned to his native village Mandiala with desire to bring a revolution. He joined the CPI(M) and started working with its front kisan organization, Kisan Sabha, and played a leading role in the Mehatpur *Byet* morcha. He returned to the UK later and now lives in the US.

22 The maximum 5 acre limit was kept, keeping in view the exigency of electoral politics of the communist parties. It was alleged that those muzaras who occupied land between 20 and 100 acres, during the Pepsu Muzara Movement, later did not even vote for the CPI (Chandan, 1979, 188; Sidhu, 2021).

23 Among the eight founding members of the NZU, Baba Mohinder Singh Thind was one of the secretaries of the erstwhile Unionist Party of pre-partition Punjab, and Partap Singh Kadia was an Akali MLA (Gill and Singhal, 1984: 1729).

24 Bhupinder Singh Mann, Ajmer Singh Lakhowal were among the earlier Presidents and General Secretaries of the Punjab unit of BKU. Balbir Singh Rajewal, current president of BKU (Rajewal), was the Secretary of the All India BKU (Gill and Singhal, 1984: 1729).

25 All Ghadrites were popularly known as Babas, experienced revolutionaries, who sacrificed their comfortable lives for the establishment of an egalitarian socio-political order.

26 The Maharashtra batch was led by Sharad Joshi of Shetkari Sangathan (Gill and Singhal, 1984: 1729).
27 This morcha received support from the kisan wing of Akali Dal, activists of Kirti Kisan Union (KKU), and sympathizers of Kisan Sabhas (Gill and Singhal, 1984: 1729).

Bibliography

Aiyar, Swaminathan and Shahnaz Anklesaria, 'Indian response is as comic as Greta's follies', *The Times of India*, February 21, 2021.

Alam, Muzaffar, 'Sikh Uprisings under Banda Bahadur 1708–1715'. *The Panjab Past and Present*, Vol. XVI-I, Serial No. 31, April 1982, pp. 95–107.

Anwar, Tarique, 'Farmers' Protest: How Protesters Have Turned Delhi's Singhu Border into a Township', *News Click*, December 23, 2020. Available at: https://www.newsclick.in/Farmers-Protest-Protesters-Turned-Delhi-Singhu-Border-Township (accessed on July 26, 2021).

Arora, Kusum, 'After Yearlong Protests, Farmers Bid Adieu to Singhu With Charity And Memories of A Lifetime', *The Wire*, December, 11, 2021. Available at: https://thewire.in/rights/farmers-protest-singhu-charityfarewell (accessed on December 17, 2021).

Arshi, Hardev Singh, 'PEPSU da Ithihasahk Muzara Ghool', *Punjabi Tribune*, *Nazaria*, March 19, 2021.

Babbar, Sundar Singh, *Babbar Akali Lehar* (Punjabi), Amritsar: Singh Brothers, 2006.

Bambeli, Vijay, 'Pagri Sambhal Jata atey Ajit Singh', *Punjabi Tribune*, February 23, 2021.

Barrier, N. Gerald, *The Punjab Alienation of Land Bill of 1960*, Durham, NC: Duke University, Program in Comparative Studies on Southern Asia, 1966, Chapters 1–3.

Barrier, N. Gerald, 'The Punjab Disturbances of 1907: The Response of the British Government in India to Agrarian Unrest', *Modern Asian Studies*, Vol. 1, No.4, 1967, pp. 353–383.

Barrier, N. Gerald, 'The Punjab Disturbance of 1907: The Response of the British Government in India to Agrarian Unrest', *Punjab Past and Present*, Vol. VIII. Part II, October 1976, pp 444–476.

BBC News, 'Karnal: Thousands of farmers hold sit-in protest', September 8, 2021. Available at: https://www.bbc.com/news/world-asia-india-58339651 (accessed on October 20, 2021).

Bhardwaj, Aakanksha N., 'Arhtiyas lend weight to farmers' stir with provisions', *The Tribune*, December 10, 2020. Available at: https://www.tribuneindia.com/news/punjab/arhtiyas-lend-weight-to-farmersstir-with-provisions 182570 (accessed on March 18, 2021).

Bhatia, Varinder, 'Explained: Who are the Punjab, Haryana farmers protesting at Delhi's borders?', *The Indian Express*, January 30, 2021.

Bhattacharya, Pritha, 'International Women's Day: 50,000 women farmers join protest at Singhu and Tikri', *Down To Earth*, March 8, 2021. Available at: https://www.downtoearth.org.in/news/agriculture/international-women-s-day50-000-women-farmers joinprotest-at-singhu-and-tikri-75834 (accessed on July 3, 2021).

Bhowmick, Nilanjana, '"I Cannot Be Intimidated. I Cannot Be Bought." The Women Leading India's Farmers' Protest', *Time*, March 4, 2021. Available at:

https://time.com/5942125/women-india-farmers-protests (accessed on March 16, 2021).

Bilga, Bhagat Singh, *Ghadar Lehar de Anfolay Varkay*. Jalandhar: Deshbhagat Yaadgar, 1989.

BusinessToday.in, 'FarmersrejectCentre'soffertoput3farmlawsonholdfor18months; want 'complete' repeal', *BusinessToday.In*, January 22, 2021 Available at: https://www.businesstoday.in/latest/economy-politics/story/farmers-rejectcentre-offer-to-put-3-farm-laws-onhold-for-18-months-want-complete-repeal285256-2021-01-22 (accessed on July 8, 2021).

Butani, Ashna, 'Teachers, doctors, engineers join protest: "We have one thing in common, we're farmers first"', *The Indian Express*, December 14, 2020. Available at: https://indianexpress.com/article/cities/delhi/farmers-protest-singhu-borderfarm-laws-7103755/ (accessed on July 3, 2021).

Chaba, Anju Aghnohotri, 'Tikait's tears turn the tide in Punjab villages', *The Sunday Express*, January 31, 2021.

Chaba, Anju Agnihotri and Harish Damodarlained, 'Who are arhtiyas, also part of the farmers' protest? What is their role?', *The Tribune*, December 15, 2020. Available at: https://indianexpress.com/article/explained/the-arhtiya-business-7098629/ (accessed on March 18, 2021).

Chand, Ramesh, *New Farm Acts: Understanding the Implications*. New Delhi: NITI Aayog, November 2020.

Chandan, Amarjit (transl. from Urdu), *Meri Aap-beeti: Autobiography of Sohan Singh Bhakna*. Ghaziabad: Copper Coin, 2014.

Chandan, Amarjit, 'Settlers' Fight for Evacuee Land'. *Economic and Political Weekly*, February 3, 1979, pp. 188–189.

Chayn, Chayn Singh, *Kirti Party dooji Sansar Jung Samey* (Kirty Party during WWII). Jalandhar: Self published, 1990.

Darling, Malcolm L. *The Punjab Peasantry in Prosperity and Debt*, New Delhi: Manohar, 1977. (Originally published by Oxford University Press in 1925).

Deol, Mandhir Singh, 'Khet Mazdoor nae vee Kisani Sangharsh chae Piaya "Seer"', *Punjabi Tribune*, January 9, 2021.

Dey, Abhishek, 'How farmer protest on Delhi borders ended: The 5 demands govt agreed to, and the 1 it didn't', *The Print*, December 9, 2021. Also available at: https://theprint.in/india/governance/how-farmer-protest-on-delhi-borders-ended-the-5-demands-govt-agreed-toand-the-1-it-didnt/779288/ (accessed on December 16, 2021).

DTE, Staff, 'Farm laws repealed in Parliament without discussion', *DownToEarth*, November 29, 2021. Available at: https://www.downtoearth.org.in/news/agriculture/farm-laws-repealed-in-parliament-without-discussion-80423 (accessed on December 12, 2021).

Dutta, Prabhash K., 'What is there in farm laws that make them so contentious?', *India Today*, December 15, 2020. Available at: https://www.indiatoday.in/news-analysis/story/what-are-farm-laws-farmersprotest-msp-1749723-2020-12-15 (accessed on July 7, 2021).

Fox, Richard G. *Lions of the Punjab, Culture in the Making*. Los Angeles: California University Press, 1985.

Gauri Lankesh News Desk, 'Pepsu Tenant Movement in Punjab for Land Ownership Rights', March 18, 2021. Available at: https://gaurilankeshnews.com/pepsu-tenent-movement-in-punjabfor-landownership-rights/ (accessed on July 15, 2021).

Gayatri, Geetanjali, 'Crossing the Threshold', *The Sunday Tribune*, Spectrum, February 21, 2021.

Ghazali, Mohammed (reported) and Swathi Bhasin (edited). 'Farmers, Cops Clash Yet Again In Haryana, Barricades Knocked Down', *NDTV*, September 30, 2021. Available at: https://www.ndtv.com/india-news/farmers-cops-clash-yet-again-in-haryana-karnal-barricades-knocked-down-2558715 (accessed on October 20, 2021).

Ghuman, Ranjit Singh and Rajeev Sharma, 'Green Revolution, Cropping Pattern and Water Scarcity in India: Evidence from Punjab', *Man and Development*, Vol. 38, No. 2, June 2016, pp. 1–20.

Ghuman, Ranjit Singh, '*Harra Inqlab ate Aarthak-Smajak Tabdeeli*' (Green Revolution and Economic Social Change). In Azad Nirmal Singh (ed.) *Punjab di Aarthakta* (Economy of Punjab). Patiala: Publication Bureau, Punjabi University, 1983, pp. 213–238.

Gill, Sucha and K. C. Singhal, 'Farmers' Agitation: Response to Development Crisis of Agriculture'. *Economic and Political Weekly*, Vol. 19, No. 4, October 6, 1984, pp. 1728–1732.

Hindustan Times, 'Farmers block KMP e-way to mark 100 days of stir', *Sunday Hindustan Times*, March 7, 2021.

HT Correspondent, 'Farmers know how to teach a lesson: Tikait to Centre', *Sunday Hindustan Times*, July, 25, 2021.

Iftikhar, Fareeha, 'Students join farmers in protest at Delhi's borders', *Hindustan Times*, December 25, 2020. Available at: https://www.hindustantimes.com/cities/students-join-farmers-in-protest-atdelhi-s-borders/story-ucyw9crn1uf16x-gtancu3n.html (accessed on July 3, 2021).

India Today, 'Ghazipur farmers' protest gets new life, hundreds flock to Delhi, mahapanchayats held in UP', February 1, 2021. Available at: https://www.indiatoday.in/india/story/ghazipur-farmers-protest-gets-new-lifehundreds-flock-to-delhi mahapanchayats-held-in-up-1764576-2021-02-01 (accessed on March 16, 2021).

India Today, 'Lakhimpur Kheri: A brief history of eight deaths', *India Today*, October 4, 2021. Available at: https://www.indiatoday.in/india/story/lakhimpur-kheri-a-brief-history-of-eight-deaths-1860566-2021-10-04 (accessed on October 21, 2021).

India TV News Desk, 'Farmers at Singhu border prepare to return to homes after year-long agitation against farm laws', *India TV News*, New Delhi, December 11, 2021. Available at: https://www.indiatvnews.com/news/india/farmers-at-singhu-tikri-delhi-ghazipur-border-dismantle-makeshift-town-return-to-homes-year-long-agitation-against-farm-laws-749017 (accessed on December 16, 2021).

India's Business Standard, 'New agri laws have potential to raise farm income: IMF's Gopinath', *Business Standard*, January 27, 2021. Available at: https://www.business-standard.com/article/economy-policy/india-s-new-agrilaws-have-potential-to-raise-farmincome-imf-s-gopinath121012700569_1.html (accessed on March 7, 2021).

Jagga, Raakhi, 'From rooftop protests, to tractor rallies, to 'Delhi Chalo': A timeline of farmers' movement', *The Indian Express*, December 4, 2020. Available at: https://indianexpress.com/article/india/explained-how-did-the-farmersprotests-become-a-massive-movement7091172/ (accessed on July 6, 2021).

Jagga, Raakhi, 'One Year of Promulgation of Farm Ordinances: Farmers mark day as Kranti Diwas, burn law copies, protest at 250 sites', *The Indian Express*, June 6, 2021. Available at: https://indianexpress.com/article/cities/ludhiana/

one-year-of-promulgation-offarm-ordinances-farmers-markdayas-kranti-diwas-burn-law-copies-protestat-250-sites-7346564/ (accessed on July 9, 2021).

Jagga, Raakhi, 'With discipline in dissent, Punjab farmers keep date with stir anniversary', *The Sunday Express*, June 27, 2021. Available at: https://indianexpress.com/article/cities/ludhiana/with-discipline-in-dissentpunjab-farmers-keep-date-with-stiranniversary-farmers-7377552/ (accessed on July 8, 2021).

Jagga, Raakhi, 'Remembering Pepsu Muzara movement: Govt. should study our past, our history...we Never gave in even during British rule', *The Indian Express*, March 22, 2021. Available at: https://indianexpress.com/article/india/remembering-pepsu-Muzaramovement-govt-should-study-our-past-ourhistory-we-never-gave-in-evenduring-british-rule-7239246/ (accessed on July 14, 2021).

Jha, Rakesh Kumar, 'Why farmers in Haryana and Punjab are up in arms against centre's farm ordinances', *English Jagran*, September 13, 2020. Available at: https://english.jagran.com/india/why-farmers-in-haryana-and-punjab-are-upin-arms-against-centres farmordinances-10016654 (accessed on July 5, 2021).

Kakhra, Arvinder Kaur, 'Kisan Andolan chae Naari Shakti da Ubhar', N*awan Zamana*, February 28, 2021.

Kamal, Neel, 'Stalemate: After 180 days, farmers say they have longer staying power', *The Times of India*, May 26, 2021. Available at: https://timesofindia.indiatimes.com/city/chandigarh/stalemate-after-180-daysfarmers-say-they-have longerstaying-power/articleshow/82957396.cms (accessed on July 9, 2021).

Kamal, Neel, 'Seven months of farm protests: Farm unions grapple with risky decision on "what next"', *The Times of India*, June 26, 2021. Available at: https://timesofindia.indiatimes.com/city/amritsar/7-months-of-farm-protestsfarm-unions-grapple with-riskydecision-of-whatnext/articleshow/83858711.cms (accessed on July 8, 2021).

Kamal, Neel, '7 months on, protesting farmers again break barricades, face water cannons', *Sunday Times of India*, June 27, 2021. Available at: https://timesofindia.indiatimes.com/city/chandigarh/7-months-on-protestingfarmers-again-break barricades facewater-cannons/articleshow/83884213.cms (accessed on July 8, 2021).

Kamal, Neel, 'Kisan Sansad drags stir out of bog R-Day march got it into', *Sunday Times of India*, July 25, 2021.

Kangniwal, Charanji Lal, 'Nili Bar da Muzara Ghool', *Punjabi Tribune*, Dastakh, November 22, 2020a.

Kangniwal, Charanji Lal, 'Amritsar da Kisan Morcha,' *Punjabi Tribune*, Dastakh, November 22, 2020b.

Kangniwal, Charanji Lal, 'Gatha doo Kisani Ghoolan dee', *Nawan Zamana*, December 13, 2020c.

Kangniwal, Charanji Lal, 'Harsa Chhina "Mogha" Morcha', unpublished paper [a]. Received from the author through email.

Kangniwal, Charanji Lal, 'Tanda Urmur de Muzara Lehar', unpublished Paper [b]. Received from the Author through email.

Kaur, Amarjot, 'Farmers' protest: Former bureaucrats, ex-Army men join hands', *The Tribune*, March 31, 2021. Available at: https://www.tribuneindia.com/news/chandigarh/farmers-protest-formerbureaucrats-ex-army-men-join-hands232797 (accessed, July 3, 2021).

Kaur, Deepinder and Atinder Pandey, 'Kisan Andolan chae Auratan de Sangrashy Gatha', *Trolly Times*, Edition 13, March 13, 2021. Available at: https://www.trolleytimes.online/edition/punjabi/edition-13 (accessed on July 4, 2021).

Kaur, Navsharan, 'Kisani Sangharsh vich Dalit Khet Mazdoor', *Punjabi Tribune*, January 8, 2021.

Kaur, Navsharan, 'Maanjog Sarbucch Adalat, Hun Sadha Gharan nu Partana namumkin', *Punjabi Tribune*, Dastakh, January 17, 2021.

Kaushal, Ravi and Sagrika Kissu, 'Women farmers celebrate International Women's Day on Delhi borders', *Matters India*, March 9, 2021. Available at: https://mattersindia.com/2021/03/women-farmers-celebrate-internationalwomens-day-on-delhi borders/ (accessed on March 18, 2021).

Khanna, Bharat, 'Writers' group from Punjab to participate in farmers protest at Delhi borders', *The Times of India*, December 6, 2020. Available at: https://timesofindia.indiatimes.com/city/ludhiana/writers-group-from-punjabto-participate-in-farmers protest-atdelhi-borders/articleshow/79591940.cms (accessed on July 3, 2021).

Kumar, Pramod, 'With anger and a song: Farmers' protest questions reform that promotes efficiency of agriculture, not well-being of agriculturists', *The Indian Express*, December 8, 2020.

Kumar, Pramod, 'The farmers' protest began a year ago. How has it lasted this long?', *The Indian Express*, June 23, 2021. Available at: https://indianexpress.com/article/opinion/columns/farmers-protest-punjabfarm-laws-7371125/ (accessed on July 9, 2021).

MA Media, 'Farmer leader Rajewal made a big statement after paying obeisance at Sri Harmandie Sahib', *MA Media,* December 13, 2021. Available at: https://mamedia24.com/farmer-leader-rajewal-made-a-big-statement-after-paying-obeisance-at-sri harmandirsahib/ (accessed on December 17, 2021).

Mahajan, Sucheta, 'Anti-British Agitation in 1907 Punjab', *Punjab History Conference Proceedings*, Fifteenth Session, 1981, Patiala: Punjabi University, 1982, pp. 209–309.

Malik, Sagar, 'Haryana standoff ends as government orders probe into Karnal', *News-Byte*, September 11, 2021. Available at: https://www.newsbytesapp.com/news/india/haryana-government-orders-probe-into-karnalincident/storyincident (accessed on October 20, 2021).

Mann, Karanbir Singh, 'The Tenant Movement in PEPSU (1948–1955)', *Punjab History Conference Proceedings*, Eighteenth Session, Patiala: Punjabi University, December 2–4, 1983, pp. 326–327.

Mishra, Kavya, 'Rooftop demonstration to a globally-recognised movement: 50 days of farmers' protest', *Opoyicentral*, January 14, 2021. Available at: https://opoyi.com/rooftop-demonstration-to-a-globally-recognised-movement50-days-of-farmers protest (accessed on July 9, 2021).

Misra, Shubhangi, 'Kamala Harris' niece Meena gives Twitter lessons on India's democracy and "anti blackness"', *The Print*, February 8, 2021. Available at: https://theprint.in/world/kamala-harris-niece-meena-gives-twitter-lessonson-indias-democracy-anti blackness/600977/ (accessed on March 19, 2021).

Mukherjee, Mridula, *Peasants in India's Non-Violent Revolution: Practice and Theory*. New Delhi: Sage, 2004.

Mukherjee, Mridula, 'Peasant Movements in a Princely State: Patiala 1937–48'. *Studies in History*, Vol. 1, No. 2, July-December 1979, pp. 216–283.

Mustafa, Faizan, 'An Expert Explains: The arguments for and against the three central farm laws', *The Indian Express*, September 29, 2020. Available at: https://indianexpress.com/article/explained/an-expert-explains-farm-acts-andfederalism-6622769/ (accessed on July 6, 2021).

Naim, Moises, 'Fads and Fashion in Economic Reform: Washington Consensus or Washington Confusion?', *International Monetary Fund*, October 26, 1999. Available at: https://www.imf.org/external/pubs/ft/seminar/1999/reforms/Naim.HTM (accessed on July 6, 2021).

National Herald, 'Why are farmer protesting?', September 26, 2020. Available at: https://www.nationalheraldindia.com/india/why-are-farmers-protesting (accessed on March 17, 2021).

National Herald, '"Why aren't we talking about this?!" Singer Rihanna extends support to farmers' protest on Twitter', February 3, 2021. Available at: https://www.nationalheraldindia.com/international/why-arent-we-talkingabout-this-singer-rihanna extendssupport-to-farmers-protest-on-twitter (accessed on March 18, 2021).

National Herald, 'Farmers protesting at Delhi borders remain resolute in seeking repeal of new agri laws', December 24, 2020. Available at: https://www.nationalheraldindia.com/national/farmers-protesting-at-delhiborders-remain-resolute-in seekingrepeal-of-new-agri-laws (accessed on March 17, 2020).

NDTV Staff, 'Punjab Farmers Returning Home From Delhi Borders Get Rousing Welcome', *Press Trust of India*, December 12, 2021. Also available at: https://www.ndtv.com/india-news/punjab-farmers-returning-to-homes-from-delhi-borders-get-rousing welcome-2647871 (accessed on December 16, 2021).

Outlook Web Bureau, 'India's New Farm Laws a Step Forward, Need to Strengthen Social Safety Net: IMF', *Outlook*, January 15, 2021. Available at: https://www.outlookindia.com/website/story/india-news-indias-new-farmlaws-a-step-forward-need-to strengthen-social-safety-net-imf/370596 (accessed on March 7, 2021).

Pain, Bedabrata, 'Watch | Noam Chomsky: Farmers Fighting For India, Beacon of Light in Dark Times', *The Wire*, June 27, 2021. Available at: https://thewire.in/video/watch-noam-chomsky-interview-farmers-protest-india (accessed on July 5, 2021).

Pal, Savinder, 'Agrarian Unrest in Punjab and Sardar Ajit Singh', *Proceedings of the Indian History Congress*, 2009–2010, Vol. 70 (2009–2010), pp. 451–464. Available at: https://www.jstororg/stable/44147692 (accessed on June 26, 2021).

Pandey, Sahil, 'Punjabi singers lend their support to farmer protest at Singhu Border', *ANI*, December 5, 2020. Available at: https://www.aninews.in/news/national/general-news/punjabi-singers-lendtheir-support-to-farmer protest-atsinghu-border20201205191944/ (accessed on July 3, 2021).

Puri, Harish K., *Ghadar Movement: Ideology, Organisation and Strategy*. Amritsar: Guru Nanak Dev University, 1983.

Rahi, Rajwinder Singh (ed.), *Meri Ram Kahani: Baba Sohan Singh Bhakna (Punjabi)*. Patiala: Sangam Publications, 2018.

Rajagopal, Krishnadas, 'Farmers' protest | Supreme Court stays implementation of 3 controversial farm laws', *The Hindu*, January 12, 2021. Available at: https://www.thehindu.com/news/national/sc-suspends-implementation-of-three-farmlaws/article33557081.ece (accessed on July 8, 2021).

Ramani, Priya, 'The Country's Fastest-Growing Newspaper', *Bloomberg Quint Opinion*, December 23, 2020. Available at: https://www.bloombergquint.com/opinion/trolley-times-the-countrys-fastestgrowing-newspaper (accessed on March 19, 2021).

Rasul, Md. Abdullah., A *History of the All India Kisan Sabha*. Calcutta: National Book Agency Private Ltd, 1974.

Sabarwal, Harshit, 'Centre is ready to make changes in farm laws, but doesn't mean there is a problem with them: Tomar', *Hindustan Times*, February 5, 2021. Available at: https://www.hindustantimes.com/india-news/clarified-if-govt-isready-to-make-changes-in-farm laws-doesn-t-mean-tomar101612509130906.html (accessed on July 3, 2021).

Sainsara, Gurcharan Singh, *Ghadar Party da Itihas (Punjabi)*. Jalandhar: Desh Bhagat Yadgar Committee, 1969.

Sethi, Chitleen K., 'How protesting farmers have kept politicians out of their agitation for over 2 months', *The Print*, November 30, 2020. Available at: https://theprint.in/india/how-protesting-farmers-have-kept-politicians-out-oftheir-agitation-for-over-2 months/554429/ (accessed on March 19, 2021).

Sharma, Aman, 'Farmer unions do not wish to be impleaded in ongoing case in Supreme Court: BKU president Balbir Singh Rajewal', *The Economic Times*, January 6, 2021a. Available at: https://economictimes.indiatimes.com/news/politics-and-nation/farmerunions-do-not-wish-to-be impleaded-inongoing-case-in-supreme-court-bku-presidentbalbir-singh-rajewal/printarticle/80137688.cms (accessed on July 14, 2021).

Sharma, Devinder, 'Markets have failed to prop up farm incomes', *The Tribune*, March 19, 2021b.

Sharma, Devinder, 'Farmers' Agitation Will Impact Global Trade', *The Tribune*, January 16, 2021c.

Shaurya, Surabhi, 'Singhu Killing: Lakhbir Was 'Lured' to Farmers' Protest Site, Had Only Rs 50 in Pocket, Claims Family', *India.Com News Desk*, October 16, 2021. Available at: https://www.india.com/news/india/singhu-border-horror-singhu-killing-lakhbir-was-lured-to-farmers-protest-site-had-only-rs-50-in-pocket-claims-family-5056472/ (accessed on October 22, 2021).

Shiva, Vandana, *The Violence of Green Revolution: Third World Agriculture, Ecology and Politics*. London and New Jersey: Zed Books Ltd., 1991.

Sidhu, Gurdev Singh, 'Kisan Morchian da Ithihas', *Punjabi Tribune*, Dastakh, November 22, 2020a.

Sidhu, Gurdev Singh, 'Kisan Sangharsh', *Punjabi Tribune*, Dastakh, December 27, 2020b.

Sidhu, Sukhdev, 'Mahitpur Byet de Safal Muzara Lehar', *Trolley Times – The Voice of Kisan Protest*, Edition 21, June 26, 2021. Available at: https://drive.google.com/file/d/1BL1ZwBGmP5aN5rpjzERUqHqpMPU6lUd/iew (accessed on July 4, 2021).

Singh, Balwinder, 'Mulakat: Dr. Ronki Ram – Kisan Andolan dee Jhamhoori Peeshan Hoor Ghoohri Hoo Rhi Hai', *Nawan Zamana*, February 28, 2021.

Singh, Balwinder, 'PEPSU dee Mizara Lehar', *The Tribune*, Dastakh, November, 22, 2020.

Singh, Balwinder, 'Kisani Sangarsh de Gouravmai Virasat: PEPSU dee Muzara Lehar da Sangarsh', *Nawan Zamana*, May, 16, 2021.

Singh, Jupinderjit, 'Nihang chief may have been part of efforts to end stir', *The Tribune*, October 19, 2021a.

Singh, Jupinderjit, 'Punjab forms SIT to probe Nihang leader controversies, background, Lakhbir Singh's Murder', *The Tribune*, October 20, 2021b. Available at: https://www.tribuneindia.com/news/punjab/punjab-formssit-to-probe-nihang-leader-controversies background-lakhbir-singhs-murder-327073 (accessed on October 26, 2021).

Singh, Mohinder, *The Akali Movement*. Delhi: Macmillan, 1978.

Singh, Partap, 'Delhi: Retired Army veterans join farmers' protest, celebrate Vijay Diwas at protest venue', *Hindustan Times*, December 17, 2020. Available at: https://www.hindustantimes.com/delhi-news/delhi-retiredarmy-veteransjoin-farmers-protest celebrate-vijaydiwas-at-protest-venue/story61iJLOCOPO58w2ql-j0LaeP.html(accessed on July 3, 2021).

Singh, Shiv Inder, 'Image that Modi government doesn't retract statements is shattered: BKU (EU) head Joginder Ugrahan', *The Caravan*, January 7, 2021. Available at: https://caravanmagazine.in/agriculture/image-that-modi-government-doesn'tretract-statements-is shatteredbkuekta-ugrahan-joginder-ugrahan (accessed on July 25, 2021).

Singh, Teja, *The Gurdwara Reform Movement and the Sikh Awakening*. Creative Media Partners, LLC, 2018.

Sunny, Shiv, 'As farmers protest, Good Samaritans at borders open their hearts and homes', *Hindustan Times*, December 02, 2020. Available at: https://www.hindustantimes.com/delhinews/as-farmers-protest-good-samaritans-at-borders-open-their-hearts-and homes/story5D8VYSs3FgsXvC8kOwscwI.html (accessed on July 26, 2021).

Sura, Ajay, 'For many visit to farmers' protest site is no less than a pilgrimage', *The Times of India*, December 22, 2020. Available at: https://timesofindia.indiatimes.com/city/chandigarh/for-many-visit-to-farmersprotest-site-is-no-less than-apilgrimage/articleshow/79849159.cms (accessed on March 19, 2021).

Suresh, Nidhi, 'Media has lost our trust': Why protesting farmers are angry with "Godi media"', *News Laundry*, December 1, 2020. Available at: https://www.newslaundry.com/2020/12/01/media-has-lost-our-trust-why-areprotesting-farmers angry-with-godi-media (accessed on March 19, 2021).

Surjeet, Harkishan Singh, 'Anti-Betterment Levy Struggle of Punjab', 1936–86: Golden Jubiliee Series No. 4, All India Kisan Sabha, May 1986.

Team TOI, '"Guardians of Protest Site" Earned Many Yellow Cards', *The Times of India* (Chandigarh), October 20, 2021.

The Economic Times, 'Delhi Chalo explainer: What the farmers' protest is all about', *The Economic Times*, December 2, 2020. Available at: https://economictimes.indiatimes.com/news/politics-and-nation/delhi-chaloexplainer-what-the farmers-protest-is-allabout/articleshow/79460960.cms?from=mdr (accessed on March 7, 2021).

The Economic Times, 'Karnal standoff ends: Haryana govt orders probe into Aug 28 incident, farmers call off sit-in', *The Economic Times*, September 11, 2021. Available at: https://economictimes.indiatimes.com/news/india/karnal-standoff-ends-haryana-govt-orders-probe-into-aug-28-incident-farmers-call-off-sit-in/articleshow/86113542.cms?from=mdr (accessed on October 21, 2021).

The Quint, 'Bloody Clothes, Swords Used to Cut Off Man's Hand at Farmers' Protest Found', *The Quint*, October 19, 2021. Available at: https://www.thequint.com/news/india/the-swords-that-were-used-to-cut-off-a-mans-hand-and-foot-at the-farmers-protest-near-delhi-last-week-have-been-found-along-with-the-bloodstained-clothes-the police-said-on-Monday (accessed on October 26, 2021).

TheTimesofIndia, 'Farmlawsdonotreformagriculture,butcatertocorporateinterests', December 12, 2020. Available at: https://timesofindia.indiatimes.com/city/chandigarh/farm-laws-do-not-reformagriculture-but-cater-to corporate-interests/articleshow/79684740.cms (accessed on March 18, 2021).

The Times of India, '100 days of Dilli Chalo: Farmers block e-ways', *Sunday Times of India*, March 7, 2021.

The Times of India.Com, 'Govt ready to suspend implementation of farm laws for 18 months; next meeting on January 22', *The Times of India*, January 20, 2021. Available at: https://timesofindia.indiatimes.com/india/govt-ready-tosuspend-implementation-of-farm-laws-for-18months-next-meeting-onjanuary-22/articleshowprint/80369144.cms (accessed on July 8, 2021).

The Tribune, 'Ready to talk to farmers, but not on repeal: Narendra Singh Tomar', *The Tribune*, Gwalior, July 1, 2021. Available at: https://www.tribuneindia.com/news/nation/ready-to-talk-to-farmers-but-noton-repeal-narendra-singh-tomar-77034 (accessed on July 3, 2021).

The Tribune, 'Situation outside BJP meeting venue in Karnal's Indri tense as farmers cross barricades put up by police', *The Tribune*, September 30, 2021. Available at: https://www.tribuneindia.com/news/haryana/situation-outside-bjp-meeting-venue-in-karnals-indri-tense-as-farmers-cross-barricades-put-up-by-police-318268 (accessed on October 21, 2021).

Thukral, Gobind, 'Punjab farmers block governor's residence to press for their demands', *India Today*, April 15, 1984. Available at: https://www.indiatoday.in/magazine/indiascope/story/19840415-punjab-farmers-block-governors-residence-to-press-for-their-demands-802946-1984-04-15 (accessed on July 26, 2021).

Times News Network, '100 days of Dilli Chalo: Farmers block e-ways', *Sunday Times of India*, March 7, 2021.

Toor, Sangeet, 'A Century apart, currents of dissent bridge the farmers' protest and the Muzara Movement', *The Caravan*, February 2, 2021. Available at: https://caravanmagazine.in/commentary/farmers-protests-Muzara-movementpunjab-land-rights (accessed on March 16, 2021).

Toor, Sangeet, 'From Trolley Times: How Women Became an Integral Part of the Farmers' Protest', *The Wire*, January 25, 2021. Available at: https://thewire.in/women/farmers-protest-women-unions-trolley-times (accessed on March 16, 2021).

Walia, Ramesh, *Praja Mandal Movement in East Punjab States*. Patiala: Punjabi University, 1972.

Waraich, Malwinder Jit Singh (ed.), *Atam Katha Baba Sohan Singh Bhakna (Punjabi)*. Barnala: Tark Bharti Prakashan, 1967.

Waraich, Malwinder Jit Singh (ed.), *Diary Baba Hari Singh Usman (Punjabi)*. Barnala: Tark Bharti Prakashan, 1991.

Waraich, Malwinder Jit Singh and Charanji Lal Kangniwal, *Babbar Akali Lehar: Samkali Dastavez (Punjabi)*. Chandigarh: Unistar, 2015.

Whitehead, Andrew, 'Freda Bedi, the 'English girl married to a Punjabi', who joined India's freedom struggle', *The Print*, March 30, 2019. Available at: https://theprint.in/pageturner/excerpt/freda-bedi-the-english-girl-married-to-apunjabi-who-joined-indias-freedom-struggle/214143/ (accessed June 29, 2021).

2 *Kisan* Protests in Punjab 1907–2021

A Literary Lineage of Resistance*

Prabhjot Parmar and Amandeep Kaur

Introduction

In *A History of Punjabi Literature*, Sant Singh Sekhon and Kartar Singh Duggal have noted that the folk songs of Punjab 'tell the tales of battles and brave warriors, describe festivals and fairs, ... stories of the farmer, the large-hearted, and of the rains which are usually kind and of crops which seldom let the peasant down' (Sekhon and Duggal, 1992: 10–11). Whether exploring themes of romance and longing with lovers like *Heer Ranjha*, *Mirza Saheban*, and *Sohni Mahiwal* or highlighting the plight of peasants, folk songs help 'the people of Punjab to express their needs, their hopes, their aspirations ... and provide a sort of catharsis for them' (Sekhon and Duggal, 1992: 13). Over the centuries, *kavishers* [troubadours], *dhadhis* [bardic singers], and other balladeers have recited and/or sung long epic poems (*vaars* and *qissas*) or their shorter versions at gatherings. Such performances in public spaces illustrate that 'the word and the music are inseparable' (Gargi, 1967: 54). Many ballads about war and strife – often interspersed with hagiographical references – that are celebrated today 'emerged as significant works of medieval Punjabi poetry' (Sekhon and Duggal, 1992: 91). Resistance and dissent have featured prominently in folk forms such as *qissas* [stories in verse], *vaars* [heroic odes and ballads], and *Jugni* [an old form of music] that are integral components of Punjabi literary tradition. With resistance as an essential characteristic, these forms have inspired Punjabi creative writers and enthralled audiences and readers. Iconic popular verses focus on resistance fusing the aesthetic with the political in response to workers, women, Dalits, or peasant movements. It is no surprise, then, that during various protest movements in Punjab, poetry and folk songs have been and continue to be recited or sung *en masse* strengthening accord and solidarity.

This article draws attention to the unfolding of this lineage during different peasant movements from the early twentieth century to the farmers' struggle in 2020–2021. As a performative genre, poetry continues to be performed predominantly in public spheres by professional bards, poets, and others suturing together the political and the aesthetic – often with

 DOI: 10.4324/9781003320005-4

allusions to the religious. Such 'storytelling performances', argues Michael Nijhawan, 'remain important sites of knowledge production and aesthetic experience' (Nijhawan, 2006: 5). During the recent year-long farmers' protest various known and less known artists and poets captured the mood and the politics of the protest to produce poems and songs. This chapter does not analyse the anatomy of various farmers' agitations, controversial agrarian bills, laws, and acts introduced in colonial or postcolonial India, or interrogate the actions of the authorities – reprisal or censorship – to quash agrarian protests. Instead, it studies selected literary responses – mostly contemporaneous – that have specific peasant agitations as their focal points. In other words, we examine representations of agitations in poems, songs, short stories, and novels rather than the factors that led to different movements or their consequences. Also, in different genres, it is not the form but content that receives our attention. While the intent of this analysis is to focus primarily on the political, it is imperative to mention that Punjabi folklore infuses the aesthetics of Punjabi literature, as evident in the following discussion of creative responses to *kisan* movements. While the chapter does not elaborate on the plight of farmers, state violence and censorship, and gender and caste issues, we acknowledge that these are significant components of the protests worthy of separate analysis.

Bookended by Prabhjot Parmar's analysis of '*Pagri Sambhal Jatta*' (1907) and the poetry written during the current farmers' protest, is Amandeep Kaur's close reading of literature that emerged during other peasants' movements, such as *Kirti-Kisan* and *Muzara*, for example. Various selections of poetry, short story, and novel considered issues affecting *muzaras* and the peasant movements in Punjab and Telangana. The treatment of *Muzara* Movement as a subject in Punjabi short story and novel has been somewhat limited; only Santokh Singh Dhir, Navtej Singh, and Jaspal Mankhera have explored this subject in some of their short stories. In the mid-twentieth century, several poets including Prabhjot Kaur and Mohan Singh, leaving aside the romantic and the philosophical, wrote about peasant struggles and their economic exploitation. Gurcharan Rampuri who was based in Vancouver wrote consistently about the have-nots and struggle against colonial and postcolonial concerns (Sekhon and Duggal, 1992: 191). The idiom of Punjabi literature, thus, is inextricably intertwined with politics of resistance and justice. Upholding these traditions, many poets, song writers, and balladeers – at home and abroad – have written about the 2020–2021 farmers' agitation.

Just before the COVID pandemic gripped the world, in his closing address delivered at the Amritsar Literature Festival on February 27, 2020, the Punjabi poet Surjit Patar stated: 'Reciting poetry in a way that each word is understood as intended is an art in itself but the larger process is the creative ideology behind the poem' (Tribune News Service, 2020). Poetic responses to the farmers' protest and the fusion of their aesthetics with religio-political symbols and imagery compel us to consider both the reading and singing of this poetry and its reception – where the visual and the aural are engaged and attentive – along with considering the 'creative ideology' that overtly positions itself with the oppressed, including those protesting at various sites. Therefore, the recent evocation of the anthem of resistance, '*Pagri Sambhal Jatta*' [Save Your Honour, O Peasant] – first sung in March 1907 during the farmers' agitation against three colonial agrarian laws once again registers the celebrated commemoration of the political and the aesthetic.

'*Pagri Sambhal Jatta*': An Anthem of Resistance

The 1907 agitation was begun with the efforts of Sardar Ajit Singh, Sardar Kishan Singh, and Lala Ghasita Ram; the two Singhs were Shaheed Bhagat Singh's uncle and father respectively and Ram was their trusted friend. Together the trio had formed the Bharat Mata Society [Mother India Society] to raise 'political consciousness' among people and to shake the roots of the British in India (Singh, 1984). Recalling the popularity of the 'historic poem' '*Pugree Sambhal Jatta*' read by Banke Dayal at the 'epoch making meeting in Lyallpur on 3 March 1907', S. Ajit Singh shares in his autobiography: '[I]t was everywhere in the Punjab resounding the skies' (Singh, 1984). Clearly, the poem struck a chord with peasants and others, demonstrating the influence of verses that simultaneously mirror the plight of farmers and galvanize them into action. '*Pagri Sambhal Jatta*' is arguably one of the most iconic poems on the condition of, and resistance by, Punjabi farmers; its titular refrain was also popularized in the 1960s through a song in S. Bhagat Singh's biopic, *Shaheed* [Martyr] (1965). The poem's repute is such that the 1907 agitation against the three colonial laws – Doab Bari Act, Punjab Land Alienation Act, and Punjab Land Colonization Act – is widely known as the *Pagri Sambhal Jatta* Movement, a befitting tribute to the power of poetry that is spoken or sung. The analogous evocation of the struggle against the three laws in 1907 and the three acts in 2020–2021 is striking.[1] Not surprisingly, the latter farmers' protest saw the resurgence of this anthem of resistance.

'Punjab folk-songs and folk romances have been a perennial inspiration to poets of the soil' (Sekhon and Duggal, 1992: 15); Dayal, who was the editor of *Jhang Sayal*, was no exception. After the piercing imagery of destroyed crops, hungry and wailing children, and impoverished peasants exploited by landlords (lines 1–5), Dayal widened the scope from fields to the nation, equating 'Hind' [Hindustan] as a 'temple' and a peasant as its 'worshipper' (line 6). His usage of the figurative language shifts in line 9 from an evocation of the nation as a contained, sacred religio-architectural space to archetypes of folk romance. People at the gathering in Lyallpur, and subsequently, other listeners and readers, would have been familiar with the reference to *Heer Ranjha*. Drawing from Punjabi folklore to resonate with the kind of unequivocal love a peasant and, indeed all Hindustanis, needed to have for their land – like that of the legendary *Ranjha* had for *Heer* – Dayal urges: 'Bravely protect your country/You are *Ranjha* and your country *Heer*' (line 9). Here, country is signified in gendered terms as a beloved. The feminization of the nation as mother or beloved is a common metaphor used in Indian literature. By 1907, the notion of '*Bharat Mata*' or Mother India was already well established. Seemingly, the metaphor of *Heer* represents undying love for one's country – what Ajit Singh was aiming for through the peasant movement. Exhorting the assembly of people, Dayal's verse would have carried an embedded message that like *Ranjha*, they should be ready to die for the love of their *Heer* – their country. (Similar usage of *Heer* as land appears in Sehrai's work discussed later in the chapter.)

Although Ranjha was killed by eating a poisoned *ladoo*, Dayal, deliberately or not, evokes reference to another folk hero and lover, Mirza, who was killed by the arrows of his beloved Saheban's brothers. 'Take an arrow on your chest' is the literal translation of *Seene te khaave teer* (line 6). In the context of the 1907 agitation, it is the peasant who is struck by the arrows of oppressive colonial laws that favoured the British and the native *zamindars*. Here, Dayal attempts to jolt the peasants out of their stupor by reminding them of their self-respect. Sardar Ajit Singh conceived of and led the 1907 movement and was instrumental in its spread to villages in Punjab; part of the success must be attributed to Dayal's poem. Furthermore, the agitation yielded results as 'all the three bills were cancelled' (Singh, 1984); peasants had successfully 'saved their honour'. The parallel between the 1907 and the recent agitation is not lost on those familiar with *kisan* movements in colonial and postcolonial Punjab. In both, poetic responses have played a major role. The continuum of such a lineage was further strengthened in the 1920s by poetic responses composed during the coming together of the revolutionary and the peasant movements.

Kirti Kaav [Peasant Poetry]: Poetry of the *Kirti* Movement[2]

After the mass movement of 1907, the political scene in Punjab was marked by the *Ghadar* Party and other revolutionary resistance events. In the late 1920s, however, an attempt was made to establish a mass movement among the peasantry with the evolution of a distinct *Ghadar-Kirti* front, which eventually culminated in the formation of the *Kirti Kisan* Party (Josh, 1979; Singh, 1994; Alaxai, 2013).[3] In line with communist politics in the mid-1920s and with an intention of forming a united front of the *Kirtis* and *Kisans*, a monthly newspaper, *Kirti* (1926–1940), served as an organ to disseminate their ideas, including through poetry. Most of the poems in the *Kirti* newspaper speak of the miserable and wretched condition of the *kirtis, as* evident from titles such as '*Dukhi Kirtian de Haarhe*', '*Kirti Dukhi Dhanad Sarkar Hathon*', '*Faryaad Dukhi Kirti*', and '*Ik Dukhi Mazdoor di Zindagi*'. The grief and misery laden poems and their titles are not surprising. In fact, some of these resonate with the poetry produced during the 2020–2021 farmers' protest movement that is discussed later in this chapter.

In addition to highlighting the shared miseries of peasants, poems published in *Kirti* combine the normative directives for the welfare of the underprivileged and the oppressed with a moral critique of capitalism and imperialism in poems such as '*Piara Vatan*' [Beloved Country], '*Shaheedi Vaar*' [Ballad of Martyrs], '*Siharfi Fariyad Dukhi Kirti*' [Complaints of a Wretched Worker], and '*Kirti Kisan*'. Considering it a symbol of hope for peasants, Giani Hira Singh Dard presents the publication of *Kirti* as the rebirth of Lenin in Punjab:

> In Punjab, through a second incarnation
> Had come Lenin once again, thought *Kirti*.
> Now would be the rule of the workers
> He said, feeling frantic
>
> (Singh, 2017: 99)

This ideological thrust manifested in many poems published in the paper. For example, the following poem by Sharaf states:

> Into the pitch, we have stepped,
> We want you to remember the fact.
> What we reared ourselves, distributed it would be,
> In abundance would it be dispersed, *Kirti*, in garden of the world
>
> (Singh, 2017: 108)

Kirti Kaav reiterates the objective of the *Kirti* Party to establish a workers' government. Since the name of the party is *Kirti Kisan* Party, it makes a clear distinction between *kirti* and *kisan*. *Kirti* is synonymous with *mazdoor* [labourer]; however, in *Kirti Kaav*, the worker and the peasant, despite being defined as two distinct groups, begin to represent the same class. For example, Vidhata Singh Tir has titled his poem 'Kirti te Kisan' (The Worker and the Peasant) and yet the 'miserable *kirti*' in the poem is actually a peasant who produces 'heaps of grain' (Josh, 1979: 140).[4]

Despite being overtly political, *Kirti Kaav* is not banal or plainly prosaic for it combines fierce nationalism with a high degree of self-criticism, in the process also revealing certain similarities with the Ghadar poetry. While the poets show their understanding of the colonial system of exploitation, there is also an unrelenting criticism of the local people for being passive. In '*Kirti-Kisano*', Munsha Singh '*Dukhi*' writes: Centuries have passed sleeping; why have you sunk into despair?/Into a state of stupor, you just keep sitting/the robbers have looted everything, leaving you penniless' (Singh, 2017: 536). Some of the poems, especially those by Firoz Din Sharaf, take the form of a conversation, wherein the worker and the capitalist address each other from their respective class positions, resulting in a call for action by overcoming religious divisions. Interestingly, peasant resistance and consciousness, in this phase, is closely tied to the national movement for independence. Thus, the poetry of the *Kirti* movement addresses – for the first time in Punjabi – the class divisions in a socialist idiom, which, later, persists in different forms in the Progressive and the *Muzara* movement.

Muzaras [Tenant Farmers] and *Biswedars* [Landlords] in PEPSU: Literary Responses to the *Muzara* Movement

Although it peaked during the 1940s and early 1950s, the origins of Patiala and East Punjab State Union [PEPSU] *Muzara* Movement can be traced back to the Punjab Tenancy Act 1868 and later to the *Praja Mandal* [*People's Association*] Movement of the 1920s and the *Kirti Kisan* Party. With its slogan of 'land to the tiller', it was directed against the *biswedars* by those tenants who had lost their hereditary property rights and now struggled for the ownership of land. It was a struggle against state repression, for exacting the amount of *batai* [share rent or share of produce] for the landlords, and a movement against the imposition of excessive land revenue, which had higher rates in the princely states (Mukherjee, 2004; Alaxai, 2013; Vaid, 2019). Mukherjee argues that the main strategy of the *Muzara* movement 'remained a combination of refusal to pay *batai*, refusal to vacate lands and resist landlords' attempts at evictions, etc., if necessary, by force' (Mukherjee, 2004: 242). This remained the broad pattern of the movement from roughly 1948 to 1952.

Jaswant Singh Kanwal's novel *Raat Baki Hai* (The Night is Still Here) is influenced by the *Muzara* Movement. In *Lok-Dushman* [The People's Enemy], Surinder Singh Narula, a contemporary of Kanwal, contextualizes the struggle as the dialectic of violence and non-violence. Joginder Bahrla's emphasis also remained primarily on poetry. In terms of its tone and tenor, three distinct moods – anger, defiance, and hope – define the poetry of the *Muzara* Movement. Activist poets like Sohan Singh Josh, Isar Singh Tamkot, Dharam Singh Fakkar, and Desraj Chajjali wrote overtly mobilizational and exhortatory verses to present the long history of the struggle and their revolutionary sensibility with an objective to create new, precise forms of expressing political demands. In his poem, '*Inquilabi Yodhia*' [The Revolutionary Warrior], Sohan Singh Josh, while exhibiting his uncompromising opposition to all forms of imperialism and considering peasants, workers, and women as the revolutionary warriors, exhorts them to collectively bring an end to the *biswedari* (Alaxai, 2013: 189).

Given the emergence of Communists as frontline activists in the movement and their inclination towards the armed struggle in the late 1940s, it is interesting to see many poems on Kishangarh – a location that became synonymous with heroism, struggle, defiance, and martyrdom. '*Saka Kishangarh*', a poem by Dharam Singh Fakkar, chronicles the incident at

Kishangarh. By contextualizing it in the broader perspective of national independence, it also constitutes resistance to the culture of tyranny advocated by the British. Elsewhere he points out:

> Kishengarh does not glorify any single individual or event, but it represents the collective effort and sacrifice of every man, woman and all inhabitants, irrespective of caste and creed over several generations.
> (Fakkar, 1940: 1)

Poems such as '*Vithia Kishangarh*', '*Kishangarh Goli Kand*', and '*Gatha Kishangarh*' also glorify the heroism and sacrifice of the villagers. The sacrificing heroes, frequently delineated as victims of the *biswedari* system, possess the capacity to liberate the collective consciousness of the *Muzaras* from fear and agony. In 'Gatha Kishangarh', the narrator, while extolling the role of the Lal Party, challenges the enemy to go back from Kishangarh:

> This land is our mother, and we are her sons
> We won't leave our land, even if the enemy
> comes in like a flood
> (Alaxai, 2013: 202)

Such poems often do not conform to formal literary conventions; instead, they tend to focus more on the direct enunciation of their political anger and their ideological principles, bordering on rhetoric and passionate sloganeering.

The history of the *Muzara* Movement and the Progressive Writers' Association (PWA) also intertwines mainly because of their investment in the communist ideal. Progressive poets like Mohan Singh, Santokh Singh Dhir, and Piara Singh Sehrai brought the *Muzara* Movement in literature through their *vaars* and ballads. Mohan Singh exhibits both romantic and progressive affiliations in his poetry. The fact that Dhir and Sehrai's poems were sung and recited at rallies organized by the party[5] testifies to the richness and accessibility of their poetry. Four themes typify the *Muzara* poetry: (a) it seeks to construct a literary expression grounded in Marxist understanding; (b) it invokes regional and folk traditions to connect with the common people; (c) there is a general call to revolt and to expose the feudal and imperialist exploitation; and (d) a graphic delineation of the sufferings of the tenants in PEPSU and reaffirmation of their right to the land. The *Muzara* poetry consciously combines the technique of socialist realism and revolutionary romanticism to represent the movement as a collective struggle. Most of these poems invariably end with the hope to establish the rule of the workers or with a call to join the other protestors or by linking resistance movements of one region with those of others. For example, Mohan Singh writes, 'Comrades, o comrades/the world will bow down to the labour' (Chandan, 1979: 22); similarly, Sehrai proclaims his belief in 'labour that will change the face of Earth' (Chandan, 1979: 58) and 'the rich and the exploiter must know. If the establishment is on their side, history is on ours',[6] thereby fostering solidarity and providing a firm basis for collective action.

Amarjit Chandan's edited collection of poems, *Telangana Tu Karwat Lai* (Chandan, 1979), includes poems written between 1948 and 1970 that incorporate some of the tenets of the Telangana and the *Muzara* movement: the call for advocating armed rebellion, the challenge of stopping state violence, and the redefining of democratic principles. Mohan Singh's ballad, 'Gajjan Singh' published in 1954 (Chandan, 1979), set in the metre and tone of 'Jagga Jamiyan'[7] and a representative of class consciousness, begins by framing itself within the voice of the folk, which is further associated with the ordinary lives of the peasants to eventually carry the message of unity, freedom, and revolution to the *Muzaras*. It is also quite literally the voice of nature, which echoes through the depiction of agricultural operations of the peasants in sync with the cyclicality of the Punjabi calendar, reminding readers, that life will be renewed:

> As came the season of spring, said the wrinkled Gajjan Singh,
> Let's gather the seeds for the sugarcane.
> Comrades, o comrades!
> Why should we look other's hands in vain?
> Here comes the Spring, here comes the hope
>
> (Chandan, 1979: 15)

The incantatory quality of the verse 'comrades, o comrades' in every stanza becomes both an exhortation and a challenge woven in musically. Here, the image of the peasant, like most other poems on the *Muzara* movement, is the image of the peasant in action which also determines the discourse of protest in the *Muzara* poetry. In the second half of the poem, the narrator relays a balladic narrative of protest and the desire of tenants for laying claim to the land in terse and truculent words: 'Comrades, o comrades!/ the tenants now demand for the lands' (Chandan, 1979: 15). The poem is replete with vegetal and floral motifs reinforced by vivid colour imagery, predominantly red and green, thereby indicating a communist idiom with agrarian hues.

Dhir's titular poem, '*Telangana Tu Karwat Lai*', (1971) is a direct call to arms, where the poet employs repetition and rhetoric of resistance to incite the people to revolt. It has larger implications in the sense that it expands the narrative through a parallel reference to Telangana and Kishangarh to include *Gaya* and *Kapilvastu* as metaphors of non-violence, to both actively engage in the historical process of struggle against capitalism and to eventually reject non-violence as a recourse to counter the systemic violence perpetrated by capitalists and feudal lords. While tyranny is an abstract concept, its execution has material and physical consequences, which Dhir demonstrates through its personification: 'Violence dances in the streets/In the town of Kapilvastu/Tyranny is thriving/In the palaces of Rishi Gautam' (Chandan, 1979: 29).

At the centre of the poem lies the idea that violence is the force of capital visited upon the people to create conditions of precarity. Dhir uses graphic imagery to describe the process by which the capitalists consume the lives of common people and defy the very notion of non-violence that Buddha had preached. In a system where the rich have 'killed the workers in the mills' or favoured 'the eviction of the peasants' and raised 'illegal taxes', making them poor and powerless, non-violence is not an option for the common people; rather, the poet imagines the ultimate political act to be the capture of power and its deployment on behalf of the oppressed (Chandan, 1979: 29–30). The militant tone and political inference make many of the poems on the *Muzara* Movement strikingly similar. For example, Sehrai's long poem, '*Telangana di Vaar*', riding on the warrior identity, chronicles the struggle of peasants in the Telangana region. It shares thematic similarity with Mohan Singh's '*Mangali*' and '*Gajjan Singh*' and Dhir's '*Boli*'. All three poems not only eulogize the guerrilla warfare tactics adopted by the peasants but also transcend temporal and geographical borders to show the interconnectedness of all those who fight for justice and land.

The language used in the ballads and *vaars* provides a fascinating insight into how these poets imagine the *Muzara* struggle. They use it to legitimize and glorify the contemporary resistance and its participants; in so doing, they construct a warrior identity, which is rooted in the cultural and religious history of Punjab. For example, Giani Bachan Singh Bakshiwala, in '*Vithia Kishangarh*', equates the strength of *Muzaras* 'with the power of Dashmesh/who made the sparrows fight hawks' (Alaxai, 2013: 198). Similarly, the evocation of the martial tradition of Guru Gobind Singh in 'Telangana di Vaar' takes the form of a call for action: 'that other efforts no more will benefit/people take recourse to sword' (Chandan, 1979: 47). Later in the poem, marked by a highly emotive theatricality Sehrai employs the metaphor of Heer, extolling the peasants' victory over the land:

> The *Kheras* had thrown Ranjha out, snatching the land Heer
> The world has changed today; pleading turned into defiance.
> The cowherd is reunited with Heer, the sword in hand of oppressor has fallen
> The sons of Earth have become *sardars* of the land again
> (Chandan, 1979: 52)

Here, land and woman become synonymous. Interestingly, while the reference to Heer enables us to discern the patriarchy of the medieval state, she is dissociated from her struggle and equated with land which must be mastered. The poets also tend to idealize traditional peasant farming as a 'natural' way of life and declare their unflinching faith in the invincibility of socialism.

Jaswant Singh Kanwal's *Raat Baaki Hai* [The Night is Still Here, 2014] set against the backdrop of the *Muzara* movement tells the story of Charan, whose hopes are dashed after he fails to secure a job on completion of his education, but later, at the behest of his friend, he joins the *Muzara* movement. The novel also weaves together a story of love and revolution focusing on the potential and dangers of love through desire, distraction, and sacrifice. Through Raj and Charan's relationship, the novelist foregrounds the idea that romance is widely incompatible with true devotion to the revolutionary cause and that the victory of love is not possible unless a revolutionary transformation is experienced in the society.

Kanwal approaches the *Muzara* agitation from a particular perspective. Through the transformation of Baba Karam Singh from a Ghadar activist to an Akali worker to a Communist revolutionary, he situates the struggle of *Muzaras* in historical continuity with the other protest movements in Punjab. His portrait of the struggle is highly idealistic, revealing how he feels the economic and the social transformation can be achieved. The postcolonial period in which it is written affects the manner in which the agrarian question is framed in the novel. Also, the representation of other *Muzaras* is partly achieved through a small re-creation of their dialogue when they participate in the meetings of *Kisan Sabhas* or protests against the *biswedars*. However, their understanding of the doctrine of revolution is very uncritical and cosmetic, as exemplified by Veeru's comment when the villagers gather to repair the breach in the riverbank to prevent flooding of their homes:

> We don't care that our houses have collapsed. We can make a living by putting up small shacks, but never abandon our claims for the land. These *Jagirdars* must be reminded of the Russian Revolution, and how the feudalism came to an end there.
>
> (Kanwal, 2014: 118)

The novel spells out a political programme for the restoration of a symbiotic relationship between the land and the peasants.

Kanwal's understanding of agrarian relations is tied to his conviction in salvation through socialist doctrine. His strength as well as weakness stems from this fervent belief. In the process of communicating the socialist ideal of the rule of the workers or distribution of land to the *Muzaras*, he turns increasingly dogmatic and rhetorical. He shows how his writing graft the omniscient narrative voice, which clearly has a conscious moral purpose, into the thought process of the *Muzaras*, even while the *Muzaras*' thoughts are imbued with party jargon. The ending of the novel where Charan goes to meet Raj also obscures some parts of the novel's representation of the peasant. However, it does celebrate the power of the people and includes collective resistance as a potential solution to the problems of injustice, clearly displaying traces of a theological faith in the advent of a utopian communist society. For example, the one-page-long last chapter is interestingly titled '*Vikas-Dhara*' and ends on an optimistic note: 'the red flags ripped apart the blue sky and the old banyan tree was waiting for a last push to fall into the pond' (Kanwal, 2014: 264).

Like Kanwal's novel, his selected short stories also foreground the socialist and Marxist ideal in their representation of the *Muzara* movement. In the eponymous short story from his collection, *Navin Rut* [The New Season, 1949], Navtej Singh presents the state of close family relations left behind after their protestor son is put into the prison immediately after independence for supporting the *Muzaras*. Through Ishar Kaur's assertion of her right to the land, the story touches upon the question of women's land rights, albeit briefly. When the other protestors arrive at Sewa Singh's fields to kick off collective farming as an act of class solidarity, Ishar Kaur, initially misunderstanding them to be hirelings of the *vadda sardar* (big landlord), screams in fear, 'They have come to grab my land. Those devils sent by the *vadda Sardar.* A Single woman's land...' (Singh, 2003: 275). However, the voice of *meri bhaun* (my land) soon turns into a collective *saadi bhaun* (our land) as the protestors celebrate the onset of the new season, metaphorically conveyed through both their decisions to collectively plough the field and to challenge the might of the *biswedar.*

The plot of Dhir's story, '*Daaku*' (The Bandits) develops through a comparison between the idyllic village of the past and the present state of wretchedness, and this indulgence seems to regulate their future hopes as well. The system which separates this dreaming of an idyllic future from the present state is the *biswedari*, which has eaten up all the resources, leaving the villagers mired in desolation, poverty, and *ujaad* (waste). Dhir consciously casts the symbol of sickle in a stereotypical and romantic frame: 'the red fragments of iron formed sickles like the second moon night. The razor-sharp rasp sharpened the edges of those sickles. Small red ambers spread out of it' (Dhir, 1950: 58). Jaspal Mankhera's short story '*Khataas*' [Sourness] focuses on the deteriorating conditions of the peasants to conclude how these *Muzara*-turned-owners are reduced back to being *Muzaras* in an agricultural system driven by capitalism, leading to debt and suicides. Through Gamdoor's retrospection on his family history, the author tends to offer a new perspective wherein the very idea that land distribution will bring prosperity and affluence to peasants and workers is presented as illusory and long lost.

After the decline of the *Muzara* movement, there are no other noteworthy political or social movements having their own distinct character until the Naxalite movement in the late 1960s. Though some small agrarian movements like the anti-levy betterment tax *morcha* (1959) and demands for land to the *abadkars* arise, they remain limited in their scope and on their influence on literature. The anti-levy movement lasted for two months and writers like Kanwal were arrested for supporting and participating in it; not surprisingly, there is hardly any literature related to it. His novel *Bhavani* is set in the backdrop of a *kisan morcha* against the imposition of illegal taxes; it does not offer much detail about the nature or location of the *morcha* and largely ignores the history that had led to it. Dhir's story '*Sipahi*' foregrounds both the struggle of members of the *kisan sabhas* to gather popular support as they march from village to village to protest against the betterment levy, and their crisis to stay relevant in village politics in the wake of rise of other factions. This village-to-village connection, seen earlier in the 1907 agitation, has emerged as a hallmark of the 2020–2021 farmers' protest.

Kalay Kanoon Te Kisan Morcha [Three 'Black Laws' and the Farmers' Protest][8]

The farmers' protest that had been taking place by the roadside and railway lines in Punjab for two months, moved to the borders of Delhi on 25 November 2020. Enroute, the farmers were stopped by heavy roadblocks and water cannons, used during one of the coldest winters experienced in North India. Undaunted, the farmers overcame all obstacles to reach the borders of the national capital Delhi; however, the city was closed to them. The restrictions imposed on the protesting farmers by the state had led to farmers settling to protest along the border of the nation's capital.[9] In so doing, they had transformed sections of busy national highways into public spheres where performance of resistance offered a powerful visual and sonic imagery. The reconfigured border – a transformative space, a threshold, an entry point – as 'a site of adjacency' with 'bodies on the line' (Butler, 2015) can be interpreted in multiple ways: denial of access – to the capital and to the government, denial of rights, discrimination against the farmers, and people's defiance against oppression are a few themes that have found their way into performances of rhythmic slogans, songs, and agit-prop poetry. Many of the well-known Punjabi poets and singer-songwriters demonstrated their support through poetry and performance at various protest sites and online. Amateur writers too had composed or shared couplets or short poems that speak of the farmers' determination and the government's apathy.

Although the intersectionality of class, caste, gender, and political affiliations – at times obvious and at others, subtle – reveals different divisions and groups, nevertheless, the farmers' protest had emerged as a united front, an alliance during a highly divisive time, both socially and politically. Attendant to these, the poetry produced during the year-long protest used intertextual figurative language reflecting the importance of unity and cohesive effort. The resistance to the three laws was a people's movement with groundswell support witnessed live on television and through social media. The intervention of technology differentiates this movement from the previous agitations, as it enabled an almost instantaneous dissemination of the protest and related creative responses at an unprecedented level.

To this end, websites and apps facilitated the collecting and sharing of verses and songs that were presented live at protest sites or recorded elsewhere; either way, their circulation facilitated unparalleled access – often in real time – to the poetry of resistance and poetry of critique. In fact, people used the internet as a tool of resistance, pushing the boundaries of the protest far beyond the heavily barricaded, razor wired, and nail studded borders that stopped protestors from entering Delhi. The border had morphed into an extended settlement seeking refuge from, and demonstrating resistance to, state violence as a collective that had adopted the peaceful path of non-violence. Finally, on November 19, 2021, the three 'Black Laws' were repealed resulting in the success of the agitation defined as farmers' victory. Selected poetry and songs offer a telling commentary of this protest movement and its success.

Illuminating the hard and sometimes dangerous work that is farming, Swami Antar Neerav addresses the state in and as 'O Bhai' [brother/man]: 'Kinnow [hybrid mandarin]/grows on thorny trees/ripens in winters/who are you scaring?' (Neerav in Gill, 2020). Using horticultural and seasonal imagery, Neerav juxtaposes the obstacles the state had installed and the hardships – sharp nails and bitter cold – that many farmers regularly endure. The shocking acts of state restriction and violence find references in various responses, comparing the protest sites to the strife-ridden national borders between India and Pakistan and, in turn, highlight the harsh treatment of citizens in their own country. Placing the threatened democratic rights and similar articulations under a magnifying lens, some comparative references draw parallels with cruelties perpetrated by the British during the colonial rule. However, it is the recurrent hagiographical evocation of the Ninth and Tenth Sikh Gurus – their resistance to the atrocities committed by the then Mughal rulers – that offers models of faith-based resolve and defiance against injustice. The narrative of martyrdom and sacrifice – commemorated by most Sikhs daily in the text of *Ardas* [Prayer] – elevates farmers as warriors who, like their Gurus, are willing to make the ultimate sacrifice. One of the rhythmic protest slogans, *Jittangay ya Marangay* [Victorious or Dead], personifies the resistance and succinctly sums up the ideology of consummate commitment to sacrifice in the name of the cause.

The performative fusion of the contemporary with the historical and the textual with the verbal and visual has created a new corpus of poetry that is no longer limited to the printed text or social gatherings. Its performance and the immediate distribution of these performances via social media bolsters the indefatigable spirit, *Chardi Kala* [High Morale] of the protestors, Sikhs and non-Sikhs. 'The determination never to give in' contends Khushwant Singh, 'came to be deeply rooted in the Sikh psyche; even in adversity, they were exhorted to remain in buoyant spirits – chardhi kala' (Khushwant Singh, 2018: 31). Considered a source of moral and spiritual sustenance, Chardi Kala nurtures the unrelenting spirit of the farmers against a government that is unmoved by their demands or plight. Satinder

Sartaj captures this spirit: 'Come see the high spirits/Our mothers stand sentinel to protect/They won't be defeated easily/Tyrant, your tyranny will not be suffered/Look, they gather courage again/This is what is Chardi Kala' (SagaHits, 2020). Perhaps, Chardi Kala is instrumental in also dealing with the extremes of weather – fierce dust storms, searing heat, heavy monsoons, and bitter cold.

Whereas literacy has traditionally been the preserve of the upper caste and upper class, oral traditions of poetry and, more recently, mass literacy movements have enabled most people from all strata of society to have access to the written word. The corpus of poetry focusing on the 2020–2021 protest crosses the divides of religion, region, geographies, gender, caste, and class. This section of the chapter considers an assortment of poems and songs whose subject ranges from the hard-working *kirti*, resistance and self-respect, youth's commitment, apathy of the government – often represented as Delhi, to political ideology and social issues and verses articulating different aspects of farmers' protest. As mentioned previously, the focus is on the power of the word, not the form. Through poetry, artists registered textual and verbal modes of protest against state violence inflicted on farmers. Poetry and song emerged as manifestations of social and political commitments of poets-song writers that compelled them to write and share the experiences witnessed in person or viewed on a live broadcast or recording. Unlike other literary forms, Punjabi poetry's reach beyond the confines of high-brow literary audience is obvious in the popularity and reciting, singing, and quoting of couplets from *Heer*, *Mirza*, or *Dulla*; or sharing the verses of Shiv Kumar Batalvi, Amrita Pritam, Lal Singh Dil, or Paash.

A scrutiny of the creative responses – oral, textual, and visual – produced during the 2020–2021 protest reveals that this vast corpus recorded in print, audio, and digital text, image, and video, in addition to voicing emotions and providing critique through different modes, has emerged as depositories of people's history. As well, these echo the literature produced during previous agrarian movements discussed above. Many of the creative writers hail from farming communities, living and/or observing the precarity, prosperity, and poverty of agrarian life. 'First and foremost, I am a farmer. I have not forgotten this, and I will never forget this', said Babbu Maan during his visit to the protest site at Ghazipur Border (PTI, 2020). However, to think that responses have not come from non-farmers would be erroneous; several poets who do not have direct connections to farming and/or reside in urban areas or live abroad in the Punjabi diaspora have written emotive verses encapsulating the condition of farmers, the protest, and other subjects; some responses have come from Pakistan. Dalits, Jatts, Punjabis, non-Punjabis, women, men, young, and old from different faiths have responded. The list consists of both established and emerging poets. However, poems produced in their thousands are not just Punjab focused – seeking a hegemonic Punjabi nationalism – but rise above differences and divisions to address issues related to *kisan* and *kirsani* [farming]. Most of the poems under consideration are from Gurbhajan Gill's online compilation of hundreds of poems, *Farmers Challenge the Ruler: Vol 1–13* (Gill, 2020). The poems in this collection are strikingly uniform in their subject matter even though their form and length vary, for example, formal poems following a rhythmic pattern, poems in blank verse, and songs in rhyming couplets.

In 'Dedicated to the Farmers' Movement', Manpreet Tiwana focuses on the reawakened sons of the soil who, upon seeing 'opposing narrative', have 'woken up' to show how attuned they are to the struggle (Tiwana in Gill, 2020). Like several other poems, its speaker is the collective voice of the farmers. 'Sown in the fields are not crops, but our fate' ascribes the abstract – fate – tactility through the act of sowing seeds (and harvesting crops). The twinning of crops and farmers' fate underpins not just financial security but the lurking threat of failure, mounting debts and possible suicide. It is important to point out that '90 percent of India's farmers can't cover the basic costs of fertilizer, seeds, pesticide and other equipment' (Shivji, 2021). The increasing costs of production have 'squeezed incomes of farmers so much that basically they are being forced to commit suicide' (Shivji, 2021). Framed against farmer suicides, the metaphor of 'fate sown in the field' gains a profoundly sad meaning. To this end, 'Suicide Note' a quartet composed by Amarjit Singh Rai Advocate draws attention to farmers' suicide by firmly situating it in the protest site through a stand-alone opening line '(At Tikri Border)'. He presents the subjugated peasant as a figure of resistance who exercises his agency to take his own life to sustain the movement, as oil is needed for a flame, blood is needed to keep alive the movement: 'Peasant powerless/Modi arrogant./To keep the flame burning/oil of blood is needed' (Rai in Gill, 2020).

Drawing attention to a life-taking menace in Punjab – drugs – Manjit Tiwana's 'Dedicated to the Farmers' Movement' together addresses both the farmers' protest and drug usage among youth (Tiwana in Gill, 2020). The poem acquires a level of militant defiance albeit with a cautionary tone. The reawakened youth who had been intoxicated under the influence of drugs, 'like hawks will strike with their claws' infusing the movement with strength and security. In a similar fashion, Harmeet Vidyarthi showcases the responsibility that Punjabi youth have demonstrated. The writer of this poem, 'Determination of Sons of the Soil', addresses Delhi – synonymous with government:

> After a long time/careless youths of Punjab have come with care/with their elders not in suitcases [carrying photographs when migrating abroad]/but seated on trolleys'. Respecting their elders, standing in support are the youth who 'the news channels defame as addicts, lazy, and absconders.
>
> (Vidyarti in Gill, 2020)

Even though Punjab is struggling with the menace of drug addiction[10] with the bulk of cases among 15–35-year-old males and children as young as nine 'hooked to drugs' (Verma, 2017), the farmers' protest poetry has shifted the spotlight on hardworking, committed, and good 'sons of the soil' who are often tarred with the same brush as the addicts. Vidyarthi continues to paint a comparative picture with reference to 'those who were dancing to the music of DJs' provocative numbers/are now dancing on the arrows laid by you [government]'. Like Swami Neerav and others, Vidyarthi alludes to the brutal curtailing of the protest by the Modi Government with sharpened iron bars and nails specially cemented into the road to prevent farmers' entry into Delhi. Poetry, thus, not only provides a critique, its imagery and metaphors also record specific acts of obstruction, intimidation, and reprisal by the state. The sons of the soil, as Vidyarthi points out, unfazed by such horrific acts, continue their protest with determination.

The assemblage of socio-religious imagery and metaphors in several poems, gesture towards a tyrannical and violent past against which the ordinary and the oppressed – often represented as meek sparrows – are transformed into warriors who fight with hawk-like ferocity. These performative texts link the past and the present to reaffirm the notion of courage and sacrifice rooted in Sikh history. In a short rhythmic poem of three stanzas, Bedi Mirpuri captures the mood of defiance at the farmers' protest on the borders of Delhi: 'We are not tired, nor will we tire/Listen carefully, O Government!/We will uproot you' (Mirpuri quoted by Gurpreet Singh Shimlapuri, 2021).

The collective pronoun 'We' represents people's power in a democracy; it clearly positions the collective voice of farmers as the speaker of the poem; a collective that locates its defiance in allusions to Sikh history. The unwavering faith in the success of the agitation is underpinned by the indomitable Chardi Kala to issue a cautionary note of inevitable defeat to the adversary. In the next stanza, the steadfast resolve of the unfatigued speaker-farmer directly references the Tenth Sikh Guru: 'We are the hawks of the Tenth Guru [Guru Gobind Singh]/taking you in talons we will soar away' (Mirpuri quoted by Gurpreet Singh Shimlapuri, 2021).

Ostensibly, written originally as a voice of Punjabi farmers – most of whom are Sikhs – Mirpuri's verse emerges as a representative voice of *all* farmers protesting at the borders along Delhi or indeed at other sites across India. Unlike Banke Dayal ('*Pagri Sambal Jatta*'), who exhorted peasants to shake off their 'languor', Mirpuri acquaints us with the farmers' tenacious resolve to hold fast and not 'return home'. Vidyarthi too makes a similar point while addressing Delhi: 'You hoped that/after crying [protesting] at your threshold for a few days/we will return home'. The avian imagery of the hawk with its powerful talons is beforehand awash in religio-spiritual narrative, reinvigorating the reader/listener with the courage needed to carry on the protest. Guru Gobind Singh, also referred to as '*Chitteyan Baazanwala*' [Keeper of White Hawks], is often depicted in paintings carrying a white hawk. Emblematic of resilience, courage, and tenacity, the hawk stands as a powerful symbol in Sikhism; more importantly because 'it is identified as the bearer of the Guru's spirit, exhorting the Sikhs to hold fast during times of oppression' (Fenech and McLeod, 2014: 149). In addition to Mirpuri and Tiwana, several other poets draw from the Sikh/Punjabi religio-cultural source and iconography to underscore the transformation of the meek into the mighty; in other words, cautioning the rulers not to underestimate the farmers.

Similarly, establishing a link between the historic and the contemporary in 'Power of Hands', Gurdish Kaur Grewal's references to, among others, Banda Singh Bahadur 'making peasants owners of land' or 'Guru Arjun fighting tyranny with immense patience' lead the reader to the unity of farmers that is informed by struggle for just cause with patience:

> 'In the struggle are
> farmers and traders too
> labourers and writers too
> villagers and city dwellers too
> Hindus and Muslims too
> Sikhs and Christian too'
>
> (Grewal in Gill, 2020)

After other references to the diversity of age, gender, and geography, Grewal focuses on unity-in-strength trope that carries with it the power to exact change and can 'topple /any tyrant ruler's throne'. In her *ghazal* of seven couplets, 'You will Regret for Centuries', Grewal forewarns the establishment on several fronts. If the opening couplet directly warns against encouraging corporatization: 'If you give wings to capitalism/You will definitely regret it for centuries' then the fifth one homes-in on political investment in communalization: 'People of all religions have come together/How will you now light the fires of hatred?' (Grewal in Gill, 2020). In a similar vein, Davi Davinder Kaur (personal communication May 28, 2021) directly addresses the crop of wheat in a lyrical poem: '*Kanke ni kanke, tu reh kirti di banke*', underscoring that it is the farmer that nurtures the crop, not the corporate.

Replete with sensory imagery, Karamjit Kaur Kishanwal's poem '*Att da Annt*' [End of Atrocities], engages repeatedly the visual, tactile, aural, and gustatory to highlight the voices of farmers against the treachery of tyrannical leaders:

> To end atrocities
> it is necessary to awaken self-respect
> we've realized
> those mocking our existence
> are not leaders
> and sugar-coated
> poisoned words of consolation can form blisters on our tongues',
>
> (Kishanwal in Gill, 2020)

Yoking together Delhi's historical and contemporary association with struggles, Kishanwal makes it a palimpsest on which yet another history is being written – on the roads by the farmers: 'On cold winter nights/ they write/on roads of Delhi/with ink of resolve/the finest poetry this era' (Kishanwal in Gill, 2020). Likewise, Gubaksh Singh Bhandal announces: 'Leaving furrows/poetry has come on the roads' ('Fields are sad', Bhandal in Gill, 2020). Employing farm imagery, Gurbhajan Singh Gill personifies the furrows in the field as 'furrowed brow' of the farmers and reminds us that the elders of this land have seen many struggles. 'Babas cut-into blocked canal openings/Harsha Chinna [village] still challenges' or 'In Malwa landlords were uprooted/by peasants in Kishangarh' are poetic salutes to the elders of resistance movements.

Punjabi Singers and Songwriters

Like poets, Punjabi singers and songwriters, many with a previous record of socio-political commitment or social responsibility, have also embodied the farmers' protest and its concerns through their music that is widely distributed via social media, especially on YouTube. For example, Babbu Maan, Harf Cheema, Kanwar Grewal, Sidhu Moosewala, Gurlej Akhtar, and Satinder Sartaj have released songs, some of which crossed four million views within a few months. Sharing of these 'solidarity-with-protest' songs allows for the creation of a visual montage – often photographed or filmed at the protest sites along Delhi borders – that provides compelling, atmospheric imagery to complement the lyrics. Through a combination of powerful aural and visual engagement, these 'set-to-music' poems seek to buttress the protest by connecting masses scattered all over the world, as though uniting public in virtual space. However, as Anastasia Denisova argues in the context of digital media and protests in Russia, '...protest publics in a virtual space does not secure the initiation of collective activism' (Denisova, 2017: 980). In other words, there is a proclivity for romanticization of resistance by many of the armchair supporters. Nevertheless, the online world forges networked resistance connections that keep the on-ground protest live through conversation; music videos afford such possibilities of expressing support and even dissent of dissent through the provision for written comments, emojis, and icons for instant 'likes' or 'dislikes'. Along with remarks of support, vitriolic and abusive comments initiate a tirade of back-and-forth insults in which many join; thus, revealing splintered political ideologies entrenched in party or regional politics. Of course, many online trolls are part of state's propaganda machinery to denounce and discredit support for the farmers' protest. The power of internet is such that during the protests, the internet services in the protest zones at Delhi borders were suspended by the government for several days, disrupting the digital flow of communication that has the extraordinary capacity to unite and, in turn, mobilize resistance. Interestingly, Mirpuri's poem discussed above was posted on YouTube in the public comments below Harf Cheema's 2020 song, '*Patshah*' [Badshah/Emperor] – a reference to Sikh Gurus.

Sung by Cheema and Grewal, 'Patshah' juxtaposes the farmers' protest with, to borrow from Nijhawan's work on *dhadi* singers, 'mythohistorical events of the Sikh past [that] become conceptually related' (Nijhawan, 2006: 196). Here, instead of a fulsome discussion of the entire song – lyrics, music, picturization – the focus is on lyrics. The notion of sacrifice becomes paramount in 'Patshah'. Borrowing from the natural and the spiritual worlds, Cheema positions the resolute farmer 'steadfast like mountains' and 'with commanding presence' and whose 'faith and patience' make him a picture to behold. His 'face glowing with spiritual light' gestures to his grounding in social justice, a constitutive element of Sikh faith. Evoking the sacrifices of the Ninth and the Tenth Sikh Gurus, the lyrics of 'Patshah' indebted to the heroic traditions of poetry, braid together heroism and martyrdom of Guru Teg Bahadur – often referred to as *Hind di Chadar* [Protector of Hindustan] – who took a principled stand to protect Kashmiri *pandits* and was executed in Delhi in November 1675 on the order of the Mughal Emperor, Aurangzeb. Establishing the parallel between then and now, the concluding line of the opening stanza, 'It's the same time for sacrifice and it's the month of *Poh* [lunar month from mid-November to mid-December]', gets even more striking when we consider the location of the protest at Singhu border that also has the state-built Guru Teg Bahadur Memorial complex. 'On the same path are walking, the sons of Guru Teg Bahadur/Let there be a divine light at Delhi border'. The allusions in lyrics and the physical site both put the historical and the current in conversation. Cheema and Grewal's location on the border and at the margins vis-à-vis the government collectively constructs protesting farmers as warriors who, like their Guru and his sons, will have to fight for just cause.

Sung in softer tones and accompanied by plaintive music, the song continues to fuse the historic and the current. The motif of sacrifice is implicit in 'Patshah's' narrative from the outset with the opening couplet equating the 'sons' – farmers – to Guru Teg Bahadur's son and grandsons – two of whom died fighting at the Battle at Chamkaur in 1705 and two executed by being bricked-up alive at the tender ages of six and eight when they refused conversion to Islam. 'Patshah' draws in the poignant reference to the *Chote Sahibzade* [younger sons]: 'In children are glimpses of Fateh Singh'. In a creative intervention, the video of the song provides a gendered interpretation when the camera focuses on two little girls at the protests as 'Fateh Singh' is mentioned. The resolute faith that Fateh Singh symbolizes posits the farmers as the ones who, inspired by the sacrifice of *Chote Sahibzade*, must possess a similar unwavering resolve not to bow to oppression. Furthermore, the sacrifices made by Guru Gobind Singh, who is praised as *Sarbansdani* – the one who sacrificed all – frames the farmers' agitation as the one that demands ultimate sacrifice.

The songs produced after the conclusion of the farmers' protests, while celebrating the victory of the common farmer over the three farm laws, do not deviate from the tone and tenor of most of the songs released during the year-long struggle. For instance, released on November 19, 2021 – the day the three farm laws were revoked – 'Jitt de Jaikaare' [Clarion Call of Victory], sung by Hasanvir Chahal, Kam Singh, and Ricky Sangha was perhaps the first song celebrating farmers' victory. In its opening refrain, the victorious farmers are regarded as 'Guru's Fauj' [Army of the Guru (an embedded reference to Khalsa fauj)]. Similarly, Virasat Sandhu's 'Fateh Morcha' [Victorious Agitation] and Resham Singh Anmol's song 'Dilliye ni jit ke tainu Punjab chalya' [Triumphant over Delhi, Punjab returns home] allude to the icons of Sikh history, the constant tussle with Delhi, and the cultural unity among various states. Even before his music company label is displayed, Virasat Sandhu's 'Fateh Morcha' video opens with an illustration of a farmer beneath which the popular tagline, 'Long Live Farmers and Workers' Unity' sets the stage for a celebratory tone of the song. An upbeat tempo with the plucking of tumbi [one-stringed instrument] as a signature link to traditional Punjabi folk music, transitions to a short montage of farmers celebrating the withdrawal of the three 'black laws'. The opening lyrics address the listener (of the music or even the government): 'Know from history/wherever we have engaged in battle/we have returned victorious'. The recurrent refrain, 'Victorious, when we return to Punjab/Delhi – nation's capital – will tell that Sardars [Sikhs] were here' employs the metaphor of a 'maidaan' [battlefield] for the protest. When repeated, 'Sardar' in the second line is replaced by 'Kisan'. While the usage of 'Kisan' has pan India connotation, when used in tandem with 'Sardars', it ascribes centrality to the Punjabi/Sikh farmers and protesters. Like several other songs, 'Fateh Morcha' also situates the current protest in the religio-historical context. As the song begins, the camera pans from right to left focusing on a few paintings, including an artistic impression of Banda Singh Bahadur, who fought for the peasants' rights in the early-eighteenth century, thus conflating historical struggles for peasants' rights and the recent protest. In addition to the complementary religious iconography in verse and images, Sandhu and co-lyricist Sukh Punia posit the protest and farmers' victory as a model for peaceful resistance: 'When generations will ask/how they had returned victorious/without weapons (arms)'. In so doing, the song presents the protest as an exemplary record for posterity. Similarly, Anmol's song too focuses on the 'future generations who would testify to the brotherhood [can be understood as harmony] of the three states – UP, Haryana, and Punjab'. The direct reference to the united stand by most of the farmers in these states can be construed as Anmol's reification of the peaceful protest by farmers: 'Leaving roses on barricades, Punjab returns home triumphant over Delhi'.

Celebrating Resistance: A Concluding Note

The rich literary tradition of Punjab presents a variety of metaphors and symbols that connote love, defiance, and resistance. Novelists, storytellers, poets, and song writers responding to farmers agitations have also included intertextual references to famous *qissas* or *vaars*, especially those of resistance. For example, Dulla Bhatti, 'a resistant hero of the land [Punjab]' (Ayres, 2009: 76), is celebrated each January during the festival of *Lohri* when people sing a centuries-old song remembering his defiance. *Dulla*, who rebelled against the Mughal Emperor Akbar, 'symbolized the prominent social force which countered the hegemony of the Mughal state' (Gaur, 2008: 33). As the 2020–2021 farmers' protest galvanized into a mass movement, people paired together the medieval narratives of resistance with the twenty-first-century struggles of farmers. In his song-poem on farmers' protest 2020, 'You Write Laws', Harbans Malwa reminds us of the lineage of defiance: 'When the spoken word was the law/the likes of *Dulla* shook the throne [establishment]' (Gill, 2020, translation by Parmar). Several references on social media pointed out that people sing about and celebrate Dulla but not many remember Emperor Akbar. Such folk-based poetic evocations immediately establish the binary of the oppressed and the oppressor and signal that centuries from today, like Dulla, it will be the farmers who will be celebrated not the rulers – or the current government. Or, as Sehrai asserts in the epigraph above that the 'rich' may have the 'establishment', but 'history' will be on the side of the oppressed. To borrow from Gaur, 'Dulla still survives' (Gaur, 2008: 37).

Notes

* This chapter is a revised version of 'Kisan Protests in Punjab 1907–2021: A Literary Lineage of Resistance', first published in *Journal of Sikh and Punjab Studies*, 29(1&2) (Spring–Fall, 2022): 163–186.

1 The three acts are Farmers' Produce Trade and Commerce Act, 2020, Farmers' Agreement on Price Assurance and Farm Services Act, 2020, and the Essential Commodities Act, 2020 and calls for a new law to guarantee Minimum Support Price for crops.

2 Unless otherwise indicated, all translations in the sections '*Kirti Kaav*' and '*Muzara* and *Biswedar* Movements' are by Amandeep Kaur.

3 With the formation of the *Kirti Kisan* Party, both the ex-Ghadarites and the Akalis contributed in reinterpreting 'the radical current of which they were a part in the formal language of socialism' (Singh, 1979: 46).

4 Bhagwan Josh, in his account of the *Kirti Kisan* Party, also points out that 'the word 'kirti' was constantly confused with the word 'peasant' after the formation of the *Kirti-Kisan* Party (Josh, 1979: 74). However, he also adds that among 'the "workers" in the Punjab 90 per cent were peasants' and the organization of the workers in Punjab 'primarily meant the organisation of the peasants' (Josh, 1979: 90–91).

5 Balwant Gargi (1985: 98) and B. Alaxai (2013: 189) note the staging of plays and *nukkad* (street) plays at the protest sites.

6 Translation by Kartar Singh Duggal in Sant Singh Sekhon and Kartar Singh Duggal (1992: 163)

7 Jagga Daku or *Jagga Jatt* was a twentieth-century heroic rebel of Punjab.

8 All translations of poems and songs in this section are by Prabhjot Parmar, unless otherwise identified.

9 The right-wing state apparatuses and media mouthpieces (notoriously known as Godi Media) promptly sprung into action to decry the protest as *Khalistani*

and anti-national, primarily because most of the Punjabi farmers are Sikhs. This is not to deny that there may have been some separatists at the protest. The right-wing party cadres and followers, along with internet trolls, inundated social media with anti-farmer and anti-Sikh slogans, posts, and memes.

10 See also Sumandeep Kaur (2021).

Bibliography

Alaxai, B. *PEPSU di Muzara Lehar: Sangarsh da Etehas*. Patiala: Sangam Publications, 2013.

Ayres, Alyssa. 'The Case of Punjab Part I: Elite Efforts'. In *Speaking Like a State: Language and Nationalism in Pakistan*. Cambridge and New York: Cambridge University Press, 2009, 67–86.

Bhattacharya, Neeladari. *The Great Agrarian Conquest: The Colonial Reshaping of a Rural World*. New Delhi: Permanent Black, 2018.

Butler, Judith. *Notes towards a Performative Theory of Assembly*. Cambridge, MA: Harvard University Press, 2015.

Chandan, Amarjit (ed.). *Telangana Tu Karwat Lai*. Amritsar: Jaspal Printing Press, 1979.

Chattha, Tohid Ahmad et al. 'Historical Perspective of Kirti Kisan Party and Its Politics in Colonial Punjab'. *Journal of the Research Society of Pakistan* 55, no. 1 (January–June, 2018), 315–324.

Cheema, Harf. 'Patshah', YouTube Video. 4:18, 28 December 2020. https://www.youtube.com/watch?v=PiY88QzYTjk

Denisova, Anastasia. 'Democracy, Protest and Public Sphere in Russia after the 2011–2012 Anti Government Protests: Digital Media at Stake', *Media, Culture and Society*, 39, no. 7 (October 2017), 976–994.

Dhir, Santokh Singh. 'Daaku'. *Sittian Di Chhan*. Jalandhar: Punjabi Publishers, 1950.

———.'Sipahi', *Sanjhi Kandh*. Jalandhar: Punjabi Publishers, 1958.

Fakkar, Dharam Singh. 'Introduction'. In *Kishengarh: The Peasant's Heroic Defense of His Land*. Sangrur: Pepsu Kisan Sabha, 1940, 1–2.

Fenech, Louis E. and W. Hew McLeod. 'Hawk'. In *Historical Dictionary of Sikhism*. 3rd ed. Historical Dictionaries of Religions, Philosophies, and Movements. Lanham: Rowman & Littlefield, 2014, 149.

Gargi, Balwant. 'New Punjabi Literature'. In Sudhi Pradhan (ed.) *Marxist Cultural Movement in India: Chronicles and Documents*. Vol. III. Calcutta: New Rooplekha Press, 1985, pp. 90–99.

———. 'Punjabi Folk Poetry'. *Asian Folklore Studies* 26, no. 1 (1967), 53–62. JSTOR. Accessed on 28 February, 2021.

Gaur, Ishwar Dayal. *Martyr as Bridegroom: A Folk Representation of Bhagat Singh*. New Delhi: Anthem Press, 2008.

Gill, Gurbhajan (ed.) 'Land [Farmers] Challenges the Rulers: Part1–13, Agriculture Based Peasants Farmers Agitation 2020'. *Punjabi-Kavita.com*. Accessed January 4 to July 29, 2021. https://www.punjabikavita.com/Kirti-Kisan-Morcha.php

Gurpreet Singh Shimlapuri. Re: *Parvaz* [Flight] (Video File). Retrieved November 15, 2021 from: https://www.youtube.com/watch?v=L29OA6ekMsg&lc=Ugw28tHxWQ3Wz0Lsl5J4AaABAg

Harp Farmer Pictures. 'Jitt de jaikaare' [Victory Anthem], YouTube Video, 4:08, 19 November 2021. https://www.youtube.com/watch?v=73k-Sw4h1Bg

Jass Records. 'Jittke Punjab Chalya' [Victorious, Punjab Returns Home] YouTube Video, 2:41, 30 November 2021. https://www.youtube.com/watch?v=KRUh7dalpEg

Josh, Bhagwan. *Communist Movement in Punjab: 1926–47.* Delhi: Anupama Publications, 1979.

Kanwal, Jaswant Singh. *Bhavani.* Samana: Sangam Publications, 2012.

———. *Raat Baki Hai (The Night is Still Here).* Samana: Sangam Publications, 2014.

Kaur, Sumandeep. 'The "Drug Menace" in Punjab: Causes, Consequences and Policy Challenges'. *Journal of Sikh and Punjab Studies*, 28, no. 2 (Spring 2021), 41–51.

Loomba, Ania. *Revolutionary Desires: Women, Communism, and Feminism in India.* London: Routledge, 2019.

Lyallpuri, Jagjit S. *Mera Jeewan, Mera Yug (My Life, My Age).* Chandigarh: Unistar, 2012.

Mankhera, Jaspal Singh. 'Khataas' (Sourness). *Basre di Laam.* Ludhiana: Chetna Prakashan, 2009, 9–21.

Mukherjee, Mridula. *Peasants in India's Non-Violent Revolution: Practice and Theory.* New Delhi: Sage, 2004.

Nandan, Inderjit. *Joginder Bahrla: Jeewan Gatha.* Barnala: Tarkbharti Prakashan, 2006.

Narula, Surinder Singh. *Neelibar.* Ludhiana: Lahore Book Shop, 1990.

Nijhawan, Michael. *Dhadi Darbar: Religion, Violence, and the Performance of Sikh History.* New Delhi: Oxford University Press, 2006.

PTI News. *Punjabi Singer Babbu Maan Meets Farmers at Ghazipur. PTI News* February 10, 2020.

Rai, Satya M. *Punjabi Heroic Tradition: 1900–1947.* Patiala: Punjabi University, 1995.

SagaHits. 'Kalawan Charhdian: Satinder Sartaj', YouTube Video, 5:19, 24 December, 2021. Accessed January 5, 2022. https://www.youtube.com/watch?v=ctav2G018rE

Virasat Sandhu. (2021). 'Fateh Morcha' YouTube Video, 2:10, 11 December 2021. Accessed January 5, 2022. https://www.youtube.com/watch?v=S_Z0C8vhos

Sekhon, Sant Singh and Kartar Singh Duggal. *A History of Punjabi Literature.* New Delhi: Sahitya Akademi, 1992.

Shivji, Salimah. 'Burdened by debt and unable to eke out a living, many farmers in India turn to suicide'. *CBC News*, March 30, 2021. Accessed April 5, 2021. https://www.cbc.ca/news/world/india-farmers-suicide-1.5968086

Singh, Ajit. *S. Ajit Singh's Autobiography: Buried Alive*, 1984. ShahidBhagatSingh.org. http://www.shahidbhagatsingh.org/index.asp?link=about_ajit1 (accessed on April 3, 2021).

Singh, Amolak. *Kirti Lehr Dian Goonjan: Kirti Kav (1926–1940).* Jalandhar: Desh Bhagat Prakashan, 2017.

Singh, Gurcharan Singh (ed.). *Babbar-Kav Sangreh.* Patiala: Publication Bureau, Punjabi University, 1988.

Singh Gurharpal. *Communism in Punjab: A Study of the Movement upto 1967.* Delhi: Ajanta, 1994.

Singh, Khushwant. *Punjabi, Punjabis & Punjabiyat: Reflections on a Land and Its People.* Edited by Mala Dayal. New Delhi: Aleph Book Company, 2018.

Singh, Navtej. 'Navin Rut'. In Poonam Singh (ed.) *Bahar Aaon Tak*. Amritsar: Ravi Sahit Prakashan, 2003, 272–276.

Tribune News Service. 'Introduce Youngsters to Punjabi Literature: Patar'. *The Tribune*. February 28, 2020.

Vaid, Chhaju Mal. *PEPSU Mujara Ghol*. Jalandhar: Punj-Aab Prakashan, 2019.

Verma, Prabal Singh. 'Punjab's Drug Problem: Contours and Characteristics'. *Economic and Political Weekly* 2017, 52 no. 3, 40–43.

3 A Tale of Two Punjabi Peasant Agitations

Comparing 1907 and 2020–2021*

Sukhdev S. Sohal

Punjab has a long tradition of peasant protests going back to the first decade of the twentieth century. For instance, the agrarian agitation of 1907 was a political manifestation of the landholding peasantry of the central districts and canal colonies of Punjab. This 'disturbances of 1907' alarmed the colonial authorities which resorted to repression to disrupt political mobilization.[1] There is an extraordinary way in which the recent agrarian agitation resonated with the past. Moreover, the Punjab peasant protests were led by 'an intellectually sophisticated and mature leadership willing to make tremendous sacrifices'.[2] The peasants protested again in Punjab and Haryana in particular and Western UP and parts of Rajasthan in general against the farm laws passed by the central government. Their mobilization and mode of protest from November 2020 got resonance of the 1907 agitation. Its scale turned pan-Indian; its prolongation gave a message of tough contestation for the government. Finally, the peasants compelled the central government to roll back farm laws.[3] With this in mind, this chapter is an attempt to see similarities and dissimilarities in the nature of peasantry, agrarian economy and political economy of the colonial state and nation state in independent India.

Peasants in Historical Perspective

Historically, peasantries emerged in order to provision emerging cities and market towns.[4] Antonio Gramsci recognized peasant society and culture to be vital in the ideas and action of subaltern classes.[5] Teodar Shanin defined peasantry having 'four essential and interlinked facets': (i) the family farm as the basic multi-functional unit of organization; (ii) land husbandry; (iii) usually animal rearing as the main means of livelihood; and (iv) a specific traditional culture closely linked with way of life of small rural communities. There are a number of analytically marginal groups which share with the 'hard core' of the peasantry but not all of its major characteristics.[6] These include agricultural labourers lacking a fully-fledged farm and rural craftsmen holding little or no land.[7] Moreover, peasants aim at 'subsistence' and produce cash crops primarily for survival and maintain their social status; farmers invest and expand the scale of operations.[8]

 DOI: 10.4324/9781003320005-5

Peasants differentiate into classes of 'small scale capitalist farmers', relatively successful petty commodity producers and wage labour.[9] Often the peasants are blamed for standing in the way of 'progress'; a failure to use land efficiently. These elite imaginings are typically espoused in order to promote policies aimed at pushing peasants off the land and turning them into labourers.[10] M. S. Swaminathan, who headed the National Commission of Farmers, provides maximal definition of a farmer as 'a person actively engaged in the economic and or livelihood activity of growing crops and producing other primary agricultural commodities and will include all agricultural operational holders, cultivators, agricultural labourers, share croppers, tenants, poultry and livestock rearing, pastoralists, non-corporate planters and planting labourers as well as persons engaged in various farming-related occupations such as sericulture, vermin-culture and agro forestry'.[11] In the present context, concepts like peasant and farmer or *kisan* are used interchangeably as majority of them fall in the category of small and marginal farmers and struggle for survival and participate in the market as well.

Peasants, Colonialism and the Agrarian Agitation of 1907

Agricultural colonization and the Land Alienation Act of 1901 were the overarching features of colonial legislation with a view to isolate and stabilize the Punjab peasantry from the inroads of merchant capital.[12] The basic purpose of creating an export zone was successfully achieved by the colonial state.[13] Nevertheless, colonialization of agrarian economy had attendant consequences in the Punjab. The value of land increased. The prices of land increased from Rs. 14 per acre in 1874 to Rs. 47 in 1900.[14] Revenue extraction by the colonial state was intensive: In 1850, the land revenue was Rs. 15 lakh and it reached to the level of Rs. 300 lakh in 1885. Its rigidity in collection was 99.1 per cent by 1890.[15] It resulted in pauperization and transfer of land from the peasants to moneylenders.[16] Moreover, the province was hit five times by famines and droughts which caused impoverishment and land transfers. The famines of 1896–1897 and 1889–1900 speedily skimmed off any economic surplus which the peasants may have generated through relatively better conditions.[17] The Indian Famine Commission (1901) reported that 'the rigidity of the revenue system forced the peasants into debt; the value of the land which they held made it easy to borrow'.[18] It pushed the peasants towards indebtedness. In 1865, it was estimated that nearly 5–6 per cent of the peasant-proprietors were in debt; it was 80 per cent in 1879.[19] In 1880, nearly 12 per cent of the debt was incurred through having to pay land revenue.[20] The peasantry passed through the processes of dispossession and differentiation giving way to tenancy cultivation. The area held by the cultivators during 1889–1907 decreased from 47.16 per cent to 37.46 per cent and the area actually cultivated by the cultivators decreased from 59.04 per cent to 46.37 per cent. There was an increase in the number of tenants from 30.55 per cent to 43.51 per cent during 1889–1907. Canal colonies had provided a demographic shift for the central Punjab peasants to move to the western Punjab. However, this relief proved temporary. There was a marked tendency among the middle peasants to cultivate as tenants to tide over economic pressure.[21]

Consequently, increase in water rates in the Bari Doab Canal area by 50 per cent and the Colonization of Government Lands (Punjab) Bill 1906 in the Chenab Colony gave an opportunity to the middle peasantry to launch and raise its voice through an agitation which was the first of its kind.[22] The raising of water rates in the Bari Doab Canal affected the landowners throughout the districts of Amritsar, Gurdaspur and Lahore.[23] The Government passed the Punjab Land Alienation (Amendment) Act in February 1906 to strengthen the restrictions regarding land alienations. Its aim was to exclude 'statutory agriculturists' for acquiring land under the Act of 1901. Moreover, this Act empowered district officers to disallow gifts of land for religious purposes, in case such gifts seemed suspect.[24] The Amendment Act accentuated the political disconnect among the urban politicians in the Punjab as they were already embittered over the British policy towards the commercial class that happened to be largely Hindu.[25] These official measures, coming in quick succession, united the rural and urban middle classes. People began to discuss politics with much less fear and with much more confidence.[26]

Peasant Mobilization for Agitation

In the agrarian agitation of 1907, new class alignments and a new mechanism of protest came into operation. Mass mobilization became a potential danger. The rural leaders also joined the protests, not only because of sympathy with the commercial classes but also from a similar fear of bureaucratic tyranny. For the first time, the professional classes were able to draw agriculturists and uneducated masses in protests against the government. Anti-government activity gained ground as new meetings and the press continued the criticism.[27] On February 3, 1907, thousands of residents of Lahore, irrespective of their caste and creed assembled to record their disapproval and emphatic protest against the Colonization Bill. Chaudhary Ram Bhaj Datta and Lala Dharam Das made fiery speeches. A resolution for the abolition of restrictions on the 'statutory agriculturists' was passed.[28] 'Grand Protest Meetings' of nearly 8,000 colonists were held in Lyallpur. Lala Lajpat Rai rushed to Lyallpur. On February 17, 1907, peasants numbering about 15,000 took part in a meeting at Lahore under the presidency of S. Gurcharan Singh.[29] Lala Lajpat Rai and Sardar Ajit Singh toured the Bari Doab area and organized land owners to support *Swadeshi* and to refuse the payment of new irrigation rates.[30] A public meeting was held at Lyallpur on March 20, 1907 where Lala Lajpat Rai, Sardar Ajit Singh, Lala Ram Bhaj Datta, Bakhshi Tek Chand and Shahabu-ud-din participated.[31] Students of the Khalsa College, Amritsar staged a hostile demonstration at the farewell visit of the outgoing Lt. Governor Sir Charles Rivaz.[32] On April 1, 1907, the *Anjuman-i-Muhibhan-i-Watan* of Lahore held a protest meeting against the Colonization Bill. Though the notice of the protest was circulated by the students only two hours earlier yet about 2,500 people, mainly 'Hindu clerks' attended it.[33] A meeting took place at Rawalpindi district on April 7, 1907, to protest against the enhanced land revenue. It was presided over by Lala Hans Raj Sahni and Lala Amolak Ram acted as Secretary. It was resolved, unanimously, to set up a sub-committee for collecting evidence about the general complaint of over assessment of the land revenue. An appeal to the Viceroy to withhold his assent to the Bill was filed.[34] With a view to sending their message, the leaders used folk idiom. Sardar Ajit Singh in his meeting on April 21 at Rawalpindi recited *Pagri Sambhal Jatta* (Peasant guard your honour) and exposed the character of the British rule.[35] Sardar Ajit Singh, in his speeches, exhorted the peasants to stop cultivation until the water rates were reduced.[36]

Pleaders and landowners took a significant lead in organizing political protests in the form of meetings and addressing them with political overtones.[37] The colonial bureaucracy considered the professional middle classes 'inimical' to the British rule.[38] The secular character of the movement popularized it among the rural and urban people. The Hindus and Muslims were asked to unite against British *zulam* (oppression).[39] Soldiers attended political meetings in which the exploitative character of British rule was pointed out.[40]

British Response to the Agitation

With the ensuing popular resentment, the government resorted to harsh measures. Prohibitory orders were imposed. A meeting was held and presided over by Lala Gurdas Ram Sawhany, a barrister and other signatories to the announcement for the meeting were Lala Amolak Ram Vakil, Lala Hans Raj Vakil, Pandit Janki Nath Kaul and Khazan Singh Barrister. The Deputy Collector summoned them to his court on May 2, 1907. A large 'crowd' of more than 20,000 assembled that day in the court compound. Court proceedings against them were stayed under the instructions of the government.[41] Resentment among the native regiments began to be considered as a fair index of the state of feeling among the civilian population. The consequences of spreading political awakening to central districts, which supplied recruits to the army and to Lyallpur which absorbed military pensioners, assumed serious significance.[42] The Military General reported to Lord Kitchener on July 2, 1907, that 'constant sedition in the ranks is undoubtedly wearing away the sense of loyalty'.[43] The colonial authorities reported 'unwillingness of the soldiers to fire upon the people to suppress disorder in the Punjab'. The bogey of 'contamination' of their men by the prevailing unrest was raised.[44] Moreover, the prosecution of the *Panjabee* (Lahore) was part of the government strategy to checkmate the new sources of political mobilization.[45]

In 1907, Denzil Ibbetson, Lt. Governor, Punjab, described the political situation in the Punjab as 'exceedingly dangerous' and mentioned about the *nai hawa* (new wave of air) that was blowing in the minds of the people.[46] The temper and tone of the newspapers owned and edited by the native Indians became a matter of 'grave anxiety' to the British administrators. Secretary to the Government of India wrote to the Director General, Post Offices, to intercept postal articles of Lala Duni Chand and Karam Das at Peshawar for three years under Section 26 of the India Post Office Act, 1898.[47] Similarly, *Anjuman-i-Khadiman-i-Hindustan,* Hoshiarpur also came under interception regulations.[48] The conservative administration of Denzil Ibbetson resorted to repression. The Home Department called for greater powers to make prosecution more a matter of executive rather than judicial.[49]

Critical Evaluation of the Agitation

In the agrarian agitation, the extremist politicians outnumbered the moderate politicians whose numbers were 26 and 17, respectively. Both groups belonged to the middle class; they were predominantly from among the educated professionals, like pleaders, teachers and journalists. The students also participated in large numbers.[50] Lala Lajpat Rai and Sardar Ajit Singh were arrested and then deported to Burma on May 7, 1907. The agitation was conducted with 'surpassing skill'. However, the repressive measures taken by the government had a 'quietening effect'. The government withdrew objectionable measures.[51] Moreover, people's reactions were directed to official measures rather than to independent actions. Colonial officers felt that the peasantry would seize all the opportunities arising out of the agitation.[52] Entrenchment in the canal colonies along with irrigational and market network put the middle peasantry in the possession of some tactical control over its own resources.[53] Lord Minto, the Viceroy and Denzil Ibbetson, Lt. Governor, Punjab, admitted that 'the troubles were largely agrarian in origin'. Other causes were attributed to the 50th anniversary of the 'Mutiny' of 1857 and the plague. These were probably articulated to underestimate the real character of the movement.[54] The movement dominated in the districts of Lahore, Rawalpindi and Lyallpur. Meetings were held in Delhi, Ferozepur, Gujranwala, Sialkot, Amritsar, Ambala, Multan, Sargodha, Wazirabad and Hoshiarpur. Its social base got widened when the educated and commercial classes revived the Swadeshi phase which perturbed the colonial authorities.[55]

Globalization, Peasantry and Farmers' Agitation of 2020–2021

In South Asia, there is a powerful legacy of rural movements that undertook struggles for the rights of farmers and peasants and agricultural labourers. In fact, rural movements have played a crucial rule in the anti-colonial struggle.[56] For the first time since neoliberal reforms were introduced in the early 1990s, a farmer protest of huge magnitude and duration was being witnessed.[57] Hanan Mollah, General Secretary of All India Kisan Sabha, identified four main characteristics of the recent farmers' movement: (i) the largest *kisan* movement; (ii) participation by about 500 organizations under the umbrella of Samyukt Kisan Morcha; (iii) a peaceful movement; and (iv) tremendous determination of the farmers.[58]

A meeting held in New Delhi under the auspices of NITI-Aayog unfolded the agenda of solving the stagnant rate of growth in agriculture by handing over clusters of 5,000–7,000 acres of farming land to corporates. Balbir Singh Rajewal, kisan leader who attended this meeting raised genuine concerns.[59] A debate ensued. The COVID-19 crisis opened 'a window of opportunity to reform' the agri-marketing system and the Modi government immediately 'grabbed' it.[60] During the raging COVID-19 wave, the central government brought in an Ordinance on June 5, 2020, relating to the farm sector. Within five days, on June 10, 2020, more than 10,000 copies of the Ordinance were burnt in 600 districts. On November 26, 2020, Constitution Day, it was decided to begin the '*Dilli Chalo* March'. The months of July, August and September were focused on protests mainly in Punjab.[61] On September 14, the farm bills were introduced in the Lok Sabha and passed on September 17 and then on September 20 in the Rajya Sabha in much haste and without voting. It exposed the parliamentary procedural lapses. The three farm laws constituted: (i) The Farmers (Empowerment and Protection) Agreement on Price Assurance and Farm Services Act, 2020 (No. 20 of 2020); (ii) The Farmers' Produce Trade and Commerce (Promotion and Facilitation) Act 2020 (No. 21 of 2020); and (iii) The Essential Commodities (Amendment) Act, 2020 (No. 22 of 2020).[62] In Parliament, the debate was 'shabbily short' and the farm laws were passed by voice vote. Those who pushed the farm laws on the last day of Parliament are from other Indian regions, where procurement doesn't work. MSP (Minimum Support Price) in those parts are like 'ghost money'.[63] These laws were meant to remove agricultural trade restrictions to give boost to the agricultural sector and generate additional income for farmers. However, farmers' leaders reacted sharply and called it an attack on the federal character of the constitution wherein agriculture is a state subject. Farmers thought that the entry of corporates would lead to a buyer's market.[64]

Corporate media hailed the laws as the ultimate solution to the agrarian crisis. The farm laws were meant to dismantle the monopoly of APMC (Agricultural Produce Market Committee) and non-mention of MSP in these laws created an alarm of serious proportions. It has been claimed that the MSP covers only 8 per cent of the farmers.[65] The farmers launched their agitation on October 1, 2020, in Punjab against the legislated farm laws by the central government. Meanwhile, Punjab passed bills to bypass central farm laws making a provision that buying below MSP was 'a punishable offence'.[66] Amarinder Singh, Chief Minister, Punjab, joined in and argued that the laws were 'clearly designed to destroy the *mandi* system in favour of a select few corporates'.[67] The government, for the first two months, ignored the protests; even labelled agitators as terrorists. The farmers resorted to '*Rail Roko*' (Stop Rail) agitation from September 25 by sitting on railtracks at strategic locations: 938 passenger trains were cancelled; 943 partially cancelled; and 105 diverted. Consequently, daily loss due to the agitation was Rs. 26 crore and revenue loss was Rs. 1,670 crore. About 3,090 freight trains could not be operated.[68]

The Samyukt Kisan Morcha gave a call to *Dilli Chalo*. After two months of agitation in Punjab, farmers moved towards Delhi on November 25. In Haryana, the BJP-led government tried to stop them by digging deep trenches, hit them with water cannons and threw tear gas shells.[69] The farm unions intensified the agitation. The agitation also began to spread to Haryana, the UP, Rajasthan, MP, Maharashtra and Uttarakhand as the Bhartiya Kisan Union (BKU) affiliates were supported by the All India Kisan Sabha and Swaraj India. The farmers, especially the youth, penetrated through barricades and reached the borders of Delhi on November 26, 2020. All entities engaged in the agitation were part of the larger entity All India Kisan Sangarsh Coordination Samiti. Lakhs of farmers pitched their tents with their tractors, trolleys, bullock carts and trawlers in four major sites at Singhu, Tikri, Ghazipur and Chilla. Three leaders gained prominence. The overall incharge at the Singhu border was Balbir Singh Rajewal; at Ghazipur, Rakesh Takait from the UP and at Tikri, Joginder Singh Ugrahan of the BKU-Ekta (U). Another leader from Haryana was Gurnam Singh Charuni. Decisions were taken unanimously after thorough discussions and farmers were addressed daily from these protesting sites.[70] The Tikri border protest stretched to 15 km on the Delhi-Bahadargarh Road, and several thousand famers were involved. The farmers carried food supplies for six months. Community kitchens (*langars*) were set up for meals. Furthermore, the farmers from Haryana started bringing truckload of vegetables from their farms and distributed them free of cost. It became a new way of protesting.[71] The BKU-Ekta (U) remained the largest peasant organization which remained active in 13 districts. It mobilized 1.5 lakh farmers, workers, women and students. It was dominated by small and marginal farmers and women.[72]

Along with the farmers, the commission agents (*arhtiyas*) joined hands to 'fight for survival'.[73] *Arhtiyas* were part of the supply chain in North West India. They were not like middlemen elsewhere as they functioned simply as agents of the procurement agencies.[74] These farm laws were expected to increase information asymmetries contributing to greater exploitation and inequities for the majority of India's small-holder farmers.[75] The farmers' agitation was deeply rooted in agrarian political economy. Davinder Sharma, an agricultural expert, stated that the farmers' income increased just 19 times in the last 40 years, while the teachers' income increased around 200 times.[76] A NITI Aayog study stated that while farmer's income in nominal terms rose 9.18 times from 1993–1994 to 2015–2016 period, the real farm income (which takes out the effect of inflation) had only doubled in 22 years.[77] The contribution of agriculture to the national GDP declined from 51 per cent in the 1950s to around 18 per cent in 2019–2020. Farmers were earning less and less from their harvests, while productivity and production went up.[78] Moreover, farming in India is dominated by small and marginal farmers. In 2011, proportion of Indians engaged in agriculture remains 54.60 per cent; agricultural labourers constitute 54.90 per cent of agricultural workforce. In Punjab, 54.2 per cent farm households are indebted, exceeding all India range of 51.9 per cent. Overall, 4.4 crore households are indebted owning land upto 4 hectares.[79] Punjab accounts for 12 per cent of the national foodgrain production and contributes about 40–45 per cent of wheat and 25–30 per cent rice to the central pool.[80] Amitabh Kant, CEO, NITI Aayog, argued that new farm laws would 'unshackle' 43 per cent of the workforce engaged in the sector.[81] A statement by a pro-government economist Ashok Gulati raised alarm when he claimed that the government cannot assure MSP from wheat and paddy throughout India.[82]

A section of the corporate houses openly supported the farm laws. The big businesses have exhausted options of making mega profits. The unfortunate paradox was that farmers became poorer and food had become more expensive. There were fears of big agricultural monopolies taking over farm lands.[83] Markets have historically failed to prop up farm incomes around the world. NITI Aayog's proposal to downsize the number of people dependent on agriculture for doubling the farm income belies logic. In the US, hardly 1.5 per cent of the population remains in agriculture. Yet farm debt had multiplied to a staggering $425 billion in 2020.[84] Meanwhile, Bihar got much attention as it had repealed the APMC Act in 2006 with the claims that it would allow farmers to sell their produce to whosoever and wherever they wished to; it would eliminate middlemen from agro-trade bringing private firms in agri-business and consequently increase farmers' earnings. However, private entities did not turn up. Between 2012–2013 and 2019–2020, procurement by public agencies in Bihar was not more than 15 per cent of total production; in Punjab and Haryana, it was at least 70–80 per cent.[85]

Farmers' Agitation: Major Features

The protests got support overseas as lakhs of Sikhs/Punjabis signed petitions in the UK, the USA and Australia demanding rollback or rethink on the new farm laws. It spread to other countries such as New Zeeland, France, Italy, Germany and Canada. They protested in front of embassies.[86] In the initial talks with the farmers, the central government admitted flaws in the farm laws and sought suggestions for amendments.[87] In these talks, 35 negotiators consisting of 32 Punjab farmers' groups and representatives of the All India Kisan Sangarsh Coordination Committee participated under the Samyukt Kisan Morcha which also conducted day-to-day proceedings.[88] Meanwhile, the Supreme Court put a hold on farm laws and formed a four-member panel which the farmer leaders immediately rejected.[89] On December 20, 2020, *Bharat Bandh* was observed with a wide response in Punjab, Haryana and other parts of India.[90]

In the age of information, national print and electronic media launched propaganda against the farmers' agitation. In response, a dedicated youth initiated a bi-weekly and bi-lingual paper *Trolley Times* as 'Voice of Kisan Protest' with a slogan 'United, will fight, will win'.[91] Its 2,000 copies were printed and distributed freely. It had inputs from the Singhu and Tikri borders. This newspaper had its readership beyond these sites.[92] It reported activities of the farmers but also broadened its scope by writing on the tenants' and peasants struggles in the 1970s and 80s in Punjab and of peasant leaders' like Teja Singh Swatantar. It also reported on the Corona virus pandemic and on youth activities. Moreover, the paper followed the template of *Ghadar* paper of mid-1910s which reported on peasants' revolts and plight of the peasants.[93] With a view to counter fake news and influence of the pro-corporate electronic and print media, which dubbed farmers as anti-national and Maoists, it was decided to set up an IT cell under Baljit Singh under the name of 'Kisan Ekta Morcha'.[94]

The farmers planned to show off their strength on Republic Day. It was decided to have a parallel tractor parade exhibiting various phases of farming and peasant life, on the model of the national parade on the Rajpath in Delhi on the January 26. Thousands of tractors were brought in from Punjab, Haryana and the Western UP. About 2 lakh farmers participated; 50,000 police personnel were deployed. Protests were also held in 20 states.[95] Attempts were made to scuttle the peaceful march when a section of the protestors reached the Red Fort on Republic Day. The police failed to protect the Red Fort. It was an attempt 'to discredit, demonize or restrict the peaceful agitation'.[96] Rakesh Takait, a kisan leader at the Ghazipur site, faced an eviction notice and water supplies were cut off. He feared violence at the hands of the local BJP MLA of UP. He refused to take water and appealed to his supporters to rush back. His tears acted as a spark. The farmers from UP, Haryana and Punjab rushed to Ghazipur. From Punjab, 2,000 tractors rushed backed to the national capital.[97] Farmers got wide support from different sections of society with donations of money and resources. *Langars* appeared on the sites. Menus ranged from *paranthas* stuffed with *paneer*, radish or potato to curries of peas and carrots and *sarso da sag* and *makki di roti*. Other items include tea, cakes, packaged drinks, *pakoras*, snacks and biscuits. With a view to beat the cold, 10,000 mufflers, socks and blankets were distributed. Water tankers, solar panels and inverters were arranged. Medical camps are organized.[98] The BKU-Ekta (U) had no dearth of funds in the initial stage and spent Rs. 7 crore, of which around Rs. 4 crore only on vehicles. Most of this was through donations. Complete transparency had been maintained in their records. The NRIs sent donations through Khalsa Aid. The World Financial Group of Canada sent Rs. 25 lakhs.[99] Villagers pooled money, installed submersible pumps for uninterrupted supply of water, water purifiers, arranged mist fans and deep freezers and even air conditioners.[100] Village-wise donations became a regular feature to sustain the agitation. In Punjab, village *panchayats* issued *diktats* like either attend farmers' stir or face fine or even boycott. A fine of Rs. 1,500 on violations of the 'order' was put up. If a vehicle broke down, the entire village contributed for repair.[101] The BKU-Ekta (U) could collect Rs. 50 lakh in the Mansa district alone. Moreover, Ram Singh Bhainibagha (U), a district president, claimed that the union spent over Rs. 25 crore in the past 11 months since the beginning of the agitation.[102] *Langar* became essential at the protest sites where people could par take irrespective of caste, creed, colour, region and religion. The farmers decided to become self-sufficient in maintaining the supply of milk and curd by bringing buffaloes to the site. Water pumps have been bored for continuous supplies.[103]

Protests brought the people together. They closed their differences.[104] A library was set up at Singhu border under the name of '*Janghi Kitab Ghar*' where books were issued free of cost and read in the tractors, trolleys and tents. This initiative proved to be a great hit.[105] New forms of entertainments like singing, social service, readings and playing games attracted the youth. Consequently, sales of liquor in rural areas dropped.[106] The government placed jammers around the area. About 31 walkie-talkie sets had been assigned to volunteers for handling security logistics and stage management.[107] Literature was published and distributed to keep the agitation in proper shape. The BKU-Ekta (U) published a booklet exposing the agri-business activities of the Adani and Ambani business groups. On farm laws, it gave a clear message: No Amendments, Complete Repeal.[108]

The farmers associated their struggle with the revolutionaries of the past, like Baba Banda Singh Bahadar who fought against the zamindari system and gave rights to the tenants.[109] Other heroes included Dulla Bhatti, who had peasant roots and revolted against Mughal Emperor Akbar in the late sixteenth century. Kartar Singh Sarabha of the Ghadar movement was remembered on his birthday. Speeches and songs mentioned the great sacrifice of Sarabha. Another Ghadarite leader Sohan Singh Bhakna was also remembered on his birthday by the BKU-Ekta (U).[110] The peasant agitation of 1907, also known as '*Pagdi Sambhal Jatta*' movement, acted as a template for the peasants. The contribution of Saradar Ajit Singh and Lala Lajpat Rai was acknowledged. The birthday of Sardar Ajit Singh was celebrated.[111] Bhagat Ravidas was remembered and so was the martyrdom of Chandra Shekhar Azad.[112] The martyrdom day of Shaheed Bhagat Singh, Rajguru and Sukhdev provided an opportunity to the youth to get inspiration. The day was celebrated at the protest sites and other towns of Punjab especially in the town Banga. Soil from Anandpur Sahib, Khatkarh

Kalan, Sunam, Sarabha and Jallianwala Bagh was carried to the protest sites near Delhi.[113] Martyrs of the *Muzara* (tenant) movement were also remembered.[114] With a view to widen the ambit of the agitation, the farmers organized *maha-panchayats* at various places in Haryana, Punjab and in Western UP. It mobilized the countryside including women. The *maha-panchayats* attracted various sections of society.[115] There were over 300 protests across the country in support of those camping around Delhi. It is worth mentioning that every fourth voter is a farmer in India.[116]

Cultural festivals like *Dussehra* were celebrated at protest sites wherein children participated in large numbers in different parts of Punjab.[117] *Lohri* was celebrated at the Singhu border and was portrayed in the poetry of Surjit Patar. One lakh copies of the farm laws were consigned to flames.[118] Folk singers turned to their best tunes composed on the themes of farming, farmers and land. Punjab has a long history of singing amidst struggles,[119] reminding one of poetry centred on farming.[120] Singers like Kanwar Grewal and Harf Cheema argued that 'songs are for people and of the people. For this it is necessary to know the people'.[121] Farmers' songs and *bolis* sung at weddings and stage shows became new modes of protest. Flags, badges of farmer unions were in huge demand. Within six months, over 5 lakh flags and 10 lakh badges have been sold.[122] Prominent singers at protest sites included Kanwar Grewal, Babbu Mann, Harbhajan Mann, Jass Bajwa, Harf Cheema, Ranjit Bawa and Harjit Harman. One song which touched the theme was '*fasla de faisle kissan karuga*' written by Kanwar Grewal.[123] The Naxalite phase of the late 1960s returned back with revolutionary songs like that of Jaimal Padda.[124] Revolutionary song '*mishala baal ke chalna*' by Mohinder Saathi was equally rallied by old and young together. It linked the late 1960s Naxalite struggle with the new peasant agitation.[125] Farmers' protests got world-wide attention when celebrities like Meena Harris, niece of Kamala Harris, Vice President of the US, climate activist Greta Thunberg, US House Foreign Affairs Committee member Jim Costa, You Tuber Lilly Singh, poet Rupi Kaur, UK MP Claudia Webbe openly supported farmers after Rihanna's one-line post 'Why aren't we talking about this?' appeared on Twitter. Farmers' body welcomed celebrity support.[126]

A significant feature of the agitation was the participation of women in large numbers. Women's participation in protests had a long history dating back to the early decades of the twentieth century. Women were given responsibilities like men.[127] Women in Haryana took training to drive tractors for the march.[128] Punjabi women shared the same political and social space as men. The recognition and respect for their contribution and active role was seen as 'a harbinger of change in a society where patriarchy runs deep'.[129] Women participated in agriculture and associated activities as labourers and also suffered from deprivation, debt and even suicides.[130] International Women's Day was celebrated on March 8th at the protest sites where thousands of women participated. Every activity, including stage, was managed by the women,[131] opening a 'new narrative of social cohesion'.[132] Their dominant presence remained at the Tikri border. The US-based *Time* magazine acknowledged their spirit of struggle 'to fight to end'.[133]

Initially, the protests took various forms. From December 26 began picketing outside Ambani–Adani-owned shops, malls and outlets. At this stage, urban middle-class groups, teachers, students and workers were roped in.[134] Stores and petrol pumps owned by Reliance were gheraoed in various towns of Punjab. Railway lines, toll plazas and shopping malls of corporate owners like Mukesh Ambani were the main targets of sit-ins.[135] Jio mobile service of Mukesh Ambani faced the wrath when 1,500 telecom towers were damaged mostly in Moga, Bathinda, Mansa, Patiala, Tarn Taran, Talwandi Sabo, Ludhiana and Faridkot. A large number of connections were surrendered mostly in rural areas of Punjab and Haryana.[136] The impact of farmer agitation was felt in foreign countries as well as Punjabi NRIs held protests in about six countries including Canada, Italy and the USA.[137] These protests forced Reliance to deny its plan to enter contract farming.[138] The pattern of protest changed with the deepening of the agitation. Punjab and Haryana were declared mostly toll-free states. By March 2021, Punjab avoided the payment of Rs. 487 crore and Haryana Rs. 326-crore worth of tolls. Only a few toll plazas continued working but the total loss, including Rajasthan, was Rs. 814.40 crore.[139]

The class character of the protest got widened with the participation of farm and industrial labourers, petty shop keepers and employees.[140] Commission agents (*arhtiyas*) lent their weight to the stir with provisions like towels, blankets, milk, flour, mattresses and toothbrushes. Water-proof tents were put up at the Singhu border.[141] Research studies have indicated that like the farmers, farm labourers also carry a huge debt which increased by 61 per cent in the last 30 years. They had little access to institutional loans and were forced to pay up to 20 per cent rate of interest.[142] Right from the outset, *dalits* assured their participation in the agitation.[143] As new farm laws were to affect rural and urban workers, small traders, consumers, these varied classes joined the stir,[144] and held rallies and conferences.[145] Farmers' leader Joginder Singh Ugrahan of BKU-Ekta (U) underlined the importance of *dalit* farm labourers in the farmers' struggle.[146] Landless labourers had their own fears with the closure of *mandis* as it would lead to loss of jobs. Moreover, the Essential Commodities (Amendment) Act could have resulted in runaway spiral of food prices.[147]

From the Kisan Sansad to Rollback

The Samyukt Kisan Morcha took the initiative to hold a parallel Kisan Sansad at Jantar Mantar, near the Parliament, with a view to voice their concerns. The sessions were held based on the pattern of parliament, presided over by the speaker, and full discussion on the issues concerning agriculture. It was a new experiment in democracy.[148] This template was followed in different areas. Kisan Sansad was also held in front of the Adani dry port in Kila Raipur, Ludhiana district.[149] Women participated in the proceedings in New Delhi and also chaired the session as well. Women also demanded 50 per cent representation in the Parliament.[150] The Kisan Sansad rejected farm laws passed by Parliament.[151]

Finally, the central government relented on November 19, 2021, on the 552nd gurpurb of Guru Nanak Dev. The Prime Minister Mr. Narendra Modi 'apologized' and accepted his 'failure to explain the laws to farmers'. The three farm laws were scrapped by Parliament without discussion. The President gave assent to the decision straightaway.[152] The decision was hailed by all within India and abroad.[153] The farmers returned to their homes after a year-long struggle. There was bonhomie of brotherhood during their departure.[154] The government lost on the farm laws due to farmers' unity.[155] It remains a 'historic victory' of 'brotherhood' with novel responsibilities on the farmer leaders. It provided inspiration to other sections of society to wage a peaceful and just struggle. It has been hailed as a 'victory of Indian democracy' and will have an 'enduring legacy'. The success of the agitation has given a message that alternative politics can be forged in times of authoritarianism.[156] However, the economic cost was stupendous,[157] especially high cost on the exchequer and manufacturers: The National Highway Authority of India, for example, lost Rs. 2,731 crore;[158] Manufacturers lost Rs. 50,000 crore;[159] and Confederation of All India Traders consisting of 15-lakh traders suffered Rs. 75,000-crore loss due to blockades. The cost which the people bore is yet to be calculated. Human cost was the loss of about 670 farmers.

India's pro-corporate media tried to paint the farmers as anti-national but failed as farmers remain the torch bearers of national culture.[160] Peasant leaders remained determined to keep the agitation non-political. No political leader was allowed to address the protesters from the stage. Yet a large number of political parties and organizations expressed solidarity with the cause of the farmers.[161] The thrust of the farmers' agitation was towards federalism.[162] There were views that the farmers must have 'a say in politics'. The agitation also had potential to 'impact global trade'.[163] World prominent agronomist and winner of the World Food Prize, Dr. Gurdev Singh Khush supported the farmers' MSP demand.[164] Eminent journalist and an expert on the agrarian economy, P. Sainth called the farmers agitation 'the largest peaceful peasants' struggle' in India. He called India 'a corporate-led state' and labelled farm laws as 'unconstitutional'.[165] Arundhati Roy called it 'unprecedented struggle in the world'.[166] Like the agitation of 1907, the present peasant struggle was secular and rooted in democratic principles. Moreover, it has been 'transformed into peoples' movement thus evolving around demands and aspirations of the working class'. It has the potential to bring about 'social transformation',[167] proving a 'new social laboratory'[168] and becoming a site to teach law and political economy through lectures of experts from law, politics, economics and farming.[169] It has gone beyond the *kisans*, as there is a broad-based engagement of the *arhtiyas*, small shopkeepers, landless labourers and social and cultural activists.[170] Those in power have been caught off guard by the songs and solidarity among the protestors on the borders of Delhi.[171] It unfolds the Punjabi character of social cohesion and camaraderie through the common kitchen (*langar*), sharing and gathering irrespective of caste, colour, creed, region and religion.[172] It has exhibited 'new paths of struggle with patience and perseverance', as movements rarely follow royal orders.[173] It has played a historic role to awaken the youth. Moreover, Punjab's farmers have staying power; coercion will backfire.[174] It has moved beyond boundaries of Punjab and has emerged as 'people's movement'.[175] Both the 1907 and 2020–2021 peasant agitations, spanning over more than 100 years, show similarities of planning, persistence and perseverance; peasants and farmers share similar fears of someone grabbing their land through legislation. The colonial financial architecture precipitated drain of wealth to England and the Indian nation state, with its neoliberal agenda, was trying to transfer wealth to few corporate houses who had taken a recent interest in agriculture.

Notes

* This chapter is a revised version of 'A Tale of Two Punjabi Peasant Agitations: 1907 and 2020–21', first published in *Journal of Sikh and Punjab Studies*, 29(1&2) (Spring–Fall, 2022): 69–92.

1 N. Gerald Barrier, *The Punjab Politics and the Disturbances of 1907*, Unpublished Ph.D. thesis (Durham, NC: Duke University, 1966).

2 Mridula Mukherjee with Avijit Ghosh, (interview), *Times of India,* Delhi, January 1, 2021.

3 'Kisan Ekta': Editorial, *Punjabi Tribune*, Jalandhar, December 2, 2020, p. 6.

4 Sydel Silverman, 'The Peasant Concept in Anthropology', *Journal of Peasant Studies,* Vol. 7, No. 1, 1979, pp. 49–69.

5 Quintin Hoare and Geoffrey Nowell Smith (Eds. and Trans.), *Selections from the Prison Notebooks of Antonio Gramsci* (London: Lawrence and Wishart, 1971), pp. 74–75, 210, 213, 273.

6 Teodar Shanin, 'The Nature and Logic of the Peasant Economy – I: A Generalization', *Journal of Peasant Studies,* Vol. I, No. 1, 1973, pp. 63–64.

7 Teodar Shanin, 'Introduction', *Peasants in Peasant Societies* (Ed. Teodar Shanin), (London: Penguin, 1971), p. 16.

8 Eric R. Wolf, 'Types of Latin American Peasantry: A Preliminary Discussion', *American Anthropologist*, Vol. 57, No. 3, June 1955, pp. 452–471.

9 Henry Bernstein, *Class Dynamics of Agrarian Change* (Halifax: Fernwood Publishing, 2010), pp. 3–4.

10 Jim Handy, 'Almost Idiotic Wretchedness: A Long History of Blaming Peasants', *Journal of Peasant Studies,* Vol. 36, No. 2, 2009, pp. 325–344.

11 The term also includes tribal families or persons engaged in shifting cultivation and in the collection, use and sale of minor and non-timber forest produce: Shagun Kapil, Pratha Jhawar, Ishan Kukroti and Sushmita Sengupta, 'Short Shrift to Rural Economy', *Down to Earth*, New Delhi, Vol. 29, No. 19, February 16–28, 2021, pp. 25–26.

12 Sukhdev Singh Sohal, *The Making of the Middle Classes in the Punjab (1849-1947),* (Jalandhar: ABS Publishers, 2008), pp. 94–95, 101.
13 Richard Fox, *Lions of the Punjab: Culture in the Making* (New Delhi: Archives Publishers 1987), Table 7, p. 57.
14 Karunamoy Mukherjee, 'Land Prices in Punjab', *Trends of Socio-Economic Change in India (1871–1961)* (Ed. M.K. Chaudhari), (Simla: IIAS, 1969), p. 533.
15 *Punjab Administration Report (1849–50 and 1850–51),* Para. 54; *Revenue and Agricultural Deptt/Revenue,* Nos. 187–190, January 1894 (NAI, New Delhi); *Land Revenue Administration Report (1889–90),* p. 4.
16 Land sales and mortgages to moneylenders: from 32,000 acres and 1,19,000 acres in 1874–75 to 74,000 acres and 2,10,000 acres in 1896–76 respectively: N.G. Barrier, *The Punjab Alienation of Land Bill of 1900,* Occasional Paper No. 2 (Durham, NC: Duke University, 1966), Appendix A.
17 *Imperial Gazetteer of India*: Punjab Series, 1908, pp. 94–95. See also, Sukhdev Singh Sohal, *Credit, Rural Debt and the Punjab Peasantry (1849–1947)* (Amritsar: Guru Nanak Dev University, 2012), p. 98.
18 Pestonji Ardesir Wadia and Gulabbhai Naranji Joshi, *The Wealth of India* (London: Macmillan, 1925), pp. 284–285.
19 Septimus Smet Thorburn, *Musalmans and Moneylenders in the Punjab* (London: William Blackwood & Sons, 1885), p. 77. *The Punjab Famine Report, 1879,* Vol. II, p. 466.
20 Hilary Calvert, *The Wealth and Welfare of the Punjab* (Lahore: Civil and Military Gazette, 1936), p. 258.
21 James Wilson, *Recent Economic Developments in the Punjab* (Suffolk Richard Clay & Sons, 1910), Appendix VII.
22 *The Tribune,* Lahore, February 3, 1907.
23 Khushwant Singh, *A History of the Sikhs,* Vol. II (Delhi: OUP, 1978), p. 157, n.18.
24 Samata R. Sharma, *Punjab in Ferment* (New Delhi: S. Chand & Co., 1971), pp. 57–68.
25 Ganeshi Mahajan, *Congress Politics in the Punjab (1885–1947),* Unpublished M. Phil Dissertation (Amritsar: Guru Nanak Dev University, 1979), p. 58.
26 *Home/Political-A,* Nos. 178–180, July 1907 (NAI, New Delhi); *Home/ Political-B,* Nos. 40–43, October 1907 (NAI, New Delhi); See also, Sukhdev Singh Sohal, 'Towards Reinterpretation of Agrarian Unrest of 1907 in the Punjab', *Punjab History Conference Proceedings* (Patiala: Punjabi University), March 16–17, 1991, p. 332.
27 *The Tribune,* Lahore, February 8, 1907; Richard G. Fox, 'Urban Class and Communal Consciousness in Colonial Punjab: The Genesis of India's Intermediate Regimes', *Modern Asian Studies,* Vol. 18, No. 3, 1984, p. 479.
28 Samata R. Sharma, *Punjab in Ferment,* p. 68.
29 *The Tribune,* Lahore, February 19, 1907; Sucheta Mahajan, 'Anti-British Agitation in 1907 Punjab', *Punjab History Conference Proceedings* (Patiala: Punjabi University), March 1981, pp. 290–309.
30 *The Panjabee,* Lahore, February 9, 1907; N. G. Barrier, *The Punjab Politics and the Disturbances of 1907,* p. 363.
31 Satish C. Mittal, *Freedom Movement in the Punjab* (Delhi: Concept, 1977), p. 45.
32 Khushwant Singh, *A History of the Sikhs,* Vol. II, p. 158.
33 Ganda Singh (Ed.), *Deportation of Lala Lajpat Rai and Sardar Ajit Singh* (Patiala: Punjabi University, 1978), p. 17.
34 Ganeshi Mahajan, *Congress Politics in the Punjab (1885-1947),* p. 82.
35 *Home/ Political-Deposit/* July 1907 (NAI, New Delhi); See also, Satya Rai, *Punjabi Heroic Tradition (1900–1947)* (Patiala: Punjabi University, 1978), pp. 12–14.

36 S. D. Gajrani, 'Agrarian Unrest in British Punjab', *The Panjab Past and Present*, Vol. XX, No. 1, April 1986, (Patiala: Punjabi University), p. 169.
37 *The Tribune*, Lahore, February 9, 19, 1907.
38 *The Tribune*, Lahore, January 7, 1905; August 27, 1907.
39 N. Gerald Barrier, 'The Punjab Disturbances of 1907', *The Panjab Past and Present*, Vol. VIII, Part II (Patiala: Punjabi University,1974), p. 457.
40 *Home/Political-A* No. 133, August 1907 (NAI, New Delhi).
41 V. C. Joshi, *Autobiographical Writings of Lala Lajpat Rai and his Speeches (1888–1919)*, Vol. I (Delhi: University Publishers, 1965), p. 124.
42 *Home/Political-A*, Nos. 148–235, August 1907 (NAI, New Delhi); *Home/Political-A* No. 133, August 1907 (NAI, New Delhi).
43 *Home/Political-A* Nos. 178–180, July 1907 (NAI, New Delhi).
44 *Home/Political-B/*, Nos. 135–145, August 1907; Copies of *India* (Gujranwala) edited by Pindi Das were seized from the possession of some soldiers at Mardan wherein ways to achieve *Swaraj* were outlined: *Home/Political Proceedings/* December 1907 (NAI, New Delhi); *Home/Political-A* Nos. 64–84, December 1907 (NAI, New Delhi).
45 *The Tribune* (Lahore), February 20, 1907; *The Panjabee* (Lahore), 9 March, 1907. *Home/Political-A* Nos. 178–180, July 1907. (NAI, New Delhi).
46 *Home/Political-A* Nos. 4–70, November 1907 (NAI, New Delhi).
47 *Home/Political-A* No. 240, August, 1907 (NAI, New Delhi).
48 *Home/Political-A* Nos. 60–61, October 1907 (NAI, New Delhi); *Home/Political-A* Nos. 64–84, December 1907. (NAI, New Delhi).
49 *Home/Political-A* Nos. 19-20, July 1907 (NAI, New Delhi).
50 N. Gerald Barrier, *The Punjab Politics and the Disturbances of 1907*, pp. 355–356.
51 *Home/Political-A* Nos. 178–180, July 1907 (NAI, New Delhi); *Revenue and Agriculture/ Land Revenue-Confidential-A*, Nos. 1–41, April 1908 (NAI, New Delhi).
52 *Home/Political-A* Nos. 154–156, October 1908 (NAI, New Delhi). See also, V. N. Datta, *Ideology of Political Elites of the Punjab (1900–1920)*, Sita Ram Kohli Memorial Lectures (Patiala: Punjabi University, 1977), p. 8.
53 Sukhdev Singh Sohal, *The Making of the Middle Classes in the Punjab (1849–1947)*, pp. 22–24.
54 *Home/Political-A* Nos. 148–235, August 1907 (NAI, New Delhi). See also, S. Razi Wasti, *Lord Minto and the Indian National Movement (1905–1910)* (Oxford: Oxford University Press, 1964), pp. 97–98.
55 *The Panjabee*, Lahore, 27 April, 1907; *Home/Political-A* Nos. 148–235, August 1907 (NAI, New Delhi).
56 Ahilan Kadirgamar and Hashim bin Rashid, 'Convergence of Agrarian Discontent in South Asia', *The Hindu*, Chennai, December 15, 2020.
57 J. K. Raja Lakshmi, 'At Ground Zero', *Frontline*, Mumbai, Vol. 27, No. 26, December 19, 2020–January 1, 2021, pp. 10–11.
58 *Times of India*, Delhi, December 28, 2020.
59 Balbir Singh Rajewal, "Kissan Andolan: Lekhajokha te Bhavikh", *The Punjabi Tribune*, Jalandhar, July 17, 2021, p. 7.
60 Ashok Gulati, 'Let's not waste a Crisis', *Indian Express*, Mumbai, October 4, 2020, p. 11.
61 T. K. Rajalakshmi, 'At Ground Zero', *Frontline*, Mumbai, Vol. 27, No. 26, December 19, 2020–January 1, 2021, pp. 10–11.
62 First and second Acts were approved by the President on 24 September and third on 26 September 2020: *The Gazette of India Extraordinary* Part II Section I, Ministry of Law and Justice, Nos. 45, 46, 47, Dated September 27, 2020.

63 Ashutosh Varshney, 'Sow Seeds of Trust', *Indian Express,* Mumbai, December 16, 2020. See also, Yoginder K. Alagh, 'One Law can't fit all', *Indian Express,* Mumbai, February 17, 2021.
64 *Times of India,* Delhi, 22 September 2020. Pulpare Balakrishnan, 'Farm Debate: Focus on access to Food', *Hindustan Times,* Chandigarh, December 25, 2020.
65 *Indian Express*, Mumbai, September 25; October 6, 2020.
66 The Bills were to pass through the Governor making it difficult to get approval: *The Tribune,* Jalandhar, October 21, 2020, p. 1.
67 Amarinder Singh, 'This is not the 1991 moment in Agriculture', *Hindustan Times,* Chandigarh, November 3, 2020.
68 *Times of India,* Delhi, November 17, 2020.
69 *Punjabi Tribune*, Jalandhar, November 27, 2020, p. 3.
70 T. K. Rajalakshmi, 'At Ground Zero', *Frontline*, Mumbai, Vol. 27, No. 26, December, 19, 2020–January 1, 2021, pp. 10–11.
71 *Times of India,* Delhi, December 4, 2020.
72 Rajni Basu, 'Long March to Peasant Unity', *Frontline,* Mumbai, Vol. 27, No. 26, December 19, 2020–January 1, 2021, pp. 15–16.
73 There is total number of 40,000 *arhtiyas* in Punjab with clerks working about 1 lakh and labourers about 10 lakh: *Times of India*, Delhi, September 22, 2020.
74 Yoginder K. Alagh, 'One Law can't fit all', *Indian Express,* Mumbai, February 17, 2021.
75 Mehta Manjula, 'A smallholder in the Agriculture Market Reform in India', *Economic and Political Weekly,* Mumbai, Vol. LVI, No. 15, April 10, 2021, p. 24.
76 *The Tribune*, Jalandhar, January 11, 2021, p. 2.
77 Report of the Committee on Doubling Farmers' Income headed by Ashok Dalwai, 2018: quoted by Joe C. Mathew, 'Smart Farming', *Business Today*, Mumbai, Vol. 28, No. 3, January 28–February 10, 2019, p. 31.
78 Shagun Kapil, Pratha Jhawar, Ishan Kukroti and Sushmita Sengupta, 'Short Shrift to Rural Economy', *Down to Earth*, New Delhi, Vol. 29, No. 19, February 16–28, 2021, p. 27.
79 *Indian Express*, Mumbai, September 23, 2020.
80 *Agricultural Handbook* (Ludhiana: PAU, 2017), pp. 2–6.
81 Amitabh Kant, 'Agriculture's Watershed Moment', *The Times of India*, September 22, 2020.
82 Ashok Gulati, 'The Farmer's Freedom to Sell', *Indian Express*, Mumbai, September 28, 2020.
83 Aunindyo Chakarvarty, 'Why big business want these farm laws', *The Tribune,* Jalandhar, January 9, 2021, p. 9.
84 Davinder Sharma, 'Market have failed to prop up farm incomes', *The Tribune*, March 19, 2021, p. 7.
85 Manish Kumar, 'The Government's Retreat from Agricultural Policy: Experiences from Bihar', *Economic and Political Weekly,* Mumbai, Vo. LVI, No. 4, January 23, 2021, pp. 14, 18.
86 *The Tribune*, Jalandhar, 1 December, 2020, p. 12. *Punjabi Tribune*, Jalandhar, December 1, 2020, p. 3.
87 Pritam Singh, 'Glaring flaws in farm laws', *The Tribune*, Jalandhar, December 9, 2020, p. 7.
88 Rajni Basu, 'Long March to Peasant Unity', *Frontline,* Mumbai, Vol. 27, No. 26, December 19, 2020–January 1, 2021, pp. 15–16.
89 *The Tribune*, Jalandhar, January 13, 2021, p. 1.
90 J. K. Raja Lakshmi, 'At Ground Zero', *Frontline,* Mumbai, Vol. 27, No. 26, December 19, 2020–January 1, 2021, p. 12.

91 *Trolley Times,* Singhu Border, Delhi, Vol. I, No. I, December 18, 2020.
92 Pankhuri Yadav, 'On the Same Page: Farmers get a Newspaper', *Times of India,* Delhi, December 20, 2020, p. 9.
93 *Trolley Times,* Vol. VI, January 12, 2021; Vol. XXI, June 25, 2021.
94 *The Tribune,* Jalandhar, December 21, 2020, p. 1.
95 *Punjabi Tribune,* Jalandhar, January 25, 2021, p. 1. *Hindustan Times,* Chandigarh, January 27, 2021, p. 8.
96 Dushyant Dave, 'The Farmers' Right to Protest', *Indian Express,* Mumbai, February 4, 2021.
97 Rakesh Takait is a son of legendary *kisan* leader Mahender Singh Takait: *Hindustan Times,* Chandigarh, January 30, 2021.
98 *Indian Express,* Mumbai, December 30, 2020.
99 *The Tribune,* Jalandhar, November 30, 2020, p. 2. *Punjabi Tribune,* Jalandhar, November 30, 2020, p. 16.
100 *The Tribune,* Jalandhar, February 21, 2021, p. 1.
101 *Hindustan Times,* Chandigarh, January 30, 2021.
102 *The Tribune,* Jalandhar, May 24, 2021, p.1.
103 *Punjabi Tribune,* Jalandhar, April 28, 2021, p. 1.
104 *Punjabi Tribune,* Jalandhar, November 30, 2020, p. 3.
105 *The Tribune,* Jalandhar, December 28, 2020, p. 2.
106 *Punjabi Tribune,* Jalandhar, December 22, 2020, p. 1.
107 *Indian Express,* Mumbai, December 30, 2020.
108 *Desh Viapi ate Lamkve Ghol da Painda Bano,* BKU-Ekta (U), January 8, 2021, p. 1.
109 Charanjit Bhullar, 'Kisan Andolan ch pae Baba Banda Singh Bahadar di soch de goonj', *Punjabi Tribune,* Jalandhar, October 17, 2020, p. 2.
110 *Punjabi Tribune,* Jalandhar, January 10, 2021, pp. 8–9; January 5, 2021, p. 5; May 25, 2021, p. 5.
111 Gurdev Singh Sidhu, 'Bar Di Abadkari ate Veehvi Sadi di Paihli Kisan Lehar', *Punjabi Tribune,* Jalandhar, November 22, 2020, pp. 8–9; See also, Chaman Lal, 'Leading Lights of *Pagdi Sambhal Jatta* Stir', *The Tribune,* Jalandhar, February 23, 2021, p. 7. Sawrajbir, 'Kisan Andolan ate *The Tribune*', *Punjabi Tribune,* Jalandhar, February 7, 2021, p. 9.
112 *Punjabi Tribune,* Jalandhar, February 28, 2021, p. 1.
113 *Punjabi Tribune,* Jalandhar, March 24, 2021, p. 1.
114 *Punjabi Tribune,* Jalandhar, March 20, 2021, p. 2.
115 *Punjabi Tribune,* Jalandhar, February 4, 2021, pp. 1–2.
116 Shagun Kapil, Pratha Jhawar, Ishan Kukroti and Sushmita Sengupta, 'Short Shrift to Rural Economy', *Down to Earth,* New Delhi, Vol. 29, No. 19, February 16–28, 2021, pp. 25–26.
117 *Punjabi Tribune,* Jalandhar, October 23, 2020, p. 2.
118 *Punjabi Tribune,* Jalandhar, January 17, 2021, pp. 1, 7.
119 Sawrajbir, 'Kissan Sangarash ate Punjab de Gayak', *Punjabi Tribune,* Jalandhar, October 16, 2020, p. 6.
120 Jasbir Kesar, 'Punjabi Kavita Vich Kisani', *Punjabi Tribune,* Jalandhar, December 20, 2020, p. 8. See also on the theme, *Punjabi Tribune,* Jalandhar, December 6, 2020, p. 10.
121 Sangeet Toor, 'Naujawan Gayak, Aagu ate Lok pakhi Syasat', *Trolley Times,* Vol. VI, January 12, 2021.
122 *The Tribune,* Jalandhar, December 13, 2020, p. 2.
123 Babbi Pato, 'Lok Pakhi Geetan di Awaz: Kanwar Grewal', *Punjabi Tribune,* Jalandhar, December 19, 2020, p. 9.
124 Inderjeet Singh Padda, 'Jaimal Padda de Geet ate Kheti Kanun', *Punjabi Tribune,* Jalandhar, December 2, 2020, p. 6.

125 Gurmeet Krhyalvi. 'Tur Gya Lokan da Albela Shayar', *Punjabi Tribune*, Jalandhar, May 21, 2021, p. 7.
126 *Times of India,* Delhi, February 4, 2021.
127 Sangeet Toor's interview with Harinder Bindu, leader, Women Wing, BKU-Ekta (Ugrahan): *Trolley Times,* Vol. I, No. III, December 26, 2020.
128 *Punjabi Tribune*, Jalandhar, January 5, 2021, p. 5.
129 Geetanjali Gayatri, 'Crossing the Threshold', *The Tribune*, February 21, 2021, p. 15.
130 Hamir Singh, 'Auratan Vee Turian Khudkushia De Rah', *Punjabi Tribune*, Jalandhar, April 20, 2021, p. 7.
131 *Punjabi Tribune*, Jalandhar, March 9, 2021, p. 1.
132 Pritam Singh, 'Sanjhivalta Di Navi Dastan', *Punjabi Tribune*, Jalandhar, March 7, 2021, p. 9.
133 *The Tribune*, Jalandhar, March 14, 2021, p. 4.
134 *Times of India,* Delhi, 28 December, 2020. Reliance claimed that 2,000 towers were damaged out of 9,000 Reliance Jio towers in Punjab. There are in total 21,403 towers are in Punjab: *Business Standard,* Mumbai, January 4, 2021.
135 *Punjabi Tribune*, Jalandhar, October 6, 7, 13, 2020, p. 9, pp. 2, 7, 9.
136 *Punjabi Tribune*, Jalandhar, December 18, 2020, pp. 2, 10. In Punjab, about 1,090 patrolling parties were deployed and 22 nodal officers were appointed to ensure that no damage was done in 27 districts: *Times of India,* Delhi, January 6, 2021.
137 *Punjabi Tribune*, Jalandhar, October 5, 2020, p. 2.
138 *Business Standard,* Mumbai, January 5, 2021.
139 *Punjabi Tribune*, Jalandhar, March 24, 2021, p. 2.
140 *Punjabi Tribune*, Jalandhar, October 7, 2020, p. 2.
141 *The Tribune*, Jalandhar, December 11, 2020, p. 1.
142 *The Tribune*, Jalandhar, March 18, 2020, p.2. *Punjabi Tribune*, Jalandhar, July 13, 2020.
143 *Punjabi Tribune*, Jalandhar, November 30, 2020, p. 3.
144 Lachhman Singh Sehewala, 'Khet Mazdoor', *Punjabi Tribune*, Jalandhar, November 5, 2020, p. 6. See also, Sukhpal Singh, 'Nave Kheti Qanun: Mazdoor varg te sambhavi assar', *Punjabi Tribune*, Jalandhar, May 3, 2021, p. 6.
145 *Punjabi Tribune*, Jalandhar, February 20, 2021, p. 2.
146 Joginder Singh Ugrahan, 'Kissan Sangarsh', *Punjabi Tribune*, Jalandhar, January 7, 2021, p. 5. See also, Navsharan Kaur, 'Kiassani Sangarsh vich *Dalit* Khet Mazdoor', *Punjabi Tribune*, Jalandhar, January 9, 2021, p. 6.
147 Rajni Basu, 'Long March to Peasant Unity', *Frontline,* Mumbai, Vol. 27, No. 26, December 19, 2020–January 1, 2021, pp. 15–17.
148 *The Punjabi Tribune*, Jalandhar, July 23, 2021, p. 1. See also its editorial.
149 *The Punjabi Tribune*, Jalandhar, July 24, 2021, p. 4
150 *The Punjabi Tribune*, Jalandhar, July 27, 2021, p. 2
151 *The Punjabi Tribune*, Jalandhar, July 29, 30, 2021, pp. 5, 10.
152 *The Punjabi Tribune*, Jalandhar, November 20, 21, 30, 2021, pp. 1, 12, i; December 2, 2021, p. 1. A SKM's five member panel was formed to negotiate with the government: *The Tribune*, Jalandhar, December 5, 2021, p. 1.
153 *The Punjabi Tribune*, Jalandhar, November 20, 2021, p. 3
154 *The Punjabi Tribune*, Jalandhar, December 12, 2021, p. 1
155 Aunindyo Chakarvarty, *The Tribune*, Jalandhar, November 27, 2021, p. 6
156 *The Punjabi Tribune*, Jalandhar, November 20, 21, 2021, pp. 6; See also P. Sainath, 'Kissan Andolan di Misali Jit de Myane', *The Punjabi Tribune,* Jalandhar, December 4, 2021, p. 8; Neera Chandhoke, 'The Enduring Legacy of Farmers' movement', *The Tribune*, Jalandhar, December 7, 2021, p. 9.
157 *The Tribune*, Jalandhar, November 21, 2021, p. 2

158 *The Tribune*, Jalandhar, November 20, December 2, 2021, p. 12.
159 *The Tribune*, Jalandhar, November 23, 2021, p. 2.
160 Surinder Singh Jodhka, 'Kisana te 'desh dirohi' da billa kiyo nahi Tikiya', *Punjabi Tribune*, Jalandhar, December 31, 2021, p. 6.
161 *The Tribune*, Jalandhar, February 12, 2021, p. 12.
162 Hamir Singh, 'Kisa Andolan', *Punjabi Tribune*, Jalandhar, October 17, 2020, p. 7.
163 Davinder Sharma, 'Time for Farmers to have a say in Politics', *The Tribune*, Jalandhar, January 16, 2021, p. 9; June 9, 2021, p. 7.
164 *Punjabi Tribune*, Jalandhar, December 3, 2020, p. 2.
165 *The Tribune*, Jalandhar, January 11, 2021, p. 2. *Punjabi Tribune*, Jalandhar, January 13, 2021, p. 7.
166 *Punjabi Tribune*, Jalandhar, January 10, 2021, p. 2.
167 Parminder Singh, 'Kisan Lehar Dia Vilankhtava', *Punjabi Tribune*, Jalandhar, January 6, 2021, p. 6. See also, Prem Singh Bhangu, 'Kissan Andolan Samajik Tabdeeli Nu Janam Devega', *Punjabi Tribune*, Jalandhar, April 17, 2021, p. 7.
168 Harwinder Bhandal, 'Navi Samajik Pathshala Vajo Kissan Sanghrash', *Punjabi Tribune*, Jalandhar, March 10, 2021, p. 6.
169 *The Tribune*, Jalandhar, March 10, 2021, p. 4.
170 Pramod Kumar, 'With anger and a song', *Indian Express,* October 8, 2020.
171 Ahilan Kadirgamar and Hashim bin Rashid, 'Convergence of Agrarian Discontent in South Asia', *The Hindu,* Chennai, December 15, 2020.
172 *Punjabi Tribune*, Jalandhar, April 5, 2021, p. 6.
173 Amit Bhaduri, 'Kisan Roh: Sidak Ne Nave Rah Khole', *Punjabi Tribune*, Jalandhar, December 15, 2020, p. 6. See also, Amit Bhaduri, 'Lehran Nahi Mandyan Hundiya Shahi Farman', *Punjabi Tribune*, Jalandhar, January 3, 2021, p. 6.
174 Ashutosh Varshney, 'Sow Seeds of Trust', *Indian Express,* Mumbai, December 16, 2020. Manat Mand, 'On Kundali Border', *Trolley Times*, Vol. VI, January 12, 2021.
175 Gurbachan Jagat, 'Sangharsh: Jeen da Eho e Salika Hunda Hai', *Punjabi Tribune*, Jalandhar, December 13, 2020, p. 6.

4 From Disunity to Unity

Organization, Mobilization Strategies and Achievements of the Recent Farmers' Movement in Punjab*

Sucha S. Gill

Introduction

There is a long history of farmers' movements in India, especially in Punjab. A glorious and successful movement of farmers' happened in Punjab during 1907. It was led by Sardar Ajit Singh, a prominent freedom fighter and an uncle of Shahid Bhagat Singh. It was against *three laws* passed by the colonial government against the farmers who organized a seven-month-long movement, which ended with the withdrawal of those acts. This is also known as *Pagri Sambhal Jatta* movement on the basis of poem written by Banke Dayal, editor of *Jhang Syal*, and read at a rally on March 3, 1907, at Layallpur, now renamed Faisalabad in Pakistan. The Patiala and East Punjab State Union (PEPSU) *Muzara* (tenant) Movement (1939–1952) fought by peasants resulted in the abolition of *Biswedari* (land lordship) in 1952. The Punjab unit of the All India Kisan Sabha was established in 1943 which fought many battles, the most prominent being against the Betterment Levy imposed by the Punjab Government on land irrigated by canals in 1959. The Telangana Peasant Struggle (1945–1949) was one of the militant movements for land ownership rights and protection of land tenure of tenants. The *Tebhaga* (one/third) Movement (1946–1947) in Bengal was for raising share of tenants to two-thirds from one-half and reducing the share of landlords to one-third. In the post-independence period, in wake of land reform legislation enacted in State Assemblies, there were several local mobilizations by tenants on landownership and protection of tenants' rights. The most prominent among these was the militant Naxalite Movement which started from West Bengal in 1967 and spread to other places to occupy the land of landlords for distribution among the poor peasants. But in the 1970s, a new farmers' movement began to take shape on issues other than land rights and protection of tenant rights. This movement was concentrated on issues of cheaper input prices and better prices of agricultural produce. Another feature of new farmer movements was that unlike earlier peasant movement, this was not led by any political party. These movements were led by a new set of leadership free from kisan wings of various political parties (Assadi,

 DOI: 10.4324/9781003320005-6

1995: Brass, 1995; Dhanagare, 1995; Gill, 1995; Hassan, 1995; Lindberg, 1995; Nadkarni, 1987; Omvedt, 1995; Gill and Singhal, 1984). These movements have been largely led by the Bharatiya Kisan Union (BKU) especially in North-West India. While in the southern states various names have been given to these movements in local languages, they had a common agenda based on lower input prices and high prices of agricultural produce along with neglect of rural development relative to urban areas. Although there have been attempts to develop All-India coordination among the state units, yet the state units have enjoyed a fairly large autonomy on the timing and process of mobilization of farmers. There is a common understanding among the farmers' unions that there is no differentiation among the different types of farmers and also between the farmers and non-farmers in the rural areas. All sections of rural population were understood to be sufferers of "urban-bias" of development and neglect of the rural areas. The Punjab unit of BKU has been part of the All India Co-ordination Committee(s) from time to time. This chapter tries to describe and analyse the recently concluded farmers' movement and is divided into five sections in addition to the introduction. Section "Origin of BKU and its Rise to Prominence in Punjab" is devoted to analysing the origin of the BKU as a new form of farmers' movement and its rise to dominance in Punjab. Section "Factionalism, Decline and Revival of BKU (under the Coordination Sangharsh Committee)" deals with the fragmentation and decline of BKU especially after it first split in 1992 and then revival of the movement after the Indian government issued Three Farm Ordinances in June 2020. Section "Spread of Farmer Movement to Other States" considers the spread of the farmer movement to other states and the formation of an apex organization, Samyukt Kisan Morcha (SKM), for directing the farmers' movement and engaging the farmers' representatives in dialogue with representatives of the Indian government. Section "Stages and Major Features of the Movement" describes the various stages of the movement and their specificities and assesses the overall nature of the movement. The final section summarizes the arguments and brings out the achievements and challenges of the movement.

Origin of BKU and Its Rise to Prominence in Punjab

The Punjab unit of BKU formerly came into existence in 1980, but it was preceded by the Punjab Khetibari Zamindara Union (PKZU) which had been established in 1972. Several rounds of struggles (1973, 1974, 1974–1975 and 1977–1978) were organized in the State under the banner of PKZU. During this period, leadership of the union passed into the hands of young non-party leaders who decided to rename it as BKU (Punjab Unit) in 1980 with active association of Sharad Joshi, a farmers' leader from the Maharashtra BKU. The transition of Punjab BKU, as an organization independent of political parties, had taken place in opposition to practices of politicians who used the support of the farming community to rise in party politics but without adequately serving the interests of the farming community. This is the reason why the BKU decided not to allow politicians, both from ruling and opposition parties, to use its platform during their struggles especially after 1980. Another factor was the change in the mobilization strategy of traditional organizers of farmers from the Communist Parties in the state. Earlier they used to organize farmers without any distinction of class or size category to fight against feudal oppression and imperialism. Due to the penetration of capitalism in agriculture following the success of the Green Revolution, there was differentiation of the peasantry into rich farmers and agricultural labourers along with the poor peasants with small and marginal holdings. The Communists decided to organize agricultural labourers independent of farmers' organization, in the Kisan Sabha, and decided to build an alliance of agricultural labourers with poor peasants against the rich farmers in their struggles for higher wages (Gill, 2000). In the wake of the changed situation, the organization of rich farmers was not on the priority list of leftist organizations in the State. At the same time, the non-left political parties like Shiromani Akali Dal and Punjab Pradesh Congress Committee had never seriously put organization of farmers on their agenda. This vacuum was filled in the state by the BKU to protect the interests of all the farmers without any distinction. The organizers of BKU, with the agenda of protecting interests of all farmers and fight against injustice to all rural areas, developed a new discourse of mobilization of farming community in the state. This discourse was strengthened on the basis of the policy framework with showed urban bias against rural development. This discourse appealed to the imagination of the entire peasantry which responded favourably to calls of the BKU on issues of low prices for agricultural inputs (diesel, electricity, fertilizers, canal water charges, seeds, etc.) and higher prices for agricultural produce, especially of wheat and rice. Very soon after, the leftist organizations like the Kisan Sabhas, had fallen in line but with a shrinking base among farmers as Kisan Sabhas were supporting only agricultural labourers for higher wages during the sowing and harvesting seasons. The issue of higher wages impacted rich as well as poor farmers as they also employed seasonal labour in the busy seasons. The BKU leadership argued that farmers could not pay higher wages due to high cost of inputs and low prices of agricultural produce which was fixed by various agencies of the government. Within a few years, the leftist organizations became marginalized and BKU emerged as the dominant organization in the rural areas of Punjab. After 1978, Punjab was infested with the problem of terrorism and leftist parties and its cadres took an open position against the Khalistani militants who retaliated against them, reducing further their capacity to work in the interest of farmers or agricultural labourers. Since the BKU leadership took a neutral position on Khalistani militants, they, therefore, could move around in the rural areas without any fear. They mobilized the peasantry on a massive scale to demand higher prices of agricultural produce especially wheat and

paddy in 1983–1984. The leadership of the BKU organized a *gherao* of the Governors' Houses of Punjab and Haryana, during March 12–18, 1984, in which 50,000–60,000 farmers participated, almost taking over the joint capital city of Chandigarh. From an organisational point of view, it was a very successful movement as it also led to the establishment of BKU units in Haryana. The movement was peaceful and self-dependent. The farmers had moved to Chandigarh on tractor trolleys carrying food and fuel while daily supplies of milk and vegetables continued to be supplied from the neighbouring villages. Earlier the farmers had stopped the entry of staff of electricity board, cooperative and revenue departments of Punjab Government as well as that of the police in the villages. The movement was successful in getting several demands conceded. Emboldened by the massive mobilization of farmers in the villages and the successful *gherao* of Governor Houses of Punjab and Haryana, the Punjab BKU declared that it would not allow the movement of food grains out of Punjab from June 10, 1984, if their demands for higher prices of grains and low prices of inputs were not met. The BKU movement was running parallel to the militant movement in Punjab. Ultimately the movement became dormant and remained so for nearly a decade. This was a direct consequence of the military operation code named Operation Blue Star on June 3, 1984, which involved military assault at the Golden Temple complex at Amritsar and at other places in Punjab to control the militant movement.

Factionalism, Decline and Revival of BKU (under the Coordination Sangharsh Committee)

During the 1980s decade, due to disturbed conditions in the state and strict conditions relating to holding of public meetings and rallies, the BKU could not organize any major mobilization among farmers. However, the union had displayed considerable resilience and survived in the difficult and disturbed situation with army and paramilitary forces occupying the state on the one hand and continued terrorist violence on the other hand. At local level, the BKU continued to be active, taking up some issues and airing the grievances of the farming community. But due to internal developments within the state and role of some external factors, the Punjab unit of the BKU split into two factions in April 1989. One faction was led by Ajmer Singh Lakhowal and another by Balbir Singh Rajewal and Bhupinder Singh Mann. With growing popularity of the BKU, a tussle started between the union leaders to occupy the top position and this meant less pressure was exerted on the government to address grievances of the followers. This was accompanied by another opportunity arriving on the scene. With the formation of the VP Singh government in Delhi, an Advisory Committee on National Agricultural Policy was established under the chairmanship of Sharad Joshi, a farmers' leader from Maharashtra. Bhupinder Singh Mann and Balbir Singh Rajewal were closer to Sharad Joshi. This further intensified the tussle for the top leadership position in the BKU. This fear came to be true when Bhupinder Singh Mann was nominated as a Member of Rajya Sabha in 1990 for six years. This split was also observed at the all India level as well in 1990 with the formation of two Inter-State Coordination Committees (ISCCs) of farmers' organization, one led by Mahinder Singh Tikait and another by Sharad Joshi. The ISCC led by Tikait took a position against the Dunkel draft while the ISCC Committee led by Sharad Joshi was in favour of globalization and freeing of trade in agricultural commodities and hence supported the Dunkel draft. Over time, Ajmer Singh Lakhowal drifted towards Akali Dal politics and also became closer to some militant groups. Although initially the Lakhowal faction had a larger support base than the other faction led by Rajewal and Mann, it began to face internal conflict on ideological grounds. A large number of activists began to question Lakhowal about his participation in Akali politics. Lakhowal, later on, got a major reward by retaining Chairmanship of the Punjab Mandi Board for ten years during the Akali-BJP coalition government of 2007–2017. Lakhowal's dabbling in Akali politics was against the BKU constitution. This also created a split in the Lakhowal faction of the BKU in 1992. The group which separated from the Lakhowal faction was led by radical leftist activists. They named their union, BKU Ekta. This set in motion the process of further splits in the BKU Ekta, all named after Presidents of the union. By 2019, there were 35 farmers' unions in the state under different names. Although some unions have been joining hands and organizing joint protests at state level, yet they have been contesting with each other for getting a dominant position among the farmers in the area of their operation/region. The united mobilizations on farmers' issues began to take shape in the first decade of twentieth century and strengthened in the second decade, especially after attempts were made by the Punjab Government to reduce the power subsidy or when there was inadequate supply of electricity at the time of transplantation of paddy or because of problems associated with market clearance of wheat and paddy. Issues such as land acquisition for highways, industrial parks, loan waivers to formers and conflict with banks/arthiyas on loan recovery have also seen limited united actions by some unions based on a common programme. The year 2020 saw the culmination of a move towards unity of action and purpose among different factions of the farmer unions. This opportunity was provided by the issuance of Three Farm Ordinances by the Union Government on June 5, 2020. Different factions of the BKU and other farmers' unions acted quickly to organize protests against these Ordinances. These Ordinances were immediately translated into Punjabi by union activists who printed and distributed them among their members and farmer leaders for discussion. This electrified the atmosphere in the rural areas and word began to spread that farmers' land and livelihood have been put under great threat due to promulgation of the Ordinances. This generated both fear and anger among the farmers in Punjab. This led to a large number of demonstrations in villages, towns and cities by some farmers of the state. Very significantly, we see for the first time in Punjab, a large number of young sons of farmers undertaking marches and demonstrations on their motorcycles and tractors. While demonstrating at various places, the youth also played the popular pro-people songs and made commitments on getting the three "black" Ordinances withdrawn. Many groups of farmers began to hold demonstrations in front of houses of elected MLAs and MPs of Akali Dal and the BJP, the coalition partners in the Union Government.

Given the level of anger against the three Ordinances, some factions of farmers' unions took initiatives to coordinate their efforts for a joint struggle against the three Ordinances promulgated by the Union Government. By September 19, 2020, this effort resulted in the formation of a Coordination Sangharsh Committee of 32 farmers' unions active in different parts of Punjab. After a call made by some farmers' unions, the focus of protest was shifted from villages, towns and cities at district level to Chandigarh, the state capital. After a major and impressive demonstration against these Ordinances in Chandigarh, members of the major unions held a meeting with the Punjab Chief Minister in July 2020 and urged him not to implement these Ordinances in the Punjab State. The Punjab Chief Minister agreed to this proposal and promised to take up this issue in the forthcoming session of the Legislative Assembly of Punjab scheduled for August 18–22, 2020. In the meantime, the Union Government converted these Three Ordinances into Three Acts by getting them passed by the two houses of Parliament in July 2020. The Shiromani Akali Dal, facing erosion of their support base among the peasantry, decided to withdraw its support to the NDA government at the centre and asked it sole representative Harsimrat Kaur Badal to resign from the Union Cabinet. The Alkali Dal voted against these bills in both Houses of Parliament. After getting approval from both Houses, the BJP-led government moved very fast in getting signatures of the President and made the Gazette Notification and converted these bills into Three Farm Acts. These developments facilitated in getting a unanimous resolution to be passed in the Punjab Legislative Assembly on August 22, 2020, that the Three Farm Acts will not be implemented in Punjab. The Punjab Chief Minister took the Leader of Opposition (from AAP) and Akali representatives on the same day to the Punjab Governor for getting his approval. The BJP did not attend the session when this resolution was passed in the Assembly. The resolution had the support of the Punjab Congress, Aam Aadmi Party and Shiromani Akali Dal. In fact, all political parties in the state, except the BJP, had committed themselves against repealing these Acts. Thus, the three Ordinances and later on these Three Farm Acts not only brought unity among different farmers' unions but also built a consensus among the political parties against the New Farm Acts. These developments opened the way for building a consensus among different sections to oppose these laws and supported the ongoing movement of the farmers. A process of fragmentation of the farmers' movement, which had started in 1992, went into reverse gear of unity in 2020 among the farmers' organizations. There was also consensus among the different unions to get the Three Acts withdrawn along with ensuring lapsing of the Parali Ordinance and not allowing passing of the Amendment of Electricity Act 2003. There was also consensus among farmers' unions to get the legal status of Minimum Support Prices (MSPs) announced for 23 commodities every year. At present framers get MSP for wheat and paddy in only a limited number of states like Punjab, Haryana, Western UP, MP, Andhra Pradesh, Telangana and Orissa and occasionally for the cotton crop. A recent NSSO survey had revealed that in 2012–2013 only 6 per cent of the farmers got the benefit of the MSP. The remaining 94 per cent of the farmers are deprived of the opportunity to sell their produce to private traders at the MSP most of the time. The private traders usually buy their produce at Rs. 350–500 per quintal less than the announced MSP in case of grains and at much lower prices in the case of oil seeds and pulses. There was a consensus among the farmers' Unions that the New Farm Acts were enacted to handover trade, marketing and storage to big corporates and also to involve them in agricultural production through contract farming. They wanted the reversal of economic policy framework, which favours big business in the country towards achieving higher welfare for the common people. Through peaceful measures, farmers were also opposing toll plazas, business interests of Ambani and grain stores of Adani. The leaders had also decided, even before the decision to shift the centre of struggle to Delhi, to keep this movement peaceful even under extreme provocations and strong measures such as *lathi* charges by police or use of water cannons on the demonstrators, or in case of arrest of union leaders. Another point of common understanding was that the movement will not be allowed to be used by any political party for its own political ends. The leaders of political parties would not be allowed to address the farmers' rallies from the stages/platform set by the Kisan Morcha. They expressed the firm opinion to enter into dialogue with government representatives whenever required. They decided to organize their protests actions at times and places under the guidance of the Coordination Sangharsh Committee. Thus, for the first time since 1984, a unity of thought in Kisan movement in organization, ideas, agenda and action came into existence on an extended scale. This is being admired and appreciated by social activists of different shades.

Spread of Farmer Movement to Other States

The movement which originated in Punjab in June 2020 began to spread to neighbouring states by July. In fact, in June 2020, when the Three Ordinances were promulgated and the farmers' union leaders of Punjab understood their potential impact on the farmers of the country, they opened their communication on this matter with farmer leaders in Haryana and UP. The BKU and other farmers' union leaders of Punjab also sent their representatives to meet their counterparts in other neighbouring states to start mobilization of farmers in their respective areas. Their purpose was to organize and mobilize for a fight against these Ordinances on a bigger scale. It was clearly understood by these leaders that mobilization of farmers in Punjab alone will not be sufficient to get these Ordinances withdrawn. They had visualized mobilization of farmers on a large scale. Although their past experience had shown that farmers' movements have been largely peaceful, Punjab leaders, in particular, emphasized that the movement has to be kept peaceful under all circumstances. They had, after all, witnessed a violent movement in Punjab during the 1980s and the damage it had done to other social movements in the state. In order to ensure the movement was kept disciplined, the various farmers' unions had created a Coordination Sangharsh Committee of 32 farmers' Union on September 19, 2020, at a meeting held in Moga. The BKU Ugrahan, another farmer union with a mass base, had also decided to support this Committee in Punjab, when their calls for various actions were announced and implemented. On November 7, 2020, a meeting of farmers' organizations from All India was called at the Rakabganj Gurdwara in Delhi, in which 400 organizations participated. In this meeting a 40 member committee was formed under the SKM for coordinated action at the All India level. It was on the insistence of SKM that a call was given for *Dili Challo, dera Dalo* (move to Delhi, sit there) and farmers starting moving towards Delhi on and after November 26, 2020.[1] The unions in Punjab had also created a cadre of volunteers who kept a watch on infiltrators and agents provocateurs during various stages of mobilizations and actions of protesters. The union leaders of Punjab had envisioned the same model at the All India level. A primary focus of the mobilization was on villages and village-level committees of organizers were created to arrange volunteers for attending site of actions and also to remain in touch with other sections of the population, especially those belonging to agricultural labourers. The members of village committees also looked after the needs of families who had left for sites of action outside the village. The village-level committees were able to mobilize a large number of persons in support of the Kisan movement in their villages. This had a cascading effect on urban areas as well, from where a large number of industrial workers and middle-class employees came out in support of the movement. When the farmers' unions decided to shift the centre of the movement from Chandigarh to Delhi, they decided to move on two routes to Delhi from Punjab. One route was through the Amritsar-Delhi national highway via Ambala and another route was the Sangrur-Delhi highway via Khanouri. The farmers began their march towards Delhi on their tractor trolleys on November 26, 2020. On the Ambala border, they faced huge opposition from a large contingent of Haryana Police who had blocked the highway with barriers of big stones and had also fitted water cannons to stop the entry of marching farmers through Haryana. The farmers continued their march after removing the big stones on the highway with the help of tractors and manual support and changed very swiftly the direction of water cannons to the other side. The Punjab farmers succeeded in crossing this barrier because the Haryana BKU, led by Gurnam Singh Chudani, had already broken police barriers on the highway to Delhi at Pipli, near Kurukshetra. After crossing Panipat, Punjab farmers found that the highway was dug deep by the police to stop them marching further. The farmers filled the road with soil with the help of tractors and continued their march. At this place, the Haryana police lathi-charged the peacefully marching farmers but this lathi-charge could not stop their march towards Delhi. After the police lathi-charge, farmers halted their march for lunch and offered the policemen food as well. Since the policemen were not carrying any food of their own, they enjoyed the food offered by protesters and left them alone. After crossing this barrier the farmers reached the Singhu border where they were stopped by Delhi Police which offered them the Nirankari Ground as a site for their *dharna* in the northern part of Delhi but the farmers insisted on reaching the Ramlila Ground. The Delhi police did not agree to this, thus, the farmers decided to have sit-in dharna at the Singhu border on the national highway. The farmers of Haryana joined them next day at this site. Another contingent of farmers, when stopped at Khanauri border, sat in dharna at that place for the night. They were allowed to march towards Delhi the next day (November 27) and reached the Tikri border of Delhi where they were stopped by Delhi police. This became the second site of dharna by the Punjab farmers. The next day, farmers of UP and Uttarakhand led by Rakesh Tikait reached the Ghazipur border of Delhi, the third site of farmers' dharna. After a call by Punjabi farmers, a large number of farmers from Rajasthan began to join this movement but were stopped on the Delhi border on the Delhi–Jaipur NH8 national highway at Jaisinghpur Khera. Thus, within a period of four days, Delhi was surrounded on all side by the farmers who were having their sit-in dharna at these four sites. Soon, farmers from states like Madhya Pradesh, Bihar, Gujarat, Maharashtra, Kerala, Odisha, Tamil Nadu, Andhra Pradesh, Karnataka and other states also joined the farmers' protests at these locations. Thus, the efforts of farmers' leaders from Punjab led to the start of an All India movement against the New Farm Acts, Prali Ordinance and the Electricity Act 2003 Amendment Bill. The demand of making MSP legally binding for buyers of all 23 agricultural commodities had been added at the insistence of farmers of those states who do not get announced MSP, even for wheat and paddy. Some of the leaders of Punjab farmers' union also became a part of SKM which was entrusted with the task of guiding the movement.

Stages and Major Features of the Movement

The farmers' movement passed through various stages and showed the potential to become the longest and largest movement of the century. It had already become larger and longer than the *Pagri Sambhal Jatta* Movement of 1907 which only lasted for six months. The present movement began from Punjab in June 2020, starting with spontaneous rallies and flag marches in the villages on motor cycles and tractors, with rallies in towns and at district headquarters by different factions of farmers' unions. It took a formal shape with the formation of the Coordination Sangharsh Committee comprising representatives from 32 unions and began to organize joint protest demonstrations. They organized the rail-roko programme to stop plying of trains in Punjab and organized a sit-in dharna on the railway tracks, blocked all Toll Plazas on highways, held dharnas in front of shopping malls and especially against stores and petrol pumps owned by Ambani and warehouses owned by the Adani group of businesses. The beginning and spread of the farmers' movement in Punjab can be called the first stage of the recent movement. At this stage, leaders of farmers' unions of Punjab established links with their counterparts in the neighbouring states. This stage lasted from the first half of June to November 7, 2020. At this stage, all the farmer unions came to agree on a common agenda of the movement. The three organizations which did not become formally part of the Coordination Sangharsh Committee virtually agreed on the agenda and action programme in principle. It was a phase of unification of the farmers' movement with leaders holding different ideologies and persuasions coming together on a common platform. There was a realization among the leaders that farmers were fighting for their existence to save their land, livelihood and farming. They were able to mobilize a large number of women and youth in the protests at various places and also against elected representatives of various political parties. The spread and intensity of the movement in Punjab isolated the Shiromani Akali Dal in the rural areas. Earlier, Akali leaders had been praising the Farm Ordinances as harbingers of a new era of prosperity in the agrarian sector of the country. They, now, took a U-turn to oppose these Ordinances. They broke their alliance with BJP-led NDA and voted against the New Farm Bill in the Parliament. This resulted in acceptance by all political parties in Punjab, except the BJP, to extend support to the farmers' movement. The farmers' unions, while accepting their support, decided not to allow political parties to use their platform for their political activities. The Punjab unions were able to attract the support of trade unions, intellectuals, poets, singers, artists, NGOs and other social organizations. Support to the unions also flowed from the *arhtyas*/commission agents, urban shopkeepers, transporters and college and university students. In the villages, all other sections of population began to support the movement with the slogan "No Farmers No Food". At that time, an impression was created that the entire Punjab, except the BJP, had risen against the Three Farm Acts.

The second stage of the movement began from November 26, 2020, when the farmers reached the Singhu border of Delhi. When the farmers were not allowed by the Delhi police to go beyond the Singhu border, they decided to start their sit-in dharna at that site. They converted their tractor trolleys as their shelters and also created a platform with a tent at a central place for addressing daily gathering of farmers. They also began to allow personalities who were extending support to the farmers' cause, to speak from this place. At the dharna sites community kitchens/*Langars* were started for feeding the demonstrators with food grains and fuel brought by farmers in their tractor trolleys. The farmers allowed visitors to the dharna and the local poor to eat from the community kitchens at a number of places. With help from some of the NGOs they made arrangements to dig up bore wells for drinking water and also built temporary toilets. At several places, doctors opened their free medical services and built temporary hospitals for helping the ailing farmers. The local villagers began to supply milk and vegetables for the community kitchens. The support of local villagers of Haryana became an important factor in sustaining the movement. It also became a valuable factor for the protection of agitating farmers coming from Punjab and Haryana at the Singhu and Tikri borders. The presence of a large number of women and young girls and boys in dharnas changed the image of Punjabi youth from drug addicts to youth with aspirations and hope for future. The participation of men, women and youth in cooking and serving food to the needy created an image of a commune where everybody took food without any distinction of caste, religion, gender or region. This revived the tradition of Guru Nanak's common community model at Kartarpur where three vital components defined it. These components were: *Kirat Karo* (participate in free labour), *Vand Chhako* (share the earnings with fellow beings) and *Naam Japo* (Devotion to God by remembering Him). All became equal through participating in the movement and by undertaking social interaction, giving a glimpse of future organization of society. The independent media took note of it and many journalists started visiting the dharna sites as if they were visiting newly created pilgrimage sites. The sites began to be visited by singers, artists, writers, intellectuals, trade unionists, ordinary men and women from middle classes. A section of retired civil servants, army men, police officers, engineers, lawyers, teachers, researchers and other professionals took a special interest in visiting the dharna sites and to extend their support to the farmers. They delivered speeches at dharna site stages and contributed in developing a new discourse of hope and aspirations for all citizens in the country. It became an occasion to relate the farmers' movement to rediscovery of the Indian Republic. There were discussions that every section of population must share in the fruits of fast economic development which India had experienced during the last four decades or more. The question of Indian prosperity and wealth of the nation being grabbed by a small section of population (1 per cent or less) became a focal point of discussion. The issues of saving and protecting fundamental rights of all sections of population, irrespective of caste, creed, gender, region or colour, also became an important part of this discourse. This had the impact of building unity among people of different religions, castes, regions and gender. This had generated a counter narrative of unity of Indians against the consciously built narrative of Hindu-Muslim divide by the ruling party at the Centre. The movement demonstrated how practically, unity among diverse people can be built during such struggles. The farmers' leaders emphasized that they were not only fighting for their own cause but also for the cause of common people who are likely to be hit by handing over trade, storage and export of grains to big private players to the disadvantage of common consumers of food and other agricultural products.

The third stage of the movement began when the Government of India seriously began the process of negotiations with the farmers by constituting a three-member committee of central ministers: Piyush Goel, Narinder Singh Tomar and Som Prakash. This committee invited farmers' leaders for talks and held 11 rounds of negotiations between December 3, 2020, and January 22, 2021. An important feature of these negotiations was that the farmers displayed deep knowledge of these laws and their implications for the farmers and common consumers, which was much better than that displayed by the ministers. The committee of ministers ended every meeting by saying that they will comeback after consultations with their senior leaders in the government. They also held one round of informal talks with Mr. Amit Shah, the Union Home Minister. The farmer leaders displayed a lot of maturity, patience and unity during the course of these negotiations. The government offered to accept amendments to these Laws but was not willing to withdraw them. The government also agreed to allow the Parali Ordinance to lapse and not to pass the Amendment in Electricity Act, 2003. Despite these concessions, the farmer leaders insisted on withdrawal of the New Farm Acts. They also added another demand that MSP be made a legal condition for purchase of all the 23 crops for which it is announced every year so that no buyer, whether private or government, could buy agricultural produce at a price less than the one announced by the government. When negotiations were going on between farmers' leaders and the three Union Ministers, someone approached the Supreme Court of India to intervene in this matter. The farmers refused to be party to this case. The Supreme Court in its hearing stayed the implementation of the Three Acts on January 8, 2021 and constituted a four Member Committee on January 11, 2021, to talk to the government and the farmers and submit its report within three months. The farmers' leaders rejected this committee and termed it biased against the farmers. One of the members, Mr. Bhupinder Singh Maan recused himself from this committee immediately. When the negotiations did not proceed further, the farmers felt that the government committee was taking farmers for a ride without yielding any tangible results and they decided to hold a Tractor March on the Ring Road of Delhi on January 26, 2021. This march was to be held parallel to the Independence Parade at India Gate. This led to the end of the third phase of the movement with talks remaining suspended till this time.

The fourth phase of the movement began on January 26, 2021. The farmers had planned to organize a colourful march on the Ring Road of Delhi. They had given a call to farmers from different states to reach Delhi on their tractor trolleys. The artists supporting the movement had prepared a variety of banners displaying slogans and demands of the movement and also bringing out the contribution made by farmers in making the country self-sufficient in food grains. There were also signboards of Sikh martyrs in various struggles in Sikh history before the arrival of the British and especially during the freedom struggle. A few days before the Tractor March there was controversy with the Delhi police on the planned route of the parade. This was settled on the evening of January 24 and it was agreed that the parade will not pass through the Ring Road but take a route in outer Delhi, passing through villages and suburbs of Delhi territory. This created two problems for the organizers. One related to the cropping up of difference of opinion among different unions participating in the Tractor March. One section, consisting of two to three unions which were not part of the SKM, insisted on holding the march on the Ring Road. This issue was raised on the evening of March 25, 2021, and these unions, sitting on the Delhi side of Singhu border, insisted on going towards the Ring Road, in the direction of Lal Quila from Mukarba Chauk. They also started their Tractor March at 9.00 AM instead of 11.00 AM, the time agreed by the SKM. The police did not stop them from crossing the barricades raised on the Ring Road in the direction of Lal Quila. The second problem the Tractor March faced was, it was supposed to start from three different locations of the Singhu, Tikri and Ghazipur borders and some sections could not be properly informed of the agreed route of the march. In spite of a large number of volunteers guiding the march, many groups lost the route. Similarly, the police personnel at different locations also faced a communication gap about route of the march. This resulted in confusion over the route agreed by the Delhi police with leaders of the SKM. During the march, although on agreed route, at several places, police resorted to lathi-charging the farmers, resulting in further confusion and injuries and arrest of several farmers. The dissenting group of farmer unions marched towards the Ring Road where they broke police barriers without any police resistance and were also joined by some followers of the Samyukta Morcha. As this group of farmers moved on the Ring Road, a section among them deviated and moved towards the gate of Lal Quila. This is the location used by Prime Ministers when addressing the nation every year on Independence Day (August 15). There was no police at the gate to stop the marchers. This section of the marchers, as planned, hoisted the *Kesri Nishan Sahib* (Gurdwara Flag) on the rampart of the Lal Quila. Another section of the marchers moved on the Ring Road towards the Income Tax Office where they were stopped by the police by firing tear gas shells on them. In this process, one of the marchers on his tractor was hit with a tear gas shell/police bullet and died on the spot. These incidents were reported by the mainstream media in distorted ways. The *Kesari Nishan Sahib*/the Gurduwara flag hoisted on the rampart of the Lal Quila, was reported as the flag of Khalistan and incidence of police lathi-charge on peaceful tractor marchers, who had deviated from the agreed route by mistake, as incidence of widespread violence by farmers. The farmers' movement was labelled as the Khalistan movement, supported by ISI of Pakistan and Khalistanis from various foreign countries. They were variously described as Maoist, terrorist and anti-nationalist (Sharma, 2021; The Tribune, 2021a, 2021b). A few days later the Prime Minister Shri Narendra Modi referred to protesters as "*Prajeevi*/parasites" (Outlook, 2021; The Times of India, 2021). This created an impression that the movement was hijacked by Sikh separatists. As a result a large number of farmers from UP and other states especially at the Ghazipur border began to leave the dharna site. The BJP leaders, along with a large number of their cadre with the help of police, began to get the remaining farmers evicted by force from the Ghazipur border. At this moment, the video of emotional Rakesh Tikait with tears in his eyes had gone viral. This resulted in movement of a large number of farmers at night from UP, Uttarakhand, Haryana and Punjab to the Ghazipur border, to show support. This emotional appeal saved the movement from getting derailed and divided. A movement which united the farmers of different regions, religions and caste, was saved from getting dissipated and destructed under a conspiracy, by prompt action of the farmers. The movement was also saved from confusion created by the social media. At this juncture, the government became even more aggressive in dealing with the movement. The government spokespersons and BJP leaders began to take tough postures against the Kisan movement, using harsh words against them as Khalistani, terrorists, prajeevi, anti-national, etc. (Pathak, 2021). The government cut the Internet connections from the dharna sites for many days so that farmers' version of the January 26, 2020, events did not reach the general public through social media. When journalists like Mandeep Singh Punia tried to record farmers' leaders version for their papers/channels, they were arrested and tortured by the Delhi police. Mr. Punia remained in police custody for several days after which the court provided him bail. The BJP leaders arranged some attacks on the peaceful dharna of the farmers in the garb of youth of local villages under police protection. When sabotage efforts and provocations did not work, the government resorted to the construction of cemented barriers with sharp and long nails fixed on the stretches of highways towards the Delhi side. This gave the impression that the Union Government was facing foreign invaders on its Delhi borders. This increased misunderstanding and a widening trust deficit between the protesting farmers (*Aandattas*) and the government. The leaders of the movement began to approach common people in villages and started organizing Khap Panchayats in UP, Haryana, Punjab and some other states. These maha-panchayats were different from the traditional caste panchayats as they did include all sections of the rural population without any distinction of caste and creed. Response to this strategy was very successful and it provided much-needed energy and support to the cause of Indian farmers. This was followed by the celebration of important events at dharna sites, such as April 14 as Ambedkar Jayanti and Baisakhi Day, May Day and other days related to the martyrdom days of freedom fighters.

The fifth stage of the movement was reached at the time of West Bengal Assembly elections held in many phases during March–May 2021. First, the SKM decided to campaign in the elections against the BJP and in favour of the Trinamool Congress. Earlier they had made a commitment that Samyukta Kisan Morcha will not support any political party or allow their platform to be used by any political party. The success of Trinamool Congress in West Bengal was hailed by the leaders of Samyukta Kisan Morcha. Second, the movement began to take up some issues beyond the domain of farmers. These were mainly related to unprecedented rise in diesel and petrol prices. They also expressed the desire to oppose the BJP in the forthcoming February 2022 elections to Punjab and UP Assembly. This also generated controversy among the various leaders of the farmers' union regarding whether to participate or not in the forthcoming Punjab Assembly elections in February 2022 (Deol, 2021). Later the Kisan Samyukt Morcha had started sending, every day, a group of 200 farmers to register their protest in front of Parliament between July 19 and August 13, 2021. They issued a whip to members of opposition parties not to allow proceeding in parliament till the acceptance of demands of the farmers. They also organized a Farmers' Parliament at Jantar Mantar, New Delhi. This irritated the BJP leadership and they started threatening protestors in UP and Haryana. In Haryana, the Chief Minister Manohar Lal Khattar, addressing party workers, gave a call to create a group of lathi wielding youth in every village to deal with protesting farmers in the state. In UP, Ajay Mishra the Union Minister of State, openly threatened the Sikh settlers in UP for participation in the farmers' movement. This provocative attitude of BJP leaders caused violence in Karnal in Haryana leading to death of a farmer in police firing. But the most serious incidence happened at Lakhimpur Kheri in UP leading to death of four farmers, one journalist and three BJP workers when son of a Union Minister attempted to kill the protestors under three vehicles at his command. This resulted in death of four farmer protestors who were returning back from a rally and one journalist. As these vehicles overturned in a narrow road with sudden appearance of a local bus on the scene three BJP workers also died. This incidence is being investigated by Special Investigating Team (SIT) under the supervision of the Supreme Court of India. The son of a Union Minister has been charged for the conspiracy to kill the farmers and is lodged in jail at present (Singh et al., 2021).

This movement, like the earlier mobilizations of the farmers by the BKU, has consciously kept itself away from established political parties to maintain the image of a non-party movement. Although some leaders of the movement have kept close personal relationship with prominent leaders of regional parties, as an organization, the movement remained non-party in nature and leaders of political parties were not allowed to address gathering/rallies/dharna for electoral purposes. This resolve was not violated during any stage of the movement. The leaders of the movement also claimed that it was movement of the entire peasantry, irrespective of class of landholdings of the cultivators. There are some scholars who characterized it as a populist movement. Lindberg, back in 1995, held the view that the peasantry had become linked to the market, where to a significant degree, price formation of agricultural produce and inputs prices are influenced by the state which regulates the conditions for the reproduction of the peasantry. This means that peasant movements are really struggles between the entire peasantry and the government. Since the post-liberalization phase, prices of inputs have already been freed and part of trade in agricultural produce is also handled by private traders. The New Farm Acts intended to hand over marketing, trade and storage to big corporate players even further. That is why the farmer movement turned against corporate players like Adani and Ambani, along with policies of the government. At the same time, the movement has also projected the slogan of "worker-peasant unity" but in practice the participation of agricultural and industrial workers remained tokenistic. The movement is dominated by landed peasantry both in terms of leadership and the cadre.[2] The farmer movement's list of demands primarily belongs to the farming peasants and the traditional slogan of the 1950s and 1960s movements, "land to the tiller" is missing, indicating that it is movement of land owning cultivators to the exclusion the tenant cultivators. Similarly, the participation of a large number of women is a new and welcome feature of the present movement but they are missing from the list of leaders guiding the movement and from the list of leaders who negotiate with the government.

Major Achievements and Challenges Facing the Movement

The movement has completed one and half year if one counts the beginning of the movement from Punjab when the three Farm Ordinances were promulgated in June 2020. But if we date the beginning of the movement to when farmers began their protest on Delhi borders on November 26, 2020, it was nearing its first anniversary. However, on November 19, 2021, on the 552nd birth anniversary of the first Sikh Guru, Guru Nanak, Prime Minister Modi unilaterally announced the repeal of three Farm Laws and appealed to the farmers to dispense with their agitation. Farmers decided to wait till these laws were actually repealed by the Government. A Cabinet meeting decided to get these laws repealed in the forthcoming session of the Parliament scheduled from the last week of November 2021 and Parliament approved the repeal in the first week of December 2021 and the Indian President immediately put his signatures of approval. On December 9, the

Secretary, Department of Agriculture and Farmers' Welfare, Government of India, wrote a signed letter to the SKM stating that (i) the government decided to set up a committee consisting of representatives of SKM, States and agricultural experts to take a decision on MSP; (ii) police cases registered against farmers for participation in agitation will be withdrawn; (iii) compensation will be paid to farmers martyred or injured during the struggle; (iv) the Electricity Amendment Bill will not be introduced in Parliament until SKM agrees; and (v) clauses 14 and 15 fixing criminal liability on stubble (Prali) burning will be deleted (Aggarwal, 2021). But this letter is silent about the demand of the SKM to sack Ajay Mishra from the Union Ministry for his son's alleged involvement in Lakhimpur Kheri massacre case. After receiving this letter the SKM decided to suspend the agitation and farmers began returning to their native places and protest sites on Delhi borders were vacated by December 15.

Along with success of the farmers' movement in getting the three controversial laws repealed, they also made many other achievements during the various stages of their mobilization. In the first place, the farmers' movement was able to reverse the trend of its fragmentation and marginalization which started from 1992 in Punjab towards unification in 2020. This was carried forward by also building unity with the farmers of Haryana. The politicians in both Punjab and Haryana had been continuously creating a wedge between farmers of Punjab and Haryana on the issue of sharing river waters of the Punjab. This division was widened during the decade long disturbed conditions in Punjab in the 1980s. The present movement, by reversing this trend of widening differences, moved fast towards developing an understanding and cooperation among the farmers of neighbouring states. This development ensured two things: one, Punjab farmers were able to pass through Haryana and reach Delhi borders because of the support given by Haryana farmers; and two, Punjab farmers are able to continue their dharna on the two sites, Singhu and Tikri, due to elaborate support given by people of Haryana in general and farmers in particular throughout its duration, in spite of many intrigues and pressures from government agencies. This unification process of farmers reached UP, Uttarakhand, Rajasthan, MP, Maharashtra and other states leading to the formation of the SKM of more than 400 farmers' unions with 40 members becoming representatives of Indian farmers. This movement, at an All India level and specifically in North-West India, was able to ensure large participation by women in a sustained manner. In the North-West India, the women had never participated in earlier mobilizations on such a scale as this time. They were supposed to remain in the villages and support household chores, taking care of cattle and related activities, while men were away on demonstrations. The participation of women at dharna sites, far away from the four walls of the houses, provided strength in more than one way. This had enriched the movement culturally by providing colour to it and adding seriousness by making men more disciplined and for keeping control of their language and behaviour at dharna sites. Their presence also helped in crossing gender barriers in cooking meals for ongoing *langars* where men could be seen cooking jointly with the women. This was accompanied by the presence of a large number of young boys and girls in the movement. It helped to improve the image of Punjabi youth from being drug addicts towards those with aspiration and commitment towards well-being of society. These developments had added necessary enthusiasm, seriousness and stability to the movement. At the country level, the movement built unity of farmers across regions, and between farmers of different religious beliefs and thoughts. The movement was able to ensure some participation of agricultural labourers from Scheduled Castes although not as much as could have been. The slogan "unity of workers and farmers" was an indicator of the unifying nature of this movement. This had become a counter slogan to the BJP of dividing people on religious lines, especially the Hindu-Muslim divide.

The dharna sites involving gathering and living together of a large number of men, women and youth from different castes, religions and regions displayed equality among the *dharnaites*. They cooked meals together, dined together and mixed with each other without prejudice. This reminds us of the model community organized by Guru Nanak in the early sixteenth century at Kartarpur, now in Pakistan. The impact of equality in living at dharna sites between men and women, people of different religions and castes may survive, albeit only partially, after people return to their villages. This may be termed the civilizing social impact of the movement which will last longer. Different dharna sites were also symbols of deepening democracy. Every day, lectures were held from stages erected at central places where speakers from different walks of life and persuasions spoke in support of the farmers' cause. This opened up the audience to different perspectives on issues relating to the movement. Here, one could find a mixture of mature ideas of seasoned leaders of farmers and enthusiasm of youth. This enhanced the consciousness of participants and generated greater tolerance towards different perspectives and viewpoints.

The lengthy duration of the movement created space for budding young leaders who were able to learn the art of addressing public rallies whilst also providing important internet and computer support for dissemination of views and ideas of farmers' leaders. These young participants have developed capability of questioning senior leaders of political parties about their performance in solving problems of the peasantry in the forthcoming assembly elections. This is an important form of social capital which the recent movement has built for future transformation of rural India. The perspective of elderly leaders also changed after working with their counterparts from other religions and regions during the course of this struggle. They also formed new friendships and fellowships among them. The experience and knowledge on how to successfully manage a movement have enriched farmers' leaders, providing them with a better understanding of agrarian issues and crisis conditions facing the country. They now have a better understanding of the importance of human and democratic rights, the need for united action by farmers, workers and other sections of working people. They have been able to better understand the mode of working of the neo-liberal economic policy and its fall outs. The prolonged period of mobilization had made the farmers' movement a focal point for dialogue and protest against wider issues troubling people in the country. The protest by farmers against the unprecedented rise in fuel prices was indicative of this. Given the weak position of elected opposition parties in the country, the farmers' movement was representing people's opposition to the unjust attitude of the present government. Finally, the peaceful nature of the movement brought great hope among the people that a very powerful government's decisions can be opposed and overturned through collective actions. This was also visible from some of the court decisions on various cases against activists and other people. These achievements make this movement historic and a turning point against the path which the country was being pushed by the ruling alliance.

The success of the movement has added to the aspirations of some leaders who were earlier opposed to contesting elections and were firm on keeping the Kisan movement away from political parties. The 22 farmers' unions and their leaders who participated in the recent farmer movement, decided to form a new party under the banner of Samyukt Samaj Morcha (SSM) to contest forthcoming elections in Punjab, leading to a split on this issue as more than ten unions decided to stay away from SSM. This can create major difficulties for future conduct of any struggle under the banner of the SKM. This can also create difficulties in saving social capital created by a long successful struggle.

Above all, the popularity of the movement in the region generated expectations among the people, particularly that in the post-movement period, after the Farm Acts were repealed, farmer leaders will be able to solve the agrarian crisis facing the farmers. But the leadership does not, as yet, have any programme to handle the present agrarian crisis. This has started a new controversy among experts and there are farmers' leaders who are in favour of the farmers' unions contesting the forthcoming elections in Punjab and UP in February 2022 (Deol, 2021; Pritam Singh, 2021)[3]. But there is no consensus on this among the leaders of SKM. Some of these issues are emotive and divisive in nature which demands attention of leaders.

On the whole the movement has wonderful achievements at its command. It was able to solicit support from many sections other than the farmers. These included agricultural and industrial workers, employees of government and banks, writers and artists, students, small traders and commission agents, youth, women, lawyers, retired civil bureaucrats and police officers. A large number of NGOs joined them in providing medical and health facilities, legal support and livelihood support to martyred farmers' families. The movement generated a culture of equality at a practical level between persons of different religions, castes, regions and gender. It created a new public discourse as a counter to the neo-liberal policy framework of development. This movement holds many possibilities for positive development in society and provides a new framework for solving agrarian crisis, saving ground water resources, adapting to the deteriorating environment and for a people-friendly model of rural life. The new discourse and peaceful nature of the movement attracted the support of Punjabi diaspora, political leaders and intellectuals at a global level. The positive effects of this recent movement will be felt in India and abroad for years to come.

Notes

* This chapter is a revised version of 'Recent Farmers' Movement in Punjab: Organisation, Stages of Mobilisation and Achievements', first published in *Journal of Sikh and Punjab Studies*, 29(1&2) (Spring–Fall, 2022): 123–141.

1 This information is based on a discussion with Jagmohan Singh Uppal, General Secretary, Bharatya Kisan Union (Dacaunda) held on July 14, 2021.

2 This observation is based on my two visits to dharna sites, first on March 9, 2021, at the Singhu Border and second on July 18, 2021, at the Tikri Border. This was also confirmed by discussions with several activists and leaders of farmers who stated that participation by agricultural labourers is largely tokenistic and only a very small number of labourers were on dharna sites. This was also confirmed by Mr. Lachhman Singh Sewewala, General Secretary of Punjab Khet Mazdoor Union in discussion with the author on October 28, 2021, at Patiala. Mr. Sewewala was involved in mobilizing agricultural workers to support the Kisan Morcha. In August 2021, agricultural labourers organized a big show by blocking one road near DC's office for their own demands and also in support of the ongoing Samyukt Kisan Morcha on Delhi borders. This has also been confirmed by Singh and Shergill (2021). In their findings, of the 460 farmers and agricultural labourers who died during the struggle, the average size of landholding was 2.24 acres but if we consider only farmers then average size of land holdings becomes 2.94 acres.

3 In the post-agitation period, there began an intensive debate between unions on whether to support participation in the forthcoming Punjab Assembly elections or not and this resulted in a major disagreement with 22 unions deciding to contest elections while ten unions deciding against it. The BKU (Ugrahan) published a long leaflet justifying its position on why it is not participating. This is likely to increase divisions between different unions of farmers with important implications for farmer struggles in the future.

Bibliography

Aggarwal, Sanjay (2021), 'A letter To Samyukt Kisan Morcha', Department of Agriculture and Farmers' Welfare, Government of India, New Delhi, December 9.

Assadi, Muzaffar (1995), '"Khaki Curtain", Weak Capitalism, "Operation Ryot": Some Ambiguities in Farmers' Discourse, Karnataka and Maharashtra'. In Tom Brass (ed.) *New Farmers' Movement in India,* Essex, England.

Brass, Tom (1995), 'The Politics of Gender, Nature and Nation in the Discourse of the New Farmers Movements'. In Tom Brass (ed.) *Ibid.*

Deol, Mandeer Singh (2021), 'Gurnam Singh Chudani Haphte lai Samyukta Morche Chon Muatal', *Punjabi Tribune*, Chandigarh, August 15.

Dhanagare, Dattatraya N. (1995), 'The Class Character and Politics of the Farmers' Movement in Maharashtra during the 1980s'. In Tom Brass (ed.) *Ibid.*

Gill, Sucha Singh and Singhal, K. C. (1984), 'Farmers' Agitation-Response to Development Crisis', *Economic and Political Weekly,* Vol. 19, No. 40, October 6.

Gill, Sucha Singh (1995), 'Farmers' Movement and Agrarian Change in Green Revolution Belt of North-West India'. In Tom Brass (ed.) *op. sit.*

Gill, Sucha Singh (2000), 'Agrarian Change and Struggle of Rural Labour in Punjab', *International Journal of Punjab Studies,* Vol. 7. No. 1, January. pp. 73–91.

Hasan, Zoya (1995), 'Shifting Ground: Hindutva Politics and the Farmers' Movement in Uttar Pradesh'. In Tom Brass (ed.) *Ibid.*

Lindberg, Staffan (1995), 'New Farmers' Movement in India as Structural Response and Collective Identity Formation: The Cases of Shetkari Sangthana and the BKU'. In Tom Brass (ed.) *Ibid.*

Nadkarni, Mangesh V. (1987), *Farmers' Movement in India.* New Delhi: Allied Publishers Private Ltd.

Outlook (2021), 'PM Parasite Reference Has Deeply Hurt Farmers: Union Leaders', *Outlook Magazine*, February 14, 2021 (Downloaded June 18). https://www.outlookindia.com/website/story/india-news-pm-modis-parasite-reference-has-deeply-hurt-farmers-union-leaders/374224

Pathak, Abhijit (2021), 'Craving for power and fetish for nationalism', *The Tribune*, Chandigarh, February 10. (Downloaded June 19). https://www.tribuneindia.com/news/comment/craving-for-power-and-fetish-for-nationalism-210182

Sharma, Vibha (2021), '32 farmer unions from Punjab not responsible for violence: Rajewal', *The Tribune*, Chandigarh, January 26. (Downloaded June 18, 2021). https://www.tribuneindia.com/news/punjab/32-farmer-unions-from-punjab-not-responsible-for-violence-rajewal-203969

Singh, Jagmohan, et al. (2021) *Tikonia- Lakhimpur Kheeri Massacre: A Fact Finding Report by all India group of democratic rights organisations*, Ludhiana, December reported by *The Wire*, on January 7, 2022.

Singh, Lakhwinder and Shergill, Baldev Singh (2021), 'Separating Wheat from Chaff: Farm Laws, Farmers Protests and Outcomes', Unpublished, Khalsa College, Patiala.

Singh, Pritam (2021), 'Kisan Jathebandian te Chon Ranniti' *Punjabi Tribune,* Chandigarh, July 7.

The Times of India (2021), 'I am seeing a new jamaat, all andolanjivis are parasites', New Delhi, February 9. (Downloaded June 18). https://timesofindia.indiatimes.com/india/i-am-seeing-a-new-jamaat-all-andolanjivis-are-parasites-pm/articleshow/80757152.cms

The Tribune(2021a), 'How extremist elements hijacked farmers' rally and Deep Sidhu's role in the chaos', Chandigarh, January 26. (Downloaded January 18). https://www.tribuneindia.com/news/punjab/how-extremist-elements-hijacked-farmers-rally%C2%A0and-deep-sidhus-role-in-chaos-203993

The Tribune(2021b), 'Tractor parade becomes violent; farmers enter Red Fort, hoist flag', Chandigarh, January 26. (Downloaded June 18). https://www.tribuneindia.com/news/chandigarh/farmers-teargassed-lathicharged-as-they-break-police-barricades-at-delhi-borders-to-enter-capital-203919

5 Contemporary Farmers' Protests and the Legacy of the 1980s

Changes in Ideology, Class Coalitions and Political Structure*

Virginia Van Dyke

Introduction

Beginning on March 12, 1984, just a few months before the Indian Army's military incursion into the Darbar Sahib complex, Amritsar, with the intention of eliminating the militants, between 30,000 and 40,000 disaffected farmers *gheraoed* the Punjab Raj Bhavan in Chandigarh for a week. This event provided a dramatic finish to a '14-month-long peaceful agitation' occurring at the height of militancy in the state.[1] Organized by the *Bharatiya Kisan Union* (BKU), before it splintered into its current fractured state, it was held in conjunction with Sharad Joshi of the *Shetkari Sangatana*, a farmers' organization based in Maharashtra and supported by the Kisan Wing of the Shiromani Akali Dal (SAD), as well as by the Kirti Kisan Union (CPI-ML) and the Kisan Sabhas of the other communist parties.[2] Motivated by the slowing of the gains of the Green Revolution, the farmers demanded that the government keep input costs low (specifically electricity prices for tube wells) and determine procurement prices for grain which took into account actual costs incurred by farmers.

Like the contemporary farmers' protests, it was characterized by peaceful crowds and *langars*. One resident of Chandigarh was quoted in *India Today*, 'With Punjab's violence as backdrop, one expected that they would set the city on fire. But one could envy their informal manners and friendly nature. We shall certainly miss them'.[3]

Several months later, on May 23, 1984, the then SAD President Harchand Singh Longowal, building on a BKU campaign demanding higher procurement prices for crops, announced the stoppage of grains moving out of Punjab along with encouraging farmers to stop repayments of loans to the government. The attack on the Darbar Sahib complex came 13 days after the announcement. P.C. Alexander, then Principal Secretary in charge of the Prime Minister's Office and close advisor to the then Prime Minister Indira Gandhi, writes in his memoir that this 'invitation to anarchy' in the context of on-going violence in the state 'was the proverbial last straw' and prompted Indira Gandhi's decision to send the army into Punjab.[4] The BKU also believed that it was the destabilizing agitation and 'the farmers' strength', seen as a threat to the state that was the real target, not Bhindranwale and his supporters.[5] Farmer activist Krishna Gandhi concurs

DOI: 10.4324/9781003320005-7

in his piece on the farmers' movement that, '...it was the economic threat of the peasant movement rather than the sporadic terrorism of the extremists that prompted the Centre's action'.[6] Thousands of farmers were arrested after Operation Bluestar and the army crackdown on the state put an end to farmer's agitations in Punjab for some time.

At the zenith, then, of the militant movement in the state, the very prominent factor of the farmers' movement, which was intertwined with protests such as the Dharam Yudh Morcha led by the SAD and Sant Jarnail Singh Bhindranwale, often gets overshadowed in the eyes of public memory and analysts by militancy, religious nationalism/revivalism and political manoeuvrings. According to Gill, '...Punjab experienced two parallel but mutually supporting movements. One was led by the Bharatiya Kisan Union (BKU) during 1983–1984. The spread of this agitation was so large that it paralyzed completely state administration in the rural areas...'.[7] As the anti-Centre Sikh nationalist agitation grew against the Congress Party led by Indira Gandhi and her policies of centralizing power and attempting to undermine the SAD, it was supported by the sympathetic farmers' movement, whose demands were also pitted against Central government policies.

While the Akalis supported the farmers' protests, the BKU 'sent Jathas of its volunteers to court arrest' in the Dharam Yudh Protests[8] and gave moral support to the Bhindranwale/Akali side of the conflict with the Nirankaris,[9] a history of mutual support that the current government draws upon in painting protestors as 'Khalistanis'.[10] Fear of the militant movement forging even closer links with the farmers' movement at that time was expressed in a piece by Pritam Singh in the *Economic and Political Weekly*, warning of an 'ominous development', that 'leaders of the BKU recently had a long meeting with Sant Jarnail Singh Bhindranwale', the union of which could 'become a powerful force'.[11]

This is not to say that there has not been substantial academic interest paid to the economic, social and political changes that were precipitated by the Green Revolution in North India and the importance of these factors in explaining political unrest in Punjab. There also has been much acknowledgment of the difficulty of teasing out multiple issues from religious revivalism to a consolidation of a newly differentiated class stemming from rising educational levels and increased prosperity.[12] However, the story of the impact of the farmers' movement on the overall level of massive anti-Centre agitations in the state, along with the reading of those protests by the Central government, may have been under told. While, by comparison, the current farmers' protests, aided by social media, poets and singers, and a small publication on the protest site called the *Trolley Times*, are constantly in focus in India and often in the international press, as well.[13] Two Punjab farmers' sons winning Olympic medals in Tokyo during the protests only added to the sense that the focus on these issues is ubiquitous.

This chapter will compare the farmers' movement in Punjab in the mid-1980s with the contemporary farmers' movement beginning in 2020 which had even a larger scale and certainly was longer lived than each of the previous individual agitations. The types of grievances, the totality of which Featherstone refers to as the 'maps of grievance',[14] the social structure and political alignments integral to the resisting community and the nature of engagement with globalizing changes are all similar in some senses, but strikingly different in others in the two examples being analysed here. What has occurred is changes in the support base of the farmers' union(s) and changes in the ideology of the leadership of the union(s), operating in a different political milieu as both the state-level and national-level political party structures have been altered. The current BJP national government is transforming both state-centre relations, as well as majority-minority relations, in moving towards a majoritarian ethnic democracy[15] and promulgating top-down society changing policies which appear to be both anti-minority and anti-poor. While the previous protests involved more tinkering around the borders of government policies to create an increasingly farmer friendly environment, the current protests were in resistance to the passage of legislation known to farmers as the *Kale-Kanun* or black laws, in a manner riding roughshod over legislative conventions, which farmers believed would alter the agricultural system entirely.

Further, the 1980s agitation ended in a draconian army crack-down in Punjab ending agitations for some time, while the contemporary sudden and unexpected capitulation of the BJP in rescinding the farm laws precipitated on-going changes in the party structure of both the impacted states of Punjab and Uttar Pradesh. There is now an emergence of a multiplicity of parties in what was previously a two-party system (actually one party in opposition to a two-party alliance) in Punjab before the Aam Aadmi Party (AAP) opened its account there in 2014. Although the farmers' political party, the Sanyukt Samaj Morcha (SSM), which emerged out of the farmers' movement, is not making much of a dent in pre-poll opinion surveys in Punjab, the issue is impacting the up-coming elections as protests continue and as parties appeal to farmers' interests. Uttar Pradesh is where the BJP is focusing its energy in efforts to hold on to this essential state. It is lobbying hard to gain the support of the Jat farmers in western UP who had been supporting the BJP and now are being wooed by the SP/RLD alliance claiming the mantel of a towering farmers' leader and Jat leader, Chaudhary Charan Singh.[16]

In the 1970s and 1980s, a newly consolidated hegemonic class of wealthier farmers confronted what they viewed as 'crisis of agriculture' because the gains of the Green Revolution prosperity were slowing. This new class of strengthened landed peasantry, dominated by middle castes (sometimes given the designation of 'backward castes' depending on state politics) had emerged first because of government policies which consolidated land plots and gave title to the 'tiller' and second because of Green Revolution policies which supported and empowered middle to larger farmers who adopted the associated technology. Following this emergence of commercialized farming and a class of capitalist farmers, and in the face of erosion of government support in subsidies and guaranteed procurement price of grains which was the basis of this new class, the Jat Sikh-dominated political party, the SAD, was interested in the formation of a farmers' union which would organize peasants in opposition to growing Marxist, particularly Naxalite, influence.[17]

The same social base that comprised the SAD, a cadre-based party with a storied history of agitational politics, supported the BKU. The BKU led a number of very successful agitations for improvements in farmers' economic as well as social and political conditions, from forcing the government to waive certain charges and taxes, to compelling tractor manufacturers to replace defective tractors, to coercing government employees to apologize and make amends for their corrupt ways. The leadership of the BKU did not have ideas of revolutionizing society or the structure of the economy; they were not ideologues. Rather the intention was to press for the best deal the farmers were able to negotiate with the government through a series of agitations, political links and through their weekly paper.

The contemporary farmers' movement, still led in Punjab by farmers' unions dominated by Sikh Jats, had less of a tie to the SAD due to political changes in the party structure in the state. The SAD, a shadow of its former self in some ways, was slow to the table in opposition to the three agricultural laws given its long time electoral alliance with the BJP and created a rift with the farmers by initially supporting the new agricultural bills. Sikh Jat farmers' support had anyway fallen away from the party over the last few elections, and there was a 'popular distrust of the self-proclaimed "farmers' party"'.[18] It was the Congress Party, not historically the party of farmer agitations in Punjab, which was carving out a new space for itself by agitating for the farmers, while at the same time struggling with internal factional conflicts. Certain socio-economic changes have been restructuring, to some degree, class relationships in the state,[19] while changes in the various spin-offs of the BKU itself has led to a rethinking and promotion of different types of class coalitions in the face of deteriorating conditions in the agricultural sector.[20]

In making this argument, I am drawing on Featherstone's questioning of why certain anti-neoliberal or anti-globalization movements share broader ideological affinities, while others may be 'exclusionary' or 'nationalistic'. These 'place-based struggles', which he terms 'militant particularisms', can take a very specific form depending on the local political and economic structure and the history and precipitating issues involved. That is, rather than struggles being part of a unified response to neoliberalism, each has its own unique response and produces different types of identities through conflicts of caste, gender and class.[21] While the commonality in the protests of the 1970s/1980s and the contemporary protests in Punjab may be the precipitating crisis of globalizing and neo-liberalizing impacts (sometimes termed the Washington Consensus) or the threat of these impacts, the response may not necessarily become, as leftist activists might hope, the unifying of such resistances as a broad-based left response. Rather agitations may 'bring unequal geographies of power into contestation'.[22] Therefore, 'exclusionary forms of the local and national' could emerge 'in opposition to forms of the global' and movements that connect different socio-economic groups may 'marginalize the grievances' of those of the weaker groups.[23]

In the 1970s and 1980s, the BKU claimed to speak for the 'rural' as opposed to the 'urban', sometimes also described as 'Bharat vs India', while more clearly speaking for a specific set of classes; the strength of the BKU was actively used against agricultural labourers.[24] Dalits in that era were compensated to show up at demonstrations and threatened if they did not. It was also the case that the BKU promoted linkages with other farmers' movements across states, in Maharashtra, Haryana and Uttar Pradesh, and brought together Hindus and Sikhs in protests at a time when the communal atmosphere had been vitiated. For this reason, it was possible to view the farmers' protests as the root of a class struggle which would lead to bridging communal identities.[25] Currently, a shift in class alliances could be mitigating the extent to which the weaker groups are marginalized from the hoped-for gains of the protests as much of the leadership of the recent stand-off at the Delhi borders have been actively promoting cross-caste, cross-class and gender-inclusive linkages with those left out of the previous protests. Concern about the external implications of a pro-corporate change in the agricultural system could smooth over, at least temporarily, internal caste and class divisions.[26]

Founding of the BKU and Growth of the Farmers' Movement

Prior to the establishment of the farmers' organizations, it was the Kisan Sabhas of the communist parties which were active in organizing the peasantry in opposition to the feudal landlords, the government or imperialism.[27] After the Green Revolution altered the class structure in the countryside, however, the strategy of the political left changed from trying to unite the entirety of the peasantry and labourers, to organizing only the small peasantry and agricultural workers in opposition to a new class of capitalist farmers, as the sharing of common interests that would unite all agricultural classes no longer existed. The CPI and the CPM both established agricultural workers unions.[28]

The strength of the Kisan Sabhas was undermined by the growth of the BKU, '...a material loss to Kisan Sabhas and the mobilizing capacity of the communists',[29] precisely as Singh argued the Akali leaders intended. Issues like 'remunerative prices' became the mobilizing slogan and issues around class exploitation ceased to mobilize groups of people reflecting a 'change in the agrarian relations'. As Mukherji poetically phrased it, 'The veterans of many a class conflict were left guessing in disbelief as their base of agrarian support slipped from under their feet'. And, he argues, as the BKU grasped the structural changes in the countryside, and became spokespersons of this new class, they were at the forefront of the 'great transformation'.[30]

The BKU, initially the *Punjab Khetibari Zimindara Union* (PKZU) (Zimindara here means landowner of any size in Punjabi, rather than Zamindar, which would refer to a large landowner or tax farmer before Zamindari abolition)[31] was founded in 1972 by the union of 11 smaller farmers' organizations, all of which were also Sikh based, at a farmers' gathering in Ludhiana. This organization was a reflection of the consolidation of a class of farmers, who not only prospered economically but also dominated the rural areas socially and politically. Although Sharad Joshi had yet to popularize the 'Bharat vs India' concept, some of the farmers who had adopted Green Revolution practices and technology joined together to speak not just for the farmers but 'the rural'. The Union was comprised largely of Sikh Jats – in fact, 96.18 per cent of the members were Jats according to Kehar Singh's survey published in 1990. They followed Sikh socio-religious conventions, meetings were held in Gurudwaras and their agitational slogans were '*Bole So Nihal, Sat Shri Akal*', etc. The Union did not attract women for the most part, although there were prominent exceptions.[32]

The impetus to form a state-wide farmers' union came from a bumper wheat crop in 1971–1972 which was met with the procurement price set lower than the year before. Farmers, concerned that their expectations of a continued growing income and increasing prosperity appeared challenged, met first with the then Punjab Chief Minister Giani Zail Singh and then with Prime Minister Indira Gandhi. Gandhi's refusal to commit to any farmer relief going forward was the driving force behind the conviction that a farmers' platform was needed.[33]

Kehar Singh also suggests that there is a political argument: as the SAD, party of the Jat Sikh farmers, lost elections in 1972, and Giani Zail Singh, a non-Jat Sikh became Chief Minister, the need for creating a pressure group type of organization presented itself.[34] There were individual political aspirations at work here, as well. Similar to the situation when Chaudhary Charan Singh, a farmers' leader and spokesperson of the 'middle castes', established the BKU as a political platform in Uttar Pradesh in 1978 when he was out of power,[35] former SAD MLA P.S. Kadian, who was one of the four very influential figures in creating the PKZU, had lost his position with the party through an ill-advised defection. The PKZU provided him with the space from which to re-enter Akali politics or, as he did ultimately, the Lok Dal (led by Charan Singh).

Union rules were in place to keep the organization apolitical, that is, office holders in the PKZU were prohibited from being office holders in any political party. The PKZU, which changed its name to the BKU in 1980 in an effort to contribute to a pan-India organization following Charan Singh's BKU, was quite adamant about this position, breaking ties with unions that did pursue an overtly political route. In spite of the continued close relationship with the Akalis, the BKU did find common ground with the Lok Dal when it believed the SAD was not aggressive enough in responding to its demands.

In the 1980s, the Indira Gandhi-led INC was in power at the Centre after a brief period of non-Congress Party rule, in which the Akali Dal had played a part. The SAD had also actively opposed Indira Gandhi's 'Emergency', and in so doing earned her animosity. Congress had just regained control of the state government in Punjab by dismissing the Akali-Janata government there, when Congress won the national parliamentary elections. The BKU had been close to both sides of this alliance as the Bharatiya Lok Dal, one of the *formateur* Parties of what became the Janata Party, was led by Chaudhary Charan Singh. In fact, the Punjab BKU lobbied for Charan Singh in the tussle of who was to be Prime Minister in the Janata Party government and supported Lok Dal candidates in the BKU's brief moment of disillusionment with the Akalis. It appeared to one observer that when Partap Singh Kadian was President of the BKU, 'the Union became almost a wing of the Lok Dal' with Kadian and 4 other leaders contesting the 1980 elections on the Lok Dal ticket after stepping down from their official role with the Union.[36] Later, however, Charan Singh lost his lustre with the Punjab BKU as he opposed the Dharam Yudh Morcha agitation.

But the relationship of the Akali Dal and BKU was not completely straight forward. Gill and Singhal argue that it is easy to see the BKU as almost an arm of the SAD and in fact Gandhi argues that government intelligence saw it this way. But there was one view that BKU-led morchas were allowed by the government to undermine the peasant base of the SAD by promoting an organization with such similar demographics and aims without the negative trappings of a political party. It is the case that during the tumultuous times of the mid-1980s, under restrictions by the State against agitational activity, the BKU was allowed a much wider freedom to manoeuvre than trade union or Kisan Sabha activity, perhaps viewed initially as less challenging to the State than the opposition parties.[37] This position changed dramatically after Operation Bluestar when the BKU declared the Central Government 'enemy number one of the farmers'.[38]

Initial demands of the PKZU were set out in a brochure written by P.S. Kadian.[39] Their demands drew from their interests of representing the 'rural' as versus the 'urban' which, as Balagopal points out, only solidifies their role as the hegemonic class by attributing to themselves the ability to speak for all farmers and all those who draw their living from the agricultural sector.[40] To counter what became known as 'urban bias' demands were for the strengthening of the rural sector. Unlike current objectives set out by farmers' unions, these included reservations for the 'rural population' in services, colleges and special quotas inside quotas for rural SCs, an end of discrimination against 'rural people' by the provision of better schools, hospitals, telephones and other infrastructure, pensions for small farmers (defined as up to 5 acres), interest-free loans for small farmers, scholarships for the children of small farmers, etc. These types of urban verses rural objectives are not included in the demands of the leadership of the contemporary protests which are limited more directly to economic issues, as will be discussed below.

Included in the objectives also were the demands which mostly benefitted the larger farmers [although all farmers are impacted by Minimum Support Prices (MSPs) and input costs/subsidies] who dominated the union which stressed the issues that inspired the creation of the union: prices of various inputs should be 'brought down' and higher procurement prices for crops should be set which took into account not only the cost of production but also the relative cost of consumer goods which had to be purchased in 'urban prices'. The Union demanded a seat at the table in the Agricultural Prices Commission and also demanded procurement prices be announced before the sowing season. The BKU also raised a whole gamut of social goals: greater respect for women, the end of overspending on celebrations such as weddings, the ending of corruption, adulteration and smuggling.

Land, of course, was a major issue. The farmers' union was adamantly opposed to land ceilings particularly since there had been several time periods when land ceilings were imposed, but always only on agricultural land. The BKU demanded that farmers with less than 10 acres should be allocated more land in order to be viable (this is an interesting demand in the light of the current situation whereby India-wide 68.45 per cent of rural dwellers own less than a hectare (2.47 acres) of land). Chaudhary Charan Singh similarly argued that small farmers should be allocated any excess land, as opposed to the landless labourers, who did not even have a place to put their dwelling, and for whom the lack of a piece of land was and is a huge impediment to a life with dignity.[41] Clearly, small farmers were included in the rhetoric and in the demands. Labourers find no place here, except possibly in being included as 'rural people'. However, the issues of small farmers were represented in the breach in actual agitations launched by the BKU[42] who were in some cases actively opposed to labourers' issues.[43] As Gill argues, 'About the particular needs of poor peasants, agricultural workers and women, the BKU has generally remained silent'.[44]

The Current Farmers' Agitations

Currently, the social, economic and political context is much different. The farmers' movement emerged as a response to specific legislation promulgated by the BJP national government designed to precipitate large scale economic restructuring of the agricultural sector. It seemed very much to be part of National government's inclination towards pro-corporate, pro-globalization policies which resonate as anti-minority (in this Sikh majority state particularly) and oriented towards the international market.

While there have been protests to national issues such as The Citizenship (Amendment) Act (CAA), which gave preferential access to Hindu, Sikh and

Buddhist immigrants from neighbouring countries with regard to applying for Indian citizenship and The Jammu and Kashmir Reorganization Act, which redefined the political status and relationship to the Centre of the Muslim majority state of Jammu and Kashmir,[45] there has not been concomitant large scale agitations in Punjab similar to the Sikh nationalist movement.[46] However, while the Sikh nationalist movement was a unifying issue between the BKU and much of the Sikh political leadership, the response to BJP government policies sparked a division in the current farmers' agitation. There was a bit of a delicate dance between ideologically motivated leadership and unions with others who fear that the united front would splinter if potentially divisive issues were introduced aside from specific issues related to agriculture. Some of the political left-associated unions have long been resisting the BJP government's moves towards adopting an anti-minority Hindutva ideology through autocratic anti-democratic means and would have preferred to broaden the protests to include these issues.[47]

Rather than one organization spearheading the movement, the recent protests were associated with 35 organizations, 32 of which were from Punjab and were organized under the umbrella of the Samyukt Kisan Morcha. They had differing ideologies or interests; some are affiliated with political parties, most were not. The unions tried to enforce a type of unity by, for example, ejecting two groups held responsible for some violence during the protests on Republic Day 2021 as they had deviated from the designated route.[48] Rather than a plethora of demands by the unions, the leadership attempted to keep laser focused on a very specific set of issues, that is, the repeal of the Modi government's new agricultural laws, along with agitating for actual legislation that will inoculate the current procurement system from being altered, although the Central government argued that it had no intention of making the feared changes. That is, the farmers were asking for guarantees that there would continue to be an MSP, and the procurement system based on *Mandis* would continue. They were also demanding the jettisoning of the Electricity (Amendment) Bill, which the farmers were concerned would eliminate free electricity or raise electricity prices as private providers would be allowed to compete with what has been a state-based system controlled by state governments. Farmers were also demanding the end of sanctions for burning paddy stubble (a practice which is a large contributor to the abysmal air quality in the area, including in Delhi), release of those jailed on charges related to the protests, compensation for families who have lost family members during the protests, and charges brought against those implicated in the Lakhimpuri Kheri murders.

There was no farmers' movement to speak of in Punjab from 1984 to 1992 as draconian laws in the state prohibited political activity until elections took place to usher Punjab into a post-conflict era. Inactivity and factionalization had weakened the farmers' representation and, according to Gill, bears some explanatory power for farmers' distress including the growth in famer suicides. Rising debt, sometimes failed crops due to weather or pest invasions, unremunerated pricing of crops, had been met with government indifference.[49]

In the run-up to what became Operation Bluestar and the fractured polity and government repression that followed, politics began to divide the formerly apolitical union which had actively opposed other farmers' unions taking the electoral politics route. Gill refers to this as 'the dual track approach to regional party politics' that is not formally aligned, but 'informal closeness'. Certainly, the BKU had supported candidates in the past. Some individuals in the BKU backed Simranjit Singh Mann in his winning bid for a Parliament seat in the 1989 elections, while Ajmer Singh Lakhowal had an important role in supporting the boycott of the elections by the Akalis in 1992 and was known to be close to Parkash Singh Badal.[50]

The BKU had split into two factions in 1988. Bhupinder Singh Mann and Balbir Singh Rajewal were divided from Ajmer Singh Lakhowal and Manjit Singh Kadian on issues to do with Union organization but also on ideology and the way forward for the farmers' movement. The Mann-Rajewal faction was in favour of liberalization of agricultural policy in line with the policies of Maharashtrian farmers' leader Sharad Joshi, notable as one of the few farmers' heads who was in favour of the Dunkel Draft of GATT which would open Indian agriculture up to globalizing impacts while withdrawing large scale government intervention of subsidies and supports. The other faction took the route more travelled by aligning with the new head of Charan Singh's BKU, Mahendra Singh Tikait.[51] (The latter is the father of the two leaders of the BKU in Uttar Pradesh currently, Rakesh Tikait and Naresh Tikait.) There is also an argument that Mann's nomination to the Rajya Sabha was the precipitating event of the split due to political jealousies.

In 1995, the BKU (Ekta) split from the Lakhowal faction. Mukherji refers to the BKU (Ekta) as the 'extreme left' re-entering the agrarian scene after a long absence.[52] A second split led to two BKU (Ekta) factions – the BKU (Ekta Ugrahan), founded by a retired service member in 2002, emerged as the largest faction and a dominant force at the protests. Gill and Singhal, writing in 1984, argued that the political left, specifically the communist parties, were ideologically committed to not allowing the strength of the larger farmers to be mobilized in opposition to the interests of the agricultural workers. The BKU, they state, has 'no such consciousness or ideological barrier' and will 'disrupt' efforts to forge unity with peasants and labourers.[53] Quite the opposite developed, however, as the BKU (Ekta Ugrahan) was aggressively reaching out in various campaigns and rallies to forge relations with labourers, as well as to other unions and groups that represent those that were previously included only as an afterthought or not included at all. This includes women. According to Bahl, thousands of women, who can be identified by their yellow *chunnis* as affiliated with the BKU (Ekta Ugrahan), can be seen actively participating, some in leadership roles, in the movement and protests.[54]

So, unlike the emergence of the BKU in the 1970s and 1980s, when it filled a vacuum that had been opened up by the left's singular focus on smaller farmers and workers, the current activity of the union represents a new move to engage with the left as well as new organizations such as the *Zameen Prapti Sangharsh Committee* (Land Rights Struggle Committee) which fights to enable Dalits to claim village land which is owed to them by law. There are reasons both of structural change, of politics and of political choices underlying this new alliance. The structural change of a shift to 'external contradictions' unites those of the lower socio-economic strata who are faced with increased farmers' distress.[55] In those struggles of small farmers, landless labourers, Dalits and women, the unifying force may be the looming threat of even more immiserization through the introduction of pro-corporate policies.

Small farmers and agricultural labourers are concerned that the erosion of government grain procurement at a set price (and the concomitant storing of that grain) will erode the system of grain distribution through the government Public Distribution System (PDS).[56] Labourers are concerned that the consolidation of large corporate farms, which they expect will be the result of the new farm laws, will change the labour market to their detriment.[57] Farmers with very small holdings who grow food for consumption to supplement their ill-paid agricultural or small-scale industrial work fear they will lose access to that land.[58]

Pramod Kumar, Director of the Institute for Development and Communication (IDC), defines the 'map of grievances' as more of an existential threat than the earlier protests in saying:

> Most of the protests in the '80s revolved largely around the enhancement of support prices, institutionalized credit system, regular supply of inputs on subsidized rates, etc. Those protests used to threaten to stop the supply of food grain to other states. Whereas now the crisis is privatization of agricultural operations and of food grain not finding a market. This protest is for survival.[59]

Prior to the most recent protests, BKU (Ekta Ugrahan) had been actively participating in or leading a number of protests or agitations, in years of 'pioneering work' in an effort to bridge caste and class divides, particularly between farmers and labourers.[60] '*Mazdoor-Kisan Ekta*' has been a major slogan of these protests. This is a challenging gulf to bridge, as the relationships can be quite hostile. There are many examples of farmers launching 'social boycotts' against landless labourers, often Dalits, which freezes them out not only from employment, but access to food, water, fodder for their animals, or even some land to use to relieve themselves, in response to wage demands.[61] However, Dalits are joining the movement as external dynamics, concern of corporate takeover of farms, compel them to put aside concerns over the internal issues of caste and class conflict, in a belief that if the farmers lose their land, they will lose their employment.[62] It is the case though, that efforts to recruit Dalits to the current protest fall short of the hoped for numbers on the barricades and it has been suggested that much unity is just for show.

For example, the BKU (Ekta Ugrahan) organized a major Mazdoor Kisan Ekta Maha rally in February 2021 along with a workers' union, the Punjab Khet Mazdoor Union (Punjab Farm Workers Union). Over 100,000 people attended including many women. Workers were asked to come to the border at Tikri on a specific day, but only a few were there. Reasons were many. Workers needed transport, could not afford to miss a day of work, and their focus in survival was on a different issue – accessing and getting paid for work done under the MGNREGA. Interviews with Dalit labourers showed that some did not understand the issues and would only show up to support farmers if they got something in return.[63]

Balagopal argued in the era of the 1980s that:

> There are two types of pressures from rural India: one, the struggle of the poor peasants and landless labourer, and the other, the struggle of the relatively better-off peasants usually called 'middle peasants' or 'rich peasants'...The movements of the rural poor fight the rural rich – the landlords and the contractors, for instance – whereas the movements of the `middle' peasants fight the urban rich and the imperialists.[64]

One could argue that now demands to overturn the farm laws are emanating from both sets. Ali argues that, 'the smaller and marginal farmers ... seem even less enthusiastic at the prospect of being left to negotiate with big agricultural interests'.[65]

The Emerging State-Level Political Structure

Certainly, the BJP's decision to rescind the laws was related to up-coming assembly elections in the affected states of Punjab and Uttar Pradesh, as the BJP faced a major alienated constituency to placate.[66] In their battle with the BJP, farmers even campaigned for and cheered the Mamata Banerjee-led Trinamool Congress' recent victory in the West Bengal elections, as it was a defeat for what seemed to be a BJP juggernaut.[67] Interviews with farmers at the camps surrounding the Delhi border resonated with anger towards the BJP, and most particularly with Modi himself. Drawing on themes of Sikh resistance and symbols of heroes and martyrs of past battles and oppression, journalist Arunabh Saikia argued, 'The resentment is so visceral and omnipresent that it is difficult to imagine in today's India, barring possibly Kashmir'.[68]

At the beginning of the protests, the strong anti-Centre sentiment in Punjab was led by the ruling Congress Party whose Chief Minister, the towering figure of Captain Amarinder Singh, aggressively supported the farmers and attacked the BJP as discriminating against and trying to destroy Punjab. In an effort to lead on farmers' issue, the Punjab government legislated against the Centre's laws even though this gesture had no real force. Captain Amarinder Singh's position, however, was undermined by the National-level Congress leaders who appointed his opponent in a factional struggle, Navjot Singh Sidhu, to be Congress Party Chief at the state level. A humiliated Singh stepped down and ultimately formed his own party, then formed an alliance with the BJP and another disaffected SAD faction led by former MP, Sukhdev Singh Dhindsa. Congress put in his place Punjab's first Scheduled Caste Chief Minister Charanjit Singh Channi; a calculated move given that Dalits are 32 per cent of the population with a history of a lack of representation. This was also a possible effort to avoid an anti-incumbency issue with a lesser-known fresh face leading the party.

There is now a five-corner contest following decades of a two-party system (Congress opposed to a BJP/SAD alliance) complicated in 2014 with the entrance of the AAP. Of these five parties/alliances, the SSM comprises some of the farmers' unions that were part of the protesting alliance. The farmers' movement which had struggled not to become aligned with political parties, to the extent of not allowing politicians access to their stage at the three camps where the protestors were staying, has split on the issue of contesting elections and or backing specific political parties. A substantial number, including the largest Union, determined to remain apolitical while continuing the struggle. The SSM is led by a projected CM candidate, Balbir Singh Rajewal, who has a history of contesting elections previously. After an aborted effort to hammer out a seat-sharing agreement with the AAP, the SSM and a farmers' party that was formed earlier, led by Gurnam S. Chaduni, will contest all the seats together in Punjab.

The real contest for the BJP is in UP where it is currently the ruling party in the state. Concerns about losing particularly West UP are paramount as UP is central to the BJP's hold on power. A major figure in the contemporary farmers' agitation, Rakesh Tikait, had been active in organizing sugarcane farmers in Western UP where their grievances were meshing with the protests against the farm laws.[69] Rakesh Tikait is the son of legendary farmer leader Mahendra Singh Tikait, who had inherited the mantel of leading the BKU in UP after the death of Chaudhary Charan Singh. Along with his brother, with whom he shares the leadership of the BKU, his political prominence has been growing. The political viability of the previously somewhat moribund Rashtriya Lok Dal (which won just one seat in the 2017 elections) has also had a resurgence in representing farmers in UP. The RLD was founded by Charan Singh's son Ajit Singh. It is now led by Ajit Singh's son, Jayant Chaudhary, and is contesting the elections in alliance with the SP which is strongly coming out on farmers' issues. The electoral battle is over who will be able to capture the non-Yadav Other Backward Classes (OBC) votes which have been central to the BJP's political equation in the state and formerly comprised the base of Charan Singh's party (splintering under the leadership of Ajit Singh).

Conclusion

One of the crucial differences between the farmers' protests of the two different eras is the linkages between states and the on-going political impact of the protests, both electoral and in terms of a pressure group. A year of camping out on the borders of Delhi brought a great familiarity with different states' leaders; it was Rakesh Tikait who re-energized the farmers in a dark, discouraged moment. Although the party configurations are different, famers' issues have become central and have changed the narrative by which parties try to mobilize support. While the BJP, for example, in UP campaigns using communal-type appeals, it is also promising to address farmers' demands. The RLD tries to gain Jat votes of farmers to combine with Muslims which is a primary support base of the SP, referring to the legacy of the farmers' leaders of previous times.

The farmers have succeeded in making their issues central to the political discussion, even if an actual farmers' party may not have electoral success. Although references to Charan Singh by the BJP may not be grounded in the ideology of his movement, his intention was to create an economic model of the economy, particularly the rural sector that did not follow the Nehruvian model of rapid industrialization at the expense of the farmers. This is then the ultimate rebuttal of the pro-corporate leanings inherent in the farm laws.

Notes

* This chapter is a revised version of 'Contemporary Farmers' Protests and the legacy of 1980s: Changes in Ideology, Class Coalitions, and Impact of Globalization', first published in *Journal of Sikh and Punjab Studies*, 29(1&2) (Spring–Fall, 2022): 143–152.

1 Prabhjot Singh, 'When Chandigarh had a Kisan Nagar', *The Tribune*, December 10, 2020.

2 Sucha Singh Gill and K. C. Singhal, 'Farmers' Agitation: Response to Development Crisis of Agriculture', *Economic and Political Weekly (EPW)*, Vol. 19, no. 40 (October 6, 1984): 1730.

3 Gobind Thukral, 'Punjab farmers block governor's residence to press for their demands', *India Today*, April 15, 1984.

4 Cited in Kirpal Dhillon, *Identity and Survival: Sikh Militancy in India 1978–1993* (New Delhi: Penguin Books, 2006), 166–167.

5 Partha Nath Mukherji, 'The Farmers' Movement in Punjab: Politics of Pressure Groups and Pressure of Party Politics', *EPW* 33, no. 18 (May 2–8, 1998): 1047, 1048, footnote 5.

6 K. R. Krishna Gandhi, 'The New Peasant Movement in Punjab', in *Peasant Movement in Modern India*, ed. Sunil Sahasrabudhey (Allahabad: Chugh Publications, 1989), 66–67.

7 Sucha Singh Gill, 'Development Crisis in Agriculture and its Political Implications – An Enquiry into the Punjab Problem', in *Political Dynamics*

and Crisis in Punjab, eds. Paul Wallace and Surendra Chopra (Amritsar: Guru Nanak Dev University, 1988), 449.

8 Gill and Singhal, 'Farmers' Agitation: Response to Development Crisis of Agriculture', 1732.

9 Kehar Singh, *Farmers' Movement and Pressure Group Politics* (New Delhi: Deep and Deep Publications, 1990), 51–52.

10 Aditya Menon, 'Khalistanis have Infiltrated Farmers' Protest, says Modi Government', *The Quint*, January 12, 2021. Some leaders of the recent protests have also criticized those whom they call Khalistanis for disrupting the protests. Yet, Ruldu Singh Mansa, leader of Punjab BKU, was suspended for 15 days for criticizing Khalistanis and indirectly, Jarnail S. Bhindranwale. Ugrahan also called out groups within the 32 Unions who are dishonest and draw on 'Khalistani money and power', Sukhmeet Bhasin, 'Fissures in farm unions over Parliament march', *Tribune News Service*, April 27, 2021. So, this interface of the legacy and meaning of Khalistan and Bhindranwale with the farmers' agitation is complex.

11 Pritam Singh, 'Growing Separatists Trend', *EPW*, 19, no. 5 (February 4, 1984): 196.

12 Brass asks in a footnote in his very important essay on the Punjab crisis, which focused largely on Centre-State relations, state-level resistance to centralization, and the personalization of politics by Indira Gandhi, whether perhaps all of this emphasis on politics misses the point. 'It is possible', he suggests, that what he termed the 'Punjab Crisis' was really at its core a reaction to green revolution inspired class changes, the results of which were exacerbated by the creation of a ready supply of educated young men for whom no white-collar jobs existed. Paul R. Brass, 'The Punjab Crisis and the Unity of India', in *India's Democracy: An Analysis of Changing State-Society Relations*, ed. Atul Kohli (Princeton, NJ: Princeton University Press, 1988), 172, footnote 2.

13 See Prateek Waghre for a discussion of media coverage, particularly social media coverage, of the on-going farmers' protests. 'Radically Networked Societies: The case of the farmers' protests in India', *Indian Public Policy Review* 2, no. 3 (2021): 41–64.

14 David Featherstone, 'Thinking Militant Particularisms Politically: Resistances to Neoliberalism in India', in *India's New Economic Policy: A Critical Analysis*, ed. Waquar Ahmed, et al. (Routledge, 2010, 1st edition).

15 Jaffrelot and Verniers refer to it as a '*de jure* ethnic democracy'; Christophe Jaffrelot and Gilles Verniers, 'A New Party System or a New Political System?', *Contemporary South Asia*, 28, no. (2020): 141–154.

16 Vibha Singh, 'Battleground UP: Amit Shah's invitation to RLD aimed at isolating Jats, say Akhilesh Yadav, Jayant Chaudhary', *Tribune News Service,* January 28, 2022. https://www.tribuneindia.com/news/nation/battleground-up-akhilesh-yadav-jayant-chaudhary-preset-united-front-says-shas-invitation-to-rld-aimed-at-isolating-jats-365025 (Accessed February, 2021). Former BJP President and current in-charge of the Assembly elections in UP, Amit Singh, is appealing to the Jats as allies in the battle with the Mughals (Muslims).

17 Kehar Singh, 'Farmers' Movements and Pressure Group Politics', 36–39.

18 Ashutosh Kumar, 'Shiromani Akali Dal (1920–2020): Ideology, Strategy, and Support Base', *Sikh Formations* 17, Issue 1–2 (2021). doi: 10.1080/17448727.2021.1873654.

19 Jonathan Pattenden and Gaurav Bansal, 'A New Class Alliance in the Indian Countryside? From New Farmers' Movements to the 2020 Protest Wave', *EPW*, 56, no. 26–27 (June 26, 2021).

20 Sinha, Shreya. 'TIF-The Agrarian Crisis in Punjab and the Making of the Anti-Farm Protests', *The India Forum* (December 4, 2020): 3–5.

21 David Featherstone, 'Thinking Militant Particularisms Politically', 263–264.
22 *Ibid.*, 265.
23 *Ibid.*, 264.
24 Gill and Singhal cite one specific example in 1979 when the then BKU President Kadian threatened violence against agricultural workers who were agitating for higher wages. Gill and Singhal, 'Farmers' Agitation', 1732.
25 *Ibid.* Mary Anne Weaver, 'Sikhs and Hindus in Punjab show rare unity', *Christian Science Monitor*, May 30, 1984.
26 "We are One': Why Punjab's Landless Dalits are Standing with Protesting Farmers', *The Wire*, January 7, 2021; Aditya Bahl, 'A New Border in an Old Republic', *Himal Southasian*, April 28, 2021.
27 Gill and Singhal, 'Farmers' Agitation', 1728.
28 Sucha Singh Gill, 'Agrarian Change in the Green Revolution Belt', in *New Farmers' Unions in India*, ed. Tom Brass (Great Britain: Frank Cass & Co. Ltd, 1995), 202.
29 Gill and Singhal, 'Farmers' Agitations', 1732.
30 Partha Nath Mukherji, 'The Farmers' Movement in Punjab', 1047.
31 Partha Nath Mukherji, 'The Farmers' Movement in Punjab', 1048, footnote 3.
32 Personal communication.
33 K. R. Krishna Gandhi, 'The New Peasant Movement in Punjab', 58–59.
34 Kehar Singh, 'Farmers' Movement and Pressure Group Politics', 36.
35 Zoya Hasan, 'Self-Serving Guardians: Formation and Strategy of the Bhartiya Kisan Union', *EPW*, December 2, 1989, Vol. 24, No. 48, p. 2664.
36 Singh, *Farmers' Movement and Pressure Group Politics*, 84–85.
37 Gill and Singhal, 'Farmers' Agitation', 1731.
38 Gandhi, 'The New Peasant Movement in Punjab', 68.
39 The document can be found in Kehar Singh, *Farmers' Movement and Pressure Group Politics* (New Delhi: Deep and Deep Publications, 1990), 25–27.
40 Kandall Balagopal, 'Rich Peasant, Poor Peasant', *Seminar*, Issue No, 352, *Farmer Power*, December 1988, 23.
41 Paul R. Brass, *An Indian Political Life: Charan Singh and Congress Politics, 1937–1961* (New Delhi: Sage Publications India Pvt Ltd, 2011), 123.
42 Gill and Singhal, 'Farmers' Agitation: Response to Development Crisis of Agriculture', 1729.
43 Singh, 'Farmers' Movement and Pressure Group Politics', 63.
44 Sucha Singh Gill, 'The Farmers' Movement and Agrarian Change in the Green Revolution Belt of North-west India', in *New Farmers' Movements in India*, ed. Tom Brass (Portland and Essex: Frank Cass & Co. Ltd., 1995), 205.
45 With regards to the Jammu and Kashmir Reorganization Act, the BJP had campaigned for years on abolishing Article 370 which gave a separate status to Jammu and Kashmir as India's only Muslim majority state and one which represented an on-going bleeding wound between India and Pakistan. It appeared to be just campaign rhetoric and too drastic to be implemented, but along with building the Ram Mandir in Ayodhya, policies and undertakings that did not seem possible are coming to pass.
46 And much less resistance to demonetization which pauperized whole segments of the society.
47 Sourav Roy Barman and Anju Agnihotri Chaba, 'Ugrahan wears his politics on his sleeve: 'Called us Pak, now Naxals', *The Indian Express*, December 13, 2020.
48 Raaki Jagga, '2 Punjab unions suspended from united front of 32 unions, barred from stage', *The Indian Express*, February 7, 2021.
49 Sucha Singh Gill, 'Farmers' Movement: Continuity and Change', *EPW*, (July 3, 2004): 2964–2965.

50 Gill, 'Agrarian Change in the Green Revolution Belt', 202–203.
51 See Mukherji for a description of the nature of the split, based apparently on interviews with those involved. Partha Nath Mukherji, 'The Farmers' Movement in Punjab', 1047.
52 *Ibid.*
53 Gill and Singhal, 'Farmer's Agitation: Response to Development Crisis of Agriculture', 1732.
54 Aditya Bahl, 'A New Border in an Old Republic', *Himal Southasian*, April 28, 2021.
55 Pattenden and Bansal, 'A New Class Alliance in the Indian Countryside?'
56 Narendra Pani, 'Farm Bills and the PDS Conundrum', *The Hindu Business Line*, November 3, 2020.
57 'For some months, we earn daily wages of Rs. 300–400 by harvesting other people's crops. Big commercial agro-firms will acquire farms and they will not hire us.' Quote from Mazabhi Sikh landless cultivator Gurmail Singh. Quoted in Anumeha Yadav, 'Why landless and marginal farmers are the backbone of farmer protests', *Newslaundry*, December 4, 2020.
58 *Ibid.*
59 Pramod Kumar, 'The farmers' protest began a year ago. How has it lasted this long?', *The Indian Express*, June 23, 2021.
60 Shreya Sinha, 'TIF-The Agrarian Crisis in Punjab', 4.
61 Pukhraj Singh, 'The Farm Law Protests Could Whitewash the Blatant Inequality of Rural Punjab', *The Wire*, December 5, 2020.
62 Sandeep Singh, '"We are One": Why Punjab's Landless Dalits are Standing with Protesting Farmers', *The Wire*, January 7, 2021.
63 Prabhjit Singh, 'In the farm laws protest, are Punjab's landless peasants getting left behind?', *Caravan Magazine*, March 22, 2021.
64 Kandall Balagopal, 'Rich Peasant, Poor Peasant', 19.
65 Asim Ali, 'Farmers' protest shows Modi's politics is caught between India's two middle classes', *The Print*, December 9, 2020.
66 Amit Shah, former BJP President and in-charge of the party election strategy in UP, gave the game away by arguing that anger over the farmers' laws would not hurt the BJP in the elections as they had been withdrawn and all was forgotten.
67 Prabhjit Singh, 'Jubilation at Singhu border as farmers celebrate BJP's defeat in West Bengal elections', *Caravan Magazine*, May 3, 2021.
68 Arunabh Saikia, 'Punjab ground report: Six months on, farm protest remains strong – and united. Where is it headed?', *Scroll.in*, February 25, 2021.
69 Shankar Arnimesh, 'Not just farm laws – sugarcane price & delayed payments also causing anger in western UP', *The Print*, February 7, 2021.

Part II

Dimensions and Dynamics of Reform, Resistance and Resilience

6 Farm Laws, Federalism and Farm Protests

Challenges for Punjab*

Pritam Singh

Introduction

> There seem to be but three ways for a nation to acquire wealth. The first is by war...This is robbery. The second by commerce, which is generally cheating. The third by agriculture, the only honest way, wherein man receives a real increase of the seed thrown into the ground, in a kind of continual miracle, wrought by the hand of God in his favor, as a reward for his innocent life and his virtuous industry.
>
> (Benjamin Franklin cited by Sova, 2018)

India's farm protests against the Indian government's agrarian policy enshrined in the 2000 farm laws brought federalism to the centre of policy debates on India's governance, and the vanguard role played by Punjabi farmers in these protests attracted national attention to the potential of Punjab in reshaping a federal future for India with a focus on agriculture in that imagined future. The three farm laws that constituted the core of the BJP government's agrarian policy provoked the largest, longest and most peaceful farmers' protests in human history. In terms of the scale of mass mobilization in India and international solidarity these protests had generated, they surpassed even India's struggle for independence.[1] Within India, the solidarity of the non-farming sectors of the population with the farmers' protest had two sources: first, the hope created by the protest as a robust and so far, successful democratic fightback against the BJP government's authoritarian mode of governance, which has been used successfully to silence all previous forms of resistance; and second, the sympathy of vast sections of India's population with the farmers, who in the popular imagination are seen as providers of food. The word *andaata* used to characterize farmers (meaning producers and providers of food) is common to many languages in India and evokes responses of respect and admiration for those who, working hard with mother earth in all weathers, continue to provide sustenance not only for their own families but also for all of society. International solidarity with the protests also had two sources: first, the perception of the movement as demonstrating the democratic vitality

DOI: 10.4324/9781003320005-9

of India – a vast 'Third World' country which has retained the important institutions of democratic governance despite massive distortions; and secondly, the perception of the movement as providing a new vision of 'development'. This new vision (eco-socialism or green socialism) gives primacy to small-scale and cooperative farming, in opposition to the vision of large-scale agrobusiness farming that has shaped capitalist policy in richer and poorer countries alike. This new vision is also critical of the attempts to create a 'socialist' alternative to capitalism, as practiced by the USSR, which focused on large-scale, collectivized farming, with the resulting destruction of small farms.[2] We discuss this new vision in some detail in the last section of the chapter.

As a marker of the BJP government's major policy initiative on agricultural governance, these laws represented the most forceful central onslaught on state's federal rights in agriculture in post-Independent India. The government brought in three Ordinances on June 5, 2020, in the name of agricultural marketing reforms and farmer welfare. All three were given hurried Parliamentary and Presidential approval, with neither stakeholder consultation nor proper parliamentary scrutiny, before becoming law in September 2020 (Singh et al., 2021).[3] These Ordinances were the following: the Farmers' (Empowerment and Protection) Agreement on Price Assurance and Farm Services Ordinance, 2020; the Farmers' Produce Trade and Commerce (Promotion and Facilitation) Ordinance, 2020; and the Essential Commodities (Amendment) Ordinance, 2020.

The farming policy of the present government as articulated through these Ordinances constituted a watershed moment in the development of the government's drive to combine the expansion of agrobusiness capitalism and increased centralized control of agriculture in India in an integrated agenda. Opposition to this integrated agenda emerged from three groups: first, from the farmers' organizations, who were fearful about the survival of their communities as a result of the takeover of the farming sector by agrobusiness corporations; second, from state governments, who were concerned about central intrusion into states' federal rights over agriculture; and third, from regional parties who suspected that these laws would further empower the government's many aggressive assaults against regional identities and aspirations. The theme of centralization versus decentralization, albeit with different nuances and varying degrees of emphasis, runs through all three strands of opposition to the farm laws. Agrobusiness corporations view centralized governance as more conducive to their interests, and the dominance of a few agro-business conglomerates facilitates centralized governance, and the combined power of the two poses existential threat to regional identities and decentralized forms of governance.

The haste with which first the Ordinances and later the Bills were rushed through provide a reasonable clue to the government's economic and political agenda.[4] There was no food emergency in the country that required that the government should act with such haste. It can be inferred, therefore, that agrobusiness interests that fund and support the BJP must have impressed upon the government the importance of using the health emergency created by COVID-19 to have these ordinances approved quickly, without attracting attention or criticism. Naomi Klein's thesis of 'Shock Doctrine', according to which governments use moments of deep crisis – economic, political or environmental – to push through controversial legislation, fits in very well with the BJP government's use of the health crisis to approve these farm laws (Klein, 2007).[5] The government, it seems, had not anticipated the scale of opposition that these measures have provoked.

Farmers' Protests against the Agrobusiness Takeover of Indian Agriculture

The central objective behind the two Bills – the Farming Produce Trade and Commerce (Promotion and Facilitation) Bill, 2020 and the Farmers' (Empowerment and Protection) Agreement on Price Assurance and Farm Services Bill, 2020 – was to encourage private investment by agrobusiness corporations, based at home and abroad, in the production, processing, storage, transportation and marketing of agricultural products both within India and overseas. For some time, there has been lobbying for foreign direct investment (FDI) into Indian agriculture by multinational agrobusiness corporations and for neo-liberal reforms in agriculture. There is already a degree of FDI in Indian agriculture, especially in contract farming for some products, but these legislations opened the way for a major increase in FDI and implementation of neo-liberal reforms in agriculture. Agricultural marketing reforms were, therefore, crucial components of these laws. One key government policy advisor viewed the laws as 'forwarding the unfinished agenda of reforms started in 1991 and the fragmented, piecemeal and patchy reforms undertaken across states to their ultimate culmination' (Chand, 2020: 3). Initiatives by the Indian government and by agrobusiness corporate interests aiming to minimize the role of the public sector and to promote privatization in the agricultural market are not new (Chadda et al., 2008; Mandal, 2020). A 2015 government report (Shanta Kumar Committee Report) named the 'Report of the High-Level Committee on Reorienting the Role and Restructuring of Food Corporation of India' hints at the dispensability of the state-regulated Public Procurement System (PPS) and Minimum Support Price (MSP) (Government of India, 2015). Balbir Singh Rajewal, the most prominent, articulate and well-informed leader of the farmers' protest, has mentioned in several publicly available lectures that he was invited to attend a Niti Aayog meeting in 2017 as one of three representatives of Indian farmers. At this meeting, a blueprint for pro-agrobusiness reforms was openly proposed. Rajewal had opposed this blueprint. In his words,

> In a Niti Aayog meeting in Delhi on 10 October 2017, the whole discussion was about agricultural reforms aimed at creating clusters of

> farms of the size of 5000 and 7000 acres which would be given on 50 years lease contracts to private corporate businesses. The initial idea of organising farmers' protests to oppose this proposal came to my mind in that meeting.
>
> (Rajewal, 2021, translation from the original Punjabi by the author)[6]

The government defended these initiatives by claiming that they were aimed at increasing the choice and freedom of the farmers to sell beyond local *mandis*, i.e. notified APMC (agricultural produce market committee) marketing yards and beyond state boundaries. The aim of the government's massive media campaign was to make its policy acceptable to the farming community. The massive farm protests demonstrated that the farming community had seen through the media campaign, and the farmers' successful counter-narrative had made it known very widely that it is the large agro-business corporations who will benefit from this freedom – both within India and abroad. The worst affected would be the marginal, small and medium farmers whose ability to bargain for pricing and contracts would be so inconsequential against the huge resources of the large corporations, that such farmers would end up economic slaves.

The Farming Produce Trade and Commerce (Promotion and Facilitation) Bill, 2020 covered wheat, rice, sugarcane and cotton, along with other products. These are the major agricultural products of Punjab and Haryana, the two major food-producing states. The mechanism for 'Dispute Resolution' between a farmer and a trader, as stipulated in the Bill, was heavily loaded against the farmer due to the unequal power relations which, in reality, exist between farmers and traders. This is particularly the case if the farmer is marginal, small or medium and the trader is a large agrobusiness corporation. There was a provision in the legislation that the dispute could be taken through various stages of the administrative/legal process starting with the sub-divisional magistrate. This provision overlooked that a dissatisfied farmer with limited resources, knowledge and time would not dare challenge the legal prowess of a powerful corporate entity. The penalty stipulated in the Bill, if a legal challenge in a dispute fails and the contract is judged to have been contravened, would also make any farmer extremely fearful about challenging a powerful corporation. Depending upon the nature of contravention of a contract, the penalty could be anywhere between 25,000 to 10 *lakh* rupees. If the contravention continued, a further penalty of between 5,000 rupees and 10,000 rupees per day could be imposed. Even a big farmer would fear such massive penalties and would not dare to mount a legal challenge.

There was no provision in the Bills for the continuity of the MSP, which is mainly relevant for wheat and rice – the two major food crops – grown in Punjab and Haryana and, to a lesser extent, in other states such as UP, Uttarakhand and Rajasthan. The Farmers (Empowerment and Protection) Agreement on Price Assurance and Farm Services Bill, 2020, instead of stipulating the MSP, merely mentions a 'remunerative price' to be contractually agreed between a farmer and 'agrobusiness firms, processors, wholesalers, exporters and large retailers'. Such a contract must also specify the 'quality, grade and standard' of the product to be sold by the farmer. The wording of the provision for changing or terminating the agreement raised more concerns about farmers' vulnerability. Section 11 of the Act stated: 'At any time after entering into a farming agreement, the parties to such agreement may, with mutual consent, alter or terminate such agreement for any reasonable cause'. Given the unequal power relations between a farmer and an agrobusiness firm, the consent of the farmer to changing or terminating a contract can be subject to powerful economic and non-economic pressures. The mechanism for dispute resolution on the contract regarding price and quality of the produce was also loaded against the farmer.

Once it became publicly known that the MSP may be abandoned, fears were expressed that outright removing of the MSP for wheat and rice, apart from alienating the farming communities in the wheat and rice producing states, might jeopardize government procurement targets which can then lead to regional food insecurity and resulting social unrest. Many government spokespersons attempted damage limitation by making announcements that the MSP would be continued. Even if those announcements could be trusted and the MSP was temporarily retained for strategic reasons, the fear was that the MSP would be used for paying the farmers only to the extent that it ensured the fulfilment of procurement targets decided by the government.[7] Once those targets were achieved, it was feared that there would be no need for the government to purchase more. After that, the farmers would lose their support structure and become vulnerable to market fluctuations which would push prices of their products down due to excess supply.

It was not beyond the realms of possibility that for the first couple of years, the Central government could encourage and incentivize big agrobusiness traders to offer higher prices to the farmers than the ones available in the APMC market yards. Once the APMC trading structures are destroyed through this rigged competition, it was feared that the farmers would be completely at the mercy of the big traders who would exploit their new vulnerability. It was this fear that had led to the two key demands of the protesting farmers: first, that the three laws be repealed and, second, that the MSP for procuring farmers' produce be made a legal right.

My reading of the government's many initiatives in the agricultural sphere, including those in the now repealed farm laws, is that their aim was to weaken the economic sustainability of the marginal, small and medium farmers so that they are forced to sell their lands to large agrobusiness corporations, either domestic or foreign owned. Farmers dispossessed of their tiny holdings will turn into wage labourers. The excess supply of such labourers in the rural economy and through economically forced migration towards the urban economy will push down wage rates and lead to increased profits for agrarian and urban capitalist enterprises. This was seen as the hidden meaning of the phrase 'transformation of agriculture' used in promoting the initiative underlying the farm laws (Singh, 2020c).

Farmers' resistance to these farming laws and the scale of the solidarity this resistance had received from a variety of social groups was demonstrated most impressively through the massively successful *Bharat Bandh* on September 25, 2020. This resistance and solidarity turned out to be the biggest political challenge the BJP has faced since coming to power for the second time in 2019.

States' Resistance against Central Intrusion into Their Federal Rights in Agriculture

From the very framing of India's Constitution in 1949 to various amendments later made to it, there has been a continuous process of invasion by the Centre into the sphere of agriculture, which in the constitution was designated as a subject to be controlled by the states. The Essential Commodities (Amendment) Ordinance 2020 took this process much further and was certainly the most devastating attack so far on the federal agricultural rights of the states. The 'One India, One Agriculture Market' slogan used by the government in promoting the laws clearly exposed the drive towards centralization implicit in the move.

There is a widespread misconception among academic and journalistic writings on the Indian political economy in general and on these latest agrarian initiatives from the Centre in particular, that the weakening of the government's regulatory regime giving more prominence to privatization, as envisaged in these deregulatory reforms, would lead to decentralization and devolution of more powers to the states (for a critical review of such writings, see Singh 2007). The roots of this misconception can be traced to a failure to recognize that the key to the shaping of India's capitalist economy has been centralized/unitarist nationalism as opposed to plural nationalisms and that the Centre has been given vast powers to build such unitarist nationalism. As a result, increasing privatization resulting from deregulatory reforms does not necessarily work against centralization.[8] The Essential Commodities (Amendment) Ordinance 2020 was the most clear-cut confirmation of the thesis that centralization and privatization in India can co-exist and, moreover, that they can reinforce each other especially if the logic of that privatization leads to strengthening the power of key business conglomerates. Strengthening centralization and privatization were, therefore, the two most prominent and inter-connected features of this proposed legislation.

The Seventh Schedule of the Indian Constitution contains three lists. List I refers to the departments/activities/subjects under control of the Centre/ Union; List II refers to those under control of the states; and List III (or the Concurrent List) refers to cases where the states and the Centre share power and responsibility. Entry 14 of the State List refers to agriculture: 'Agriculture, including agricultural education and research, protection against pests and prevention of plant disease'. If we were to deduce from this that agriculture is a state subject under the Constitution, that would be formally correct. However, other provisions of the Constitution in the Centre/Union List and in the Concurrent List have provided legal justifications for Central interventions in the sphere of agriculture. In general, national goals and imperatives are invoked in order to use these Union and Concurrent List provisions. In some cases, Central intrusions into agriculture have been made without any constitutional sanction at all. The states can be constitutionally deprived of all powers, including in the sphere of agriculture, under provisions mentioned in Part XI of the Constitution, which discusses 'relations between the Union and the states'.

Under Article 248 in Part XI, the Centre has residuary powers of legislation relating to any item which is not mentioned in any of the three lists. Under Article 249, the Central Parliament has the power of legislation regarding any subject, even in the State List, if the Centre considers this to be necessary 'in the national interest'. There is no similar provision in the Constitution of any other federal country. Even the 1935 Act made during British Rule in India – whose format was the basis for drafting the Constitution of independent India – did not have a clause giving such overriding powers to the Centre.

Entry 33 in the Concurrent List limits the power of states in agriculture and empowers the Centre by stating that both the state and the Union government can legislate regarding production, trade, supply and distribution of a range of foodstuffs and agricultural raw materials. The Sarkaria Commission on Centre-State Relations had pointed out that the Centre had used Entry 33 in the Concurrent List to enact in the Parliament the Essential Commodities Act, 1955. This Act had disproportionately empowered the Centre in the management of agriculture, and it was the 2020 Amendment of this Act that was now being brought in to further increase the powers of the Centre in the agricultural sector.

Entry 34 in the Concurrent List mentions 'price control', once more giving scope for the Centre to impose control over agriculture and invade the powers of the states. The Government of Tamil Nadu recognized that Entries 33 and 34 in the Concurrent List had a damaging impact on state autonomy in the sphere of agriculture, and in its memorandum to the Sarkaria Commission, it demanded that Entries 33 and 34 are transferred from the Concurrent List to the State List. West Bengal's Left Front government led by Jyoti Basu went even further in demanding in its memorandum that not only the existing entries in the Concurrent List but also those in the Union List that constrict the states' jurisdiction in agriculture should be deleted and that 'agriculture, including animal husbandry, forestry and fisheries, should be exclusively a states' subject...The recent trend, with the Centre progressively encroaching in the sphere of agriculture, must be reversed'.[9] What was happening, through the 2020 Amendment of the Essential Commodities Act 1955, was not only the opposite of what Tamil Nadu and West Bengal had rightfully demanded but, in fact, would have increased the power of the Centre yet more.

The manner in which the Amendment was pushed forward using Ordinances was also extraordinary. Indira Gandhi used the Emergency (1975–1977) to make harmful amendments that curtailed the power of the states over education and forestry. This government was using the health emergency caused by COVID-19 to push this amendment through – using Ordinances – to cause devastating damage to the powers of the states in the sphere of agriculture. The scale of the threat posed by this proposed legislation to the states' already limited autonomy can be understood from these words:

> The Central Government may, for carrying out the provisions of this Ordinance, give such instructions, directions, orders or issue guidelines as it may deem necessary to any authority or officer subordinate to the Central Government, any State Government or any authority or officer subordinate to a State Government.
>
> (Section 12 of the Farmers' Produce Trade and Commerce (Promotion and Facilitation) Bill, 2020)

This alarm bell about the emasculation of powers of the states by federal powers could only be ignored if state leaders had a very limited vision of politics.

The undermining of autonomy of the states cannot be more starkly implied than in the words in Section 16 of the *Farmers (Empowerment and Protection) Agreement on Price Assurance and Farm Services Act*, 2020:

> The Central Government may, from time to time, give such instructions, as it may consider necessary, to the State Governments for effective implementation of the provisions of this Act and *the State Governments shall comply with such instructions*. (italics added)

Thus, no scope was left for any escape for a state government from these Central directives.[10]

The Ordinance's attack on the limited revenue resources of the states was also clear in the provision that 'no market fee, cess or levy' could be levied by a State APMC Act or any other state law on the agricultural market transactions taking place outside the APMC marketing yard. After depriving the states of the sales tax revenue they earned earlier and replacing it by a centrally controlled GST, and then resisting paying compensation to the states for this loss of revenue, indicates another clear attempt to weaken the states financially and make them more dependent on the Centre.[11]

Aside from the vertical tensions between the Centre and the states caused by the agrarian reforms associated with the now repealed farm laws, the reforms had the potential to generate new, horizontal tensions between states and class conflicts aligned with inter-state tensions. Agriculturally dependent states such as Punjab and Haryana, and the farmers of those states, would be the most adversely affected due to the weakening of the MSP structures. In contrast, industrially advanced states such as Gujarat and Maharashtra and the big business interests (especially agrobusiness interests) based in these states would be beneficiaries as a result of increased and easier access to foodstuffs and agricultural raw materials from other states. This would have increased regional and class tensions. Such tensions always lead to justifying stronger central powers to manage these tensions.

The MSP was already a centrally governed policy instrument designed to shape the cropping pattern of Punjab, and to a lesser extent of Haryana, towards two principal food crops. This instrument was used to incentivize farmers to grow and market wheat and rice to overcome food scarcity and dependence on PL 480 food aid from the USA (Singh, 2008). Having achieved national food self-sufficiency through the Green Revolution that ravaged the ecology of Punjab and Haryana, the Centre was on the brink of causing economic and social ruin for the peasantry in these two states through the project envisaged under the repealed farm laws. The Centre should, instead, be rewarding and compensating these two states for the damage the Green Revolution had caused to their ecological resources and health of the people. Though the farmers in other states of India are not as directly reliant on the MSP system as are the farmers of Punjab and Haryana, and to a lesser extent the farmers of UP, Uttarakhand and Rajasthan, they are still apprehensive about the takeover of agriculture by corporate agrobusinesses. Additionally, there has been increased awareness among farmers of other states where the MSP system did not operate about the existence and operation of the MSP system. They had therefore demonstrated visible support to the farmers' organizations protesting on the borders of Delhi.

Together with Tamil Nadu, West Bengal and Jammu & Kashmir, Punjab has a proud history as part of the vanguard of the movement for greater federal devolution of powers to the states. Sardar Parkash Singh Badal, the former Chief Minister of Punjab once emphasized his commitment to federalism by stating that the Anandpur Sahib Resolution is the past, present and future of Akali Dal politics[12] but unfortunately, Akali Dal was uncertain whether to support or oppose these laws. At first, it supported the laws because of its political partnership with the BJP, but then, faced with wholehearted opposition from Punjab's farming community and pressure from rank and file of the party, the representative of Akali Dal in the BJP-led NDA government, Harsimrat Kaur Badal, was forced to resign her Ministership. Captain Amarinder Singh, the Chief Minister of Punjab till recently before being replaced by Charanjit Singh Channi as the new choice for the post by his party's central leadership, had written an excellent English translation of the historic Anandpur Sahib Resolution, along with an introductory note for the entry on the Resolution in the *Encyclopaedia of Sikhism* edited by the late Professor Harbans Singh (Amarinder Singh, 1992). His endorsement of the Resolution is complete as there is not even a word of criticism by Amarinder Singh. Every entry in the *Encyclopaedia* is a document of lasting importance, and it is a sign of the intellectual, political and moral weakness of most Punjabi politicians that Amarinder Singh has now been criticizing the Anandpur Sahib Resolution. Amarinder Singh has further weakened his pro-federal credentials by his recent launch of Punjab Lok Congress with which he hitched an alliance for the 2022 Punjab Assembly Elections with the anti-federalism BJP (Singh, 2021f, 2021h). The late Harkishan Singh Surjeet, the CPM leader, once made an important contribution to strengthening the wording relating to the federal dimensions of the Anandpur Sahib Resolution though unfortunately he later moved more towards unitarist/centralist nationalism.[13] Punjab's political leaders, intellectuals, opinion makers and social activists need to recover the moral and intellectual strengths to again become vanguards in the struggle for federalism in India. The struggle for federalism and diversity is also the struggle for democracy. The weakening of federalism contributes to the concentration of economic and political power at the Centre and the rise of authoritarian political tendencies and practices.

Regional Aspirations/Identities against Hindutva Centralism

The increased central intrusion through these Acts into the federal agricultural rights of the states had alarmed all the states, though the BJP-ruled states had either remained silent or endorsed the central government's moves. The increasing centralization is viewed by regional groups as a threat to the solidity of regional interests, aspirations and identities. The troubled relations with Shiv Sena and Akali Dal, two of the oldest allies of the BJP, are manifestations in different ways of the tension between the ideological perspectives of centralist Hindutva and of the regions (Singh, 2020b). The tension over the farm Acts led to resignation of the Akali Dal representative Harsimrat Kaur Badal from the Union Cabinet; this was the first resignation ever from a BJP-led government at the Centre over a policy issue. The BJP-controlled coalition government in Haryana, with its regional ally in Dushyant Chautala's Jannayak Janata Party, remained under constant tension, because the deputy chief minister Chautala was being forced by farming organizations to support their campaigns against the farm laws.

Though different in many other respects, the BJP and Congress are both centralist in their political goal of building a single unified Indian national identity. Therefore, both are opposed to the articulation of regional identities. The Congress's distrust of regional identities was guided by the Nehruvian project of building one unified Indian nationhood after India gained freedom from British Rule (Chandra et al., 2007). It was partly this project which was responsible for not acceding to the Muslim League demand for regional devolution of powers as outlined in the Cabinet Mission proposals. It was rejection of the Muslim League demand and Cabinet Mission proposals by the Congress leadership led by Nehru which eventually led to the partition of India (Jalal, 1985). Nehru was also a strong believer in central planning as a strategy for capitalist industrialization of India and this led him to push for centralization (Desai, 1959, 1975, 1984, 2004; Bettelheim, 1968; Chakravarty, 1989). Additionally, central planning in the Nehruvian strategy was not merely an economic project; it was also seen as a political project to unify the nation by using central planning to reduce inter-regional disparities through regulation and allocation of centrally-controlled public sector investment in different regions (Singh, 2008). The Nehruvian project was ostensibly 'secular' in character but the fact that Hindu majoritarianism was structural, it had the consequence of entrenching Hindu majoritarian bias in Indian institutions (Singh, 2015; Rehman, 2016; Mohapatra, 2017; Deshpande and Palshikar, 2019). Nehruvian centralization, wedded to strong Indian nationalism, created crucially the conducive ideological, cultural and institutional space for the emergence of Hindu version of strong Indian nationalism.

Despite the continuity and similarity provided by shared centralism between Nehruvian Congress perspective on Indian nationalism and Hindutva nationalism, the crucial difference between Nehruvian Congress-inspired nationalism and BJP–RSS-inspired nationalism is that the latter is explicit in its ideological commitment to build Hindu India. This ideological adherence to build unified Hindu India leads to BJP showing a much more aggressive approach than the Congress towards centralization. Its propagation of 'One India, One Agriculture Market' in defence of its farming policies articulated through the farm acts, the aggressive promotion of Hindi over regional languages (far more than the Congress ever did during its reign), its decision to scrap Jammu and Kashmir's constitutional status and statehood, and its New Education Policy are some of the key indicators of the BJP's aggressive centralization agenda. In October 2021, the central BJP government extended the powers of Border Security Force beyond the initial 15 km limit from the international border to 50 km limit (Jagat, 2021). More recently, this government amended the service rules of India's civil service cadre to further strengthen the central government control over that cadre (Menon, 2022) The significance of these measures, along with the farm laws, must be seen as links in the same chain of aggressive centralization agenda being pursued by the current BJP regime.

The BJP sees the emergence of regional nationalist identities such as Tamil identity and Bengali identity, to name just two regional identities in the states which have Hindu religious majority but strong history of opposition to Hindu/Hindi identity, as obstacles to the emergence of transregional Hindu identity in India. Conversely, the more articulate proponents of regional identities such as the anti-caste Tamil thinker and politician Periyar E.V. Ramasamy viewed regions as spaces of 'counter-hegemonic force' against Brahmanical Hinduism (Dhanda, 2021). Just as the BJP views regional identities with suspicion – as a subversion of its agenda to create an overarching Hindu identity – the regions suspect the BJP vision to be one aimed at the annihilation of regional identities. The tension between the states – the locations of different regional identities – and the Centre over the farm acts has contributed to heightening regional fears about the BJP's unitarist Hindutva agenda.

The Left in India, especially the parliamentary Left represented by CPI and CPM, is increasingly oriented towards centralized nationalism and has surrendered to the flawed discourse of 'unity and integrity of the country' (Singh, 2002). As a result, it has not been able to capture the progressive potentialities of regional nationalisms in India especially in opposition to centralized Hindu nationalism (Singh, 2008a, 2009). However, two developments are now slowly making the Left rethink about its perspective on regional identity. One relates to the involvement of the Left-oriented farmers and agricultural labour organizations in the recent farmers protests against the farm laws. This involvement has brought them in contact with many farmers' organizations from Punjab which have articulated strong positions on the farm laws as attacks on the federal rights of the states in agriculture. The second relates to the dynamic of the politics in Bengal where the Left has been strong for many decades but has now been reduced to an opposition status with the strong emergence of the regionally based party All India Trinamool Congress (popularly known as TMC) led by Mamata Banerjee, the current chief minister of Bengal. In the recently concluded assembly elections in Bengal, Mamata Banerjee, by articulating the aspirations of Bengali regional identity against the Hindu identity that was vociferously projected by the BJP during the election campaign, was able to convincingly defeat BJP. The farmers' organizations had actively campaigned against the BJP in this election, and the active role played by Punjab-based organizations during the campaign against the BJP seems to have played a decisive role in shaping the election results in constituencies with substantial numbers of Sikh voters.

The farmers' movement has played a critical catalyst role in drawing attention to the anti-federal and anti-regional implications of the farm laws and Hindutva centralism. It was this combined force of the farmers' movement and regional identities which forced Prime Minister Modi to eventually concede defeat on November 19, 2021, on its centralist agenda articulated through the farm laws.

The Ecological Dimensions of the Farm Laws and Centralized/Corporate Agriculture

We have discussed the three main nodes of resistance (farmers, states and regional identities) to the BJP government's farm laws, and all these nodes have shown one common concern; namely, the weakening of the states' federal agricultural rights through an increasingly centralized agrobusiness restructuring of Indian agriculture. Nevertheless, it is important to mention, even if briefly, the ecologically damaging fallout and the anti-federal implications of that ecological damage if these laws had been put into operation. These two inter-connected dimensions of destruction of ecology and the weakening of federalism have remained almost completely unexamined in the current debates on this issue.[14] The destruction of locally and state-based agriculture and its incorporation into all-India and global agricultural marketing systems would have led to increased transportation. An increase in transportation everywhere leads to an increase in carbon emissions, pollution, ecological destruction and damage to the health of all living beings, human and non-human. It is the antithesis of the 'self-reliance' (*Aatmanirbharta*) which the BJP government has been falsely proclaiming as its aim.

There is also a need to start rethinking the wider importance of agriculture in the 'development' discourse. Both traditional right-wing thinking (such as Rostow's stages of growth or Lewis' dual economy model) as well as dominant left-wing thinking (Stalin's collectivization is an extreme strain) view development and growth as a path of moving from agriculture to industry to services. In the era of global climate change, where the planet earth faces an existential threat from global heating and loss of biodiversity resulting from traditional economic growth paths, whether of the traditional right or the traditional left, the centrality of farming and of farming ways of life, compatible with ecological sustainability, needs to be rediscovered. The eco-socialist vision – as a critique of both the traditional right-wing and traditional left-wing modes of thinking – is an attempt to grapple with the ecological challenge humanity is currently facing (Singh et al., 2021).

Eco-socialist vision is the new paradigm of re-organizing economy and society in such a way that such re-organization is compatible with ecological sustainability. This vision is a critique of the twentieth century's two main alternative politico-economic paradigms – capitalism and traditional socialism of the Soviet variety (see Singh and Bhusal, 2014 for further elaboration).

Eco-socialism's critique of capitalism is focused on critiquing the main driver of capitalist mode of accumulation namely profit-maximization. Capital in search of profit looks upon every natural resource – human labour, land, water, air, forests, animals, birds, mines, etc., from the viewpoint of exploiting that resource for profit maximization. An individual firm in a capitalist economy is engaged in competition with other rivals in the market to survive and outcompete. This competitive pressure leads an individual firm to focus, in the short run, on exploiting every available natural resource in the least cost-effective and the most profitable way for itself without any consideration for the externalities, i.e., the macro-economic environmental implications of its business strategy, not only in the medium or long run but also in the short run. This neglect of externalities is intrinsic to capitalism because if the collective state-level regulation of pricing the externalities in the decision-making process of an individual firm has to be imposed, it will lead to the erosion of the main institutional regulatory mechanism of capitalism, i.e., the market. Because of the operation of external and internal economies of scale, capitalism as an economic system tends towards concentration and centralization of capital which leads to the rise of monopolies and international conglomerates. So far, the legislative infrastructure of capitalist states has tried to reduce this anti-competitive monopolistic tendency of capitalist accumulation through various anti-monopoly legislations to restore the essential characteristic of capitalism, i.e., the competitive market. However, despite the enormous paraphernalia of anti-monopoly legislations, the monopolistic power of big corporations has expanded beyond any level reached before in the history of capitalism. In the same way as regulatory mechanisms of capitalist states have not been able to overcome the inevitable consequence of market competition, i.e., monopolization, the environmental regulatory mechanisms of these states will not be able to defy completely the anti-environmental implications of the profit-maximizing objective of the firms involved in competitive market structure of capitalism. Therefore, the idea floated by some theorists of capitalism that capitalism can become green capitalism is structurally flawed. That capitalism is inherently destructive of nature is central to the eco-socialist critique of capitalism (Singh, 2021e). This does not mean that eco-socialists reject green reforms under capitalism; what they reject instead is the inherent capacity of capitalism to protect ecology and ecological balance (Singh, 2022).

Eco-socialist critique of capitalism also looks upon capitalism from the angle of consumption. Capitalist accumulation and expansion require expanding consumption to the point of even creating fictitious needs and deliberate obsolescence (Panayotakis, 2011). This unceasing expansion of consumption creates enormous amount of waste to the point where the rate of waste generation becomes higher than the planet's capacity to absorb that waste. It is this excess of waste generation over waste absorption which leads to pollution of land, water and air; and this pollution, in turn, damages the quality of the availability of these natural resources and the health of human and non-human beings (Rogers, 2006).

Eco-socialist critique of the old Soviet style socialism is based on the recognition that though those regimes rejected the market logic of capitalism and replaced it with the regulatory instrument of central planning, the objective of that planning had one commonality with one central objective of capitalism, i.e., continuous economic growth without any consideration for its environmental consequences. The managers of this growth, obsessed socialist regimes, believed that through central planning, they would be able to achieve greater efficiency than that achievable under capitalism by avoiding waste which was unavoidable under capitalism. They hoped that through this higher economic growth rate, they would be able to win the ideological battle with capitalism by demonstrating to the world that socialism was a better socio-economic system than capitalism. The central planners believed in the gigantism of large-scale production in both industry and agriculture and in the worship of technology in achieving that gigantism. Undoubtedly, one of the stated objectives of that unceasing growth, gigantism and technology was social-economic equality that is unachievable under capitalism. This social objective was admirable but the dominant factions in these regimes did not understand or appreciate that unceasing growth had adverse ecological consequences. Some socialist ecologists who tried to highlight the possible ecological and social disasters that will result from this growth obsession were either ignored and, in some cases, ruthlessly purged and punished. Those socialist ecologists eventually proved correct. The Soviet-type economies were big ecological disaster stories. The Chernobyl nuclear disaster in Ukraine in 1986 was just one of those disasters that the world came to know.

In the sphere of agriculture, the Stalinist collectivization in Soviet Russia by ruthlessly destroying small family farms for the purpose of large-scale industrialization of agricultural production is one of the most known environmental, social, economic and political disasters of the Soviet-type regimes.

Eco-socialists, therefore, reject both the paradigms of capitalism and its claimed alternative, i.e., Soviet style socialism. Different types of capitalisms (Anglo-Saxon, European social democratic and Asian) and socialisms (Chinese, Vietnamese and North Korean) fall within the same spectrum of capitalism and socialism, though Cuba did show some departure by emphasizing and encouraging organic agriculture (Singh, 2008b).

Informed by the ecological failures of capitalism and Soviet-style socialism, ecological socialism advocates a different development paradigm based on reorganization of the existing chemical and industrial agriculture regime towards a new regime of small-scale, local, family and cooperative farming that is organic and natural in character (Singh, 2010a, 2010b, 2014). The transition path towards that ecologically oriented agriculture requires innovating and embedding new modes of energy use and concomitant agricultural practices (Singh and Singh, 2019a) which can, in the case of Punjab, draw upon the ecological teachings of Guru Nanak and other Sikh gurus (Singh and Singh, 2019b). This transition path is a new road map that critiques the existing regime of agriculture that is centralist and points towards one that is decentralist. The struggle for federalism is a struggle also for that decentralist regime of agriculture which is a move away from that chemical/industrialised farming mode to one that is oriented towards natural and organic farming.

Punjab's farmers' organizations have so far shown only a limited understanding of the ecological dimensions of the existing chemicals-oriented Green Revolution strategy in Punjab and, even less of the strategy of agrobusiness takeover of Punjab agriculture which is at the core of the farm laws these organizations had fought against. Disengagement from the agrarian strategy supported by these farm laws involves fighting against centralization of agriculture and upholding the federal rights of Punjab to initiate an autonomous agrarian strategy suited to the ecological conditions of the Punjab, albeit within the constraints impinging on Punjab due to the state being placed in the web of Indian centralist capitalism and global capitalism. The extent to which these constraints can be overcome has not been fully tested. Struggling to weaken these constraints has to be at the centre of politico-economic strategies of the farmers' organizations. The fact that the farmers' organizations have drawn such wide-ranging degree of mass support in their struggle, unparalleled in Punjab's recent history, is a sign of hope that they can dare to move towards ecologically oriented agriculture, that the present conjuncture and needs of future generations demand.

Some individuals and NGOs such as Kheti Virasat Mission (Sharma, 2017), All India Pingalwara Society founded by Bhagat Puran Singh and Dalit agricultural organizations such as Punjab Khet Mazdoor Union (Singh et al., 2021) have already shown through their organic agricultural practices the potential for moving forward towards ecological agriculture in Punjab. La Via Campesina (meaning the peasants way), an international peasant movement, is coordinating the international struggles for natural farming which now are mainly concentrated in Latin America and Africa (Singh, 2021g). Those are inspiring experiences for Indian and Punjabi farmers to draw upon. A serious opposition to the anti-federal centralized capitalism in India demands putting decentralized and ecologically oriented agriculture at the centre of that opposition. The farmers' protests in defeating the agro-business oriented farm laws that were aimed at centralization of economic and political power and centralized governance of agriculture in India has opened the potential for moving towards the alternative path of decentralized and ecologically oriented agrarian future.

Conclusions

It is only through concerted and collective action of the organizations representing marginal, small and medium farmers that the multi-dimensional destructive turn in economic policy symbolized by these farm laws has been reversed temporarily by the success in getting these laws repealed. However, the danger still exists in the long run of centralized agrarian strategy being redeployed. It is also in the economic interest and moral duty of all political groups and state governments that stand for federalism, pluralism and ecological sustainability, to coordinate their efforts to oppose this move. The struggle for federalism and diversity is also the struggle for democracy. The weakening of federalism contributes to the concentration of economic and political power at the Centre and the rise of authoritarian political tendencies and practices which are also anti-ecological in their orientation.

One indicator of the sincerity and commitment of those making coordinated efforts to reverse the policy package contained in these farm laws would be for them to declare, that in any future central government they may be part of, they would never introduce such pro-agrobusiness capitalism, anti-federalism and anti-ecology laws and would look anew at the Constitutional provisions in order to increase the power of the states in agricultural management. There are other areas too, such as industry, finance and education, where federal devolution must be fought for (Singh, 2008), but agriculture being linked to the land and source of food remains the most crucial area in which states must obtain the right to retain their autonomy.

Protecting agriculture as a state subject within Indian federalism and resisting the influence of agrobusiness capitalism would be India's key economic, political, social and cultural battle in the coming years. Grasping the seriousness of this issue would be a critical prerequisite of developing the perspective to strengthen federalism, decentralization, diversity, democracy, local farming, small-scale farming, cooperative farming and ecological sustainability.

Farming organizations have still to develop an understanding and awareness of the ecologically destructive nature of existing agricultural practices especially in the so-called Green Revolution belt of Punjab and Haryana. The ecological destruction of Punjab in general and its rural sector in particular will intensify if the agrobusiness strategy enshrined in these farms laws is not defeated and pushed back for good. The fight for Punjab's federal rights in agriculture is closely linked with the strategy to move towards more autonomous agrarian strategy oriented towards ecological agriculture. A broader and deeper understanding of the strategy towards ecological agriculture would involve understanding of the eco-socialist or Red/Green vision of agriculture. Some initial steps, which can be called transition steps towards that direction, have already been taken by some individuals, NGOs and agriculture labour organizations. Learning from similar international experiences in Latin America and Africa would further enrich the understanding of the historic need for transition towards the eco-socialist vision of decentralized agriculture.

Notes

* This chapter is a revised version of 'Farm Laws, Federalism and Farm Protests: India and Punjab', first published in *Journal of Sikh and Punjab Studies*, 29(1&2) (Spring–Fall, 2022): 245–266.

1 An exhaustive account of the scale and degree of international solidarity attracted by these protests would be a fit subject for a substantial research project. As one small indicator of international interest based just on my individual engagement with this subject, I note that I have spoken at webinars and given interviews for print media, radio and TV (not counting UK and India) in the USA, Canada, Australia, New Zealand, France, Pakistan, Sri Lanka, Bangladesh and Slovenia. My articles on the subject have been published in French (Singh, 2020f, 2021a) and Spanish (Singh, 2021b), as well as the ones

published in English, Hindi and Punjabi, and pieces are likely to be published in the coming months in Italian, German and Portuguese.

2 For a set of brief elaborations of the eco-socialist vision and reflections on the farm laws and farmers' protests from this perspective, see P. Singh (2020f, 2021a, 2021b, 2021c, 2021d).

2 The materials from two earlier articles – (Singh, 2020c; Singh et al., 2021) – have been so extensively used in this article that the relevant passages have not always been cited here except in those cases where a specific point refers to the earlier articles. It is strongly recommended that Singh et al. (2021) be read for an in-depth examination of many aspects of the political economy of these laws, policies and protests that have a bearing on argument developed here, which focus mainly on aspect of federalism, farm laws and farm protests.

4 Since the three Ordinances were later introduced as Bills in Parliament to become Acts or laws, the words Ordinances/Bills/Acts or laws are used interchangeably in the paper.

5 Klein (2007) developed this argument in the context of the rise of neo-liberalism as a policy doctrine. She argues that governments seize upon disasters – environmental, economic and political – in order to push through policies and programmes to advance neo-liberal management of economy, politics and society.

3 Rajewal has also argued consistently that these farming laws, if not repealed, would open many more avenues and paths of central intervention into federal rights of states in agriculture.

7 For a more detailed examination of different dimensions of the MSP system, see Singh and Bhogal (2021a, 2021b). See also Singh and Bhogal (2021c). For a critical examination of the government claims on retaining the MSP and APMC, see Singh (2020e).

8 For an elaboration of this thesis, see Singh (2008). See also Singh et al. (2020) for book review panel discussion on the book.

9 For a more detailed investigation of the constitutional centralism in Indian agriculture, see Chapter 5, 'Centre-State Relations in Agriculture and their Implications for Punjab Agriculture' in Singh (2008) and for the assault of these farming laws on states' federal rights in agriculture, see Singh, 2020a.

10 See also Singh (2020a) for further elaboration.

11 Punjab' Finance Minister Manpreet Badal has estimated that Punjab alone would lose Rs 4,000 crore revenue per year because of this farming initiative of the Centre (*Punjabi Tribune*, 2020).

12 A retired Punjab civil servant, also named Pritam Singh, who worked for many years under different governments in Punjab, including those led by Akali Dal, and had proximity to many top Punjab politicians, shared with me this proclamation made by Sardar Parkash Singh Badal.

13 An Akali leader confided this in me, and his view was that it was widely known in Akali and CPM circles that during the 1970s when Surjeet had close ties with the top Akali leadership, he had a significant role in influencing their thinking. Surjeet is known to have influenced the wording of the Anandpur Sahib Resolution (1977 version) issued by Sant Harchand Singh Longowal as the President of Shiromani Akali Dal. The Akali leader who confided in me was not judgmental about Surjeet's role – he was neither appreciative nor critical of the role played by Surjeet in shaping the wording of Anandpur Sahib Resolution.

14 Singh et al. (2021) remains the only scholarly contribution so far that puts ecology at the centre of the analysis when examining the farm laws and drawing attention to the digital capitalist strategy underpinning these laws. It also draws attention to the regional implications of the agrarian agenda behind these laws.

Bibliography

Badal, Manpreet. '*Kheti Billan Naal Punjab Nun Har Saal 4000 crore rupai da nuksaan hovega*' (The Farming Bills will lead to 4000 crore rupees annual loss to Punjab). *Punjabi Tribune*, September 19, 2020, p. 2.

Bettelheim, Charles. *India Independent*. London: MacGibbon & Kee, 1968.

Chadha, Rajesh, Davenport, Scott, and Elumalai, Kannan. *Competition and regulatory reform in Indian agricultural markets, International Workshop, Agricultural Trade Liberalisation and Domestic Market Reforms in Indian Agriculture*, 2008. Accessed March 5, 2021. Available at: https://www.researchgate.net/publication/271474881_Competition_and_Regulatory_Reform_in_Indian_Agricultural_Markets.

Chakravarty, Sukhamoy. *Development Planning: The Indian Experience*. Delhi: Oxford University Press, 1989.

Chand, Ramesh. 'New farm acts, understanding the implications', *NITI Working Paper Series 1/2020. National Institution for Transforming India, Government of India*, 2020. Accessed March 10, 2021. Available at: https://niti.gov.in/sites/default/files/2020-11/NewFarmActs2020.pdf.

Chandra, Bipin, Mukherjee, Mridula, Mukherjee, Aditya, Mahajan, Sucheta, Panikkar, K. N. (eds.). *India's Struggle for Independence: 1857–1947*. Penguin India, 2017.

Desai, Akshay, Ramanlal. *Social Background of Indian Nationalism*. Bombay: Popular Prakashan, 1959.

Desai, Akshay, Ramanlal. *India's Path of Development: A Marxists Approach*. Bombay: Popular Prakashan, 1984.

Desai, Meghnad. India: Emerging Contradictions of Slow Capitalist Development. In: Robin Blackburn ed. *Explosions in a Subcontinent*. London: Penguin, 1975, pp. 11–50. Included also in Desai 2005.

Desai, Meghnad. *Development and Nationhood: Essays in the Political Economy of India*. New Delhi: Oxford University Press, 2005.

Deshpande, Satish and Sanjay Palshikar (eds.). *Sectarian Violence in India: Hindu–Muslim Conflict, 1966–2015*, India: Orient BlackSwan and EPW, 2019.

Dhanda, Meena. Closing address to the International Conference 'Anti-Caste Thought: Theory, Politics and Culture', University of Wolverhampton, UK, October 30, 2021 (unpublished).

Government of India. *Report of the high-level committee on reorienting the role and restructuring of Food Corporation of India*. Government of India, New Delhi, 2015.

Jagat, Gurbachan. 'BSF imbroglio in Punjab'. *The Tribune*, October 31, 2021.

Jalal, Ayesha. *The Sole Spokesman: Jinnah, the Muslim League and the Demand for Pakistan*. Cambridge: Cambridge University Press, 1985.

Klein, Naomi. *The Shock Doctrine: The Rise of Disaster Capitalism*. Random House, 2007.

Mandal, Monika. 'India's uninspiring record of deregulating farming could explain why many are worried about new laws.' *Scroll.in*, December 4, 2020. Accessed March 10, 2021. Available at: https://scroll.in/article/980171/indias-uninspiring-record-of-deregulating-farming-can-explain-why-many-are-worried-about-new-laws.

Menon, Jaya. 'Amendments to IAS cadre rules can cause irreparable damage to spirit of cooperative federalism: Tamil Nadu CM to PM Modi'. *The Times of India*, January 23, 2022.

Mohapatra, Subas (ed.). *Indian Society and Culture*, Taylor and Francis, 2017.

Panayotakis, Costas. *Remaking Scarcity: From Capitalist Inefficiency to Economic Democracy*. London: Pluto, 2011.

Rajewal, Balbir, Singh. '*Kisan Andolan: Lekha Jokha ate Bhavikh*' (translation; Farmers' Struggle: Current Assessment and its Future). *Punjabi Tribune*, July 17, 2021, p. 7.

Rehman, Mujibur (ed). *Communalism in Postcolonial India: Changing Contours*. India: Routledge, 2016.

Rogers, Heather. 'Garbage Capitalism's Green Commerce'. *Socialist Register 2007 Coming to Terms with Nature*, 2006, 231–253.

Sharma, Divya. 'Technopolitics, Agrarian Work and Resistance in Post-Green Revolution Indian Punjab'. PhD diss., Cornell University, 2017. Accessed February 8, 2011. Available at: https://ecommons. cornell.edu/handle/1813/59067.

Singh, Amarinder. 'Anandpur Sahib Resolution'. In Harbans Singh (ed.) *The Encyclopaedia of Sikhism*. Patiala: Punjabi University, 1992, pp. 133–141. (The author's name is mentioned as 'M.A.S. (Maharaja Amarinder Singh of Patiala)'.

Singh, Pritam. 'Political Economy of Nationalism: Minority Left and Minority Nationalisms vs Mainstream Left and Majority Nationalism in India'. *International Journal of Punjab Studies,* 9, no. 2 (July–December 2002): 287–298.

Singh, Pritam. 'Political Economy of Centralisation in India: Some Critical Notes from a Decentralist Perspective'. In B. Nayak (ed.) *Nationalizing Crisis: The Political Economy of Public Policy in Contemporary India*. Delhi: Atlantic Publishers, 2007, pp. 17–45.

Singh, Pritam. *Federalism, Nationalism and Development: India and the Punjab economy*. London/New York: Routledge, 2008 (Second Indian reprint 2019).

Singh, Pritam. 'Political Economy of the Third Front in India'. *Contemporary South Asia*, 16, no. 4 (December 2008a): 465–469.

Singh, Pritam. 'Contemporary Global Capitalism: Multi-pronged Crises'. *Economic and Political Weekly*, (October 11, 2008b), 43(41): 36–40.

Singh, Pritam. 'Left and the Third Front'. *Economic and Political Weekly*, XLIV, no. 12 (March 21, 2009): 8–11.

Singh, Pritam. 'Capitalism, Nature and Eco-Socialism'. *Economic and Political Weekly,* XLV, no.12 (March 20, 2010a): 29–33.

Singh, Pritam. 'Interrogating Marxian, Neo-classical and Green Perspectives on the Contradictory Implications of Third World/Asian Development and Poverty'. In Sucha Singh Gill, Lakhwinder Singh and Reena Marwah (eds.) *Sustainability of Asian Economic Development*. New Delhi: Routledge, 2010b: 149–163.

Singh, Pritam. 'The Competing Theories of Development and Underdevelopment: A Critical Evaluation from an Eco-Socialist Perspective'. *LIMES Plus,* XI, no. 3 (September–December, 2014): 117–146.

Singh, Pritam. 'Institutional Communalism in India'. *Economic and Political Weekly*, 50, no 28 (2015): 48–56.

Singh, Pritam. 'Centre's Agricultural Marketing Reforms Are an Assault on Federalism', *The Wire*, June 20, 2020a. Accessed February 8, 2021. Available at: https://thewire.in/agriculture/agriculture-marketing-reforms-federalism.

Singh, Pritam. 'As cracks in NDA Widen, Is BJP Ideology Compatible with Regional Identities'. *The Wire*, September 22, 2020b. Available December 10, 2020. Available at: https://thewire.in/politics/bjp-punjab-akali-dal-shiv-sena-regional-alliances.

Singh, Pritam. 'BJP's Farming Policies: Deepening Agrobusiness Capitalism and Centralisation'. *Economic and Political Weekly*, 55, no. 41 (October 10, 2020c): 14–17.

Singh, Pritam. 'BJP's Agrarian Agenda: Strengthening Agro-Business Capitalism and Weakening Federalism'. *Radical Socialist*, December 4, 2020d. Accessed January 15, 2021. Available at: http://www.radicalsocialist.in/articles/national-situation/906-bjp-s-agrarian-agenda-strengthening-agro-business-capitalism-and-weakening-federalism.

Singh, Pritam. 'Glaring flaws in farm laws'. *The Tribune*, December 9, 2020e.

Singh, Pritam. 'Les agriculteurs contre l'agenda agro-industriel de Modi'. *Le Grand Continent*, 22 décembre, 2020f. Accessed January 20, 2021. Available at: https://legrandcontinent.eu/fr/2020/12/22/les-agriculteurs-contre-lagenda-agro-industriel-de-modi/.

Singh, Pritam. 'Aux sources de la révolte paysanne en Inde: capitalisme de l'agrobusiness et centralisation', *CONTRETEMPS REVUE DE CRITIQUE COMMUNISTE*, 26 janvier, 2021a. http://www.contretemps.eu/inde-modi-bjp-capitalisme-agrobusiness-mouvement-paysan/?fbclid=IwAR1h1Uhc51enzvGavQ_VeoFet6QELny75dP3ciTxmmU3hnxzYQYEo8Qz4Eg.

Singh, Pritam. 'INDIA, Las raíces de la revuelta campesina: contra el agronegocio capitalista y la centralización', *viento sur*, 30 ENERO, 2021b. Accessed September 20, 2021. Available at: https://vientosur.info/las-raices-de-la-revuelta-campesina-contra-el-agronegocio-capitalista-y-la-centralizacion/?fbclid=IwAR3GMZjvbl_2_rfo_PFIX7UzmxGzSwGJ39OKCnmVMUN0ak1zJAKLkR7N6UA.

Singh, Pritam. 'Behind the Indian Farmers Struggle', *Anti-Capitalist Resistance*. February 10, 2021c. Accessed January 25, 2021. Available at: https://anticapitalistresistance.org/behind-the-indian-farmers-struggle/.

Singh, Pritam. 'Indian farmers confront agribusiness and Hindu nationalist agenda of Modi'. *Red and Green Labour*, February 21, 2021d. Accessed April 15, 2021. Available at: https://redgreenlabour.org/2021/02/21/indian-farmers-confront-agribusiness-and-hindu-nationalist-agenda-of-modi-government/.

Singh, Pritam. 'Capitalism, Ecology and Eco-socialism'. In V. Upadhyay and P. Singh (eds.) *Global Political Economy: A Critique of Contemporary Capitalism*. Delhi: Aakar, 2021e, pp. 353–375.

Singh, Pritam. '*Punjab de sehaj bodh ton tutdian*' (translation: 'Losing touch with the common sense of Punjab'). *Punjabi Tribune*, November 2, 2021f.

Singh, Pritam. 'A Global Peasants' Movement for Sustainable Healthcare', *The Wire*, April 17, 2021g.

Singh, Pritam. 'Amarinder Singh's Fall to Political Irrelevance Will Go Down in History'. *The Wire*, November 5, 2021h.

Singh, Pritam. 'Green Reforms and Individual Interventions in the Green New Deal Transition to Ecosocialism'. In Leigh Brownhill, Salvatore Engel-Di Mauro, Terran Giacomini, Ana Isla, Michael Lowy, and Terisa Turner (eds.) *The Routledge Handbook of Ecosocialism*, London: Routledge, 2022: 235–241.

Singh, Pritam. and Bhogal, Shruti. 'Misunderstanding the MSP: A properly thought-out resolution requires the untangling of many aspects of farm laws'. *The Indian Express*, January 8, 2021a. Accessed January 15, 2021. Available at:

https://indianexpress.com/article/opinion/columns/farm-laws-protests-farmers-govt-talks-msp-apmc-mandi-7137463/.

Singh, P. and Bhogal, Shruti. 'Interrogating the MSP Regime, Farm Laws and Agrarian Future in India'. *Millennial Asia*, 12, no. 3 (December 2021b): 332–349.

Singh, Pritam. and Bhusal, Lok Nath. 'Austerity, Welfare State and Eco-Socialism: With Special Reference to the United Kingdom'. *Economic and Political Weekly*, XLIX, no. 39 (September 27, 2014): 111–118.

Singh, Pritam. and Singh, Nadia. 'Political Economy of Bioenergy Transitions in Developing Countries: A Case Study of Punjab, India'. *World Development*,124(C), 2019a). 104630.

Singh, Pritam. and Singh, Nadia. 'The Ecological and Social Teachings of Guru Nanak'. *Sikh Review*, 67 (12) 2019b: 31–34.

Singh, Sukhpal and Bhogal, Shruti. 'MSP in a Changing Agricultural Policy Environment'. *Economic and Political Weekly*, 56, no. 3 (2021c): 12–18.

Singh, Sukhpal, Thandi, Shinder Singh., Narang, Harpreet Kaur. and Singh, Pritam. 'Did Indian Federalism Fail Punjab?' *Journal of Sikh and Punjab Studies*, 27, no. 1 (2020): 157–179.

Singh, Tanya, Singh, Pritam and Dhanda, Meena. 'Resisting a 'Digital Green Revolution': Agri-logistics, India's New Farm Laws and the Regional Politics of Protest'. *Capitalism Nature Socialism*, 32, no. 2 (June 2021): 1–21. Accessed August 25, 2021. Available at: https://www.tandfonline.com/doi/full/10.1080/10455752.2021.1936917.

Sova, Chase. 'Why the founding fathers wanted Americans to be farmers'. *Quartz*, March 20, 2018. Accessed July 15, 2021. Available at: https://qz.com/1233436/why-the-founding-fathers-wanted-americans-to-be-farmers/.

7 'Modernist' Teleology and Futures of Agriculture

Making Sense of the Punjabi Farmers' Movement of 2020–2021*

Surinder S. Jodhka

Introduction

In the last week of November 2020, a large contingent of farmers from Punjab began their march to the national capital demanding immediate repeal of three newly enacted laws concerning agriculture. They were joined on their way, in large numbers, by their fellow farmers from Haryana. Defying all the odds and crossing all the hurdles, they managed to reach the borders of Delhi on November 26–27. Their numbers kept swelling by the hours, going up to around 300,000 over the next few days. They settled in for the winter, staying put at the borders of Delhi, despite the harsh weather. On January 26, their strength rose to nearly a million, as many more of them arrived from across the country on a special call to show their strength. Thus, when India celebrated its Republic Day in the capital city and paraded its military might to the Indian public and the world, the farmers drove their tractors on belt roads of the city, in a parallel display of strength.

The farmers kept sitting on the borders of Delhi for a whole year, until their primary demand, the withdrawal of the three laws was conceded. On the morning November 19, 2021, the Indian Prime Minister announced the withdrawal of the three laws in a specially telecast message. It was the day of Gurupurab, the birth anniversary of the founder of Sikh faith, Guru Nanak. No one had expected such an announcement. Given the near complete lack of trust of the Union government among the farmers, they kept sitting until the laws were formally repealed by the Indian Parliament ten days later. Before they withdrew their year-long sit-in on the borders of Delhi, they also wanted assurance on their related demands. The Union government conceded to almost everything the farmers asked for. This included the passing of legislation the Indian Parliament, which would ensure a Minimum Support Price (in MSP) for a large number of crops produced by the Indian farmers across the country. Thus, making farming a part of the rights-based livelihood system.

The year-long sit-in of the farmers on the borders of national capital has perhaps been the most significant social and political movement in

DOI: 10.4324/9781003320005-10

the contemporary history of India. The nature and extend of farmers' mobilization would be comparable to any other movement anywhere in the modern world. Though the numbers of farmers present at the Delhi borders during the year kept fluctuating, their resolve to fight for their demands remained firm. Their spirit, their courage, their conduct and their organizational discipline was a source of surprise for many. Perhaps the most bewildered were the 'pro-regime' intellectuals, journalists and opinion makers.

Though the ruling establishment had sensed that the new laws were unlikely to be welcomed by the farmers, they had hoped that the looming pandemic would discourage them from stepping out to protest and they would eventually reconcile to the intended changes. This is clearly evident from the fact the three laws were initially introduced as 'ordinances' by the Union Cabinet in the month of June 2020, without the mandated feedback from the Indian public and consultations with the stake holders (Aiyar and Krishnamurthy, 2020). They were subsequently passed by the Indian Parliament, during the second half of September 2020, when India was experiencing its first peak of COVID-19 infections and the country was under a national lockdown.

The resolve of the farmers also seemed to have bemused, albeit pleasantly, the critiques of the Union Government of India led by Mr. Modi. The opinion 'Someone had finally found the courage to stand-up to the undemocratic and authoritarian power that ruled the country' was echoed by a wide range of 'left-liberal' intellectuals and political activists from across the country (Singh, 2021). Many of them would have normally looked at such protests of the landed Jatts of Punjab and Jats of Haryana with a sense of suspicion, if not outright scorn. The visible Sikh religious symbols and slogans of the Punjabi farmers displayed proudly and loudly in their gatherings, no longer seemed to attract any objections from the secularist elite of Delhi. Even the Communists of Kerala and Bengal appeared mesmerized by the Punjabi songs of singers like Kanwar Grewal and Harf Cheema and their open use of the Khalsa symbols and the militant religious Sikh greetings/slogans that the congregations on Delhi borders echoed in their *pandals* and on the micro-YouTube channels.

As the movement kept gaining in strength and support over the next few weeks, many of the farmer leaders too expressed their amazement. The statement that 'they had not expected the kind of groundswell of support from farmers of the region and from such a wide spectrum of the Indian society, and even the outside world', was repeated by many speakers at meetings over the next few weeks and months, while complimenting those sitting on the *dharnas* (Ellis-Petersen, 2021).

> This is no longer a movement of the farmers of Punjab and Haryana, or of India. This has become a much bigger movement, a global movement. We are being supported by people from across the world. We have become a source of their hopes as well,

farmer leader Balbir Singh Rajewal often repeated in his speeches at the Singhu Border.

How do we make sense of such an unexpected and unanticipated mobilization? Several answers to this question or explanations have been attempted. Some well-meaning experts described the farmers' movement as something similar to the peasant uprisings of the nineteenth and twentieth centuries, invoking categories like 'moral economy' to understand and explain the anger and anguish of the protesting farmers.[2] Many journalists and pro-state economists described the movement simply as a struggle for continued state patronage and support, by those involved in farming as an occupation, since the farm unions had been demanding an assurance on extending the MSP regime and further expanding its scope. Or, was this movement merely an assertion of rural dominant castes and rich farmers who were anxious of their future and wary of losing their dominance in the local and regional contexts in the emerging power structure and shifting class balance in favour of the urban-based corporate capital?[3]

While there may be an element of truth in some of these explanations, the protesting farmers were certainly not 'subsistence-oriented peasants'. They were enterprising cultivators, who used a wide range of farm inputs and produced primarily for the market. They have been doing this for decades. Beyond farms, they have also been integrated into the larger economic, social and political life of the nation and the world. Their organizations have been named 'unions' because they functioned like the trade unions of urban factory workers, as interest groups, meant to bargain with relevant 'others' on their behalf. However, the latter two explanations are too instrumental and do not explain the overwhelming support that the movement received, particularly the financial and emotional support of the Punjabi diaspora, living far away from the farm lands of Punjab, and the younger generations, who often express a distaste for agriculture as a possible occupation.

This chapter is an attempt at exploring the sources of the 'surprise' and basis for why these protests struck such a deep chord and argues for a need to examine its cultural roots with a historical and anthropological lens. It begins by providing a brief context to the farmers' movement and the three farm laws. The next section provides a brief overview of the contemporary history of Indian agriculture with a regional focus on Punjab, a kind of revisit. The last section attempts a critical engagement with the popular ideas of the inevitability of the decline of agriculture and a demise of agrarian cultures. The concluding section goes on to argue for a historical and sociological understanding of the agrarian cultures rather than a pre-scripted teleology that takes the end of agriculture for granted and is accompanied by a discussion on the idea of developmentalism, which sees the end of village and agriculture not only as inevitable but also a desirable accomplishment for a nation trying to modernize itself, its ultimate self-realization.

The Context

As is evident from the above discussion, the immediate context of the year-long sit-in on the borders of Delhi, led by the farmers from Punjab, was the enactment of three laws by the Union government, done without any real consultations with the relevant stakeholders. In the Indian legal system, agriculture is listed as a subject where provincial governments have autonomy of legislation and governance. However, given the nature of India's weak federal structure, the Union government often manages to compromise provincial autonomy. The enactment of the new laws was an example of such an overreach.

Of the three laws, two were newly drafted 'Acts' and one an 'Amendment' to a pre-existing law. The first of these, 'The Farmers' Produce Trade and Commerce (Promotion and Facilitation) Act, 2020', proposed to 'liberalize' the sale and purchase of agricultural commodities, specifically of food grains. The apprehension of the farmers was that it would have undermined the pre-existing marketing framework and opened-up trading of farm produce outside the Agricultural Produce Marketing Committees (APMC), the *mandis*. The mandis were put in place by different state governments (although, not all) as part of a supporting structure for the surplus producing farmers of the state at the time of the Green Revolution which began in the 1960s and 1970s. Agencies of the Union government began to procure food grains through the APMC at an assured MSP determined by it, to shore up its own food reserves for running the public distribution system (PDS) across the country. The new law made no reference to the existing MSP regime or its future and raised the suspicion that the MSP would be done away with entirely. The second legislation, the 'Farmers (Empowerment and Protection) Agreement of Price Assurance, Farm Services Act, 2020', provided a framework for contract farming, where farmers could directly enter into agreements with one or more buyers to produce a specific crop, which the latter would purchase at a pre-fixed price. Provisions of contract farming had already been in place at the state level but the new law proposed to bring it into a common national framework. This law, too, made no provision for any kind of price security to the cultivators. Provisions provided for dispute resolution were also source of anxiety for the farmers, since they saw these as skewed in favour of the buyers.

The third law was an amendment of the existing law named 'The Essential Commodities (Amendment) Act, 2020'. The new amendment proposed to do away with the existing limits on storage of cereals, pulses, oilseeds, edible oils, onions and potatoes. They were to be no longer listed as essential commodities, which would have opened up the possibility of their being hoarded by those with the resources and storage facilities, namely corporate capital. Farmers feared that the real intention of the government was to provide corporate capital an opportunity to enter agricultural markets to earn big profits. Such a provision would have also implied an eventual withdrawal of price security to the farmers, exposing them to the vagaries of a market dominated by big corporates. Together, the three new laws were designed to open up the agricultural sector to an active commercial engagement by the big corporates, who could purchase, store and even dictate to the farmers what crops to produce, through the contract farming system.

While the farmers, particularly those from the north and north-western states of Punjab, Haryana, Rajasthan and Uttar Pradesh, found everything in the new laws as being against their interests, and a sell-off to corporate capital, the pro-government economists insisted that the new laws would help the farmers immensely. Chand articulated this perspective clearly in the following:

> ...the three policy reforms undertaken by the Central government through the three new Acts are in keeping with the changing times and requirements of farmers and farming. If they are implemented in the right spirit, they will take Indian agriculture to new heights and usher in the transformation of the rural economy. The reforms have generated optimism for India to become a global power in agriculture and a powerhouse for global food supply. The reforms carry the seed for farmers' prosperity and transformation of the rural economy and to make it a growth engine of the Indian economy.[4]

Why did the farmers not recognize what was good for them? For the Union government, the problem lay primarily in their inability to comprehend the laws and them being manipulated by certain oppositional political interests. When the farmer organizations were initially called for discussions by the central government, at the early stage of the protests, they were given presentations by government officials on the various clauses and to emphasize the point that they had not actually understood the new laws. A senior minister even suggested that the concerned ministry and its officials, who were engaging with farmers, ought to prepare better-quality powerpoint presentations, in simple and clear language, to remove the farmers' doubts about the new laws. Some mainstream television channels too repeated this narrative, through their reporting and their discussions, with 'experts'. They invariably tended to accuse the 'leaders' of the farmers of collaborating with opposition politicians to fool the *bhole-bhale kisan* (naive farmers).[5]

This was not simply a case of statist propaganda against a popular movement. There was also an underlying appeal of such an argument among the urban middle classes, who have increasingly come to be the hegemonic social group. It is their perception of agriculture and its place in their visions of India's futures that have come to increasingly dominate India's mainstream political agenda. It is in this context that the next section makes a brief revisit to the contemporary history of Indian agriculture.

Revisiting Indian Agriculture[6]

When Robert Clive won the battle of Plassey for the British East India Company in 1757 and the Company established its rule over parts of Indian territories, their first target was to secure rights over the revenue collected from agricultural lands. Envisaging an endless capacity of Indian peasant to pay taxes, they initiated formalization of the existing arrangements of revenue administration through a range of reforms, called the land settlements. By the time they managed to reach Punjab after defeating the Sikh forces in 1849, they had experimented with a range of land revenue systems. However, they formalized land relations everywhere, hoping to maximize their share of the revenue collection. As the demand for raw cotton in Britain escalated after the Industrial Revolution, they also ensured through their revenue policies that the Indian cultivators shifted to cultivation of cash crops like cotton over cereals. Their policies also introduced a new legal framework, which enabled the creation of a market for the sale and purchase of agricultural lands.

As is well known, the British colonial administrators popularized the view that the pre-colonial rural India had a hopeless economy, which had been stagnant for centuries and millennia, caught in the whirlpool of caste and a self-imposed culture of isolation from the outside world. As they propagated to the world outside, the colonial and Orientalist narratives framed the Indian culture as having had no history of technological progress (Inden, 1986). The local people purportedly surrendered to the vagaries of nature and the ideology of *karma*. In reality, however, the agrarian economy of the region during the pre-colonial period had not been a 'backward' system or a homogenous social and economic universe that had been eternally stagnant. As historical research has shown, the Indian cultivators had evolved a range of sustainable systems, including modes of irrigating their fields with wells and ponds (Chatterjee and Rudra, 1989). They did not depend only on rains. Indian agriculture also produced a substantial surplus. Thriving urban centres and flourishing political empires of the ancient and medieval times were a proof of this. Much of the wealth that the empires possessed, and in search of which the European colonizers came to India in the first place, was sourced primarily from its agrarian riches, the origin of which mostly lay in its diverse agrarian crops, spices and indigo.

Commenting on the economic vibrancy of the region, historian David Ludden, for example, sums up the historical evidence on the pre-colonial period, particularly the period immediately before the British established their rule in the region as follows:

> In the fourteenth century, South Asia became a region of travel and transport connecting Central Asia and the Indian Ocean. This redefined the location of all its agrarian territories... New technology, ideas,

> habits, languages, people and needs came into farming communities. New elements entered local cuisine. People produced new powers of command, accumulation, and control, focused on strategic urban sites in agrarian space. By 1600, ships sailed between China, Gujarat, Europe, and America. ... A long expansion in world connections occurred during centuries when a visible increase in farming intensity was also reshaping agrarian South Asia. .... Regional formations of agrarian territory came into being, sewn together by urban networks...
>
> (Ludden, 1999: 113)

Questioning the assumptions of the colonial view, he shows how certain communities moved across regions, resulting in significant changes in the agrarian economies, as also in the social composition of cultivating classes. Speaking about the present north-west of India, he writes how the drying up of the Saraswati River forced the Jat farmers of Rajasthan region to move 'into the upper Punjab doabs and into the western Ganga basin in the first half of the second millennium' (*Ibid.*, 117). He continues:

> All these trends combined to open new agricultural territories from Panipat to Sialkot along very old trade routes running from Kabul to Agra. By the sixteenth century, Jalandhar and Lahore were thriving towns surrounded by lush farmland. Wheat lands expanded west of the Ganga and in Punjab doabs astride trade routes and around old trading towns where distinctively urban commercial and administrative groups were already prominent... As farmland expanded in spaces between the plains and high mountains, new opportunities for trade arose at ecological boundaries, and this stimulated more commercially oriented production and processing. By the sixteenth century, tobacco, sugarcane, honey, fruits, vegetables, and melons fed Punjab commercial life, along with profits from sericulture, indigo, and all the elements of cloth manufacturing.
>
> (*Ibid.*, 117–118)

The decadence of Indian agriculture started during British rule, particularly in the eastern regions, where they established their rule first, after the battle of Plassey in 1757. As mentioned above, their only aim of colonizing the region during the initial decades seems to have been driven by a greed for extracting land revenue, which produced economic and social disasters. A move to the cultivation of cash crops, such as cotton for export and for its use in the newly opened cloth mills in their emerging industrial cities of Britain meant lesser production of the cereals required for local consumption. Their policies also killed the local craft and industry, leading to a massive de-urbanization of India and a significant increase in the rural population and their dependence on the agrarian economy.

The frequent famines caused by the shifting cropping patterns in different part of the subcontinent and a general sense of desperation in the countryside produced anger against the colonial rulers. It manifested itself in a series of 'peasant movements' during the first half of the twentieth century. Some of these movements were led by the Congress Party under the leadership of Gandhi, while others were helmed by communists. They all demanded a change in the political regime and restoration of their rights over the lands they cultivated. It was in this context that the agrarian question became an urgent priority with the native political elite who inherited power from the colonial rulers after Independence in 1947.

Rural Development and Agrarian Change

The early initiatives by the independent Indian state were in the form of legislative interventions that attempted to restore ownership right to tillers of the land and provide them security of tenure. Land Reform legislations enacted by the state governments on the directives of the Union government produced mixed results. They did help in reducing the hold of intermediaries and traditional *zamindaris* in some parts of the country, but did so only in those states where the cultivating peasants could build sufficient pressure on local state functionaries. The government of India also introduced a Community Development Programme (CDP) hoping that the villages would work cooperatively towards rebuilding local communities, as Gandhi had envisaged. However, these initiatives had very limited success in improving the productivity of land (Moore, 1966).

By the late 1960s, the Nehruvian state managed to find the resources to invest in modernizing its agrarian economy. Helped by some global agencies, and using the new technologies developed elsewhere, India moved on to a path of increased productivity. Though confined to a few promising pockets, state investment in agriculture provided an impetus to its growth and, within a just a decade or so, the country was producing enough food for its rapidly growing population. The Green Revolution was made possible as much by the enterprising farmers as by the kind of investments that the Indian state made in establishing agricultural infrastructure. From the construction of dams and canal networks to setting up agricultural universities, marketing networks and making provisions for cheap credit from institutional sources on a 'priority' basis, the Indian state played a critical role in enabling its farmers to pursue the path of intensifying production. The idea of Green Revolution, as a concept, steadily spread to other 'less-developed' regions of India as well, though the required investments in agricultural infrastructure are no longer forthcoming from any agency of the Union or state governments.

Envisaged in North America, the Green Revolution was a technology-driven programme focused on increasing the productivity of land. It assumed that an increase in income would eventually also 'trickle-down' to the poor. However, empirical research showed that this was not happening and the number of those living below a subsistence level of nutrition, the poverty-line, was quite large. The Union government responded to this by introducing special programmes targeting the poor. These initiatives were put together into a single scheme called the Integrated Rural Development Programme (IRDP). The IRDP was replaced with the Mahatma Gandhi National Rural Employment Guarantee Act (MGNREGA) during the early 2000s.

Neo-liberal Reforms and the 'Decline' of Agriculture

The neo-liberal reforms of the early 1990s fundamentally changed the orientation of the Indian state towards agriculture and its farming populations. The broader orientation of the Indian economy also began to change. Once liberalization was unleashed, the private corporate sector began to grow rapidly. Thus, the size of the national economy expanded. But the corporate economy was at first largely focused on the high-end service sector, which did not generate many jobs. Thus, unlike the 'classical' growth trajectories of the industrialized nations of the global North, even when the share of India's agriculture in national income declined rather rapidly, a much larger proportion of the workforce remained employed in agriculture. Such a decline in the relative size of agrarian economy in terms of its value addition has produced many imbalances, going beyond the sphere of income and employment.

The growing size and power of the urban and corporate economy marginalized its agrarian economy in the national imagination, the effects of which began to also be felt by those working in the sector. For example, the earlier growth in agriculture had given enough incomes and aspiration to the landowning classes/castes to educate their wards, hoping that they would find employment outside the village. However, the ones who controlled corporate capital preferred their own and only those from the urban upper castes and urban educated individuals with the required cultural capital, leaving those coming from agrarian backgrounds in the lurch.

As the power and influence of the corporate capital grew, it also began to diversify its economic enterprises beyond traditional manufacturing and business outsourcing in IT services and software. Agriculture and food processing began to attract them as avenues of possible investments and incomes. The growing size of the urban middle-classes and its increasing penchant for consumption provided a sure source of demand for processed food. Processed food products could also be exported to emerging markets abroad. To the neo-liberal policymakers of the Indian state, these appeared to be the most desirable solutions for an agricultural sector complaining of crises for a long time. However, given the diversity of legal frameworks governing agricultural lands and the restrictions put in-place against the purchase or leasing-in of agricultural lands by corporates, as a measure of protection to the farmers, corporate capital could not easily enter the agricultural economy. It is in this context that the Union government decided to enact the set of three new laws that would make it easier for the big corporations to enter the agricultural sector, on their own terms.

Punjab, the Regional Trajectories[7]

The partition of the subcontinent in 1947 and the subsequent political history of the region have produced a strong centripetal tendency, with the central government acquiring a much stronger position over the provincial states. As indicated above, the passing of the three laws by the Union government without any meaningful consultations with the state government and other stakeholders is another clear evidence of such a process. While this has often been discussed and debated at the political level, the diverse realities on the ground are rarely spoken about. The historical dynamics of agrarian regions, during the pre-colonial and colonial period were very diverse. These diversities continue to be significant even today. The agrarian trajectory of Punjab has been very different from that of other regions and the national narrative of agrarian realities today.

The Indian Punjab is among the smaller states of the union, covering just around 1.5 per cent of its total geographical area, and a little over 2 per cent contribution to its total population. However, the region has had a distinctive identity, shaped by its history, culture and linguistic distinctiveness. Until around the early 1990s, Punjab had been the richest state of the country with the highest per capita income. The sources of its prosperity had been its vibrant urban centres and a thriving agriculture.

It was not the post-independence state initiatives alone that helped the region develop its agrarian economy. Punjab had occupied a special status during the British rule as well. It was among the last territories to be conquered by the British colonizers, and they treated it very differently. The British recruited a section of the Punjabis into their army, who even fought wars for them, outside the subcontinent, including during the two World Wars. They also saw Punjab as a region with a potential for agricultural growth. Given that a good number of rivers flowed through the region, they invested in building a network of canals and moved sections of the Sikh farmers from its central and eastern districts to the newly irrigated lands of western Punjab, thus setting up the 'Canal Colonies' (Ali, 1988). The Sikh farmers returned back to their native districts after the Partition bringing with them the experience of entrepreneurial farming.

The post-colonial state too saw Punjab as a region with exceptional potential for agricultural growth. Confronting serious food deficits during the early decades after its independence, the Union government looked at Punjab as one of the most suitable regions for rapid economic growth. The first major irrigation and hydro-power project set-up after independence was primarily to serve the agricultural lands of Punjab. Though the construction of the legendary Bhakra Nangal Dam on the River Satluj had been visualized by the pre-independence Punjab government, its construction was completed in 1963, just a few years before introduction of the Green Revolution technology in the region. As an extension of the Bhakra Nangal project, the region saw the laying of an extensive network of canals, reaching up to parts of Rajasthan and Gujarat. The hydro-power generated by the project too became a cheap source of electricity for the tube-wells extensively used for irrigation in the region and their numbers steadily grew.

As indicated above, Punjab had been agriculturally a vibrant agrarian region even during the colonial period and it continued to record a positive growth during the first few decades after independence, despite all the social and political disruptions caused by the Partition. Punjab's agriculture grew at an impressive rate of 4.6 per cent during 1950–1964,[8] improving India's food supplies.[9]

However, in the emerging geo-political and intellectual environment of the time, countries like India were being seen as 'Malthusian time bombs' (see Kumar, 1999: 44). According to this view, their rapidly growing population could not be sustained by the slow pace of growth in their ability to produce food. This was also seen as a source of 'worry' by the western political powers in a world marked by the Cold-War. They advocated technology driven solutions to such perceived challenges. The hybrid high-yielding variety (HYV) of seeds being developed in North America during the 1950s were seen as a way out for newly independent countries like India, which could be saved from an impending human and political crises, it was argued.

The western powers succeeded in selling this idea to the Union government of India and the HYV seeds arrived in the country in the mid-1960s. They were introduced as a package programme for 'revolutionary' growth of the agricultural economy. The 'package' called Green Revolution included use of chemical fertilizers, a variety of pesticides and herbicides and an extensive use of agricultural machinery. This package came with a variety of incentives, such as cheap credit from commercial banks and subsidies on farm inputs. It was around this time that the state governments were encouraged to also put in place a marketing network in the form of mandis for assured procurement of the farm produce. In order to build its own stocks of food grains for the PDS, the central government began to procure food grains through the newly set-up mandis at a pre-declared MSP, which was decided after calculating all the costs incurred by the cultivators, including the costs of labour. This new technological revolution in agriculture was to be supported by a network of scientifically trained professionals who were to be educated in the newly set-up agricultural universities, the first of which was set up in Punjab at Ludhiana in 1962.

The success of the new seeds was premised on availability of assured irrigation. The canal network and water flowing from the Bhakra Nangal project would have strengthened Punjab's claim for being selected as a prime site for the experiment. Though a large number of districts were selected from different parts of the country for the experiment with HYV seeds, Punjab was at the forefront of all this.

Given that the logic of new technology was about feeding the growing population and production of food-grains, the new HYV seeds were initially used for wheat cultivation, which is also a staple food of the Punjabis. However, it was soon realized that a large proportion of the Indian population ate rice. Though rice cultivation was not unknown in the region, it was a marginal crop. Rice needed a much larger volume of water than was available at most times of the year in the region. With new sources of irrigation becoming available, cultivation of rice was no longer a difficult proposition. It also turned out to be an economic and ecological boon for those pockets of the state that experienced perpetual water-logging, made worse by the newly constructed canals in these regions. Tube wells that irrigated paddy remedied the problems created by the water seeping in from the canals and kept the fields ready for *rabi* crops later in the year (Shergill, 2005). Cultivation of paddy also came with other incentives. The Food Corporation of India (FCI) eagerly procured it, which soon made it a viable commercial crop for the Punjabi farmers. Given its wider market, locally and abroad, farmers could often sell it at a price higher than the MSP to private traders. Some varieties, like the Basmati, for example, continue to be sold at a much higher price in the open market than the MSP available in the *mandis*.

As expected, Punjab turned out to be the most successful case in terms of adoption of new technologies and increase in agricultural productivity. While the average growth rate of the agricultural sector for the entire country in the period between 1961–1962 and 1985–1986 was 2.6 per cent, the corresponding numbers for the state of Punjab alone were 6.4 per cent, the highest across all the states. The neighbouring state of Haryana followed Punjab with 4.7 per cent and Gujarat, with a 3.4 per cent growth rate, was placed third during this period.

The adoption of HYV seeds was also much more extensive in the state of Punjab. Against the national average of 31 per cent for 1974–1976 and 54 per cent for 1983–1985, the total area under HYV seeds in Punjab was 73 and 95 per cent, respectively, significantly higher than in any other state of the country. This was true also for use of other inputs such as chemical fertilizers, pesticides, tube wells, tractors and other machines. For example, by 1984–1985 Punjab had 4642 tractors per 1 lakh gross cultivated area against the national average of 230 (Singh and Kohli, 2005: 286–289). With increased use of technology, Punjab was also able to bring almost all of its cultivable land under farming. The prosperity produced by its agricultural sector made Punjab the state with the highest per capita income.

Such an extensive adoption of the new technology was made possible because of its acceptance by different classes of cultivators in Punjab. However, although new technology was supposed to be scale neutral, it certainly wasn't resource neutral, as John Harriss argues (Harriss, 1987). Along with the large landowners, the smaller landholders too, took to the new seeds, but many did not have the resources required for all the inputs, that had to be necessarily purchased from the market. They borrowed money, often from informal sources. The commission agents, the *arhtiyas*, in the newly set-up mandis did not hesitate to lend as long as they promised to bring their farm produce to them for sale. Thus, rural Punjab saw rapid mechanization of agriculture. Even those without the resources to buy tractors, shifted from the traditional bullocks, preferring to instead hire machines from the bigger landowners. Everyone was soon integrated into a market-oriented agriculture. Smaller landowners used their family labour more intensively, often getting a slightly higher yield per acre from their farms as compared to the more resourceful bigger farmers (Bhalla and Chadha, 1983).

Punjab agriculture also witnessed a significant change in its cropping pattern. The variety of crops sown in Punjab came down from 21 in the year 1960–1961 to only 9 by 1990–1991 and this has remained so thereafter. Wheat and rice emerged as the two most popular crops. The area under crops other than wheat during the *rabi* season declined from 62.74 per cent in 1960–1961 to 17.12 per cent in 2004–2005. The change was much bigger for the *kharif* season and the area under rice cultivation increased ten-folds, from a mere 6.05 per cent in 1960–1961 to a whopping 63.02 per cent in 2004–2005.[10]

Caste, Class and Power

Use of new technology and HYV seeds also implied shift to a far more intensive agriculture. Cultivation of crops like paddy required much more labour, and it was needed throughout the cropping season. Machines also helped bring the barren and uncultivated lands under cultivation. Land owners began to increasingly self-cultivate, preferring to hire wage labour over leasing their lands out to tenants and *siris*. *Siris* worked as attached labourers but were paid a share of the produce, generally one-fifth, for their labour input. With a significant increase in productivity of land, this was no longer acceptable to the farmers. They preferred hiring them on annual wages, as *naukars* or farm servants but also often kept them tied by paying them wages in advance and keeping them perpetually indebted. In addition, they hired a much larger number of casual labourers. Demand for labour was particularly high during the peak farm operations, such as sowing, harvesting and paddy transplantation.

As elsewhere in the subcontinent, land and labour relations in rural Punjab also have a caste dimension. Almost the entire population of *Dalits*, who make up nearly one-third of the total state population, are landless. They had traditionally been the source of agricultural labour for the landowning castes. Land ownership was caste-centric too. Most of the agricultural land is owned and cultivated by the *Jatts*. Besides Jatts, Punjab has some other castes who own and cultivate land. They include *Rajputs*, *Gujjars*, *Sainis*,

Labanas and *Kambojs*. These communities are either confined to a few pockets of the state or they are mostly owners of small and marginal holdings. Jatts too are internally heterogenous in terms of their holding size. However, almost all the big landowners are Jatts and they have been part of the regional elite of Punjab. They were the group that gained the most from the British colonial policies of recruitment in the armed forces and the granting of land titles, as mentioned above.

The success of Green Revolution strengthened their hold over the rural economy and regional politics. Introduction of electoral democracy after independence enabled them to quickly emerge as the regional ruling elite. Their rise to power at the regional level further helped them consolidate their position in the village and the agrarian economy. The increasing demand for labour and growing formalization of labour relations tended to produce frictions in their relationship with the Dalits. The older *jajmani* ties disintegrated fast with most of the traditional caste occupations of the servicing castes becoming redundant.

Seeing their position change in the emerging capitalist agrarian economy, the labouring poor began to unite to demand better wages. However, the farmers found a solution to the growing assertion of the local Dalits by utilizing labour from poorer regions of the country. A large number of the labouring poor began to arrive in Punjab from the eastern districts of Uttar Pradesh and Bihar. They initially came only for the peak season activities, arriving for the wheat harvesting and staying back until paddy transplantation. Over the years, some of them began to stay through the year, working as regular farm servants, replacing the local Dalits. With increasing mechanization of agricultural processes, such as harvesting of wheat and paddy, and paddy transplantation, during the post-1990s, demand for this labour too has been declining.

However, the caste question has not gone away and continues to be conflictual, although the nature of caste conflict between Dalits and Jatts seems to have shifted from the axis of class to a question of dignity and citizenship. Though sharply divided across *jatis*, they all ask for a dignified space in the village life. The traditionally dominant Jatt Sikhs continue to see themselves as a superior people even when this idea receives no ideological sanctity from their religious traditions. They often see any form of Dalit assertion as a challenge to their authority, which occasionally leads to inter-caste tensions and conflict (Jodhka, 2002, 2003, 2015).

The landowning Jatts have also been looking outwards, aspiring to diversify their sources of income by investing in urban trade and educating their wards (Jodhka, 2006). Many of the richer farmers have themselves become *arhtiyas* in grain mandis and have diversified their economic portfolios in other ways (Sinha, 2020). The Jatt Sikhs of Punjab have also been among the most mobile communities of the subcontinent and have been emigrating abroad in large numbers, mostly to the countries of Europe, North America and Australia. However, even when they leave the village and country along with their families, they tend to not sell their agricultural lands. This has produced a vibrant land tenancy market (Bansal, 2020). This also keeps them connected to their 'roots'. Some of the smaller cultivators in the region have also been exiting from agriculture to pursue their careers in the non-farm economy. They too tend to lease-out their land for cultivation to enterprising farmers with the resources and the required farm equipment.

Such a practice of reverse tenancy has kept the average size of *operational holdings* relatively large in the state. As per the Agricultural Census of 2015–2016, on an average, as many as 86 per cent of India's operational holdings were in the size category of small (less than 2 hectare) and marginal (less than 1 hectare). Together they cultivated 47 per cent of all the cultivated area. In contrast, only 33 per cent of the operational holdings in Punjab fell in the small and marginal categories and they accounted for only 9 per cent of the state's total cultivated area. Punjab had 33 per cent of its operational holdings in the category of medium (4–10 hectares) and large (above 10 hectares), and together they cultivate two-thirds of its total cultivated area. The remaining 34 per cent of the holdings were in the semi-medium size category with 2–4 hectares of land cultivating 25 per cent of the land. Nationally, only 5 per cent of all the operational holdings fell in the two upper (above 4 hectares) categories with 29 per cent of the total area under cultivation.[11]

Futures of Punjab Agriculture

In the recent national discourse, Punjab and its agrarian economy is invariably presented through its negatives: depleting water tables, growing farmer indebtedness, lack of alternative sources of employment, declining incomes and a general sense of social fragmentation, reflected presumably in widespread drug addiction among its youth. While there is an element of truth in some of this, they surely do not provide a complete picture of the ground realities of Punjab agriculture.

As mentioned above, in the post-independence period, Punjab emerged as the most prosperous state of India in terms of its per capita income and remained so until the early 1990s. The shift in India's development trajectory during the early 1990s unleased new forces of economic growth. The prolonged conflict in the region around the question of Khalistan during the 1980s also dented the Punjab economy. While agricultural growth picked-up in rest of the country, Punjab saw a dip and grew by only 1.6 per cent during 2005–2006 and 2015–2015 when the national average was 3.5 per cent. The growth rate of agriculture in Punjab currently stands at around 2.3 per cent. Its position in the national economy has since been declining and it currently stands at number 10 among the major states of the country.

However, the reason for the relative decline of Punjab is not to be viewed in its agricultural sector alone. In fact, agriculture continues to do reasonably well in the state, primarily because the average size of its operational holdings is much higher than the national average. Punjab also has the best infrastructure required for agriculture in the entire country. An average agricultural household in Punjab still generates the highest monthly income (23,133), followed by Haryana (18,496) and Kerala (16,927).[12] Punjab has also done well in reducing the work force employed in agriculture. As per the Periodic Labour Force Survey (PLFS) 2017–2018, against the national average of 44.14 per cent, agricultural sector in Punjab employed only 26 per cent of its workers aged above 15 years.[13] Even in rural Punjab, agriculture does not provide employment to a majority of the resident workers. In the same year only 40.68 per cent of the rural workers, including landless labourers, were employed in agriculture.

Agriculture remains the most important economic activity in the state's economy and its social life. A significant proportion of the urban trade and industry are allied to agriculture. Punjab ranks fourth in terms of the number of agro-processing units in the country, after Andhra Pradesh, Tamil Nadu and Telangana. The sector added 44 per cent to the total gross value added by the manufacturing sector and employed about 46 per cent of the total workers employed by registered factories.[14] Punjab also continues to be ahead of other states in terms of productivity of food grains (wheat and rice) and the surpluses it generates. During the year 2017–2018, average per hectare yield of cereals in Punjab was 4,733 kg against the national average of 2,661 kg.

This is not to deny an absence of 'negatives' or 'crises' in rural Punjab and its agrarian economy. These have been well-known for quite some time. As is the case with the rest of India, agriculture in Punjab has been under severe stress since the early 1990s. While rice cultivation made sense for a limited while, it is no longer a sustainable crop for the state. Unregulated and subsidized exploitation of ground water has begun to produce a serious ecological crisis for the local agrarian economy, effects of which are already visible. Declining returns and rising costs have further strained the farming population of Punjab. This is clearly reflected in their growing indebtedness[15] and increasing incidences of suicide (Singh et al., 2016). The increasing desperation for going abroad among the rural Punjab youth is also indicative of the severe stress the cultivating households feel today.

The local elite has been acutely aware of these crises, as also the cultivating farmers. When water tables go down, they are the ones whose cost of installing a new or deeper tube-well substantially goes-up. The agenda of crop diversification has been around since 1986 when a committee headed by S.S. Johl had prepared a Report on the subject for the Punjab government. While the proposal of replacing paddy with other crops has been forcefully advocated by many 'outsiders', in the absence of any concrete alternatives and initiative offered to the farmers, it is unlikely to be taken seriously. The way forward from these crossroads is difficult but certainly not impossible. The recent proposal by the Union government and by a section of the establishment economists to let the free market take care of all the problems of India's agrarian economy has only deepened the anxiety felt by the farmers of Punjab, and elsewhere.

Farming, Developmentalism and Agrarian Cultures

Turning our focus back to the farm protests 2020–2021 and on farmers who sat on the roads surrounding Delhi, occupying parts of the major highways connecting the national capital to different parts of the country, how can we make sense of their remarkable resilience and determination? They sat through the harsh winter and the peak summer temperatures, sleeping on metalled roads. More than 700 protesting farmers died, mostly at the protest sites around Delhi, due to hardships related to weather and living conditions. Sitting in their thousands at the protest sites, far away from their homes and villages, also implied a significant expenditure, every day that they wouldn't be bearing lightly. How could we then explain their resilience and ability to carry-on such a sit-in for a whole year?

The answer is perhaps simple. Treat it as it presented itself to be: the articulation of a voice demanding to be heard. As Kanwar Grewal put it in one of his songs: '*fasla de faisle kisan karega*' [those who cultivate shall have the right to decide what to grow on their lands]. This was a struggle for democratic rights, for being recognized as citizens. Agriculture is not merely an occupation of a subject population in an empire, where the peasant cultivates land only at the will of the supreme power, the king, and as per his directives.

The popular and establishment narrative on Indian agriculture has come to be framed through the twentieth-century theories of economic growth, inscribed in textbooks of economics and other social sciences. The narrative goes somewhat like this: All societies go through certain phases of evolution. Early human life was primitive, when homo-sapiens lived like other animals, struggling to collect food for their survival. Agricultural innovations were the first major revolutions in human history. This made it possible for the kin groups to live together, at one place, along with others, forming rural settlements. Agricultural surpluses also enabled the emergence of urban centres, a new elite, and eventually new forms of political authority, the king. The next major revolution to occur in human history was the discovery of inanimate sources of energy; the industrial revolution in countries of Western Europe. In due course, they all became urban. Even agriculture was subsumed by it, turning it into a bourgeois enterprise. While all this was accomplished by Western Europe during the nineteenth century, the developing world, the present-day Global South, is still striving to 'catch-up' with the developed world. The narrative also marks these two groupings of countries as being characterized by distinct values or culture, often described as 'modern' versus 'traditional'.

However, the actual history of the world does not begin or end with the nineteenth- and twentieth-century Western Europe. Patterns of change and development have continued to be significantly diverse across regions. The above narrative also provides no space for the colonial history of plunder and the consequent 'backwardisation' of regions like India (Washbrook, 1993). However, this textbook narrative of human history came to be the hegemonic view of the world during the second half of the twentieth century and it continues to hold sway even today. Built into this view is also a larger narrative of human 'evolutionism' and 'developmentalism'. The world is thus assumed to have evolved out of tradition to modernity; from myth to reason; from collective will to individual agency. Modernity, as sociologist Gurminder Bhambra argues, invoked the ideas of *rupture* and *difference*. Its advocates underlined that the societies of the modern West had gone through a process of a temporal rupture, which implied a complete break from the agrarian ways of life of the past. The modernist conception of the world simultaneously also equated the agrarian societies of the non-Western world as being similar to the pasts of Western Europe. The difference between the West and the non-West was thus constructed in a manner that the two were viewed as being at different stages of their evolutionary process (Bhambra, 2007).

Such a view found considerable favour with the urban-centric professional middle-class elite that emerged under the colonial patronage in countries like India and inherited political power from the colonial masters. The models of change proposed by 'development studies' (the economists) and 'modernization theories' (sociologists and anthropologists) during the early decades after the decolonization of countries like India, in many ways reinforced the colonial view of underdevelopment as a natural stage in the process of evolution of the developing countries of the Global South into developed countries, at par with those of the Global North. Thus, agriculture has no place in the elite imaginations of the futures of their countries. And, in their frames of imaginations, farmers certainly have no ability or right to propose an alternative vision, even when it concerns their own lives and livelihoods. The mainstream narratives of modernity and developmentalism frames them as infantile, and thus having no claim to an agency of their own.

The protesting farmers saw themselves as citizens of the country, with a sense of entitlement. Their being from the relatively better-off position helped them sustain the movement. However, this was not a movement only of the cultivating farmers. It was also an assertion of farming cultures, embedded in which are the regional cultures. The new laws would have not only changed the way agriculture is done but would have also brought in a new corporate economy into the regional heartlands. It was this that explains the overwhelming support that the movement was able to generate across sections of Punjabis, particularly the Sikhs, from across the world. The movement was thus also a refusal and resistance to subjection and subjugation of regional culture to a view of market-driven national culture. Further, farming cultures also go beyond those who are directly involved in agriculture as an occupation and counted by official surveys. Despite structural conflicts and limitations (Jodhka, 2021), they could build solidarities across neighbouring castes, communities and classes. The Punjabi farmers' choice of Panjabi as a mediating language for their politics was precisely to articulate their interests in an inclusive language.

The source of surprise was thus not simply the ability of farmers to be able to stand up firmly and make their views on their futures heard, but at the very idea that they even ought to be having a view. While this surprise is easy to explain among the establishment economists, left-wing intellectuals and even farm leaders felt the pressure of the 'mainstream narrative'. It was the confidence and firmness of the so-called lay farmers, and the larger solidarities across genders, castes and classes that they had been able to forge that kept the movement going. Perhaps the most critical cultural resource that kept the Punjabi farmers going was their ability to invoke Sikhi, institutionally, such as the sustained langars; and emotionally, through the active and consistent use of everyday Sikh slogans.

Notes

* This chapter is a revised version of 'Agriculture and Citizenship: Making Sense of the Farmers' Movement of 2020-21', first published in *Journal of Sikh and Punjab Studies*, 29(1&2) (Spring–Fall, 2022): 187–206.
1 See Yogendra Yadav's piece in *The Print*, December 30, 2020, 'Why the farmers' movement is no longer what the Modi govt thinks it is'. https://theprint.in/opinion/farmers-movement-no-longer-what-modi-govt-thinks-it-is/576380/.
2 See a discussion organized by the Centre of Policy Research on March 18, 2021, and argument made by Harish Damodaran, available on YouTube https://www.youtube.com/watch?v=sfxTN9qJL9o&t=4712s.
3 Ramesh Chand. 2020. 'New Farm Laws: Understanding the Implications'. Niti Working paper Series 1/2020. http://niti.gov.in/sites/default/files/2020-11/NewFarmActs2020.pdf. Accessed July 08, 2021.
4 See, for example, a series of stories by Zee Television, Hindi, by its main news reader, Sudhir Chaudhary. https://www.youtube.com/watch?v=rXG5fRbBtk4.
5 This section of the chapter expands some of the arguments I presented in my *Economic and Political Weekly* editorial on the subject (Jodhka, 2020).
6 This section partially draws from an earlier piece on the subject (Jodhka, 2021).
7 Bhalla et al. cited in Kumar (2019: 43).
8 As cited by Kumar (*Ibid*.: 43) India's food availability per capita increased from 144.1 kg per person per annum in 1951 to 171.1 kg per person per annum in 1961.
9 Toor et al. cited in Lakhwinder Singh et al. (2016) https://thi.ucsc.edu/wp-content/uploads/2013/04/Vision-for-Economic-Development-in-Punjab.pdf. Accessed February 24, 2021.
10 *Economic Survey*, Punjab 2018–2019: 63–64. Available at: https://www.esopb.gov.in/static/PDF/EconomicSurvey-2019-20.pdf
11 *Ibid*., p. 64.
12 *Ibid*., p. 40.
13 *Ibid*., p. 40.

14 There is a large volume of literature on the growing indebtedness of Punjabi farmers and its different manifestations in the popular culture and everyday life. See, for example, Sidhu and Gill (2006), Shergill (2010), Singh et al. (2017), B. Kaur (2021), and T. Kaur (2021).

Bibliography

Aiyar, Yamini and Krishnamurthy, Mekhala. 'On farm laws, how the Centre faltered', *Hindustan Times*, December 2, 2020 (Downloaded June 29, 2022). https://www.hindustantimes.com/analysis/on-farm-laws-how-the-centre-faltered/story-44IpmLCZ2Pz0PFKnYOJgfJ.html

Ali, Imran. *The Punjab under imperialism, 1885–1947.* Princeton, NJ: Princeton University Press, 1988.

Bansal, Gaurav. 'Tenancy and Accumulation: A Study of the Capitalist Farm Sector in Punjab'. *Journal of Agrarian Change*, 2020. Vol. 10 (2): 28–47. http://ras.org.in/tenancy_and_accumulation. Accessed February 24 2021.

Bhalla, Gurdarshan Singh and Gopal Krishna Chadha. *Green Revolution and Small Peasant: A Study of Income Distribution among Punjab Cultivators.* New Delhi: Concept Publishing House, 1983.

Bhambra, Gurminder Kaur. *Rethinking Modernity: Postcolonialism and the Sociological Imagination.* London: Palgrave, 2007.

Chatterjee, Sumita and Ashok Rudra. 'Relations of Production in Pre-Colonial India'. *Economic and Political Weekly*, 1989. Vol. 24 (21): 1171–1177.

Ellis-Petersen, Hannah. 'Roaring crowds, roti and Rihanna: the view from a Delhi farm protest camp'. *The Guardian*, February 12, 2021 (Downloaded June 29, 2022). https://www.theguardian.com/world/2021/feb/12/roaring-crowds-roti-and-rihanna-the-view-from-a-delhi-farm-protest-camp

Harriss, John. 'Capitalism and Peasant Production: The Green Revolution in India'. In T. Shanin (ed.) *Peasant and Peasant Societies.* 227–245. London: Blackwell, 1987.

Inden, Ronald. *Imagining India.* Cambridge: Blackwell, 1990.

Jodhka Surinder Singh. 'Caste and Untouchability in Rural Punjab'. *Economic and Political Weekly*, 2002. Vol. 37 (19) May 11: 1813–1823.

Jodhka Surinder Singh. and Prakash Louis. 'Caste Tensions in Punjab: Talhan and Beyond'. *Economic and Political Weekly*, 2003. Vol. 38 (28): 2923–2926.

Jodhka Surinder Singh. 'Beyond "Crises": Rethinking Contemporary Punjab Agriculture'. *Economic and Political Weekly*, 2006. Vol. 41 (16): 1530–1537.

Jodhka Surinder Singh. *Caste in Contemporary India.* London and New Delhi: Routledge, 2015.

Jodhka Surinder Singh. 'Indian State and the Future of Agriculture: The Government Intervention Puts Indian Agriculture in the Grip of Corporates', *Economic and Political Weekly* (Editorial), 2020. Vol. 55 (49): 8.

Jodhka Surinder Singh. 'Changing Modes of Agriculture in Punjab', *The India Forum.* 02 April, 2021. https://www.theindiaforum.in/article/changing-modes-agriculture-punjab. Accessed February 24, 2021.

Jodhka, Surinder Singh. 'Why Are the Farmers of Punjab Protesting?' *The Journal of Peasant Studies*, 2021. Vol. 48 (7): 1356–1370.

Kaur, Bhupinder. 'Indebtedness among Farmers of Punjab', *Economic and Political Weekly*, 2021. Vol. 56 (26–27): 14–21.

Kaur, Tript. 'Of Half-moon Nights and Peasant Tragedy: Reading Rural Distress and the Green Revolution in Gurdial Singh's *Adh Chanani Raat*'. *Economic and Political Weekly*, 2021. Vol. 56 (26–27): 30–36.

Ludden, David. *An Agrarian History of South Asia*. Cambridge: Cambridge University Press, 1999.

Kumar, Richa. 'India's Green Revolution and Beyond: Visioning Agrarian Futures on Selective Readings of Agrarian Pasts', *Economic and Political Weekly*, 2019. Vol. 54 (34): 41–48.

Moore, Barrington Jr. *Social Origins of Dictatorship and Democracy*. Middlesex: Penguin, 1966.

Shergill, Harjinder Singh. 'Wheat and Paddy Cultivation and the Question of Optimal Cropping Pattern for Punjab', *Journal of Punjab Studies*, 2005. Vol. 12 (2): 239–250.

Shergill, Harjinder Singh. *Growth of Farm Debt in Punjab: 1997 to 2008*. Chandigarh: Institute of Development and Communications, 2010.

Sidhu, Rajinder Singh and Sucha Singh Gill. 'Agricultural Credit and Indebtedness in India: Some Issues', *Indian Journal of Agricultural Economics*, 2006, Vol. 61 (1): 11–35.

Singh, Gian, Anupama, Gurinder Kaur, Rupinder Kaur and Sukhvir Kaur. 'Indebtedness among Farmers and Agricultural Labourers in Rural Punjab', *Economic and Political Weekly*, 2017, Vol. 52 (6): 51–57.

Singh, Lakhwinder, Kesar Singh Bhangoo and Rakesh Sharma. *Agrarian Distress and Farmer Suicides in North India*. Delhi: Routledge, 2016.

Singh, Nirvikar and Deepali Singhal. 'The Green Revolution in Punjab, India: The Economics of Technological Change', *Journal of Punjab Studies*, 2005. Vol. 12 (2): 285–306.

Singh, Prem. 'Let the farmers' lead', *The Indian Express*, January 18, 2021 (Downloaded June 29, 2022). https://indianexpress.com/article/opinion/let-the-farmers-lead-7151460/

Sinha, Shreya. 'The Politics of Markets: Farmer-Trader Relations under Neoliberalism in Punjab, India'. *Journal of Agrarian Change*, 2020, Vol. 20 (2): 255–269.

Washbrook, David. 'Economic Depression and the Making of "Traditional" Society in Colonial India 1820–1855', *Transactions of the Royal Historical Society*, 1993. Vol. 3 (1993): 237–263.

8 Reforming Agricultural Markets for Agrarian Transformation

Potential Implications of Repealed Farm Acts for Punjab*

Sukhpal Singh

Introduction

The now repealed Union Acts on agricultural markets were brought in, first as ordinances in June 2020 and later as Acts in September 2020. This enactment was accompanied by farmer protests for their repeal in Punjab since September 2020 and later across north India. The farmers were at the borders of Delhi for more than a year and the Acts were put on hold by the Supreme Court of India until further notice in early 2021 itself. After many rounds of talks between the government and the farmer unions, there was a deadlock for more than 10 months before the three Acts (two new and one amended) were unilaterally announced by the Prime Minister to be repealed in November and were repealed by the Parliament in November 2021 itself. Meanwhile, hundreds of farmers lost their lives in the protest. Although there were two new Acts (The Farm Produce Trade and Commerce Act, 2020 – popularly known as Agricultural Produce Market Committee (APMC) *mandi* bypass Act – and the Farmers' (Empowerment and Protection) Agreement on Price Assurance and Farm Services Act, 2020 – commonly called the Contract Farming Act, 2020, besides the amendment in 2020 to the Essential Commodities Act (ECA), 1955, the Contract Farming Act 2020 was the most controversial as it was also not just about markets alone unlike the APMC Mandi bypass Act, 2020, as contract farming (CF) takes the market to the fields and has serious production and resource use implications.

Punjab has been one of the important agriculturally grown states as reflected in yields as well as farm input use besides commercialisation of crops where even food crops are grown mostly for the market. The fertiliser use is double that of India on per hectare basis and 94 per cent of paddy and 79 per cent of wheat produced are sold in the market. Until recently, this outcome can be seen as a case of state-managed capitalistic growth of agriculture in the state. During the last decade (2010–2020), however, the trend rate of growth of area, production and yield in Punjab became negative for most crops with the exception of paddy, barley, maize and oilseed in terms of production. The two crops of wheat and paddy ended up occupying 82 per cent of the Gross Cropped Area (GCA) of the state by 2014–2015,

 DOI: 10.4324/9781003320005-11

leading to heightened level of issues of groundwater depletion, stagnant farm incomes (Singh and Singh, 2020) and, therefore, an urgent need for crop diversification which has not progressed at all despite several attempts at it (Bhogal and Vatta, 2021). The increasing dependence of farmers on markets for inputs and output has led to higher cost of cultivation resulting in indebtedness, suicides and depeasantisation of the small and marginal farmers and displacement of labour due to excessive mechanisation (Singh and Singh, 2020). Punjab was also a pioneer in perishable produce CF in India since the 1990s and had significant experience of CF. Given this background, this chapter examines the implications of the repealed Acts from the farmer perspective and draws lessons from it in order to make sense of the proposed agricultural market reforms. It is particularly important to see whether adequate measures were being proposed to protect the small farmer interest under liberalised and pluralistic but mostly private-run market structures for their future viability. The 'The ECAA and FPTCP&FA, 2020' section brings out potential implications of the ECAA, 2020 and APMC Mandi bypass Act 2020 and the 'The Union CF Act: Design Issues' section analyses the major issues and implications of CF and examines aspects of the repealed Union CF Act 2020 followed by major lessons and ways forward in the 'Conclusions and Ways Forward' section.

The ECAA and FPTCP&FA, 2020

Two new Union laws aimed to create a 'one-nation, one-market' framework in what is essentially a federal nation, though with a unitary bias wherein, according to the sharing of legislative powers in the Indian constitution, agriculture and agricultural markets are under the domain of State governments. The third legislative measure was an amendment to the ECA, to remove uncertainties regarding stocking limits on food commodities, which were provided for under the ECA to contain price volatility, a too common a feature in commodity markets in India.

ECAA, 2020

The stated purpose behind these laws was to provide better price discovery for the farmer and to make agricultural markets attractive to private investment, as stated in the Statement of Objects and Reasons of the Essential Commodities (Amendment) Bill 2020:

> While India has become surplus in most agricultural commodities, farmers have been unable to get better prices due to lack of investment in cold storage, warehouses, processing and export as entrepreneurs get discouraged by the regulatory mechanisms in the Essential Commodities Act, 1955. A High-Powered Committee of Chief Ministers who examined this issue, recommended removal of stringent restrictions on stock,

> movement and price control of agricultural foodstuffs for attracting private investments in agricultural marketing and infrastructure.
>
> (GoI, 2020)

In effect, the three Acts aimed to provide ease of doing business for India's corporate sector right from procurement to stocking, processing and retailing as value chain players. Therein lay the apprehensions of the protesting farmers who had spent more than one year camping at the Haryana and UP borders outside Delhi. In addition to the protesting farmers, the repealed Acts attracted serious opposition from as many as seven States – Punjab, Chhattisgarh, Delhi, Rajasthan, Kerala, Tamil Nadu and West Bengal – which passed resolutions against these new Acts (HT, 2021; IE, 2021), various farmers' unions, many civil society organisations and a large number of political parties, despite the government claiming and highlighting various benefits of the new Acts at several fora and in Parliament. The Governments of Punjab, Rajasthan and Chhattisgarh even amended these laws in their State assemblies to nullify their application to their States (Rajalakshmi, 2020).

The amended ECA intended to promote investments in cold storage, warehouses, processing and export infrastructure, provided for relaxation for major cereals, edible oilseeds and oil, pulses and onion and potato crops though that was still not an absolute freedom from the ECA. This relaxation allowed regulation of stock by government only in extraordinary circumstances which could include war, famine, natural calamity of grave nature or extraordinary price rise.

The amended ECA, 2020, permitted government to impose stock limits if prices rose about 100 per cent of the previous year/5-year average retail price for horticultural produce and 50 per cent in the case of non-perishables. Further, it stated that such orders would not apply to a processor or value chain participant of any agricultural produce if its stock limit was lower than or just equal to its installed capacity for processing or demand for export in case of an exporter. The definition of a value chain participant included farm producer, processor, packer, storing entity, transporter and distributor, where in each stage, value was added to the product.

These ECA relaxations sound good from the perspective of various value chain participants but would not really have helped farmers directly. Only some Farmer Producer Organisations (FPOs) might have been able to use it for storing their produce for better prices and/or processing/value addition. Moreover, FPOs could benefit only if they had warehouses and were involved in processing, storage, packing, transport and distribution – any activity which added value.

The consumer benefit of this relaxation was not a given as it might actually end up leading to larger hoarding, and therefore, higher consumer prices. The more important aspect of this ECA reform was to do away with export bans that can really translate to indirect benefits for the farmers by giving them stable market access to exports. However, the 2020 imposition of complete ban on onion exports (by Director General of Foreign Trade) with little regard for the provisions of the amended ECA 2020 on perishable produce did not inspire any confidence among investors that the regulations would be consistently followed.

Although the Statement of Objects and Reasons of the Act claimed that India has attained surpluses in most agricultural commodities, data on per capita availability tell another tale. Between 1961 and 2018, the increase in availability of cereals was only about 26 grams per person per day – a mere six per cent increase over more than five decades. The overall foodgrains availability per person per day grew only by a paltry three per cent or 15 grams over this period. In case of pulses, the availability was actually 14 grams lower per day that was a 21 per cent decline over these years, and gram availability dropped by 13 grams or 43 per cent over this period, despite some of the supply coming from imports (IASRI, n.d.).

Added to this poor showing on per capita availability are the levels of hunger and malnutrition that can only worsen with food inflation (Kumar, 2021). Therefore, the 'de-fanging' of the ECA would have provided windfall gains for monopoly traders and companies who speculate on prices while turning into a nightmare for poor consumers who depend on the market to buy their food supplies, which includes some farmers who are net buyers of foodgrains, despite a reasonably well-run Public Distribution System (PDS) under the National Food Security Act, 2013.

The Farmers' Produce Trade and Commerce Act, 2020

The FPTC Act intended to promote efficient, transparent and barrier free inter-State and intra-State trade of farm produce outside the physical premises of markets or deemed markets notified under various State agricultural produce marketing legislations. It also sought to create a facilitative framework for electronic trading. However, as its intent was to bypass the existing (APMC) Mandi system, it was also referred to as the 'Mandi bypass Act' (Narayanan, 2020).

Prior to the enactment of new Acts of 2020, and after their repeal, under the State APMC Acts, there was a notified market area, and all notified crops or commodity produces were to be transacted within the designated APMC yards and sub-yards. Alternatively, buyers seek permission under the amended APMC Acts – as per the model APMC Act, 2003 and later the Model Agricultural Produce and Livestock Markets (APLM) Act, 2017 – from the local APMC for buying outside the mandi or undertaking CF (the latter is also under a separate law on CF modelled on the lines of 2018 Model Contract Farming and Services Act in some states). The produce, however, could still be subject to the same taxes and levies as the produce transacted inside the market yard.

The repealed Act would have created a new 'trade area' outside the APMC market yards/sub-yards where any buyer with a Permanent Account

Number (PAN, an income tax ID in India) could buy directly from farmer-sellers and the State government could not impose any tax on such transactions. However, the 2020 action by Haryana government to stop neighbouring UP farmers from selling paddy at Minimum Support Price (MSP) in Haryana even after the new Acts had come into force showed that inter-State barriers are not so easy to remove by regulation unless States come on board (The Statesman, 2020).

More significantly, the FPTC Act categorised transactions between traders either within a State or across States as farmer's produce. This expanded classification defied logic as once the primary transaction is completed, the farmer is not involved in subsequent transactions. This was similar to FPOs, which perform pre and post-farming operations, seeking exemption from income tax on the ground that they dealt with the produce raised by their members who were farmers and were exempt from income tax. The payment system provided by the new Act, i.e. payment by the trader on the same day or within a maximum of three days was worse than what was already provided under the APMC Act in some States like Madhya Pradesh (MP) since 1986, where payment for produce bought in the market yard had to be made on the same day to the farmer-seller. The MP APMC Act even provides for MSP as the starting point for auction when it states:

> provided that, in the market yard, the price for such notified agricultural produce of which support price has been declared by the State Government shall not be settled below the price so declared and no bid shall be permitted to start, in the market yard below the rate so fixed.
> (MPSAMB, 2005, p. 37)

So far as the role of FPOs in value chains or farm produce markets is concerned, the FPTC Act provided for e-markets by FPOs, although one was not sure how many of them could make use of this opportunity given their poor capital and professional resources. This was similar to APMCs allowing private wholesale markets by such collectives and many such markets exist in Maharashtra.

In what could be adverse to FPOs, they were treated as farmers under the Union Act. Section 2-b of the Act, as it stated: '"farmer" means an individual engaged in the production of farmers' produce by self or by hired labour or otherwise and includes the farmer producer organisation'. This, despite the fact that FPOs are not involved in production as most of them carry out pre- and post-production operations such as aggregation, trading and value addition.

At the same time, the trading role of the FPO was explicit in Section 4-1 which stated:

> Any trader may engage in the inter-State trade or intra-State trade of scheduled farmers' produce with a farmer or another trader in a trade

area: Provided that no trader, *except the farmer producer organisations* or *agricultural co-operative society*, shall trade in any scheduled farmers' produce unless such a trader has a permanent account number allotted under the Income-tax Act, 1961 or such other document as may be notified by the Central Government.

(The Gazette of India Extraordinary, 2020, p. 43)

This duality could create problems. Moreover, FPOs were not explicitly named as a part of the definition of person on the buying side, while cooperatives and co-operative societies were. There was even a separate payment mechanism proposed and rules provided for FPOs. It was not clear why this was needed and why producer members' own agencies like Amul needed to be told by government when and how to pay their members.

Inadequate Rationale for New Trade and Commerce Act

It had been argued and believed by most lay persons interested in the issue of farm laws and many experts that APMC markets had become monopsonistic (a market characterised by a single buyer) due to collusion among traders in these markets, did not discover prices efficiently and suffered from poor modern infrastructure. Therefore, it was reasoned out that farmers needed to be given a choice of channels and better price discovering markets like private wholesale markets, e-markets or new trade areas where farmers and buyers could just negotiate a price mutually.

First of all, it was questionable if the agricultural produce directly sold by farmers could be described as 'trade and commerce' as they did not engage in trade and commerce, as also pointed out by farmer unions. Therefore, one could argue that agricultural marketing could not be legislated as a trade and commerce activity which would have brought it under the ambit of Entry 33 of the Concurrent List, paving the way for Union legislation. To support this point, trade transactions between an APMC-licensed trader and another APMC or outside trader who buys from this trader are anyway not under the purview of APMCs, as the APMC Act deals only with farmer-level sale of produce: the first transaction between farmer and buyer directly or through a Commission Agent (CA) and not subsequent transactions (Singh, 2021). Therefore, much ambiguity would have been avoided and farmers' apprehensions not raised if such subsequent transactions, which qualify under 'trade and commerce', had been separately legislated upon under the Union List where Entry 42 has inter-State trade and commerce as its scope.

The view that APMC markets were *sarkari* or were not democratic in most States was not true as vibrant elections are held in major States like Gujarat, Maharashtra and Karnataka. That APMCs are not government bodies is clear from a recent statement in the Gujarat Assembly where it was stated that Gujarat has 227 co-operative APMCs and 30 private APMCs and only two new private markets had come up during the last two years. Only some States like Punjab have not conducted elections for APMCs for decades now and all office bearers are nominated.

On the issue of infrastructure, even as early as 2015, 83 per cent of APMC markets had godown facilities, 66 per cent had covered platforms, 76 per cent had drinking water facilities and 65 per cent had toilet facilities. Furthermore, 38 per cent of these markets had farmer rest houses, 15 per cent even had cold storages, 29 per cent had drying platforms and 22 per cent had grading facilities (LSS, 2019, p. 12).

Another argument for bringing in new Union Acts was that the States were not reforming markets fast enough and adequately. Evidence (LSS, 2019), however, speaks to the contrary. Even before the Union government's ordinances in 2020, the States had started to implement the Model Acts drafted by the Union Ministry of Agriculture and Farmer Welfare, which indicates the extent and speed of reforms. By June 2018, a total of 23 States had permitted direct purchase from farmers, 21 allowed e-trading, 23 had single point levy of market fee and 22 issued single-trading license for the entire State. In addition, 22 States/Union Territories (UTs) had allowed private wholesale markets, 20 permitted CF and 15 even freed fruits and vegetables from APMC regulation altogether.

To add to the irony, just when the ordinances were brought in during 2020, 27 out of India's 29 States and two UTs had already implemented most of the provisions: single license, single-point levy of market fee, direct marketing and private wholesale markets, through amendments to their APMC Acts. Even as recently as 2019, the 15th Finance Commission's report for 2020–2021 introduced performance-based grants for States to incentivise them to adopt the model APLM Act, 2017, the model Agricultural Produce and Livestock Contract Farming and Services (Promotion and Facilitation) Act, 2018 (APLCFA or Contract Farming Act) and the model Land Leasing Act (Rawal et al, 2020).

Paradoxically, although the basic objective of the new Acts was to open up agricultural markets for both buyers and farmer-sellers, the Union Acts would have brought re-regulation in some States instead. For instance, Bihar had done away with APMC regulation in 2006, while Sikkim and Kerala never had any. This could have gone against the argument for freeing of markets, if the new laws were allowed to go ahead, though no regulation of markets need not be desirable, as the experience of Bihar has shown (Singh, 2015; Bera, 2021).

Why Were Farmers and *Arthiyas* Protesting? Would APMCs Have Died?

The fear expressed by farmers and their unions about MSP arose from the absence of a level-playing field between the new trade area and APMC market yards and sub-yards. There were supposed to be no taxes in the new trade area, in contrast to significant buying costs in APMC market that were as high as 8.5 per cent in Punjab, including the 2.5 per cent charge by the commission agents (CAs or *Arthiyas*). Therefore, due to lower buying cost, the traders and even agents could move out of the APMC market yards and start buying from new trade areas (non-APMC areas). Another apprehension was that the Union government could also proactively shift its own buying agencies to the new trade area to buy directly from farmers. This would have still given access to MSP for farmers but the CAs could suffer as then they would not have been able to charge hefty commission which has been increasing along with every hike in MSP over the decades.

The 2020 directive of the Food Corporation of India (FCI) to the Government of Punjab to arrange to pay farmers for their produce bought by the FCI in Punjab directly into their bank accounts and not through the CAs was also a clear signal that Union government agencies were not keen to maintain the *arthiya* as an intermediary. The FCI was reported to have even offered to pass on the 2.5 per cent commission earlier paid to the *arhtiyas*, to the farmers as an incentive for receiving direct payment. However, the FCI would have still purchased from the APMC mandis like how the Cotton Corporation of India did in case of cotton during the kharif season of 2020, without involving and paying the *Arthiyas*.

That existing APMC mandis would have faced a crisis if the new Act came into force was clear from the already available reports which suggested that trade was moving outside the APMC markets and the State governments were lowering the market fee and other cesses to retain some competitive position as seen in MP (Arora, 2020; Kakvi, 2020; Siddique, 2020; Dwary, 2021).

The apprehension about MSP and public procurement disappearing (Singh, 2020) arose against the backdrop of the Acts coming in the context of some recent policy documents like the Shanta Kumar Committee Report of 2015 and the Commission for Agricultural Costs and Prices (CACP) reports suggesting reduced procurement and an end to open-ended procurement from States like Punjab to cut down buying costs of FCI. It was feared that FCI itself might start procuring directly from the new trade area to cut down its buying costs like market fees and *arthiya* commission.

The argument this these new Acts were aimed at bringing new investment in agriculture was based on misplaced hope if one went by the experience of Kerala which never had an APMC Act or Bihar which repealed the APMC Act in 2006 (Singh, 2018) or Maharashtra which delisted fruits and vegetables from APMC in 2018. It is important to note that laws cannot replace policy. Therefore, a policy has to be in place to get the agricultural sector and markets going. New investments need incentives, and not just ease of doing business.

More importantly, from the viewpoint of the farmers, perceived changes in the 'social contract' between farmers in some States and the Union government lay at the root of the apprehensions which resulted in protests and their unyielding positions. This social contract is seen in the form of government not only promising farmers an MSP for 23 crops but also procuring some of them (mainly wheat and paddy) since the 1960s and farmers responding to it by adopting new varieties and investing in farming which led to sufficient production of foodgrains in India over the decades. It was feared by farmers that government was not keen to stay committed to this promise and its delivery because it was providing a bigger space and role for private players in this domain. In any case, proposals like deficiency price payment without direct procurement by government suggested a reduction in public procurement by some government bodies like CACP and Shanta Kumar Committee comments were also seen from this perspective by the farmers.

In popular understanding of the farmers, the role of the state would have transformed from providing a supportive framework for the agricultural sector to one that just facilitated, even encouraged corporate operations. There was, thus, fear of withdrawal of the state from agricultural markets suddenly and leaving it open to the private sector to engage with farmers without adequate protection of the law or support of the state agencies.

The Union CF Act: Design Issues

CF is growing in importance globally with the Food and Agriculture Organisation (FAO) reporting that by the turn of the century (2000), 45 per cent of cash crop and livestock farmers were growing under contract (Chazovachii et al., 2021). CF has been in practice in India since the 1960s in the seed sector across States and in other farm produce in many states like Punjab, and Haryana since the 1990s with the Pepsi Foods undertaking tomato, chilly and potato CF. There is a widespread practice of CF across crops, States and agencies (public, private and multinational) in India covering dozens of crops and livestock products with hundreds of CF projects or schemes, for domestic processing or for export. Further, CF has been legal in most States as per the model APMC Act 2003 of the union Ministry of Agriculture and Farmer Welfare (MoAFW), and later, under a separate Agricultural Produce and Livestock Contract Farming and Services (promotion and facilitation) [APLCF&S (P&F)] Act, 2018 like in Tamil Nadu and Odisha (GoI, 2018).

Globally, there have been issues with the CF practice (USAID, 2015; Chazovachii et al., 2021) like side selling, mistrust and dissatisfaction among contract growers about company practices and, therefore, unwillingness to continue or withdrawal from contracts (Ruml and Qaim, 2020) though contract farmers earned higher returns despite spending higher on production than that by non-contract farmers (Loquuias et al., 2021) although not in all situations (Ragasa et al., 2018). The role of CF in stabilising farm income as a part insurance against market risk has also been noted (Bellemare et al., 2021). In India, the practice of CF has also led to exclusion of small farmers as contracting agencies prefer larger farmers to reduce their transaction costs (Singh, 2002, 2004; Kumar, 2006) with a few exceptions in some regions and some crops (Pritchard and Connell, 2011; Singh, 2012, 2013; Sharma and Singh, 2015; Sharma, 2016a, 2016b) as sometimes small farmers self-select themselves out when large farmers are part of the CF program (Ze-ying et al., 2018). The exclusion of smallholders has led to research and policy concerns on the inclusiveness of agribusiness models globally (Melese, 2012). There is no doubt that CF generally benefits farmers compared with existing channels of marketing (Singh, 2002; Kumar, 2006; Kaur and Singla, 2018). Studies have refuted claims of the contracting agencies that they are in partnership with famers or the claimed farmer benefits, and studies find that farmers are not willing to take up CF due to the stringent quality standards and rejection of farm produce (Ray et al., 2021) and global agencies like FAO are now designing and advocating responsible contracts (FAO and IISD, 2018).

The Farmers (Empowerment and Protection) Agreement on Price Assurance and Farm Services Act, 2020 (Contract Farming Act) stated that its mandate was:

> to provide for a national framework on farming agreements that protects and empowers farmers to engage with agribusiness firms, processors, wholesalers, exporters or large retailers for farm services and sale of future farming produce at a mutually agreed remunerative price framework in a fair and transparent manner.
>
> (GoI, 2020a)

The use of the term 'farming agreement' itself was unusual as it was being confused with other arrangements like sharecropping or leasing agreements.

The biggest problem was that it was being confused with *corporate farming* (corporates farming on leased or owned land). The confusion between CF and corporate farming created by the Act was so significant that the Rajasthan Amendment Bill, 2020 (GoR, 2020, p. 4) stated:

> Where under a farming agreement, sponsor undertakes the farming by deploying his/its manpower, the sponsor shall be liable to remove his manpower from the agriculture farm/field from the next date of termination of the farming agreement and in the event of manpower of the sponsor continuing in the agricultural farm/field, the sponsor shall be liable to pay damages to the farmer to the tune of such amount as may be notified by the state government from time to time which shall not be less than one thousand rupees per bigha per day.

The Act seemed to protect farmer's land when it stated in Section 14: 'No farming agreement shall be entered into for the purpose of (a) any transfer, including sale, lease or mortgage of the land or premises of the farmer...'

(GoI, 2020a, p. 5). But since the 'production agreement' was defined as 'where the sponsor agrees to provide farm services, either fully or partially and to bear the risk of output, but agrees to make payment to the farmer for the services rendered by such farmer' (GoI, 2020a, p. 2), it raised doubts as to how could a farmer be paid for the services rendered, and not for the produce? How could the sponsor bear risk of output when it was produced by the farmer? The sponsor can only reduce farmer's market risk as it agrees to buy in advance at a pre-agreed price.

The above aspects of the Act raised doubts whether it was more about land leasing and corporate farming, rather than CF. If that was so, then this Act violated the land leasing Acts of many states which still restrict farmland leasing with only a few exceptions of some categories in some States. And, it is important to recall that the Union government's 2018 model Contract Farming and Services Act had also provided for land leasing in the Act (Singh, 2018). So, it was more about providing it by design, not a default or lacunae in the Act and the Rajasthan government amendment Bill, 2020 can't be faulted for (mis)interpreting it.

The 'trade and commerce agreement', another type of CF agreement in the Act was defined as 'where the ownership of commodity remains with the farmer during production and he gets the price of produce on its delivery as per the agreed terms with the Sponsor' (GoI, 2020a, p. 2). It was nothing but about direct purchase which is not the appropriate transaction under any CF Act besides the fact large retailers were mentioned as contracting parties. The global and the Indian truth about large retailers or food supermarkets is that they don't have contract agreements with farmers and buy directly without any advance commitment of price (Singh and Singla, 2011).

The Act linked bonus and premium over and above the guaranteed price, with mandi price or electronic market price which was anti-CF in nature. The contract price, like many other basic aspects of a contract, should be left to the parties to negotiate. This can't be tied to any other channel especially APMC price as the very rationale for bringing this law was to provide an alternative channel to farmers and create competition due to the perception that APMC markets were not seen as discovering the prices efficiently. Therefore, going back to the same mandi did not speak very well of the Act.

This Act left out many sophisticated aspects of modern CF practices like contract cancellation clauses and damages therein, and 'tournaments' in CF where farmers are made to compete with each other and paid as per relative performance, although this is banned in many countries. The very basic aspects of CF like acreage, quantity and time of delivery were not specified which is a must for any law regulating it as these are mandatory aspects of such an arrangement whether with supply of inputs or otherwise. In fact, the 2003 model APMC Act had such provisions and even a model CF agreement. Therefore, it required properly thought-out regulation but the new Act fared poorly on that count.

Further, it is surprising that despite keeping the dispute settlement outside the purview of civil courts, the CF guidelines stated that a farming agreement must meet the ordinary requirements of contract law to be valid just like other contracts (GoI, 2020b). If these contracts were not to be dealt with by civil courts, then why this condition? These guidelines also stated 'when a sharecropper is involved in the agreement, he may be made responsible for receiving and using any inputs from the sponsor, for the cultivation of produce of the appropriate quality and for production by using good standard practices' (GoI, 2020b, p. 2). This was again faulty as CF agreement by a contracting agency is always with a landowner or a lease operator, and not with a farm worker or a labour tenant.

The above discussion shows that the repealed union CF Act was more about facilitation and promotion of the CF mechanism rather than its regulation. That the Act went all the way to facilitate CF was clear from the fact that it mentioned that the stock limits Act (ECAA, 2020) would not apply to contract farmed produce. Why should this provision of another Act be specifically mentioned in this law which has nothing to do with this law directly or indirectly? Finally, the proof of any law is in its implementation but so far as protection of farmer interest is concerned, this Act left much to be desired in its design itself.

Implications of CF in Punjab: Exclusion and Reverse Tenancy

In Punjab, only 31 per cent of the operated agricultural landholdings are small or marginal and they account for just 8 per cent of the operated area. On the other hand, large farms (above 10 hacs) account for just 7 per cent of all farms but cultivate 26 per cent of land and they along with another 28 per cent semi-medium farms (4–10 hacs) who had 43 per cent of operated area, accounted for 69 per cent of all operated area of the state. Further, there is one tractor for every three farm workers now. The operating farmers are only 20 per cent of all workers and only marginally higher than the farm worker proportion in total (16 per cent) (Singh and Singh, 2020). Small farmers in the state have been moving out of agriculture due to the phenomenon of 'reverse tenancy', leasing out their land to bigger operators like medium or large holders who have the resources and linkages for modern farming or agribusiness. Importantly, Punjab is the only state in India where the size of operational holdings is increasing instead of decreasing (Singh, 2012). In Punjab, by 2010–2011, 55 per cent of the operated area was with the tenants with leased in area accounting for 48 per cent of the operated area and the average size of the operated holding of a tenant was double that of an owner operated although the owned land did not differ across types of farmers. Further, 83 per cent of tenant farmers owned tractors compared with 55 per cent of owner farmers and 78 per cent had power operated tube wells compared with 61 per cent of owner farmers. A majority of them also employed permanent farm servants compared with only 25 per cent of owner farmers. The semi-medium and large farmers accounted for 48 per cent and 34 per cent of the leased in area respectively, with another 14 per cent being with the semi-medium farmers in 2010–2011. The small farmers accounted for only 4 per cent of the leased in area (Shergill, 2016). In Hoshiarpur, 43 per cent farmers leased in land (Chatterjee et al., 2020).

During the first phase of CF in Punjab in the 1990s, the contracting companies (HLL, Pepsi and Nijjer) preferred large growers for contract production, perhaps to avoid problems of dealing with too many small growers, and the average contract grower holdings were as large as 72 acres each in case of MNCs and 22 acres each in case of a local contracting firm (Singh, 2004). Further, CF led to concentration of operated land and even reverse tenancy (Singh, 2002) and even in 2007, 56 per cent of contract farmers had leased in land and 51 per cent of them even more than 10 acres each. Thus, 33 per cent of them had operated holdings of more than 25 acres each, 46 per cent of 10–25 acres and only 20 per cent had less than 10 acres each (Shrimali, 2014).

The CF programme excluded small farmers in most cases as firms specified eligibility conditions like landholding, irrigation and education. Contract farmers had average holdings much larger than the average size of a holding in the state (9.5 acres) (Asokan and Singh, 2006; Singh, 2008) and there was 'no marginal farmer (in the size group of below one hectare)... operating under CF. A handful of small farmers (in the size group of one to two hectares) were operating' (Kumar, 2006). Yet another study noted 'the majority of the acreage registered in the project (CF by PAFC) is held by larger farmers, who tended to receive greater benefits from participation' (Witsoe, 2006). Even Nijjer Agro worked mostly with medium-sized farmers who had on average 13 acres of land and only 6 per cent farmers were small or marginal (Dhillon and Singh, 2006). Markfed, a parastatal agency, placed advertisements in local newspapers asking farmers willing to grow at least three acres of basmati paddy under CF to contact its district managers (Singh, 2012).

In 2014–2015, the three major contracting companies active in the Khanna area of Ludhiana district (PepsiCo, Mahindra & Mahindra and Technico Agri Sciences) preferred to work with larger farmers; one of them requiring a minimum operational holding of seven acres for a farmer to be eligible to be contact grower (Sinha, 2020). In chicory and sugar beet CF, the two CF agencies mostly excluded marginal and small farmers from their operations. Only one firm had 6 per cent of its all-contract farmers who were small despite the fact that 28–32 per cent of the farmers in their operating areas were marginal or small. Operated land holdings of contract farmers in both cases were double that of their non-contract counterparts and even owned holdings were larger (Kaur and Singla, 2018). Therefore, CF has led to perpetuation of reverse tenancy in the state which leads to control of land and benefits of farming being taken away by leases rather than small land operators or owners (Singh, 2020a).

Conclusions and Ways Forward

Though CF is an important mechanism for diversification, in reality, it is more about who does CF, why and how, which can help or hinder diversification. In order to ensure better farm incomes from new crops, it is important to ensure that contracts are fair and balanced and reduce farmer's market and production risk of new crops.

As far as local groups or agencies of small farmers are concerned, there is a striking absence of any farmers' or producers' organisations in Punjab. Compared to 2.2 per cent of the farmers in India being members of some agricultural association or other and 4.8 per cent being self-help groups, the corresponding figures in Punjab were only 0.3 per cent and 1.5 per cent respectively (Witsoe, 2006). This neglect of smallholders is further reinforced by the absence of non-governmental organisations (NGOs) working in the agricultural sector of the state (Singh, 2012) which has been noted earlier as well (Singh, 2004). The farmers' organisations and NGOs could have intervened in CF situations as intermediaries to protect the farmer and broader local community interests. It is also important to realise that CF need not be promoted for all crops, farmers and regions, and the State should play more of a regulatory role rather than a promotional one. Credit support to CF projects by the State is crucial. State policy, including CF, needs to be changed in favour of small producers (Singh, 2012). It was ironic that a corporate joint venture with a foreign wholesaler (Tata-Total Produce) was the first and only agency in Punjab to organise fruit and vegetable producers into producer companies (PCs) though it never worked (Singh, 2012). Punjab has been a laggard in promotion of PCs unlike many other States (Singh and Singh, 2014; Singh, 2021a).

For CF to succeed, both regulation and policy are needed, and one can't do the job of another. Contract should be fair to both the parties and enforcement mechanism should be clear and credible. There should be promotion of grades and quality standards among growers besides credit support and extension provision by public agencies, and State should not promote CF in non-viable situations or intervene too much, and incentives should be time bound and short term. Most importantly, competition in CF among buyers is a must to avoid opportunism by buyers and give choices to farmers to receive competitively discovered prices and other benefits (USAID, 2015). Many times, government projects in the contract crop can drive away private agencies from CF (Lambrecht and Ragasa, 2018).

Further, since Indian farmers are marginal or small, they can't deal with large buyers on their own even if they are brought under CF by some corporate agencies. Therefore, group contracts should be either part of the legislation or encouraged by policy incentives to make the mechanism inclusive and effective for farmers. The government can facilitate such contracts through credit and extension facilities like in Thailand (Singh, 2005). Also, India has thousands of PCs which are very business-like entities of farmers, and they can play a role in making CF deliver the objectives of farmer income enhancement by facilitating CF with smallholders, and also undertaking it on their own (Singh and Singh, 2014; Singh, 2021a).

It is important to ask: Can one size fit all in a diverse country like India in its markets and institutions? For example, Punjab may be ready for CF or direct purchase but not Odisha. Some States have functional APMC infrastructure while others have none or have dismantled it like Bihar did with the stroke of a pen in 2006. Do we need more mandis or more deregulation? Would only more mandis do, or do we need more functional and effective mandis?

It is also important to recognise that Indian agri-produce markets are decentralised and dynamic. One agrees that the APMCs in some States are inefficient and ridden with corruption and malpractices, but is moving away, the solution? Should we abandon the existing structures which would amount to throwing away the baby along with the bathwater, or should we reform the APMC markets as they are the last resort for millions of marginal and small farmers who would never be attractive to corporate buyers whether individually or collectively through FPOs?

The decision to do away with APMC regime on grounds of inefficiency and monopsony is similar to the argument against practicing democracy. Should we give up democracy or federalism because it is not working smoothly? If self-reliance is the purpose of these reforms, should it be achieved through corporates or through people's agencies like APMCs and FPOs?

Finally, it is important to realise that whatever expansion CF and direct purchase may witness, India's large mass of marginal and small farmers would need public and private wholesale markets which need to be reformed in terms of free licensing for better competition, e-payment of market fee, ensuring open auction, better facilities, representation of PCs in APLM governance and even denotification of Commission Agents/*Arthiyas* as MP did in 1985, though it is not widely known and discussed even today. The reform of APLM markets is important as they serve as competitors to CF and 'direct' purchase practiced by food supermarkets and other buyers, and even proposed private wholesale markets, and can help improve the terms offered by direct buyers and contracting agencies to growers as contract/direct prices are unfortunately benchmarked to APLM prices and the repealed CF Act, 2020 also took this route to contract price determination, to some extent.

More recently, in November 2021, after the repeal of the Union Farm Acts, in the same month, Punjab repealed the Contract Farming Act of 2013 (PVSS, 2021a) and has also undone all reforms in the APMC Act from 2006 to 2017 by disallowing all private channels like private wholesale markets, direct purchase or public–private partnership in agricultural markets (PVSS, 2021b). This only takes Punjab back to the pre-2003 days and will do no good for the farmers of Punjab who desperately need new channels for their existing and new crops and produce.

Note

* This chapter is a revised version of 'Contract Farming for Agrarian Transformation? Experiences from Punjab in the Context of Union Contract Farming Act, 2020', first published in *Journal of Sikh and Punjab Studies*, 29(1&2) (Spring–Fall, 2022): 227–44.

Bibliography

Arora, S. By amending Model Mandi Act, MP has pushed its agricultural sector into throes of uncertainty, *Indian Express*, December 21, 2020.

Asokan S. R. and G. Singh. *Contract farming of Medicinal Herbs and Organic Crops in India*, CMA Monograph No. 224, CMA, IIM, Ahmedabad, 2006.

Bellemare, M. F., Y. N. Lee and Novak, L. 'Contract Farming as Partial Insurance'. *World Development*, 2021, 140(C).

Bera, S. 'What trade freedom did to Bihar farmers', *Mint*, March 8, p. 8, Ahmedabad, 2021.

Bhogal, S. and K. Vatta. 'Can Crop Diversification Be Widely Adopted to Solve the Water Crisis in Punjab? *Current Science*, 2021. 120(8), 1303–1307.

Chatterjee, S., Krishnamurthy, M., Kapur, D. and Bouton, M. 'A study of the Agricultural Markets of Bihar, Odisha and Punjab', CASI, University of Pennsylvania, Philadelphia, 2020.

Chazovachii, B., C. Mawere and L. Chitongo. 'Sustainability of Centralised Contract Farming among Tobacco Smallholder Farmers in Makoni North District, Zimbabwe'. *Cogent Social Sciences*, 2021, 7, 114.

Dhaliwal, H. S., M. Kaur and J. Singh. 'Evaluation of Contact Farming Scheme in the Punjab State', Dept. of Eco., PAU, Ludhiana, 2003.

Dhillon, S. S. and N. Singh. 'Contract Farming in Punjab: An Analysis of Problems, Challenges and Opportunities'. *Pakistan Economic and Social Review*, 2006, 44(1), 19–38.

Dwary, A. Madhya Pradesh *Mandis'* Revenue at One-Third in January, To Rent Out Space, *NDTV.Com*, February 12, 2021.

FAO and IISD. *Model Agreement for Responsible Contract Farming*, with commentary. Rome: FAO, 2018.

GoI. *The Essential Commodities Amendment Bill, 2020 (As introduced in the Lok Sabha)*, Ram Vilas Paswan, Minister of Consumer Affairs, Food and Public Distribution, September 14. New Delhi, Government of India, 2020.

GOI. *Model Act (The State/UT Agricultural Produce and Livestock Contract Farming and Services (Promotion and Facilitation) Act, 2018*, February, MoAFW, Dept. of Agriculture, Cooperation and Farmers' Welfare, Government of India, 2018.

GoI. *The Farmers Produce Trade and Commerce (Promotion and Facilitation) Bill*, No. 10 of 2020, Ministry of Agriculture and Farmer Welfare (MoAFW), Government of India, 2020.

GoI. The Farmers (Empowerment and Protection) Agreement on Price Assurance and Farm Services Bill, No. 11 of 2020, 2020a.

GoI. *The Farmers (Empowerment and Protection) Agreement on Price Assurance and Farm Services Bill*, No. 11 of 2020 – Guidelines for Farming Agreement, 2020b.

GoR. *The Farmers (Empowerment and Protection) Agreement on Price Assurance and Farm Services (Rajasthan Amendment) Bill*, No. 31 of 2020, Govt. of Rajasthan, 2020.

HT. 'West Bengal passes resolution against three farm laws, sixth state to do so', *Hindustan Times,* Online, January 28, 2021.

IASRI. *Agricultural Research Data Book 2017*, Indian Agricultural Statistics Research Institute. ICAR, New Delhi, n.d.

IE. 'TN adopts resolution against Centre's farm laws, seventh state to do so', *Indian Express*, Chennai, 2021.

Kakvi, K. 'New laws paralyse 70% of MP's Mandis in six months', *News Click,* December 7, 2020.

Kaur, P., and Singla, N. 'Can Contract Farming Double Farmers' Income?' *Economic and Political Weekly*, 2018, 53(51), 68–73.

Kumar, P. 'Contract Farming through Agribusiness Firms and State Corporation: A Case Study in Punjab'. *Economic and Political Weekly*, 2006, 41(52), 5367–5375.

Kumar, M. 'Food Stuffs Market Regulation: The Essential Commodities (Amendment) Act 2020 and After'. *Economic and Political Weekly*, 2021, 56(49), 15–19.

Lambrecht, I. B. and C. Ragasa. 'Do Development Projects Crowd-Out Private Sector Activities? Evidence from Contract Farming Participation in Northern Ghana'. *Food Policy*, 2018, 74, 9.

Lok Sabha Secretariat. *Agriculture Marketing and Role of Weekly Gramin Haat*s, Standing Committee on Agriculture, 62 Report, January 3, LSS, New Delhi, 2019.

Melese, A. T. 'Contract Farming: Business Models that Maximise the Inclusion of and Beenfits for Smallholders in the Vlaue Chain'. *Rev. dr.unif.*, 2012, 17(1–2), 291–306.

MPSAMB. *M P Krishi Upaj Mandi Adhiniyam*, 1972 (MP Act No. 24 of 1973), up-to-date amended Act, MPSAMB, Bhopal, 2005.

Narayanan, S. 'The Three Farm Bills: Is This the Market Reform Indian Agriculture Needs?', *The India Forum*, November 27, 2020.

Pritchard, B. and J. Connell. 'Contract Farming and the Remaking of Agrarian Landscapes: Insights from South India's Chilly Belt'. *Singapore Journal of Tropical Geography*, 2011, 32 (3), 236–252.

PVSS. The Punjab Contract Farming (Repeal) Bill 2021, Bill No. 36-PLA-2021. Punjab Vidhan Sabha Secretariat (PVSS), Chandigarh, 2021a.

PVSS. The Punjab Agricultural Produce Markets (Amendment) Bill 2021, Bill No. 35-PLA 2021. Punjab Vidhan Sabha Secretariat (PVSS), Chandigarh, 2021b.

Ragasa, C., I. Lambrecht and D. S. Kufoalor. 'Limitations of Contract Farming as a Pro-Poor Strategy: The Case of Maize Outgrower Scheme in Upper West Ghana'. *World Development*, 2018, 102, 30–56.

Rajalakshmi, T. K. 'State governments in Punjab, Chhattisgarh and Rajasthan get their acts together and pass amended farm Bills in their State Assemblies', *Frontline*, December 4, 2020.

Rawal, V., S. Patel and J. Pais. 'The political economy of agricultural market reforms – an analysis of the farmers' produce trade and commerce (promotion and facilitation) Act, 2020', SSER monograph No. 20/4, SSER, New Delhi, 2020.

Ray, N., G. Clarke and P. Waley. 'The Impact of Contract Farming on the Welfare and Livelihoods of Farmers: A Village Case Study from West Bengal'.

Journal of Rural Studies, 2021 published online. https://doi.org/10.1016/j.jrurstud.2021.06.003.

Ruml, A. and M. Qaim. 'Smallholder Farmers' Dissatisfaction with Contract Schemes in Spite of Economic Benefits: Issues of Mistrust and Lack of Transparency'. *The Journal of Development Studies*, 2020. https://doi.org/10.1080/00220388.2020.1850699.

Shergill, H. S. 'Growth of Cash Rent Tenancy and Modernization of Land Lease Market in Punjab'. In L. Singh and N. Singh (eds.) *Economic Transformation of a Developing Economy: The Experience of Punjab.* India: Springer, 121–139, Chapter 6, 2016.

Sharma, N. 'Determining Growers' Participation in Contract Farming in Punjab'. *Economic and Political Weekly*, 2016a, 51(2), 58–65.

Sharma, N. 'Does Contract Farming Improve Farmers' Income and Efficiency? A Case Study from Punjab'. *Economic and Political Weekly*, 2016b, 51(40), 63–69.

Sharma, N. and S. P. Singh. 'Agricultural Diversification and Contract Farming in Punjab'. *Journal of Economic and Social Development*, 2013, 9(3), 38–51.

Sharma, N. and S. P. Singh. 'Exploring Contract Relationships in Punjab: A Case Study of Potato and Basmati Paddy'. *Journal of Land and Rural Studies*, 2015, 3(2), 165–186.

Shrimali, R. *Spaces of Corporate Control in Agriculture: A Critical Study of Contract Farming in the Indian State of Punjab*, PhD thesis, York University Toronto, 2014.

Siddique, I. 'Amid new farm laws, pandemic, Madhya Pradesh mandis take a hit', *Indian Express*, December 14, 2020.

Singh, P. and I Singh. 'Political Economy of Capitalist Development in Punjab's Agriculture'. *Agrarian South*, 2020, 9(2), 197–227.

Singh, S. 'Contracting Out Solutions: Political Economy of Contract Farming in the Indian Punjab'. *World Development*, 2002, 30(9), 1621–1638.

Singh, S. 'Crisis and Diversification in Punjab Agriculture: Role of State and Agribusiness'. *Economic and Political Weekly*, 2004, 39(52), 5583–5590.

Singh, S. 'Role of the State in Contract Farming in Thailand: Experience and Lessons'. *ASEAN Economic Bulletin*, 2005, 22(2), 217–228. (Now *Journal of Southeast Asian Economies* from 2013).

Singh, S. 'Marketing Channels and Their Implications for Smallholder Farmers in India'. In McCullough, E. B., Pingali, P. L. and Stamoulis, K. G (eds.) *The Transformation of Agri-food Systems: Globalization, Supply Chains, and Smallholder Farmers.* Rome: FAO and London: Earthscan Press, 2008, 279–310.

Singh, S. 'Institutional and Policy Aspects of Punjab Agriculture: A Smallholder Perspective'. *Economic and Political Weekly*, 2012, 43(4), 51–57.

Singh, S. 'The Practice of Contract Farming in India: Making It Inclusive and Effective'. *Food Chain*, 2013, 3(3), 137–154.

Singh, S. 'Reforming markets, lessons from Bihar', *The Tribune*, Chandigarh, February 6, Op ed. Agriculture, page 9, 2015.

Singh, S. 'APMCs: The other side of the story', *The Hindu Business Line*, Opinion, January 24, 2018.

Singh, S. Farmers' apprehensions about role of mandis, terms of procurement under new laws need to be addressed, *The Indian Express,* December 3, 2020.

Singh, S. 'Ownership v/s Control: Changing Dynamics of Land Use in Liberalised Agricultural Context of India'. In D. K. Mishra and P. Nayak (eds.) *Land and*

Livelihoods in Neoliberal India. Singapore: Palgrave Macmillan, 2020a, 57–70, Chapter 3.
Singh, S. 'Food Security and Markets: Understanding the Protests over India's Changing Social Contract with Farmers', *The Hindu Centre for Politics and Public Policy*, Chennai, March 15, 2021.
Sinha, S. 'Betting on Potatoes: Accumulation in Times of Agrarian Crisis in Punjab, India'. *Development and Change*, 2021, 51(6), 1533–1554.
Singh, S. and T. Singh. *Producer Companies in India: Organisation and Performance*. New Delhi: Allied, 2014.
Singh, S. and Singla, N. *Fresh Food Retail Chains in India: Organisation and Impacts*. New Delhi: Allied, 2011.
Singh, S. *Understanding Performance and Impact of Producer Companies: Case Studies across States and Promoters in India*. Ahmedabad: CMA, IIM, Final report, March, 2021a.
The Gazette of India Extraordinary. The Farmers' Produce Trade and Commerce (Promotion and Facilitation) Act, 2020, Part 11, Section 1, Ministry of Law and Justice, New Delhi, September 27, 2020 (Downloaded June 20). https://prsindia.org/billtrack/the-farmers-produce-trade-and-commerce-promotion-and-facilitation-bill-2020
The Statesman. *Farmers from UP Stopped from Entering Haryana to Sell at Paddy at Government Run Mandis*. September 29, 2020.
USAID. *Building Enabling Environment for Contract Farming Success*, Policy Brief 6, February, 2015.
Witsoe, J. 'India's Second Green Revolution? The Sociological Implications of Corporate-led Agricultural Growth'. In Devesh. Kapoor (ed.), *India in Transition: Economics and Politics of Change*. Philadelphia, PA: Centre for the Advanced Study of India, 2006, 1–33.
Ze-ying, H., X. Ying, Z. Di, W. Chen and W. Ji-min. 'One Size Fits All? Contract Farming among Broiler Producers in China'. *Journal of Integrative Agriculture*, 2018, 17(2), 473–482.

9 *Mera Pind, Mera Sabhyachar, Mera Virsa*

Understanding Sikh Diaspora Support for the Punjab Kisan *Morcha**

Shinder S. Thandi

Introduction: Formation of the Sikh Diaspora

A century and a half of Sikh overseas migration resulted in the scattering of Sikhs all over the globe, with total number in the diaspora now estimated at around 2 million, out of global Sikh population of around 25 million. Well over 80 per cent of the Sikh diaspora is now concentrated in two major regions – Europe, with majority still in the UK, and North America, with Canada having a larger share.[1] This formation occurred during several migration waves, with each wave having its own specific context and features, causing Sikhs to venture overseas. Overseas migration began in the 1860s after re-appraisal of Sikhs by the British due to their role during the Indian Mutiny of 1857 but gathered pace over the next half a century. Thus, by the outbreak of World War 1, Sikh communities were well established in various overseas locations in southeast and east Asia, Australia, New Zealand, Fiji, East Africa, UK and on the Pacific coast of North America, especially around the porous borderlands between the USA and Canada (Mangat, 1969; Ballantyne, 2006; La Brack, 2008; Shamsul and Kaur, 2011). The spread and settlement of these pioneer overseas communities reflected the changing socio-economic conditions in Punjab: new opportunities offered by British army recruitment with Sikhs classified as one of the favoured 'martial races'; new information on jobs available overseas as policemen or security guards ('*jagas*') to protect the expanding British empire, and deteriorating economic conditions and shrinking opportunities at home 'pushing' Sikhs to go overseas to seek their fortunes (Tan, 2005; Streets, 2010; Thandi, 2017).[2]

However, by the 1920s, a series of anti-immigrant policies, especially in North America, Australia and New Zealand, severely limited the further expansion of Sikh migration, except in clandestine forms. However as favourable conditions re-emerged after World War 2, initially in war-damaged UK, we see beginnings of the golden period of Sikh migration. The mass movements of the 1950s and 1960s to UK and from the mid-1960s to the USA and Canada, to the Gulf States in the 1980s and the more recent movements since the 1990s to newer locations such as Greece,

DOI: 10.4324/9781003320005-12

Italy and Spain in southern Europe and Norway and Sweden in northern Europe, largely had rural roots, mainly in villages of central *Doaba* districts of Jalandhar and Hoshiarpur (Tatla, 2004; Thandi, 2017). This in a way reversed the earlier trend during the British army recruitment period when migration flows from the *Malwa* and *Majha* sub-regions tended to be more common. Moreover, with many of the pioneer migrants from *Malwa* and *Majha* loosening or in many cases, totally breaking ties with their homeland localities, especially in countries such as Malaysia, Singapore and Fiji, the newer post-war *doaba* migrants were in a position to sustain strong economic, cultural and political ties with their villages, consequently helping this sub-region to become economically more developed relative to others.

Nowadays most doaba villagers are transnational, with pioneer migrants or their children and grandchildren settled across all parts of the diaspora. However, with growing awareness of the relative success of overseas doaba Sikhs, overseas migration from the *Malwa* and *Majha* districts also began to increase over time. Furthermore, new employment opportunities in the post-1980s decades opened up horizons for a diverse range of Punjabi migrants, especially from those previously under-represented, whether in terms of religion, caste or sub-region, making all Punjabis closely inter-connected within a globalized world. The sub-regional dimensions of Sikh migration have relevance for at least two inter-related reasons. First, as the most developed and globalized sub-region, arguably as result of extensive overseas migration, the doaba sub-region does not suffer from agrarian distress to the same degree relative to the Malwa sub-region. Second, the predominantly doabia Sikh diaspora communities were familiar with the plight of Malwa farmers, such as incidence of debt, suicides and cancer, and had already developed a narrative which blamed these ills squarely on the Indian government. So it was not surprising when farmer protests started, initially in Malwa, doabian Sikhs gave them their overwhelming support.

To conclude this section, a century and half of overseas migration means that Sikhs can be considered a classic example of a truly transnational community, with global mobility and growing global visibility. Historical experiences demonstrate that Sikhs developed an acute sense of mobility, a sort of rootlessness, which compels them to move in light of the changing socio-economic environment (Thandi, 2017). So, after their initial settlement in a foreign country, many move again to another country sometime later, and then to another. In fact, many Sikhs have experienced thrice or multiple migrations over the past century and a half. For instance, Sikhs who first ventured abroad to Malaysia, Fiji, Singapore or the UK, then migrated to Australia, New Zealand, Canada or the USA, have resettled again within these locations. This sense of 'nomadism' or 'rootlessness' became more acute in the contemporary age of globalization where new digital technologies enables Sikhs to remain connected and exchange information on a 24/7 basis, wherever they may be settled.

Sikh Diaspora's Homeland Orientation

Unlike the expectations of most assimilationist theorists in migrant-receiving countries, the vast majority of overseas Sikhs have stayed attached to their Sikh identity and continued to maintain links with their homeland, whether only symbolically (that is, perceiving Punjab as their ancestral or sacred homeland) and/or materially. Thus, many continue to sustain familial, economic, financial, philanthropic, cultural and political connections with Punjab albeit at varying levels depending on the relative time period of overseas settlement (Thandi, 2014b). In the age of globalization, with massive expansion in flight routes and availability of cheap air travel and advances in and diffusion of digital technologies which allow instant and almost free global connectivity via the internet and social media, not only have homeland linkages strengthened and become circular and multi-layered, they have also expanded to include intra-diaspora networks, creating dense transnational practices among the global Sikhs (Thandi, 2014b). The latter proved to be an important dimension in concerted diaspora lobbying during the recent farmers' agitation.

Acknowledging the growing importance of diaspora communities as non-state actors in the global political economy, the extensive literature emphasizes two potential diaspora roles. The first role as a *positive* one, where diasporas have the capacity to economically and socially develop their homelands through various forms of financial assistance such as remittances, both financial and social, foreign direct investment, philanthropic funding for modernizing villages and providing rural education, health and civic infrastructure, among others (Thandi, 2000).[3] The second role as a *negative* one, where diasporas have the capability to finance insurgency or separatism, creates communal tensions or wreck peace accords.[4] There are many examples of both types of roles played by diasporas, sometimes simultaneously, although each has its own specific context. Generally speaking, we can say that a conflict-generated diaspora (formed after individuals are 'pushed out' of their homeland as refugees or asylum seekers due to state repression) compared to a diaspora formed through voluntary migration, will be more problematic for the homeland state.[5] The foregoing may seem a rather simplistic differentiation, largely because it implies that diasporas are a homogenous group with all migrating during the same time period or under similar conditions, when clearly that is often not the case, except in cases of extreme humanitarian crisis. Often diasporas form over a period of time, during different waves and in different contexts and comprise of different categories of migrants – unskilled and skilled, rural and urban, young and old, male and female and dependent or bread winner – making diasporas a very heterogeneous group. We discussed this heterogeneity in the context of formation of Sikh diaspora above. With this limitation in mind and given diasporas retain an emotional attachment to their homeland, albeit to different degrees, they can be mobilized by their hostland-based organizations in pursuit of activities which can be considered positive or negative or both. Thus, active diasporas can use identity politics in a variety of ways to exert an impact or leverage over their homelands, often to the annoyance of their homeland governments. According to Benedict Anderson, pioneer of the concept of Long Distance Nationalism, a diasporan:

> While technically a citizen of the state in which he comfortably lives, but to which he may feel little attachment, he finds it tempting to play identity politics by participating (via propaganda, money, weapons, any way but voting in the conflicts of his imagined *Heimat* (homeland).... this citizen-less participation is inevitably non-responsible – our hero will not have to answer for, or pay the price of, the long-distance politics he undertakes.
>
> (Anderson, 1991: 13)

Although Anderson provides a succinct explanation of diaspora nationalism, one can question his concluding words, albeit written before acceleration of globalization processes, in so far as they relate to diaspora support for farmers. Their involvement is not always risk-free as the global reach of the nation-state has also stretched and deepened and many do bear some of the negative consequences which may arise from their involvement in homeland politics. Since Anderson's original contribution, many other scholars have explored diaspora's multi-layered motives for involving themselves in identity politics, especially if they nurse a grievance against their homeland government.

Sikh Diaspora's involvement in homeland politics has a long history going back to the early part of the twentieth century. We can take two examples to illustrate this: first, the *Ghadar* movement, which had its origins in California over a century ago and had the objective of freeing India of British colonial rule[6] and, second, diaspora's support for the Khalistan movement in Punjab in the 1980s to establish a Sikh Homeland where Sikh sovereignty would be paramount.[7] Of course, both the Ghadar *lehar* and the Khalistan movements failed, although for several qualitatively different reasons, strong memories of both movements linger on, especially of the latter which still has a significant, although a minority voice, among sections of the Sikh diaspora.

To elaborate further on the failure of the two movements, the Ghadar movement's hope of bringing down British rule in India was doomed right from the start given the enormity of the task, total manpower available to them, botched preparations due to poor co-ordination and serious miscalculations by its leaders. Some describe the movement as a utopian pipe-dream led by misguided individuals who were duped into thinking that a revolutionary path was even possible to defeat an expanding Empire. However, having said that, the Ghadar rebellion scared the British, making them take it seriously and respond by a series of repressive measures in India.[8]

Despite the emotional outrage, trauma and anger expressed by the Sikh community after the attack on the Golden Temple by the army ordered by Prime Minister Indira Gandhi, this did not translate into mass support for the overseas Khalistan movement. Almost 14 years of violence and killings sanctioned by the Indian state (through the police and para-military forces) and militant organizations, had turned most of the Sikhs in Punjab against the Khalistani organizations as the community yearned for peace and communal harmony. In the diaspora too, support was only forthcoming from a small section of the Sikh community and militant activities had, in fact, polarized opinion leading to high tensions and even violence.[9] Further, the anti-Sikh violence in Delhi and in some other cities following the assassination of Indira Gandhi by her Sikh bodyguards in November 1984, again created outrage at the gruesome killings of thousands of innocent males, but it did not translate into support for Khalistan, rather only generated even greater anger against successive Indian governments for their failure at not delivering justice to the victims and their families.

Diaspora's Growing Influence on Hostland Politics

In the discussion above, we have shown how diasporas continue to play an important role in their homelands and how their linkages have become more dense and multi-layered. We should also be noted that these linkages are no longer just uni-directional, i.e. from diaspora to homeland as previously conceptualized, but have become multi-directional and circular, that is, from the homeland to different nodes and intra-nodes of the diaspora and vice versa. These have evolved, strengthened and deepened over the years due to globalization processes discussed earlier. The emergence of these dense transnational practices means that daily events in the homeland are transmitted instantly to diaspora locations. These events are also transmitted within diaspora communities through the emergence of a vibrant Sikh/Punjabi owned media, be it newspapers, radio stations, television channels or other online platforms. The role of online media, especially social media, is also an important factor in understanding diaspora's support and extensive mobilization for the protracted farmer agitation in India.

There is, however, another important dimension to diasporas which is highly important and unique but remains under-researched, especially in the context of diaspora's role in host country politics. After all, many diaspora communities have lived in their adopted countries for several decades and assimilationist and integrationist forces will have impinged on political and social attitudes and behaviours over the generations. A good indicator of the impact of these forces is diaspora's increasing participation in domestic politics of these countries. This political participation happens in multifaceted ways but two major forms are noteworthy: first, by joining established political parties and participating in elections at different levels of government and, second, by establishing advocacy organizations to lobby hostland governments to protect and promote community interests and also to engage in associated national and global networking.[10] There are, of course, some outstanding examples from early migration history which illustrate political activity of overseas Sikhs: Sophia Duleep Singh's activism during the suffragette movement in the 1910s in the UK, Makhan Singh's role in establishing and leading the trade union movement in Kenya in the 1940s and Dalip Singh Saund, the first Sikh US Congressman from California during 1957–1963, showing much concern for California's farmers and US's hostile immigration policies. As the period of Sikh settlement increased, so did electoral participation in domestic politics, although extent of involvement was always contingent on local political conditions and opportunity structures. When we look across different Sikh diaspora nodes today, we see that the degree of Sikh participation in electoral politics, especially at the highest levels, is most advanced in Canada, then perhaps in the UK and USA. In these countries, Sikhs and other Punjabis are active in domestic politics at different levels of government – city council, municipal, state or provincial and federal. This is not to suggest that in older settlement countries like Singapore, Malaysia and New Zealand, individual Sikhs did not participate in domestic politics, as they certainly did, but their overall number remained limited. The important point being made here is that by entrenching themselves in corridors of political and social power in their adopted countries, enables them to have some leverage over policies implemented. It also provides them an opportunity to mobilize political support for a specific cause, such as farmers' protests. We will come back to these important multifaceted aspects of diaspora's role later in the chapter.

Diaspora Mobilization for '*Kaley Kanoon*' (Black Laws)

As news of farmer protests against the three farm Ordinances, later becoming Acts, began to percolate to different diaspora locations, there was an immediate response in terms of 'what could they do' to show support to their kinfolk back home. This question was constantly raised in workplaces, *gurdwaras*, community centres and the Sikh/Punjabi media. Right from the beginning there was little focus on learning about the actual details on the pending legislation, but a unanimous consensus that this was yet another example of Indian government's conspiracy to harm Sikhs and Punjab. The community was already aware of the adverse agrarian conditions, such as rising farmer indebtedness, increasing landlessness and farmer suicides, being experienced by Punjabi farmers over the past decade as these were discussed on a regular basis in the Sikh/Punjabi media. Many members of the diaspora had also participated in annual rallies to commemorate anniversaries of Operation Bluestar and absence of justice against perpetrators of Anti-Sikh pogroms in Delhi in November 1984 and were aware of the political and human rights issues. The Khalistani organizations, who often organized these rallies, in fact, had gone a step further and developed their own anti-India narrative that was continually recited by their leaders at these rallies. According to this narrative, the ills inflicted on Punjab, such as farmer suicides, drug addiction and environmental destruction, were all parts of Indian government's deliberate policy to destroy Sikhs and the dream of Khalistan.[11] So the introduction of these new farm laws fitted well into the existing narrative believed by many Sikhs about injustice in India.

Diaspora support for the farmer agitation gained wider support and attitudes became even more entrenched after call by farmers' organizations to take their protest to Delhi. As has been well documented, serious attempts were made by the Haryana BJP government, working in close alliance with its parent government in Delhi, to stop the peaceful march through acts of brutal repression. Tear-gas shells, water cannons, digging of trenches, concrete barricades, police baton charges and preventative arrests were used on farmers at Shambhu and a few other places to stop them moving forward on National Highway 1, the old Grand Trunk Road, towards Delhi. These brutal attacks on peaceful protestors enraged the Sikh diaspora and later the global community, as images of Indian police firing water cannons were constantly played and replayed by major global news media outlets such as BBC, CNN, Bloomberg and Al Jazeera. All attempts to stop the farmers moving towards Delhi failed and as protestors approached Delhi, negotiations between the farmers' organizations and government law enforcement agencies resolved that farmers could camp peacefully at Singhu and Tikri and later Ghazipur, on the borders of Delhi. The '*Dilli Chalo*' movement and the state repression that followed was a critical turning point for the Sikh diaspora. Thereafter they started mobilizing support for farmers, defend human rights and the right to peaceful protest. The farmers' protest was now also becoming globalized through processes discussed below.

Diaspora support for farmers was organized and demonstrated in different ways. Almost all gurdwaras in major countries of Sikh settlement made immediate appeals for funds to offer financial support to farmers, enabling them to continue their struggle. Media reports and author's personal conversations with many members of the *sangat* and committee members at different gurdwaras in the UK and USA indicated that anything from US$30,000 to US$100,000 was raised by such appeals by each gurdwara over a period of several weeks, especially after the farmers began to consolidate their communal living in camps at Singhu, Tikri and Ghazipur. This occurred despite the fact that most countries had lockdown rules which either closed or limited the gathering of sangats in gurdwaras. The audio-visual Punjabi media, especially television channels and radio stations, engaged in almost blanket coverage of farmer protests and held regular discussion on the issues. Some media outlets had either embedded their own journalists in the camps or employed other journalists to send daily updates directly from the camp sites. The media also made funding appeals on a daily basis and often reported on how the collected funds were being utilized to ensure transparency. In California, USA and Canada, several business and truck company owners made direct appeals to their employees and truck drivers to donate money towards the farmers' cause and some individuals were reported to have donated as much as US$5,000 each. A number of NGOs stepped up to the challenge by both raising funds and sending much needed materials for the camps – blankets, mattresses, medicines, portable toilets, diesel, books, bottled water and food parcels – to raise their morale, provide warmth and help sustain the movement. Much of this financial and material assistance came via intermediaries based in India.[12] Khalsa Aid, a British NGO that has been operating around the world, as well as in India, for over 20 years, providing humanitarian aid in emergency situations, made extra efforts to serve the perceived needs of the farmers.[13] In addition to the above collective forms of support, several wealthy individuals or groups with past history of philanthropic work or new to it, took it upon themselves to offer *seva* in different and creative ways – to fund *langars* enroute to camps or at the camps, donate nutritional food such as almonds, heaters, ventilators or volunteer their medical services etc.[14]

Instant images of gratification shown on social media of this diasporan seva only acted to boost funding efforts to support farmers at these camps, especially as it was both a very chilly winter and an ongoing public health crisis caused by the COVID-19 pandemic. There can be no doubt that many diasporans would have returned to Punjab to show support and participate in the movement had there not been a pandemic and almost universal restrictions on international travel. They had done so before, for instance, enthusiastically supporting the Aam Aadmi Party (AAP) during the 2014 Lok Sabha and 2017 Punjab Assembly elections. At that time, many diasporan Sikhs had pinned their hopes on AAP as it was promising corruption-free Punjab, which many of them were desperately seeking given their negative experiences of Indian bureaucracy. Diaspora support came in the form of both finance and manpower with AAP claiming 2,500 diasporans returning in 2017 in response to its '*Chalo Punjab*' campaign.[15] Their support appeared particularly significant in 2014 as the party managed to capture 4 of the 13 parliamentary seats in the Lok Sabha at its first attempt. However, the expected diaspora influence seemed to vanish in 2017 as AAP's internal and organizational problems erupted openly with the party only able to capture 20 Assembly seats across Punjab and more significantly only 2 in the doaba region where most diasporan Sikhs hail from.

In addition to financial support, which could then be transformed into material goods for the camps, diaspora communities mimicked the tractor rallies of farmers. News reports indicate around 50 cities spread across the globe, especially in areas of high Sikh settlement, saw Sikhs hold tractor or car rallies in support of farmers. One of the largest of these was the Tractor Rally spearheaded by young people of the Jakara Movement in the Bay Area of California, home to one of the largest concentration of Sikhs in the USA. It was reported that 10,000 vehicles drove across the Bay Bridge from Oakland to the Indian Consulate in San Francisco, taking two hours rather than the normal commute of 20 minutes.[16] This also happens to be the region where the Ghadar Party was founded and undertook many activities, including publishing its own newspaper, *Ghadar.* Canadian Sikhs also held a large car rally in Brampton to end at the Indian Consulate and a *kisan* rally from Calgary to Edmonton to coincide with the one organized by the *Samyukt Kisan Morcha* (SKM) in Delhi on India's Republic Day, January 26, 2021.[17]

The use of social media by Sikhs, especially WhatsApp, Instagram, Facebook, YouTube, in raising awareness of the farmer movement, discussing issues behind the protests, providing updates, etc., can't be underestimated. Many advocacy groups such as the Sikh Coalition, United Sikhs, Sikh American Legal Defense and Education Fund, Turbans 4 Australia, National Sikh Youth Association (UK) and others had already amassed considerable experience in online networking, campaigning and fundraising. Several Sikh Advocacy groups emerged to resist the tremendous surge in hate crimes against Sikhs following the Twin Towers bombings on '9/11' (September 11, 2001), to raise awareness about the Sikhs and engage in legal struggles for recognition of Sikh religious symbols such as the turban, *kirpan* and *kara* in schools and workplaces. So by the time the farmer protests began, their online infrastructure was already in place to start campaigns on raising awareness and lobbying policymakers. Social media was used extensively by the younger generations, especially university and college students and they emerged as the most assertive and articulate activists in spreading the message and countering the official Indian government narrative at rallies and on online platforms. Many of these students also held meetings at their own and other campuses to raise awareness and engaged in creating art, music and merchandise such as T-shirts and posters, to raise donations. Naindeep Singh, Executive Director of the Jakara Movement emphasized the unique role being played by young people who, he argued, had lived their lives as 'cultural brokers' and were well positioned 'to provide fresh perspectives and bring in new groups'. Manpreet Kaur, Communications Director for Jakara went further and expressed the anguish faced by diaspora Sikh youth in the following moving way:

> We are sitting so far away from what's happening on the grounds, but feel every emotion as though we are there – we cry with those crying, we smile with those dancing and singing folk songs, we laugh with those creating witty jokes and songs. We're sitting on the edge of our seats, inspired and in awe.[18]

For the first time since the trauma of Operation Bluestar, this new generation of diaspora-born children also began engaging with their parents, discussing reasons behind the farm protests, learning about their own family lineage and heritage and history of their ancestral homeland. If Operation

Bluestar served as a lesson in Indian politics for them, the farmer agitation was now a lesson in agricultural economics and workings of Indian federalism. This constructive engagement had the effect of not only consolidating their Sikh identity but also cemented both inter-generational and intra-generational solidarity.

A unique aspect of diaspora support, not witnessed before to the same extent or in the same way, was diaspora engagement with representatives of domestic political, civic and labour organizations. This engagement was helped immensely by the fact that these organizations had experience of working with members of the Sikh community on various other political or labour campaigns. Sikhs, representing their community organizations, approached their local or municipal councils, to lobby in support of farmers. Many also wrote to their elected representatives at city, state or federal level, to raise awareness of farmers' issues, violation of human rights of peaceful protestors, blocking access to the Internet and curtailment of press freedom and more generally about police repression and abuses of democracy in India. These lobbying efforts yielded positive results at all levels. The Canadian Prime Minister Justin Trudeau supported the farmers' right to protest and criticized Indian government's handling of the peaceful protests which created a diplomatic row,[19] and many US Congressman – Representatives and Senators – also condemned India for its repression of peaceful protests and undemocratic practices in January 2021. At about the same time, around 78 Indian-American organizations and gurdwaras in the USA sent a joint letter to US President Biden requesting him to convey a strong message to the Modi government on human rights violations of peaceful protestors. These organizations also expressed concern over how some handles on social media were mischievously proposing a repeat of the 1984 pogroms against Sikhs which, they argued, would only raise tensions among Indian Americans.[20]

In the UK, more than 100 Members of Parliament and Lords, signed a letter circulated by UK MP Tanmanjeet Singh Dhesi to the Prime Minister Boris Johnson, asking him to declare his support for the protesting farmers and raise the matter with the Indian government on his forthcoming visit there.[21] Finally, an e-petition campaign to 'urge the Indian Government to ensure the safety of protestors and press freedom' was signed by over 100,000 British citizens, crossing the threshold necessary to guarantee a parliamentary debate. The debate took place on March 8, 2021, lasted one and half hours and covered many aspects of the farmer agitation. Many MPs urged the UK government to call out India's human rights abuses and for limiting press freedom. The Government Minister, whilst conceding that human right violations and limits on press freedom were not acceptable, said they were not able do anything about the farm legislation as this was an internal matter for India.[22] Needless to say, the debate upset the Indian government and its response was swift as we will discuss later in this chapter. The above examples are, of course, serious global rebukes of the Indian government coming from the highest level of politics and were challenging the Indian government 'anti-national' narrative that had been promoted after the Republic Day events in India.[23]

In terms of support from citizen organizations, including those representing the Indian diaspora, there was an overwhelming positive response to affirm solidarity. For instance, in February 2021, the Global Indian Progressive Alliance, representing some 20 Indian diaspora organizations from across the world, issued a statement in support of protesting farmers, for repealing the farm laws and urging the Indian government to recognize the right to peaceful protest. Pointing to the haste and undemocratic nature of Farm Laws, the Alliance stated:

> As progressive Indians, we are again disturbed to see the ramming through of laws without any attempt at consensus building. There has been no discussion with other political parties, citizen groups, affected stakeholders or academics in developing bills and passing them through Parliament, suppressing even the parliamentary debate process.[24]

In the USA, 87 farmer organizations and allied agroecology, farm and food justice groups delivered a solidarity statement in support of the unified, peaceful and dignified farmer struggle, to the leader of SKM which was managing the protests on behalf of 40 plus Indian farmers' unions. Showing astute awareness of the issues at stake, Sophia Murphy, Executive Director of the Institute for Agriculture and Trade Policy was reported as saying:

> Liberalising markets without taking into account farmers' political voice and protecting against concentrated buyer power makes a mockery of what markets should stand for; we denounce the three farm bills, the lack of consultation with farmers and their organisations, and stand in solidarity with the brave stance India's farmers are taking.

In a similar vein and with their members' own experiences in mind, Jim Goodman, President of the National Family Farm Coalition was reported as saying:

> We are honoured to join the Institute for Agriculture and Trade Policy, Rural Coalition, Grassroots Global Justice, and 83 additional organisations standing in solidarity with the farmers and farm workers in India who have been protesting for 85 days to protect their minimum price guarantees. We have been forced to accept low farm prices and we support their demands for economic parity – fair prices and living wages – to defend their livelihoods, their food sovereignty and the future of their republic.[25]

A report by Bhasin in *The Tribune* of March 2021 stated that more than 100 labour, community and civil society organizations in Canada and other countries issued a joint statement in solidarity with farmers of India.[26] The above are only some examples to demonstrate that Sikh advocacy groups across North America, Europe and Australasia worked hard to raise awareness of farmer grievances, urging civic, labour and diaspora organizations to write letters of support to elected representatives and help with fund raising. Mobilizing and lobbying at this level is unprecedented in Sikh diaspora experiences.

Diaspora Motives for Farmer Support: Identity and Livelihoods over Profits

There are numerous motives behind the widespread, diverse, enthusiastic and emotional involvement of the Sikh diaspora in the farmer agitation but only the major ones will be identified and discussed in this chapter. An important overarching motive is related to the strong sense of empathy with Punjabi farmers given that a large component of the Sikh diaspora comes from Sikh Jat farming families, with many still owning agricultural land back in Punjab.[27] This land is usually operated by their family members, other relatives or co-villagers or by those from neighbouring villages and usually under some annual contractual agreement. A Jat's attachment to land is a well-known aspect of Punjabi culture and folklore. This landholding, no matter how meagre, is considered an important part of their identity or being (*haund*), family ancestry, social and political status and a memory of previous lifestyle and livelihood. It is also a landed asset which can be endowed to future generations. Any perceived threat to this mental equilibrium will not be tolerated. Over time, many Sikh migrants worked hard, often taking advantage of any overtime that was available, to accumulate savings and used them to purchase more land in their ancestral village or nearby to add to their meagre inherited share. They also saw this purchase both as a landed asset expected to rise in value over time and as financial investment for earning a steady income.

Ownership of land means many diasporan Sikhs receive considerable amount of annual income (*hala*) from those actually cultivating it. This annual rental income comes in useful in setting up their children in the diaspora, as maintenance funds for their home in the village, a handy sum for holidays or as part of wedding expenditure during their visits home. Some diasporans also utilize these funds in philanthropic ways, helping to modernize their villages or for providing rural education and health services and building sports facilities in their neighbourhood. Whilst it is true that some families, especially those who migrated several generations ago, sold their land when they acknowledged that their children were unlikely to return or care much about their family land, a significant majority of first and second generation Sikhs still continue to hold on to their land, however small and unviable. In any case, a sharp fall in agricultural land prices over the past few years stalled selling of land, with many biding their time and hoping for a rebound.

Just as important as owning land, most diasporan Sikhs have brothers, sisters and cousins, other relatives and friends back home whose livelihoods are highly dependent on income earned through farming operations. If their livelihoods are perceived to be in danger, it should not surprise us if diaspora Sikhs would want to offer every support to eliminate that risk. Government statistics show that only a small proportion of Sikh Punjabi farmers are large landowners and if anything the vast majority are small and marginal farmers with landholdings of less than 2 hectares and their numbers are increasing whilst the average size of their landholding is decreasing (Sood, 2016). In fact, due to agrarian distress, many farming families are highly dependent on financial remittances sent by their overseas family members, preventing them from falling into debt and enabling them to eke out a decent level of living. The extent of landlessness or depeasantization in Punjab has been rising and farm laws have only acted to instil new fears in the minds of many marginal farmers that they may also be pushed to the edge of landlessness and poverty, especially given that alternative employment opportunities are almost non-existent (Singh et al., 2009). Many such marginal farmers were actively involved in the agitation and diaspora Sikhs expressed a strong sense of empathy towards them.

Besides the close and strong family, village and community comradery discussed above, there are two further factors worth noting in understanding motives for diaspora support. First, all political parties of Punjab have their chapters in most countries of Sikh diaspora settlement. As leaders of all of these parties, except the BJP, came out against the new farm laws, their diaspora-based members were compelled to publicly demonstrate their opposition and joined the rallies and engaged in fundraising. Second, it is worth remembering that there is continuity in some occupations in the diaspora and farming or agriculture-related activities remains an important source of livelihood for many diaspora Sikhs – for example, banana cultivation in Woolgoolga, Australia, dairy farming in the Waikato region of New Zealand, berry farming in Abbotsford, Canada and fruit, nut and vegetable farming in California's Central Valley in the USA. So we would expect these farming communities to show empathy and solidarity and offer support, especially given they are fully aware of the challenges which face farming and farmers in their own environments.

To reiterate an old saying, often, unfortunately used in derogatory ways towards Punjabi farmers by Indian urban middle classes, that 'there is only one culture in Punjab, it is agriculture', took on a new meaning in a very creative and positive way during this agitation. The fact that farming practices are so deeply embedded into the culture, psyche, ethos, values and essence of a Sikh farmer, clearly manifested themselves in public displays and affirmation of community's rich cultural heritage in terms of religious values, rituals and folk music. Baba Nanak was, after all, a farmer for many years whilst founding a new community at Kartarpur.[28] Cultural performances staged at the camps demonstrated to the outside world the depth and richness of this agrarian folk culture, with many folk singers, *dhadi jathas*, poets, musicians, dancers, actors and *gatka* experts volunteering to entertain there. Thus, farming and culture were shown to be intertwined and inseparable in the Sikh tradition. Through these performative acts the overwhelming sentiment evoked, both in India and in the diaspora, was that a farmer's village (*pind*), culture (*sabhyachar*) and heritage (*virsa*) were under attack by a ruthless government that had been captured by 'exploitative' Indian and global agrifood corporates.

Indian Government Reactions to Sikh Diaspora support for Farmers

The Indian government has always closely monitored activities of its diaspora communities through its diplomatic missions and consulates, more so of Sikhs given the support and encouragement given by some sections of the Sikh diaspora to the Khalistan movement since the 1980s. It would be an understatement to say that many Sikhs since 1984 have felt deeply alienated from the Indian state, irrespective of the political party holding power. The army attack on the Golden Temple during Operation Bluestar, lack of justice for victims and their families after the anti-Sikh pogroms in Delhi and some other Indian cities, dubious 'black lists' of alleged diaspora-based 'terrorists', disappearances and unlawful detentions, have made the Sikh community cynical of Indian government intentions, creating a huge trust deficit. When the Indian government's negative comments about overseas Sikhs went into over-drive at the start of the farmer agitation, with government Ministers and the pro-Modi Indian media linking the protests to Khalistani elements, many Sikhs saw this as an excuse for demonizing the farmer movement.[29] But as we discussed earlier, diaspora support for farmers came from almost the whole social and political spectrum of the Sikh community, from young and old, rich and poor, progressives and conservatives, those with and without farmer background, Jats and non-Jats, as well as from those who were pro-Khalistan and those historically and very vocally opposed to the Khalistan movement. So, at the community level at least, the strategy of labelling the heterogeneous diaspora supporters of farmer agitation as anti-nationals or Khalistanis, did not work and if anything only intensified anger against the government and resulted in even greater efforts in galvanizing support. The government's response was to increase intelligence gathering by instructing its missions abroad to monitor rallies in support of farmers and keep records on anti-farm reform protesters. It is possible that some of this intelligence was utilized by the Indian government as indicated in recent news reports on refusal of entry at Delhi airport to philanthropist Dhaliwal and revoking of OCI cards and long-term visas to many diasporans.[30]

India prides itself in being the largest (parliamentary) democracy which gives voting rights to all but this is only one and a limited aspect of human freedom. Other measures such as the Human Freedom Index are more comprehensive and inclusive and India scored 6.43 out of 10 in this index in 2020, placing it 111 out of 162 countries.[31] Viewed from this perspective and with India constantly repeating its claim on the global stage as the world's largest democracy, arguably the most serious damage to its carefully nurtured global image was done by diaspora lobbying. The large number of statements and letters in support of farmers from governments, government agencies and civic and labour organizations was beginning to expose India's global image. The Indian government hated being tarnished by accusations of human rights violations, blocking of access to internet at camp sites, curtailment of press freedom by jailing or intimidating journalists who dared to question government policies and blatantly using the National Investigation Agency to intimidate farmer leaders and diaspora organizations funding them and went on the offensive.

Two examples are worthy of note which demonstrate India's immediate reaction to foreign government remarks. First, on December 4, 2020, India's Ministry of External Affairs (MEA) called in Canadian diplomats for a rebuke after Prime Minister Justin Trudeau voiced concern about human rights violations of peacefully protesting farmers during a Facebook Live session. The Ministry called his comments 'unwarranted' and amounted to 'unacceptable interference' in India's internal affairs which risked damaging bi-lateral ties between the two nations.[32] The pro-Modi Indian media went further and questioned Trudeau's motives, along with his and his Sikh Defence Minister's alleged personal links to the Khalistan movement and accused both of them of pandering to Sikh voters in Canada. This diplomatic spat was just another example of the troubled relations between India, Canada and the Sikh community ever since Operation Bluestar.[33] The second example relates to Indian Government's reaction to the British parliamentary debate on farmer agitation on March 8, 2021, mentioned above. Displaying great anger at comments made by some MPs during the debate, India's Foreign Secretary Harsh Vardhan Shringla summoned Alex Ellis, the Delhi-based British High Commissioner, the next day and is reported to have told him that the debate represented 'gross interference in the politics of another democratic country' and many MPs were deliberately misrepresenting events in India to engage in vote-bank politics.[34] Hitting back at the debate, the Indian High Commissioner in London also released a similar statement on Twitter:

> We deeply regret that rather than a balanced debate, false assertions – without substantiation or facts – were made, casting aspersions on the largest functioning democracy in the world and its institutions.

> [...] When aspersions are cast on India by anyone, irrespective of their claims of friendship and love for India or domestic political compulsions, there is a need to set the record straight.[35]

Needless to say, this is the usual response from the Indian government whenever its practices, especially on human rights and press freedom, are criticized. But in this case, criticism of India came from all quarters of the world and was challenging the Indian narrative on necessity of farm reforms to enrich farmers, their alleged acceptance by majority of farmers except a minority, role of vested foreign interests and India as a tolerant multi-faith democracy. It was becoming clear, even to many independent observers, sustained hostility by the government towards farmers and their supporters, whether at home or abroad, its use of intimidatory tactics through 'political abuse' of the National Investigation Agency to serve notices to many individuals, curbs on press freedom and jailing of journalists reporting on farmer protests and internet blackouts at camp sites was beginning to tarnish the 'carefully cultivated image of Modi as a world statesman'.[36] It is worth remembering that Modi, when Chief Minister of Gujarat, was refused a visa to enter the USA in 2005 till he became Prime Minster, for his alleged tacit support for Hindu extremists in the Gujarat carnage in 2002 which left 2,000 people dead.

Sikh diaspora's support for farmers also created tensions between Sikhs and Punjabis and some sections of the Indian diaspora at the community level at several locations. Non-Sikh Punjabis were lukewarm in their support unlike the Sikhs themselves given the latter's lesser emotional attachment to land and their urban origin but overall, there were more tensions between Sikhs and non-Punjabi Hindus than among the Sikhs and Hindu Punjabis. In a way this was not surprising given the past history of troubled Sikh-Hindu relations, especially in Canada, associated with alleged involvement of Khalistani operatives in the bombing of Air India's 'Kanishka' flight which killed 329 people and the subsequent botched trial by the Canadian judicial system. The Khalistan movement had also created tensions among Sikhs themselves which still persists today in different forms.[37] However, this time, a new element, of pro-Modi Hindutva groups, unhappy at the criticism levelled at Modi, their personality cult-like hero, entered the scene to show support to 'Hindu nationalist' government's farm laws by holding '*Tiranga Yatra*' or rallies. Some of these rallies, especially in Brampton in Canada and Sydney in Australia, ended up in threats of intimidation, violence and vandalism and also began to develop a religious dimension.[38] In Canada a 'war of words' in different Indian languages played out with the Punjabi media mostly supporting the farmers and media in other Indian languages supporting the Modi government. In Ontario, when the *Hindu Forum Canada* sponsored billboards on major highways thanking Prime Minister Modi for sending COVID-19 vaccines (but not thanking Germany or the USA who also sent them) and at a time when Indians at home were struggling to get them and thousands of farmers were protesting, was perceived as provocation and raised tensions.[39] One widely reported case was that of a Haryana youth, Vishal Jood, a self-labelled 'Tirangi Warrior', who was found guilty and sentenced to jail for attacking Sikhs in a series of incidents in Sydney, despite petitions by Haryana's Chief Minister Khatter to the Indian foreign ministry to intervene on his behalf.[40] I use the above examples not to give the impression that actual Sikh-Hindu violence was widespread, because it clearly wasn't, but only to draw attention to the fact that tensions were running high in some places and community leaders and the police had to appeal for calm and not to spread hatred.[41] This, however, was not the case with the very venomous and visceral 'war' over the social media which did not abate during the agitation period.[42]

Some Conclusions

As discussed in the first section, although Sikhs started migrating overseas over a century and half ago and settled and resettled in different locations, many have still not lost contact with their ancestral homeland. Homeland orientation has only strengthened but a long period of settlement abroad has also resulted in growing outreach in their hostlands and within the globally dispersed Sikh community. All these three dimensions – homeland orientation, hostland orientation and global networking – are crucial in understanding the extent, depth and scope of diaspora support for the farmer agitation in India during 2020–2021.

To elaborate further on the little discussed second feature, first, given the long settlement period, Sikhs began participating in domestic politics, representing their local communities at different levels of government and began holding important positions from City Mayors to Ministers in federal or central governments. Canada is an excellent example of the latter as many Sikhs have been elected to the Canadian Parliament over the years and, in fact, since 2016, there have been more Sikhs in the Trudeau Cabinet than in India.[43] This not only raised the profile of the global Sikh community but also gave them some leverage to influence decisions and policy making. Second, the lengthy period of settlement resulted in upward social mobility, enabling the community to create strong institutions and advocacy networks which work to accommodate their religious, political, social and cultural needs. The existence of these advocacy groups and their associated networks meant Sikhs became relatively experienced and successful at engaging in dialogue not just among themselves but also with other communities and governments to defend their religious values and identity, outward religious symbols and community interests in their adopted homes. We have demonstrated in this chapter how these advocacy networks were mobilized to demonstrate solidarity and offer all forms of support to Punjabi farmers protesting against the ill-conceived farm laws passed by the Modi administration in 2020. This diaspora activism was also important in raising global awareness of farmers' issues which put the Indian government on the back-foot under world's gaze.

There can be no doubt that Sikh diaspora mobilization in support of farmers was unprecedented. It was undoubtedly the most widespread, diverse and unifying mobilization which included mass participation by women and diaspora-born younger generations never seen before. This mobilization needs to be contrasted with the earlier mobilization during the Khalistan movement which only ended up polarizing and dividing overseas Sikh communities, tarnishing community's image which took some time to rectify. Overall, therefore, the nature, extent and success of mobilization in support of farmers represent a watershed moment in Sikh diaspora experience, signalling the political maturing of the Sikh global community.

The totally unexpected U-turn taken by Modi to revoke the farm laws on November 19, 2021, which also happened to be day of Guru Nanak's 552nd *gurpurab*, was welcomed unanimously by all, especially the farmers and the Sikh diaspora. Whilst actual reasons for repealing the farm laws and why at that juncture, will probably never be made public, one can only speculate that the decision was made because of a combination of domestic and foreign compulsions confronting the Modi government. Whilst the Indian media tried to spin Modi's decision as that of a decent, courageous, considerate and compassionate person, other commentators hailed it as victory for strength of Indian democracy in which subaltern voices cannot ultimately be ignored. Of course, the decision to revoke the laws could have been made much earlier in the year, so what changed? More nuanced explanations point to the unexpectedly protracted and popular nature of the agitation coupled with political imperatives, especially given that Assembly elections in five states were imminent, particularly in the populous state of Uttar Pradesh which is usually considered a critical barometer of the national mood and governance. The sustained support for farmers coming from many of these states gearing up for elections rattled the Modi government and repealing farm laws can be seen as an exercise in damage limitation. The laws were repealed very rapidly by Parliament, in fact, within ten days of Modi's public announcement. Externally, the perceived negative impact of farmer's movement on Modi's global image was equally important. The emergent image of an authoritarian Hindu nationalist, abusing democratic norms to silence critics and devaluing human rights by not condemning rising violence against religious minorities, was beginning to conflict with his strategically manufactured image of a global statesman during multi-lateral dialogues, and this must have been troubling for him, forcing him to climb-down despite presiding over an enormous majority in Parliament and a doting Indian media. The forthcoming assembly election results will demonstrate what, if any, political damage the farmers' agitation caused to the BJP and its allies.

Three speculative but important questions to end on are, first, what will future mobilization and support for farmers be like if their demands or conditions for ending the agitation, and as agreed by the central government, are not fulfilled? If the demands are not fully met, will there still be an appetite and widespread support for another agitation? Second, will SKM be able to maintain farmer unity given that some of the kisan unions entered the electoral fray causing divisions among them? Or will the unity maintained during the 2020–2021 agitation prove to be one-off, unique example? Finally, given growing divisions among farmer unions, especially in Punjab, will the diaspora continue to offer unconditional support in a similar and sustained way or will supporters lose interest? With the Punjab Assembly elections being held only a couple of months after the end of the farmer agitation and a general election only two years away, the next few years could witness unsettling times unless the agrarian issues remain at the forefront of political discourses and meaningful policies to safeguard farmer interests are implemented.

Notes

* This chapter is a revised version of 'Mera Pind, Mera Sabhyachar, Mera Virsa: Understanding Sikh Diaspora Support for the Punjab Kisan Morcha', first published in *Journal of Sikh and Punjab Studies*, 29(1&2) (Spring–Fall, 2022): 267–290.

1 It is always difficult to find accurate data on the total Sikh population. If we go by the latest Indian census data, there are 16 million Sikhs in Punjab, another 5 million outside Punjab, scattered in various States and Union Territories, adding to 21 million and with further 2 million estimated to be living overseas, makes a total of 23 million. However given potential accounting errors, the Indian census figures for Sikhs can be safely raised by 10 per cent, and numbers in India would then be 17.6 million in Punjab plus 5.28 million in the rest of India, making a total of 23 million. With estimated 2 million as part of the Sikh diaspora, makes the total global Sikh population to be 25 million.

2 For a detailed discussion of the push and pull factors that explain Sikh overseas migration see (Thandi, 2017) in the *Brill Encyclopedia of Sikhism*.

3 Both Merz et al. (2007) and Brinkerhoff (2008) have several case studies which show different contexts in which diasporas can play a positive role.

4 See a number of case studies in Smith and Share (2007) and a survey of existing literature in Koinova (2018).

5 There are many examples of such conflict-generated diasporas becoming more active in supporting self-determination or separatism for their homelands. In the case of Sikhs, there is some evidence to suggest that Sikhs who were able to settle abroad as asylum seekers, sometimes referred to as political migrants, in the 1980s/1990s, were more active in the Khalistan movement. See Mahmood (1996) and Tatla (1999).

6 The Ghadar movement still continues to attract academic interest, especially from diaspora based scholars. For some recent publications see Malini Sood (2001), Maia Ramnath (2011) and Seema Sohi (2014). Also see several articles in special issue on the Ghadar Movement in the *Journal of Sikh and Punjab Studies* edited by Sukhdev S. Sohal in 2019 and accessed March 19, 2022 at: http://www.giss.org/jsps_vol_26.html.

7 There is now comprehensive literature on the Khalistan movement but both Deol (2003) and Shani (2011) provide interesting perspectives. However, in terms of detailed discussion on diaspora mobilization for Khalistan, Tatla's 1999 book on *The Sikh Diaspora: Search for Statehood*, remains unchallenged.

8 For an interesting discussion on British responses to Ghadar, see Condos (2017), pp. 198–215.

9 Tatla (1999) has an excellent discussion, based on his close reading of Punjabi vernacular sources, on rising tensions both within the Sikh community and in Sikh relations with other Indian communities.

10 Currently there is no conceptual framework to measure the degree of influence exerted by Sikh diaspora lobbies in hostland politics, so clearly more research is needed. For interesting case studies of lobbying in the USA by other diasporas and their influence, or lack thereof, on US foreign policy, see DeWind and Segura (2014).

11 The author has attended many such rallies in London's Hyde Park and Trafalgar Square and vividly remembers the 2019 rally which marked the 35th anniversary of 1984 and heard many such speeches.

12 For instance, a 20-year Californian resident, Satwinder Singh Bagga and his friends collected Rs 10 lakh to undertake mineral water *seva* for marching farmers. See 'NRI from California spends lakhs on mineral water for protesting farmers', *The Tribune*, January 25, 2021.

13 Khalsa Aid was founded by Ravinder (Ravi) Singh in 1999 after, apparently being shocked, at seeing the plight of refugees in Kosovo. Singh aligned his organization's values under the Sikh ideology of '*sarbat da bhalla*' (welfare of all mankind). Two Sikhs, representing Brampton in Canada, Tim Uppal (Member of Parliament) and Prabmeet Singh Sarkaria (Member of Provincial Parliament) and Mayor of Brampton, Patrick Brown, nominated Khalsa Aid for the Nobel Peace Prize for their humanitarian work.

14 There are too many donations by wealthy individuals or families to list here but three examples are noteworthy. First, Raja Dhaliwal of Canada, through his World Financial Group, donated Canadian $50,000 towards *langar seva*. This money was donated via Khalsa Aid as it was already operating in the camps. For details see report by Sukhmeet Bhasin 'More support, aid pouring in from NRIs for protesting farmers at Delhi', *The Tribune*, November 29, 2020. Second, California based philanthropist farmers, Tut Brothers, who have rural roots in Jalandhar, donated 30 quintals of almonds to farmers camping on Delhi borders. These were sent through their relatives. See news report 'NRIs send 30 quintal almonds for protesters', *The Tribune*, December 4, 2020. The four Tut brothers had earlier donated around Rs 55 million in 2004 to install an imported water filtration plant to keep water clean in the *Sarovar* that surrounds the Golden Temple. Third, Dubai-based businessman and Chair of *Sarbat Da Bhalla Charitable Trust*, Dr SP Singh Oberoi, vowed to help farmers with what they deemed as necessary: team of 18 specialist doctors, essential medicines, 5 ambulances, 20 tons of dry food, fodder for horses, reflectors for tractor-trollies to prevent accidents, 3,000 blankets, 3,000 jackets and 12,000 sleepers. See *The Tribune* report 'Farm Stir: Anger pours on to streets', December 5, 2020.

15 See *Financial Express Online*, 'Around 2,500 NRIs return to Punjab to back AAP in Assembly elections', January 13, 2017.

16 The Jakara Movement is a grass roots level youth movement led by past or current university and college students. They have been active over the past decade in raising awareness and advocating action on hate crimes and human rights violations in Punjab. For a report on the Bay Area rally see Vandana Menon (2020) 'Children of kisaans': The global Punjabi diaspora speaks up for the farmers protesting in India' *Scroll*, December 14, 2020.

17 See report by Sukhmeet Bhasin 'NRIs to hold car rallies in Canada to support farmers' tractor march on Jan 26'. *The Tribune*, January 25, 2021.

18 Quoted in Vandana Menon (2020).

19 See Sadanand Dhuma 'India Throws a Trudeau Tantrum', *Wall Street Journal*, 10 December, 2020.

20 See the news report 'Global Indian Diaspora sends roses to Indian missions as mark of love to farmers', *The Tribune*, February 14, 2021.

21 See 'If protesting farmers are abused, it will make movement stronger: British MP Dhesi', *The Tribune*, January 30, 2021.

22 Full text of the debate published in Hansard can be accessed at Press Freedom and Safety of Protesters: India-Hansard-UK Parliament.

23 The Indian government released a statement through the MEA in February 2021 in response to growing international criticism of its dealings with farmer protests. The statement defended India's position and claimed 'it is unfortunate to see vested interest groups trying to enforce their agenda on these protests, and derail them. This was egregiously witnessed on 26 January, India's Republic Day' and 'some of these vested interest groups have also tried to mobilise international support against India'. To read the full statement see Government of India, Ministry of External Affairs, 'Press Statement on recent comments by foreign individuals and entities on the farmers' protests', February 3, 2021.

24 See *Press Trust of India* report 'Global Indian diaspora seeks repeal of farm laws', February 1, 2021.

25 Both statements are taken from a *Tribune* news report 'US farmer groups deliver solidarity statement to Indian farmers, *The Tribune*, February 20, 2021.

26 See Sukhmeet Bhasin's report 'Canadian civil groups out in support of Indian farmers', *The Tribune*, March 3, 2021.

27 No generalization is implied here as the author is well aware of many relatively smaller Sikh groups from non-farming backgrounds among the Sikh diaspora. Although no data or research exists on these groups, the vast majority have shown sympathy and support, maybe for different reasons, including religious affinity.

28 For an excellent discussion of Nanak's life at Kartarpur see latter part of Gurinder Singh Mann's opening chapter 'Baba Nanak and the Founding of the Sikh Panth' in Jacobsen, Mann, Myrvold and Nesbitt (2017).

29 There are many examples of statements from Government Ministers and other BJP spokesmen that try to link farmer agitation with the Khalistani movement. One example deserve a special mention. During the Supreme Court hearing on farmer agitation and their forthcoming march on Republic Day, the Attorney General (AG) K. K. Venugopal made a statement to the Chief Justice that 'Khalistanis have infiltrated into the protests'. This was confirmed after a senior advocate P S Narasimha, representing the Consortium of Indian Farmers Association which supported the farm laws, stated that groups like 'Sikhs for Justice' are involved in the protests against the laws. The AG said he would file an affidavit and IB reports the next day. It appears no such affidavit or IB reports were filed as there is no information in the public domain on their filing. See *Times of India* report 'Khalistan supporters have infiltrated farmer's protest: Attorney general to SC', January 12, 2021.

30 For example, see report by Aman Sood, 'NRI Darshan Singh Dhaliwal refused entry for 'backing' farmers' protest', *The Tribune*, October 24, 2021 and another report a few days later 'OCI cards, visas of farm protest backers revoked', *The Tribune*, October 27, 2021.

31 The Human Freedom Index was developed jointly by the Cato Institute, Fraser Institute and the Liberales Institut of the Friedrich Naumann Foundation for Freedom. According to the *World Population Review* website

> The Human Freedom Index places each country on a scale of 0 to 10, where a score of 10 represents the most freedom, for personal freedom and economic freedom. Each country's human freedom index is an average of the two.

> *Personal freedom* is the freedom of an individual to have freedom of opinion and expression, freedom to come and go, equality before the courts, and security of private property. *Economic freedom* consists of personal choice, freedom to compete in markets, protection of person and property, voluntary exchange, and allowing people to prosper without intervention from the government or economic authority' (italics added).

Further details and full report at: https://worldpopulationreview.com/country-rankings/freedom-index-by-country (accessed March 10, 2021).

32 See report in the *New York Times* 'Indian Farmers' Protests Spread, in Challenge to Modi', December 4, 2020.

33 Sikh community's anger against Canada and India was clearly visible when a Canadian think tank known for its conservative leanings, Macdonald-Laurier Institute (MLI), released a controversial report written by a senior journalist Terry Milweski, which argued that Khalistan was basically a Pakistan project created to harm India. The report appeared to make a number of unsubstantiated allegation against *Sikhs for Justice*, a pro-Khalistan advocacy group behind the global Khalistan Referendum 2020 campaign but the report also cast doubts on Sikh advocacy in general. In the forward written by Ujjal Dosanjh (a former British Columbia Premier well known for his anti-Khalistan stance) and Shuvaloy Majumdar (Munk Senior Fellow for Foreign Policy at the Macdonald-Laurier Institute, and former Director of Policy to Canadian Foreign Ministers) it warns Canadians about Sikh human rights advocacy groups who are engaged in providing a 'steady and predictable drumbeat of victimization, persecution and genocide commemoration, presented as steps to assist a community in need of healing' (p. 5). This appeared to jive with Indian government narrative on Canadian Sikhs and unsurprisingly, the Indian Government and Indian media lapped it up implying 'we told you so'. Sikh Community leaders and 50 plus academics asked the Macdonald-Laurier Institute to withdraw the report but it is still available on their web-site.

The *Sikhs for Justice* took out a defamation lawsuit against both Terry Milweski and MLI, seeking millions in damages. Recently a court ruling by a Canadian Judge meant that the defamation case will now go to full trial unless both parties reach a settlement. See report by Murtaza Ali Shah 'Sikh group scores first win in defamation case involving allegations of Pakistan's backing', *Geo News*, November 6, 2021, https://www.geo.tv/latest/380712-sikh-group-in-canada-scores-first-win-in-defamation-case-over-allegations-of-pakistans-backing (Accessed March 10, 2021).

The MLI report is available at: 0200820_Khalistan_Air_India_Milewski_PAPER_FWeb.pdf (macdonaldlaurier.ca) (accessed March 10, 20221).

34 See 'India protests farmer protest debate in UK house, summons high commissioner', *The Times of India*, March 10, 2021.

35 As above.

36 See Tavleen Singh 'Mishandling of farmers' agitation has damaged PM Modi's carefully cultivated image as a world statesman', *Indian Express*. February 7, 2021.

37 One interesting example of continuing tensions was cancellation of talks on farmer agitation at the University of British Columbia and Simon Fraser University in Vancouver, Canada in April 2021. Hartosh Bal, political editor of *Caravan*, a respected and progressive news magazine based in Delhi in India, who has been highly critical of Indian government's human rights record and its use of repressive measures against protesting farmers, was invited by the Punjabi Studies program at UBC to give an online talk about the ongoing farmers' struggle in India. He was also invited to a similar online talk at Simon

Fraser University. A group of Sikh activists objected to the talk as he was the nephew and alleged to be supporter of the late K. P. S. Gill, the Police Chief in Punjab at the height of the Khalistan movement. They held Gill responsible for killings and disappearances of hundreds of Sikh youth in the 1980s and early 1990s. As a result of activists' pressure, both talks were cancelled. For more details, see Gurpreet Singh 'UBC pressured by Sikh activists to cancel daring journalist's appearance on panel' and 'Canada's laughing-stock universities cave in twice to community gatekeepers by cancelling Indian journalist's talk' in *The Georgian Straight*, April 1 and April 25, 2021.

38 See the following news reports on Canada and Australia 'Indian diaspora holds Tiranga rally in Brampton for stronger ties with Canada', *The Tribune*, March 1, 2021 and 'Australia threatens deportations after attacks on Sikhs', *The Tribune*, March 4, 2021.

39 For further details, see Rishi Nagar 'Farmers' revolt is dividing the Indian diaspora in Canada', *Calgary Herald*, April 24, 2021.

40 See report by Sandeep Dikshit 'Attack on Sikhs in Sydney: Haryana youth Vishal Jood pleads guilty', *The Tribune*, September 2, 2021.

41 With rising tensions between Sikh and Hindu communities, especially among youth, attempts were made to jointly condemn them although not all agreed to sign a public statement. See report by Kathleen Calderwood, 'Tensions boil over in Sydney's Indian community as farmers' protests in Delhi continue', *ABC Western Sydney* March 15, 2021.

42 The exchanges became particularly vitriolic after a number of well-known global celebrities such as Rihanna, Greta Thunberg, Trevor Noah, Meena Harris (lawyer and US Vice President Kamala Harris's niece) and a number of Hollywood actors such as Susan Sarandon and John Cusak among others tweeted their support for farmers. Punjabi celebrities such as singer-actor Daljit Dosanjh, musicians Jay Sean (Kamaljit Singh Jhooti) and Dr Zeus (Baljit Singh Padam) and Indo-Canadian You-Tube host Lilly Singh, also tweeted support for farmers, troubling the Modi government and its celebrity supporters such as Bollywood actor Kangana Ranaut.

43 The first Trudeau government in 2016 had four Sikh MPs in the Cabinet, although after the recent election, the number has gone down to 2, Harjit Singh Sajjan and Kamal Khera. Harjit Singh Sajjan, Defence Minister since 2015 was transferred in a Cabinet reshuffle to become Minister for International Development and Minister Responsible for the Pacific Economic Development Agency of Canada. His position was given to Anita Anand, an Indian-Canadian with Punjabi roots. Kamal Khera, Sikh MP from Brampton West and one of the youngest females elected to Parliament, became the Minister for Seniors. Also interestingly, Sikh-Canadian Jagmeet Singh, leader of the New Democratic Party (NDP), again emerged as the 'kingmaker' after Trudeau's Liberal Party failed to win a clear majority in Parliament.

Bibliography

Anderson, Benedict. *Imagined Communities: Reflections On the Origin and Spread of Nationalism*. London: Verso, 1991.

Ballantyne, Tony. *Between Colonialism and Diaspora: Sikh Cultural Formations in an Imperial World*. Delhi: Permanent Black, 2006.

Brinkerhoff, Jennifer M. (ed). *Diasporas and Development: Exploring the Potential*. Boulder: Lynne Rienner Publishers, 2008.

Condos, Mark. *The Insecurity State: Punjab and the Making of Colonial Power in British India*. Cambridge University Press, 2017.

Deol, Harnik. *Religion and Nationalism in India: The Case of the Punjab*. London: Routledge, 2003.

DeWind, Josh and Segura, Renata Segura (eds.). *Diaspora Lobbies and the US Government: Convergence and Divergence in Making Foreign Policy*. New York: New York Press, 2014.

Jacobsen, Knut., Mann, Gurinder Singh, Myrvold, Kristina, and Nesbitt, Eleanor. (eds.). *Brill's Encyclopedia of Sikhism, Volume 1: History, Literature, Society, Beyond Punjab*. Leiden: Brill Publishers, 2017.

Koinova, Maria. *Diaspora Mobilizations for Conflict, Routledge Handbook of Diaspora Studies*. London: Routledge, 2018.

La Brack, Bruce. *The Sikhs of Northern California, 1904–1986*. New York: AMS Press, 1988.

Mahmood, Cynthia, Keppley *Fighting for Faith and Nation*. Philadelphia: University of Pennsylvania Press, 1996.

Mangat Jagjit, Singh. *A History of the Asians in East Africa c. 1886 to 1945*. London: Oxford University Press, 1969.

Merz, Barbara, Chen, Lincoln and Geithner, Peter. (eds.). *Diasporas and Development*. Harvard: Global Equity Initiative, Harvard University, 2007.

Ramnath, Maia. *Haj to Utopia: How the Ghadar Movement Charted Global Radicalism and Attempted to Overthrow the British Empire*. Oakland: University of California Press, 2011.

Shamsul, Amri, Bahauddin and Kaur, Arunajeet. *Sikhs in Southeast Asia: Negotiating an Identity*. Singapore: Institute of Southeast Asian Studies, 2011.

Shani, Giogio. *Sikh Nationalism and Identity in a Global Age*. London: Routledge, 2007.

Singh, Karam, Singh, Sukhpal and Kingra, Harmeet, Singh. 'Agrarian Crisis and Depeasantisation in Punjab: Status of Small/Marginal Farmers Who Left Agriculture'. *Indian Journal of Agricultural Economics*, 2009, Vol. 64, No.4, October–December, pp. 585–603.

Smith, Hazel, Stares, Paul. (eds.). *Diasporas in Conflict: Peace-Makers or Peace-Wreckers?* Tokyo: UNU Press, 2007.

Sohi, Seema. *Echoes of Mutiny: Race, Surveillance and Indian Anticolonialism in North America*. Oxford: Oxford University Press, 2014.

Sood, Malini. *Expatriate Nationalism and Ethnic Radicalism: The Ghadar Party in North America*. London: Routledge, 2001.

Sood, Ranjana. 'Land Structure and Status of Land Holdings in Rural Punjab'. *Advances in Economics and Business Management*, 2016, Vol. 3, No. 5, April–June, pp. 430–432.

Streets, Heather. *Martial Races: The Military Race and Masculinity in British Imperial Culture 1957–1914*. Manchester: Manchester University Press, 2010.

Tan, Tai Yong. *The Garrison State: Military, Government and Society in Colonial Punjab 1849–1947*. New Delhi: Sage, 2005.

Tatla, Darshan Singh. *The Sikh Diaspora: The Search for Statehood*. Washington: University of Washington Press, 1999.

Tatla, Darshan Singh. 'Rural Roots of the Sikh Diaspora'. In Ian Talbot & Shinder Thandi (eds.) *People on the Move: Punjabi Colonial, and Post-Colonial Migration*. Karachi: Oxford University Press, 2004, pp. 45–59.

Thandi, Shinder Singh. 'Sikh Migration' Section IV. In Knut A. Jacobsen and Gurinder Singh Mann (Editors-in-Chief) and Kristina Myrvold and Eleanor

Nesbitt (Associate Editors) *Brill's Encyclopedia of Sikhism, Volume 1: History, Literature, Society, Beyond Punjab*. Leiden: Brill Publishers, 2017.

Thandi, Shinder Singh. '*Vilayati Paisa*: Some Reflections on the Potential of Diaspora Finance in the Socio-Economic Development of Punjab'. *International Journal of Punjab Studies*, 2000, Vol. 7, No. 2, pp. 323–341.

Thandi, Shinder Singh. 'The Punjab Paradox: Understanding the Failures of Diaspora Engagement'. *Diaspora Studies*, 2014a, Vol. 7, No. 1, pp. 1–14.

Thandi, Shinder Singh. 'Sikh Migration, Diasporas and Transnational Practices'. In *Oxford Handbook of Sikh Studies*. New Delhi: Oxford University Press, 2014b, pp. 545–559.

10 Enhancing Visibility, Extending Solidarity

Women's Participation in the 2020–2021 Farmer Protests*

Swaroopa Lahiri

Introduction

On November 19, 2021, Indian Prime Minister Narendra Modi took the entire nation by surprise when he announced his decision of rolling back the controversial farm bills that had sparked widespread protests throughout the country for over a year. In September 2020, three farm bills had been hastily passed in the Indian Parliament: the Farmers' Produce Trade and Commerce (Promotion and Facilitation) Bill, the Farmers (Empowerment and Protection) Agreement on Price Assurance and Farm Services Bill and the Essential Commodities (Amendment) Bill. These farm acts, colloquially referred to as the 'black laws', had stirred up much controversy and uproar because of their intent to liberalize the agricultural sector at the expense of some farmers' incomes and autonomy. Small and marginal farmers who are often debt-ridden and have very little bargaining power vis-à-vis powerful agro businesses were expected to be the worst hit (Economic and Political Weekly, 2020). Modi's televised speech in November included an apology to all the people of the country and claimed that since the government had failed to convince a certain section of the farmers on the benefits of the bills, the bills would be revoked. On November 29, the Indian Parliament swiftly passed the Farm Laws Repeal Bill 2021 without much discussion or opposition.

The steadfast protests played a crucial role in pressurizing the government to cancel the laws. While protests had erupted in September 2020 after the bills were passed, they gained momentum in late November 2020 as farmers from Punjab, Haryana, Uttar Pradesh and Rajasthan stormed toward the national capital, New Delhi, and made their base on its borders. The farmers remained undeterred by the dipping mercury, Khalistani (Sikh separatist movement) or anti-national allegations and the police's various efforts to quash the protests. The two most prominent border protest sites were Tikri and Singhu located on the Delhi-Haryana border. In a span of days, Singhu and Tikri were rapidly transformed into vibrant bustling spaces that highlighted continuity between dissent and everyday life. *Langars* (a Sikh hallmark of free community meals served by the community kitchen), including pizza *langars*, massage centers, tattoo parlors, makeshift

 DOI: 10.4324/9781003320005-13

gym and libraries were sights that greeted visitors (Tagore, 2021). In sync with the Sikh ethos of *sewa* (selfless service), amenities such as medicine shops, a dental camp and laundry facilities had also been set up (Sinha, 2020a, 2020b). Poems by Punjabi revolutionary poets Lal Singh Dil and Sant Ram Udasi were recited by young children with fervor. Posters, slogans and speeches made ample reference to Sikh religious vocabulary and the Sikh people's longstanding contributions to the Army, their role as the nation's *annadata* (food provider) and their inherent revolutionary spirit.

There are several dimensions that made these protests, sometimes termed as the 'largest protest in human history', stand out, especially with respect to previous protests in the country. The sheer scale and organizational prowess depicted in the protests, along with extensive media coverage, resulted in significant global attention and solidarity with the protesters. For instance, Justice for Migrant Women sponsored a one-page advertisement in *The New York Times* that included a letter of support for the farmers' protest signed by 75 organizations working for diverse causes (the majority of which are not related to farmer-specific issues). Another aspect that made the protests all the more remarkable was the overwhelming presence and active participation of predominantly Punjabi and Haryanvi women. In the aftermath of the purported success of the movement, this chapter focuses on women's participation in the farmer protests through a brief historical examination of women's involvement in protests in India and by exploring the impetus for participation in the farmer protests for different groups of women based on caste and socio-economic backgrounds and experiences. The chapter also analyzes the nature of participation in the protests and its implication for gender relations in the future, especially once women have returned to their hometowns or villages.

Historical Background on Women's Involvement in Protests in India

Women in India have a long history of association with social protests, dating back to the colonial era and the freedom struggle. The modes of participation, the degrees of participation and the rationale behind participation have varied depending on the cause, class identity and external environment. It is impossible to list all such instances especially since many contributions are poorly documented but this section attempts to put the spotlight on some of these protests to illustrate the breadth of causes and tactics employed. Two relevant peasant movements that included active and overt participation by women were the *Tebhaga* Movement of 1946–1947 and the Naxalite Movement of 1967–1971 (Singha Roy, 1992). The *Tebhaga* Movement, supported by the Bengal Kisan Sabha, was initiated by sharecroppers, agricultural laborers and poor peasants against the *Jotedars* and *Zamindars* (rich peasants and landowners) and demanded the sharecroppers' right to retain two thirds of the agricultural produce. While women from the protesting households cooked for the activists, sheltered them and secretly delivered messages, they also openly retaliated against the landowners, including the women of the landowning households, by defiantly carrying paddy claimed by landlords to their own houses (Singha Roy, 1992: 56). They even adeptly converted their domestic tools such as broomsticks and traditional vegetable cutters to weapons when shielding the protesters against the wrath of the police (Singha Roy, 1992: 58).

The Naxalite Movement, often seen as an extension of the *Tebhaga* Movement, featured a similar variety of participation tactics from women, such as grabbing crop produce, meal preparation, sheltering injured protesters and serving as communication agents. It is important to note that while women took part in these movements, they were driven by their class identity rather than their gender identity. The participating women were from the agricultural labor class and resisted not only the police and the male landowners and rich peasants but also the women belonging to the landowning households who were seen to be complicit in the exploitation of the laborer class.

Apart from socio-economic status, the characteristics of the political field affect the issues and struggles that women choose to support. Ray meticulously unravels the complexities of women's movements in India by comparing the movements in Bombay (present day Mumbai) and Calcutta (present day Kolkata) (Ray, 2000). The main puzzle that she investigates is why different issues were taken up by women of both cities when they shared a similar social and political history, especially during the colonial period. Women in Calcutta rallied behind the causes of unemployment, wage discrimination, literacy, electricity and water (practical concerns) whereas women in Bombay were more aligned to the Western feminist movement and took up gendered or 'feminist' issues (strategic concerns) such as sexual harassment, patriarchy and violence against women (Ray, 2000: 5, 24). The reason behind this divergence is the nature of the political field: Calcutta had a hegemonic political field with the Communist Party of India (M) dictating women's issues whereas Bombay had a fragmented political field where independent women's organizations were setting the agenda (Ray, 2000: 42). Leftist political parties and their associated women's wings prefer to focus on class based issues such as poverty and unemployment. Gender issues are taken up occasionally but only when they do not overshadow the broader agenda. On the other hand, independent organizations can afford to pursue explicitly feminist issues since they are not accountable to political parties.

Environmental protests often garner staunch female support as women are generally regarded as the custodians of familial well-being. Examples include the 1973 *Chipko* Movement, the 1980 Anti-Nuclear Power Plant Protests, 1984 protests against Union Carbide after the Bhopal blast and the 1985 Narmada Dam protests (Bhowmick, 2020). While eco-feminist scholars have argued that women have an innate relationship with nature, it is in fact the gendered division of labor, and in particular, women's reliance on the natural environment to collect firewood and fodder that also make them recognize the pressing stakes of the issue at hand (Agarwal, 1992: 147–148).

Gender identity, notably of a mother, has been emphasized in some movements that were explicitly spearheaded by women. The concept of motherhood has been widely deployed in conflict ridden zones as a tool of intervention and a call for peace. Schirmer (1993) developed a political motherhood framework whereby women use traditional maternal qualities such as care, nurture and responsibility and concern for the vulnerable people in order to make strides into the public sphere either during or post conflict. Schirmer illustrates how in the case of Latin America,

> these women use the image of the weak and powerless female to their advantage as a protective means for mobilization, resistance and survival. As in the bread riots of the past centuries, these women represent the defiant transformation of the powerless victim into the political actor.
>
> (Schirmer, 1989: 4)

Two examples of movements that capitalized on the motherhood trope can be found in the North Eastern states of Manipur and Nagaland. The *Meira Paibis* (fondly called the Mothers and Grandmothers of Manipur) and the Naga Mothers' Association (NMA) started off with social cleansing activities such as prohibition of alcohol and narcotic abuse in public places but soon shifted gears and entered the field of peace activism to protest against issues such as insurgency, Indian Army oppression and extrajudicial killings. The most common tactics adopted by the NMA for peace activism were peace marches and rallies, followed by dialogue, mediation and prayers, strongly adhering to a non-violent mode of protest (Vernal, 2015:105). The NMA precisely played the mother card to make their voices heard. The 'mother' as defined by the NMA didn't have to be a biological mother but one who could display the quintessential maternal qualities such as unconditional love, care and nurture (Vernal, 2015: 100). Motherhood is a convenient intervention tactic because it is not viewed as too radical to become untrustworthy as it is merely considered kitchen politics. NMA's kitchen politics revolved around inviting rebel members of their tribe home and counseling them to make them realize the gravity of their actions.

While the NMA has generally promoted motherhood within a non-violent and socially conformist framework, in the neighboring state of Manipur, motherhood has been weaponized in a dramatic and socially deviant manner. On July 15, 2004, following the brutal rape and subsequent killing of a woman named Manorama by the Indian Army, a group of 12 middle-aged *Meira Paibis* stripped in front of the then Assam Rifles Headquarters,

Kangla Fort. They held banners labeled 'Indian Army Rape Us' and 'Indian Army Take Our Flesh' and claimed to be 'Mothers of Manorama' expressing fury at the way the Indian Army treated Manorama and demanding the withdrawal of the Armed Forces Special Powers Act.

Chakravarti (2010) argues that the demonstration was utterly shocking yet poignantly effective because

> as "Mothers of Manorama", the *Meira Paibis* deployed the trope of motherhood to shock and shame the army, whom they rendered as disobedient and wayward sons. By simultaneously insisting on their maternal status and inviting rape, they made the very act of viewing their naked bodies fraught with the horror of primeval taboo and oedipal guilt. By doing so they turned the shame of rape back on Manorama's rapists.
>
> (54)

She further mentions that this act could be seen as a new bold language of protest whereby the state, international laws and other institutions are circumvented and not approached for delivery of justice or at least not considered as the only avenues of recourse (Chakravarti, 2010: 50). In addition, this message was extraordinary enough to be covered extensively by the national media and sent shockwaves all over the country.

Several features of previous women's protest movements help us to understand women's key role in the 2020–2021 farmer protests. Substantial mobilization by local political parties as well as women's organizations was pivotal in generating awareness and gaining mass support. The participation methods ranged from traditional responsibilities of food preparation, managing households in the absence of men and peaceful sit-ins at the protest sites to leadership roles such as delivering speeches, sloganeering and overseeing event arrangements. While different women had different motivations for showing up to the protests, like in past protests, their household roles and identities fueled their resistance. Being custodians of familial well-being, the fact that the farm laws threatened to disrupt household well-being served as an important driving force. For a certain section of women who had lost their husbands or sons due to the agrarian crisis, their identities and experiences as 'widows' or 'mothers' were highlighted.

At the same time, past protests were usually localized, at least for the most part. The farmer protests saw women, including a significant proportion of elderly women, having a prolonged presence at the national capital's protest sites, located at a considerable distance from home and devoid of the accustomed privacy. The participation of elderly women, often the most determined and resilient of the lot, mirrored the 2019–2020 Citizenship Amendment Act (CAA) demonstrations, where grandmothers who had previously never ventured out of their homes, assembled at Shaheen Bagh in Delhi, braving the harsh winter for a peaceful sit-in that championed equality and justice for the future generations. Even then, the Shaheen Bagh protest was principally composed of women residing in Delhi whereas the farmer protests had some women walking for days to reach the protest site.

Women's Mobilization in the 2020–2021 Farmer Protests

Women's massive turnout at the protests was both spectacular and intriguing. As Neelam Ghumaan, the general secretary of Janwadi Istri Sabha Punjab (an organization that advocates for women's rights) pointed out,

> it is so difficult to organize women on social issues. They don't even know their own rights as daughters, wives or mothers. They hardly come out against their own social discrimination. But as soon as you talk about their economic rights, they step out and become a part of the organisation.
>
> (Toor, 2020a, 2020b)

Much of the credit for robust female participation in the protests can be attributed to the efforts of farmers' unions such as the Bharti Kisan Union Ekta Ugrahan (BKU-Ekta Ugrahan) in organizing extensive on-ground mobilization and awareness campaigns and in trying to establish inter-caste solidarity (Sinha, 2020a, 2020b). Harinder Bindu, the state president of the BKU-Ekta Ugrahan's Women's Wing and a relentless activist fighting for farmer and laborer rights deserves special mention (Toor, 2020a, 2020b). While in Punjab, she efficiently helmed the creation of new units and organized training and meetings for both men and women. Men were taught to perform domestic responsibilities in the absence of their wives who were attending meetings and encouraged to involve female members of their families in political discussions and activities. Women were trained to be partners and collaborators rather than passive supporters. Partnership was not only reflected when women stayed at the protest sites, the movement gave women flexibility in terms of the method of participation. Hence, it ensured that all women who wanted to participate were able to participate in some way or the other, given their respective constraints.

Once the protests reached Delhi, Bindu, a single mother left her teenage son with her family and made her way to the Tikri protest site (Jaswal, 2021). In Tikri, her main job was to monitor the supply chain and make sure that necessities were always in stock. Apart from supply chain management, her typical day at Tikri was packed with activities: morning meetings with the union, checking up on women protesters and motivating them, overseeing stage performances and crowd management and interacting with media personnel.

The women who had gathered at the Singhu and Tikri protest sites were mainly from Punjab and Haryana. They were a diverse group and cut across class, caste, literacy and age divides. They ranged from Jat women of large landholding families to landless Dalit agricultural laborers. The sites simultaneously had the presence of young, technology savvy and educated women and grandmothers who had received no formal education. While women were naturally vocal about the dangers presented by the three bills, they simultaneously brought their gendered experiences, concerns and demands to the protest.

Apart from the daily newspapers, a number of weekly news magazines such as Frontline, Outlook, India Today and Time carried front cover images of women protestors along with lead stories which increased women's visibility and diversity during the agitation. *Trolley Times*, a newspaper launched by the farmers to become their mouthpiece and represent their voices exemplify this diversity of women protesters in their various illustrations.

Time magazine's choice to feature women protesters on its cover changes the question of visibility for women farmers. Although women participating in agriculture is hardly news, they are merely imagined to be part of a larger agricultural community, bereft of any distinction as a social group. The Kisan Long March in 2018 would be a good example in this context where women would feature as participants in the images circulated in popular media but bore no gendered distinction. The image the Time magazine chose for its front cover highlights the gendered dimension of their participation and vouches for the powerful leadership that women demonstrated in the protests. The front cover has women of all ages, including grandmothers, a baby and a young girl (Time, 2021). Some choose to cover their heads with the *chunni* (traditional long scarf) which is a marker of Sikh religion and Haryanvi culture aimed to protect the modesty of the woman (the practice of *purdah)*. Yet, they still defy the broader connotations of *purdah* such as the gendered partitioning of space and behavioral expectations through their prolonged presence at a public protest site. The images of the woman carrying her baby and the young girl convey that women's social roles are no longer limited to their traditional gendered duties of caregivers. Rather, they translate into a more capacious notion of a dissident community with a common political goal. The young girl's presence and solidarity imply that the event is also a political lesson in progress with future generations at stake.

On the other hand, one *Trolley Times* illustration depicts three elderly women who refuse to adhere to the ablest and ageist presumptions about participation in political struggles. In fact, throughout the protests, the elderly women had been among the most resolute and had categorically refused to budge from the protest site until and unless the laws were repealed. A featured story in the first edition of *Trolley Times* mentioned an elderly woman who abandoned her coveted sweater knitting project and signed up for the protest despite poor health conditions. Her reasoning was simple and she used the sweater as a metaphor for aspirations and prized possessions: 'If I don't go to the protest now much that has been knitted will unravel, including my son's dreams, your father's earned land' (Kaur, 2020). The *Trolley Times* image also strongly condemns the Chief Justice of India's patronizing remark about why women and elders were kept in the protest. Such a remark strips women of their agency that includes the right to protest and the clubbing of women and elders portrays women as infirm and helpless people who are in continuous need of assistance and guidance.

Women's Motivations for Participation

The social imaginary of a farmer in India is a male figure as captured by the popular term *kisan bhai* (farmer brother). Showing up to the protests in solidarity with the farming community meant asserting their independent identity as farmers and gaining recognition as farmers for many women (Kaur and Sekhon, 2021; Kaushal and Kissu, 2021). Women in agriculture have been historically disadvantaged compared to their male counterparts. A long list of factors are to be blamed (Agarwal, 1994: 298). Socio-cultural norms such as the prevalence of *purdah* restrict their mobility and make it more likely for agricultural extension officers to target male household heads for technology diffusion and training. The use of the plough by women is a social taboo and so they need to rely on hired workers or male members of the family for ploughing their fields but their ability to command labor is limited. Women also typically have lower access to financial, informational and institutional resources due to lower ownership of assets such as land and cash, lower literacy rates including digital literacy and less awareness. In India, for example, only about 13 per cent of women own agricultural land. Applying Kabeer and Subrahmanian's (1996) gender disadvantage framework to agriculture, women farmers face three sets of disadvantages: *gender-specific disadvantage* (domestic division of labor, prevalence of purdah/female seclusion and other restrictive socio-cultural norms, fewer assets), *gender-intensified disadvantage* (lower literacy rates, lower occupational mobility, lower levels of self-esteem due to social conditioning) and *imposed gender disadvantage* (limited access to extension services and information, institutional biases).

The new farm laws would have sharpened the existing gender inequities in agriculture and would have more adversely impacted women (MAKAAM, 2020). Since women farmers suffer from low mobility and generally sell small quantities of inferior produce, they mainly tend to sell their produce to local private traders who, over the course of time, become familiar and trusted figures. These traders often double up as informal credit lenders and provide support for other agricultural needs. The dismantling of the Agricultural Produce Market Committees (APMCs) markets (*mandis*) would have hit women harder since the mandis enabled price discovery for the women farmers – in fact, for many women, it served as the only source of price discovery. In addition, the mandis' proximity to the villages is especially convenient for women who cannot afford to travel long distances on a regular basis due to socio-cultural norms and domestic duties. The new laws would have triggered the entry of bigger, alien players and would have severely undermined women's existing networks of market access. Most women farmers simply do not have the bargaining power, the requisite negotiation skills or literacy levels to deal with powerful businesses and risk being completely sidelined in a corporatized agricultural sector.

In addition, India's current wave of feminization is occurring under distress circumstances (Pattnaik et al., 2018). Women's involvement in agriculture is negatively associated with the average size of landholdings and is positively associated with poverty and total farm area under food grains. In other words, poor women with smaller landholdings who mostly cultivate food grains are stuck in the agricultural sector. These women are also increasingly confronted with a hostile agricultural landscape characterized by water scarcity, fragmented plot sizes, mechanization and the difficulty of accessing labor. Farming is becoming a loss-making profession in many states, with cultivation costs routinely exceeding the crop sales revenue. Once hailed as the cradle of the Green Revolution, the euphoria has long died down in Punjab. The state is now bogged down by a severe agrarian crisis as a result of rapidly depleting groundwater resources, rising costs of production notably lease land rentals and mounting indebtedness. Farmers and agricultural laborers are caught in a spiraling debt trap due to high capital and technology investments necessitated by the Green Revolution and dwindling farm incomes (Singh et al., 2017). The surge in suicide rates, especially in the *Malwa* region, highlights the dire situation. Women who have lost husbands and other male members of the family to suicides suddenly find themselves in the role of primary breadwinners. Women who have access to land and were previously excluded from working in the fields due to family customs now grapple with the unfamiliar tasks of cultivation and agricultural decision-making in a collapsing agricultural landscape. For the landless women, there exist very few opportunities for paid labor in Punjab since the cultivation of the two dominant crops wheat and rice is heavily mechanized (Singh, 2021a, 2021b, 2021c). If suicide was driven by the inability to repay debts, women frequently inherit the deceased member's debt in addition to fending for their families. An assessment of landholding status of families post-suicide in the *Malwa* region shows that landholding size reduces irrespective of the category of the farmer (marginal, small, semi-medium, medium, large) and sometimes even leads to instances of landlessness (Padhi, 2012: 22–24). It is hardly surprising then that a large number of widows from the suicide afflicted *Malwa* region turned up at the protests notably on December 16, 2020, as the farm bills were expected to worsen the factors that compel suicide. The pandemic served as a tipping point because the lockdowns drastically cut down the income avenues for many debt-ridden women and participation in the protests provided them with an outlet to vent their frustrations and anger (Toor, 2020a, 2020b; Gayatri, 2021).

The Dalits are particularly hard hit, especially the Dalit women. Caste is an important determinant of social relations in rural India. In Punjab, for example, the Dalits generally live at a lower altitude than the upper caste landowning families so that the latter do not have to touch water already used by Dalits (Suresh and Saxena, 2021). Dalits' homes are also labeled as places where the sun never rises – since there is a general belief that the wind blows from the east, the upper caste farmers refuse to experience wind coming from the side of the Dalits and hence ensure that Dalits remain in the western side of the villages (Suresh and Saxena, 2021). Along with social discrimination, Dalits simultaneously face economic discrimination with severe implications for household welfare. Bakshi (2008) calculates an index of access to land for cultivation in India and establishes that while non-Dalit/Adivasi group's index is 1.16, the index for Dalits is 0.45. Simply put, this means that the land owned by Dalits is less proportionate to their share in the population and that Dalit households are disadvantaged in terms of land ownership, compared to other social groups.

While the all India figure is 0.45, the figure for Punjab from where most Dalit protesters showed up is abysmally low: the index of access to land for cultivation for Dalits is 0.09 whereas non-Dalit/Adivasi groups have an index of 1.68. Even though the indexes are calculated using slightly dated data from 2004 to 2005, the extent of inequality is startling. More recent figures aren't encouraging either. As per Census 2011, Punjab has the highest proportion of Scheduled Caste population in the country (32 per cent) yet Dalits barely own 2.3 per cent of the agricultural land in the state (Dastidar, 2021a, 2021b). The 1961 Punjab Village Common Lands Regulation Act technically reserves one third of the village common land (*shamlat* land) for use by the Dalits (Sharma, 2021). However, that regulation is rarely enforced on the ground and common land often ends up being controlled by rich landowners or is sometimes even earmarked for development projects. Members of organizations such as Zameen Prapti Sangharsh Committee (ZPSC) who are fighting to challenge land inequity participated in the protests not only to repeal the farm acts but also to shed light on the plight of Dalits in the agricultural sector. In fact, right after Punjab's first Dalit Chief Minister Charanjit Singh Channi assumed office in September 2021, the ZPSC mobilized Dalit women who turned up outside the district administration complex and demanded equitable land distribution and the implementation of the Land Ceiling Act (Singh, 2021a, 2021b, 2021c).

Since the majority of Dalits do not own land for cultivation, their agricultural livelihoods as laborers are entirely dependent on upper caste landowners. The Green Revolution compelled several farmers to mechanize their operations, shrinking agricultural labor work opportunities for the landless. Some of these workers then started working at the APMCs and the proposed dismantling of the APMCs would have eliminated an important source of income for them (Sinha, 2020a, 2020b). Another lingering fear was that the new farm laws would have ushered the advent of contract farming and increased Dalits' precarity by depleting their earnings as agricultural laborers and snatching other benefits that they currently enjoyed. A quote from a female member of the Punjab Khet Mazdoor Sabha voiced this concern:

> The three black laws will hit us harder than it will hit the farmers. If corporations are allowed to enter the system, we will be robbed of small perks our employers give us such as wheat for Rs 2 per kg and 400 units of electricity to our homes.
>
> (Deol, 2021)

Dalit women face double marginalization along caste and gender lines. In addition to taking care of their homes and bearing their domestic responsibilities, they work on the fields and get paid much less than their male counterparts for the same amount of labor. They tend to have little to no bargaining power with respect to their employers who almost always happen to be male landowners. Furthermore, Dalit women are subject to widespread sexual harassment at the hands of the landowners. When they visit the village common land to gather fodder for the cattle, they are often bombarded with taunts and casteist remarks (Sharma, 2021). The farmer protests did include some Dalit women but their number was much less in comparison to the number of women from higher socio-economic backgrounds. This was partially due to the existing social hierarchies in their communities. In that sense, the protest sites could be considered as bubbles – the attempts to erase caste distinctions at the sites by using the slogan *kisan mazdoor ekta zindabad* (long live the unity of the farmer and the laborer) did not have spillover effects outside the boundaries of the sites. Even at the protest venues, the Dalits were sidelined for the most part when it came to delivering speeches or being at the forefront of other activities. For the Dalit women, a practical factor contributed to their small presence: transport problem. This quote by Paramjeet Longwal, general secretary of the Zameen Prapti Sangharsh Committee illustrates this:

> Tractors and trolleys are owned by *zamindars* [landowners], that is the *kisans* [farmers] and so we had no way to come. They would take upper caste women...I had mobilized close to 600 Dalit women and half of them dropped out because of a transport problem.
>
> (Suresh and Saxena, 2021)

Nonetheless, a few fiery Dalit women activists and leaders such as Nodeep Kaur had a powerful and impactful presence at the protests.

On the other hand, some women from landholding households had a slightly different motivation: protecting their land. There was a common perception that the farm acts would snatch land away from landowners and reduce them to bonded laborers in their own fields. In fact, in 1907, there was an eerily similar movement to the 2020–2021 farmer protests called the *Pagri Sambhal Jatta* movement spearheaded by celebrated revolutionary Bhagat Singh's uncle Ajit Singh. It was launched against three British laws related to agriculture which threatened the autonomy and land ownership rights of Punjabi farmers. The farm acts were Doab Bari Act, Punjab Land Colonisation Act and the Punjab Land Alienation Act (Brar, 2020). For the traditional landowning Jat-Sikhs, land is not only a source of sustenance but a cultural asset. Land, irrespective of size, is sacred and intrinsically tied to the honor and ancestry of the family. Elderly women insisted that the protests were essential to protect the interests of the future generations by ensuring that their land remained in the family (Shergill, 2020).

Several women were also concerned that the laws would have a direct adverse impact on their households' kitchens as well as on other indicators of gender equality (Salam, 2020; Gupta, 2021; Talwar, 2021). Women's assets such as gold and utensils are the first to be auctioned off in times of crisis and repaying of debts. Due to the prevalence of patriarchal customs, declining farm incomes would more strongly affect the nutritional intake and educational opportunities of women as they typically have very low levels of intra-household bargaining power. BKU's state committee leader Sukhwinder Kaur echoes this sentiment:

> Women are already cornered in this industry because we don't own any land. If women are unable to run their households, they will be forced into prostitution. Every time there is an agrarian crisis, women are impacted first and the most.
>
> (Deol, 2021)

Modes of Participation and Representation

Media reports documenting the farmer protests were sprinkled with phrases like 'women of steel', 'women helm the stir', 'women take reign' and 'women take the lead' and lauded the grit, determination and leadership skills of women. Women themselves described the movement as revolutionary and confidently stated that they were naturally prepared for sacrifices as they hailed from the land of Bhagat Singh with ancestral ties to the freedom struggle and an inherited revolutionary trait (Bhatnagar, 2021; Singh, 2021a, 2021b, 2021c). Women participants who died during the protests were referred to as 'martyrs' as the fight against the farm laws was viewed as a noble cause.

Apart from the sit-in at the Delhi protest sites, women had been instrumental in sustaining multiple protests in their home states, at locations such as toll plazas and shopping malls. In some instances, women had taken over agricultural tasks to enable men to leave for the protest sites or had adopted a rotational strategy that permitted them to balance their domestic responsibilities with their presence at the Delhi border protests. They had also ensured a steady supply of rations and other essential items to the sites.

At the Delhi border protest sites, women juggled a range of activities such as cooking *langar*, singing revolutionary songs, performing skits, delivering speeches and managing the events on the stage. Their leadership streak was particularly evident on Women Farmers' Day (January 18, 2021) and International Women's Day (March 8) when all events were entirely organized and led by all-women crews (Bhatnagar, 2021; Kaushal and Kissu, 2021). A new publication, *Karti Dharti*, was launched by a group of women to provide a platform for diverse voices, notably women's voices, related to the farmer protests. The prevalent motto was to stand shoulder-to-shoulder with men (commonly referred to as brothers) and fight as equal partners and stakeholders. One particular illustration from *Trolley Times* with women in the foreground raising the farmer union BKU-Ekta Ugrahan flag captures this sentiment.

Women's performances amalgamated their identities as farmers and as family members of men who had suffered as a result of a failing agricultural sector. They employed both radical forms of participation such as burning effigies of the advocates of a neo-liberalized agricultural sector – IMF-World Bank, corporate honchos Adani and Ambani and the Prime Minister Narendra Modi – and tractor rallies as well as performative gendered practices of mourning. The female driven tractors on Republic Day signaled an attempt to shatter male monopoly on agricultural technology, to shun societal expectations about women's behavior and claim recognition and visibility as women farmers in their own right. Simultaneously, women lamented the loss of their sons and husbands who had committed suicide due to acute indebtedness by holding their portraits high (Iftikhar, 2020). The photographic presences of those who had died forged a site of revolutionary remembrance and brought an affective charge to the crisis. In the context of the farmer protests, the most interesting form of performance by women was the *Pitt-Siapa* (Kopal, 2021). *Pitt-Siapa* is a Punjabi mourning ritual performed only by women which entails weeping, beating up their chests and foreheads and singing songs bemoaning the death. However, in this case, women used the ritual to curse and wish for the death of Narendra Modi with the phrase '*Modi mar jaa tu*' (Modi go die). This act in itself can be classified as bold defiance since women were weaponizing their traditional emotional labor responsibilities to assign a death verdict to the most powerful man in the country. This transgression not only undermined the authority of the Prime Minister but also emphasized the agency of the politically marginalized women bound by the dictates of patriarchy.

Implications of Women's Participation for Gender Relations

One of the most striking aspect of women taking part in the farmer protests was that the vast majority of them came from the states of Punjab and Haryana, the heartland of the patriarchal belt in India. According to Caldwell (1978), the patriarchal belt is characterized by undervaluation of women's work, subordination of women through restrictive behavior codes and the intertwining of family honor with female virtue, high fertility rates and a preference for male children. A penchant for male children supported by female feticide and female infanticide practices is indicated by the dismal child sex ratio in both states: 846 females for 1,000 males in the 0–6 age group in Punjab and 834 in Haryana as compared to the national figure of 919 (Census of India, 2011). Caldwell (1978) states that despite their blatant exploitation, women in the patriarchal belt rarely fight back overtly because they have been socialized since a very early age to embrace traditional gender roles defined by religious teachings.

Kandiyoti (1988) builds on Caldwell's notion of the belt of patriarchy and coins the term 'classic patriarchy'. In areas of classic patriarchy, women seldom display overt acts of resistance and often figure out ways to accommodate their interests within the system through participation in 'patriarchal bargains' that reflect their constraints. The nature of the 'patriarchal bargain' is defined by class, caste and ethnicity. In societies where classic patriarchy is prevalent, early marriages of women and control and subordination of women are common. Women's labor and progeny are fully appropriated and women's contribution to production is rendered invisible. Under classic patriarchy, women of higher caste and class are more likely to follow *purdah* or female seclusion that serves as a marker of status. As coping mechanisms, women in these regions use interpersonal strategies that maximize their security through emotional manipulation of their sons and husbands. There is a premium on age and older women grease the wheels of the patriarchal system by abetting the infliction of gender injustices they themselves had gone through as daughters-in-law. When classic patriarchy is threatened by new market forces, the introduction of capital or economic impoverishment, women resist transition and seek to claim their part of the 'patriarchal bargain' – protection in exchange for subordination and propriety. This is because the alternative range of options for women to enhance their security is limited.

Punjab and Haryana embody many traits of classic patriarchy with their profligate dowry practices and appropriation of women's labor including reproductive labor. Women are conditioned to believe that their domestic contribution is not valuable and are barred from exploring wage employment due to caste barriers. Jat-Sikh women complain that they are restricted from seeking wage employment even in the face of economic duress since their caste privilege renders paid employment a social taboo (Padhi, 2012: 45–46). In Haryana, female shortages due to adverse sex ratios and agrarian needs had led to bride prices but this practice did not translate into an elevated status of women. Instead, bride prices were paid for physically strong women who could fulfill the family's agricultural labor needs – widow remarriage was also encouraged for the same purpose (Chowdhry, 1994: 60, 120). On the other hand, in Punjab, many widows were forced to remarry close family relatives so that any property rights they had inherited as a result of widowhood would remain in the family (Kaur, 2011).

Women's feisty participation in the farmer protests hence appeared in stark contrast to the socio-cultural fabric of Punjab and Haryana. The protest sites had witnessed fluid gender roles with men and women equally sharing kitchen duties. Men who had previously never cooked were now serving food to women and respecting and recognizing women's labor (Natt, 2020). They saw this as nothing short of a revolution as well as an eye-opening experience – as one of the male protesters put it, 'My wife and I alternate between home and the protest site. Being at the protest has made me realize that cooking itself is a full-time job and my wife does so much more with the same time' (Gayatri, 2021). The tractor rally by women was enthusiastically supported by men despite the tractor's traditional masculine connotation – in fact, some women were taught how to drive tractors by men at the protest sites. Activists had taken advantage of such a large female gathering to spread awareness about women's rights and motivate them to stand up for themselves. For some women, protesting had truly been a transformative experience (Bhowmick, 2021; Gayatri, 2021). This was especially true for women who had spent most of their lives within the confines of home and had rarely interacted with the outside world. There was a growing optimism that the protests had stirred women's consciousness and improved self-perception and were a stepping stone for gender equality movements that had so far occurred unevenly in the country, including in Punjab. The participants were expected to return as enlightened women free from the shackles of gender stereotypes with the resolve to challenge the state and regressive patriarchal customs back home.

However, there is skepticism about whether participation in the protests can dramatically alter gender relations, especially within the household since social conditioning of women is deeply entrenched. Previous protests such as the *Tebhaga* movement did not lead to notable changes in gender relations even though women fought side by side with the men. The women were simply expected to return to their original role after the protests had ended. There is an age factor involved too: older women are more likely to want to revert to the status quo after the protests are over (Gayatri, 2021). This desire can be explained by the classic patriarchy discussion mentioned earlier. Older women with limited options for independent economic survival rely heavily on the patriarchal bargain especially since they have already fulfilled their end of the bargain (subordination and propriety) in their initial years. For them, the sole goal of the protests was to repeal the farm acts. Furthermore, the same protest sites that ensured gendered labor sensitization and the weakening of rigid gender roles also became spaces of female objectification and multiple sexual harassment incidents, including an alleged gang rape (The Tribune, 2021).

Conclusion

The farmer protests raging at the Singhu and Tikri borders of Delhi were characterized by historically unprecedented levels of participation from primarily Punjabi and Haryanvi women belonging to various socio-economic classes, castes, age groups and professions. Refusing to be mere spectators, women had turned into active participants, leaders, security guards and organizers in Singhu and Tikri and simultaneously cultivated smaller protests in their home states. There were numerous reasons behind such a powerful involvement: some women wanted to be recognized as independent farmers who were equally, if not, more adversely affected by the farm laws due to inherent gender inequality in agriculture. Other women were opposing the laws because they would shrink many farmers' household incomes and impact household welfare, especially women's nutritional intake and educational opportunities. For Dalit women, possibly the most marginalized group, the laws would have compounded the economic hardships they already faced due to the intersection between gender and caste. Most of the remarkably resilient elderly women feared that the farm acts would endanger familial land ownership: a marker of family honor. The modes of participation ranged from cooking, rallying, delivering speeches and slogans to performative acts that mourned deceased family members and challenged authority and patriarchy.

The protest sites had been transformed into flourishing spaces of increased gender equality where cooking duties were evenly distributed, women's traditional labor was valued and women participants were treated as equal partners. Several women, especially younger women, claimed that the protests were an eye-opener in terms of how they should perceive themselves and boosted their morale and self-respect. However, it is uncertain whether participation in the protests would translate into improved gender relations and create dents in the patriarchal society over time. The introduction of the farm laws was essentially seen as an economic issue and it is usually relatively easier to garner women's support for economic causes. In any case, involvement of women in previous peasant movements in Punjab, albeit on a much smaller scale, did not result in much change in gender relations. Mobilizing women on gender issues is a tedious task, especially in deeply patriarchal settings such as Punjab and Haryana. Historically, men have solicited and appreciated women's solidarity and support for social issues but it remains to be seen whether female participation in the farmer protests succeeds in becoming a launch pad for gender equality movements in Punjab or for the country at large.

Note

* This chapter is a revised version of 'Enhancing Visibility, Extending Solidarity: Women's Participation in the 2020-21 Farmer Protests', first published in *Journal of Sikh and Punjab Studies*, 29(1&2) (Spring–Fall, 2022): 291–304.

Bibliography

Agarwal, Bina. 'The Gender and Environment Debate: Lessons from India'. *Feminist Studies* 18, no. 1 (1992):119–158.

Agarwal, Bina. *A Field of One's Own: Gender and land rights in South Asia.* Cambridge: Cambridge University Press, 1994.

Bakshi, Aparajita. 'Social Inequality in Land Ownership in India: A Study with Particular Reference to West Bengal'. *Social Scientist* (2008), 39 (9/10): 95–116.

Bhatnagar, Amil. 'Women Take the Lead at Singhu, Say There Is No Question of Going Back'. *The Indian Express*, January 19, 2021. Accessed March 20, 2021. https://indianexpress.com/article/cities/delhi/women-take-the-lead-at-singhu-say-there-is-no-question-of-going-back-7151801/.

Bhowmick, Nilanjana. 'How Women Have Changed India Through Political Protests'. *Time*, January 15, 2020. Accessed June 18, 2021. https://time.com/5765702/india-protests-women/.

Bhowmick, Nilanjana. '"I Cannot Be Intimidated. I Cannot Be Bought." The Women Leading India's Farmers' Protests'. *Time*, March 4, 2021. Accessed June 15, 2021. https://time.com/5942125/women-india-farmers-protests/.

Brar, Kamaldeep Singh. 'Explained: Separated by over a 100 Years, What Connects the *Pagri Sambhal Jatta* Movement with Ongoing Farmers Protests?' *The Indian Express*, December 7, 2020. Accessed March 10, 2021. https://indianexpress.com/article/explained/explained-recalling-pagri-sambhal-jatta-movement-and-what-connects-two-farmer-movements-in-punjab-separated-by-over-a-100-years-7094916/.

Caldwell, John C. 'A Theory of Fertility: From High Plateau to Destabilization'. *Population and Development Review* (1978): 553–577.

Census of India 2011. Govt. of India.

Chakravarti, Paromita. 'Reading Women's Protest in Manipur: A Different Voice?' *Journal of Peacebuilding & Development* 5, no. 3 (2010): 47–60. Accessed March 10, 2021. http://www.tandfonline.com/doi/abs/10.1080/15423166.2010.305597731461

Chowdhry, Prem. *The Veiled Women: Shifting Gender Equation in Rural Haryana 1818–1990*. Delhi: Oxford University Press, 1994.

Dastidar, Riddhi. 'For Women at the Farmers' Protests in Delhi, the Farming Laws Aren't the Only Issue'. *The Swaddle*, January 20, 2021a. Accessed March 14, 2021. https://theswaddle.com/for-women-at-the-farmers-protests-in-delhi-the-farming-laws-arent-the-only-issue/.

Dastidar, Riddhi. 'India's Suffering Female Farmers Have the Most to Lose'. *Foreign Policy*, April 13, 2021b. Accessed November 15, 2021. https://foreignpolicy.com/2021/04/13/indias-suffering-female-farmers-have-the-most-to-lose/.

Deol, Taran. '"We Can Lead a Revolution" – Women Take Centre Stage at Farmer Protests at Singhu Border'. *The Print*, January 18, 2021. Accessed October 12, 2021. https://theprint.in/india/we-can-lead-a-revolution-women-take-centre-stage-at-farmer-protests-at-singhu-border/587871/.

Economic and Political Weekly. 'Farmers' Protests: What Are the Main Concerns Regarding the Farm Bills Passed by the BJP Government?', December 11, 2020. Accessed January 20, 2021. https://www.epw.in/engage/article/farmers%E2%80%99-protests-what-are-main-concerns-regarding.

Gayatri, Geetanjali. 'Crossing the Threshold: Agitation against Farm Laws Turns the Spotlight on Punjabi Women'. *The Tribune*, February 28, 2021. Accessed April 15, 2021. https://www.tribuneindia.com/news/features/crossing-the-threshold-215517.

Gupta, Vivek. 'Women Rise in Anger at Farm Law Protests Breaking Patriarchy and Stereotypes'. *The Leaflet*, January 2, 2021. Accessed March 10, 2021.

https://www.theleaflet.in/women-rise-in-anger-at-farm-law-protests-breaking-patriarchy-and-stereotypes/.

Iftikhar, Fareeha. 'Widows, Mothers of Farmers Who Died by Suicide Join Stir at Delhi's Tikri Border'. *Hindustan Times*, December 17, 2020. Accessed March 22, 2021. https://www.hindustantimes.com/delhi-news/delhi-widows-mothers-of-farmers-whodied-by-suicide-join-stir-at-tikri/story-iTZsmlr1pqWVVn722N-ZlVI.html.

Jaswal, Srishti. 'Meet Harinder Kaur "Bindu", the Farmer Leader Running the Tikri Protest'. *Newslaundry*, January 25, 2021. Accessed April 10, 2021. https://www.newslaundry.com/2021/01/25/meet-harinder-kaur-bindu-the-farmer-leader-running-the-tikri-protest.

Kabeer, Naila, and Ramya Subrahmanian. *Institutions, Relations and Outcomes: Framework and Tools for Gender-Aware Planning*. Brighton, UK: Institute of Development Studies, 1996.

Kandiyoti, Deniz. 'Bargaining with Patriarchy'. *Gender & Society* 2, no. 3 (1988): 274–290.

Kaur, Gurmit. 'Customary Law and Widow Remarriage: Its Implications and Effects on Colonial Punjabi Women'. In *Proceedings of the Indian History Congress*, vol. 72, pp. 828–835. Indian History Congress, 2011.

Kaur, Jaswinder. 'Sweater'. *Trolley Times*, Volume 1, Edition 1, December 18, 2020.

Kaur, Navjotpal, and Sumeet Sekhon. 'Women Take Lead Roles in India's Farmers' Protest'. *The Conversation*, January 7, 2021. Accessed March 10, 2021. https://theconversation.com/women-take-lead-roles-in-indias-farmers-protest-151981.

Kaushal, Ravi, and Sagrika Kissu. '"World Is Changing": Sea of Women Farmers Throng Borders of Delhi to Celebrate International Women's Day'. *NewsClick*, March 8, 2021. Accessed May 10, 2021. https://www.newsclick.in/%E2%80%98World-Changing-Sea-Women-Farmers-Throng-Borders-Delhi-Celebrate-International-Women-Day.

Kopal. 'When the Women Mourned Modi'. *KartiDharti*, February 2021. Accessed May 10, 2021. https://kartidharti.com/article/when-women-cried-for-modi-602f0ce455cd2.

Natt, Navkiran. 'From Tikri's Kitchen'. *Trolley Times*, Volume 1, Edition 2, December 22, 2020.

'Not in the Interest of Women Farmers!'. MahilaKisanAdhikarManch (MAKAAM), September 30, 2020.

Padhi, Ranjana. *Those Who Did Not Die: Impact of the Agrarian Crisis on Women in Punjab*. SAGE Publications India, 2012.

Pattnaik, Itishree, Kuntala Lahiri-Dutt, Stewart Lockie, and Bill Pritchard. 'The Feminization of Agriculture or the Feminization of Agrarian Distress? Tracking the Trajectory of Women in Agriculture in India'. *Journal of the Asia Pacific Economy* 23, no. 1 (2018): 138–155.

Ray, Raka. *Fields of Protest: Women's Movements in India*. University of Minnesota Press, 2000.

Salam, Zobia. '"We Have to Look After Our Homes as Well as the Movement": Women at Farmers' Protest'. *The Wire*, December 6, 2020. Accessed April 8, 2021. https://thewire.in/agriculture/women-farmers-protest-dilli-challo.

Schirmer, Jennifer. 'Those Who Die for Life Cannot Be Called Dead: Women and Human Rights Protest in Latin America'. *Feminist Review* 32 (1989): 3–29.

Schirmer, Jennifer. 'The Seeking of Truth and the Gendering of Consciousness: The CoMADRES of El Salvador and the Conavigua Widows of Guatemala' in '*Viva': Women and Popular Protest in Latin America*, edited by Sarah A. Radcliffe and Sallie Westwood, 30–65. London: Routledge, 1993.
Sharma, Shreya. 'Punjabi Dalit Women Fight Multiple Battles Rolled into One at Farmers Protest'. *Kaur Life*, February 24, 2021. Accessed January 10, 2022. https://kaurlife.org/2021/02/24/punjabi-dalit-women-fight-multiple-battles-rolled-into-one-at-farmers-protest/.
Shergill, Sunny. 'Meet the Women behind the Indian Farmers' Protests'. Agriculture | *Al Jazeera*, December 21, 2020. Accessed April 10, 2021. https://www.aljazeera.com/features/2020/12/21/meet-the-women-behind-the-indian-farmers-protests.
Singh, Avtar. 'Dalit Women Seek Implementation of Land Ceiling Act in Punjab'. *Hindustan Times*, September 21, 2021a. Accessed January 5, 2022. https://www.hindustantimes.com/cities/chandigarh-news/dalit-women-seek-implementation-of-land-ceiling-act-in-punjab-101632239593917.html.
Singh, Gian, Anupama Uppal, Gurinder Kaur, Rupinder Kaur, and Sukhvir Kaur. 'Indebtedness among Farmers and Agricultural Labourers in Rural Punjab'. *Economic and Political Weekly,* 52, no. 6 (2017): 51–57.
Singh, Mausami. 'Farmers' Protest: Women of Steel Lead the Way'. *India Today*, January 15, 2021b. Accessed April 8, 2021. https://www.indiatoday.in/india/story/farmers-protest-delhi-borders-women-protesters-grandmothers-mothers1759530-2021-01-15.
Singh, Navsharan. 'Women Farmers at the Delhi Protest Ask, 'What's for Us in These Laws?'. *Scroll*, January 18, 2021c. Accessed March 10, 2021. https://scroll.in/article/984300/women-farmers-at-the-delhi-protest-ask-whats-for-us-in-these-laws.
Singha Roy, Debal K. *Women in Peasant Movements: Tebhaga, Naxalite and After.* Manohar, 1992.
Sinha, Jignasa. 'Protest Site Draws "Sewa" – Medicine Stalls, Laundry Service, Temple & Library Come Up'. *The Indian Express*, December 11, 2020a. Accessed March 15, 2021. https://indianexpress.com/article/cities/delhi/protest-site-draws-sewa-medicine-stalls-laundry-service-temple-library-come-up-7100228/.
Sinha, Shreya. 'The Agrarian Crisis in Punjab and the Making of the Anti-Farm Law Protests'. *The India Forum*, November 28, 2020b. Accessed January 8, 2021. https://www.theindiaforum.in/article/agrarian-crisis-punjab-and-making-anti-farm-law-protests.
Suresh, Nidhi, and Shivangi Saxena. 'For Dalit Farm Protesters, Battle Continues to Confront Caste at Two Levels'. *Newslaundry*, December 13, 2021. Accessed January 5, 2022. https://www.newslaundry.com/2021/12/13/for-dalit-farm-protesters-battle-continues-to-confront-caste-at-two-levels.
Tagore, Anita. 'A Field of Solidarity and Protest'. *The Indian Express*, January 12, 2021. Accessed May 10, 2021. https://indianexpress.com/article/opinion/columns/farmers-protest-singhu-border-laws-7143741/.
Talwar, Sanskriti. 'How Women Farmers in Punjab Mobilised against the Farm Laws'. *BehanBox*, January 4, 2021. Accessed March 10, 2021. https://behanbox.com/2021/01/04/how-women-farmers-in-punjab-mobilised-against-the-farm-laws/.
Time Magazine. Double Issue. March 15, March 22, 2021.

Toor, Sangeet. 'Caught between Debt and Landlessness, Punjab's Protesting Women Assert Fight for Rights'. *The Caravan*, December 13, 2020a. Accessed February 20, 2021. https://caravanmagazine.in/commentary/farmers-protests-women-punjab-singhu-tikri-delhi-farm-bills

Toor, Sangeet. 'Women's partnership in the worker-farmers' movement'. *Trolley Times*, Volume 1, Edition 3, December 26, 2020b.

Trolley Times. Volume 1 Edition No. 2. December 22, 2020.

Trolley Times. Volume 1 Edition No. 3. December 26, 2020.

Tribune (2021) 'Women Activists Demand Safety at Protest Sites, Say Time to Look'. *The Tribune*, May 19, 2021. Accessed July 10, 2021. https://www.tribuneindia.com/news/punjab/women-activists-demand-safety-at-protest-sites-say-time-to-look-255253

Vernal, Triveni Goswami. 'Motherhood as a Space of Protest: Women and Armed Conflict in North-East India'. PhD diss., Gauhati University, 2015.

Index

Note: Page numbers followed by "n" denote endnotes.

For Product Safety Concerns and Information please contact our EU
representative GPSR@taylorandfrancis.com
Taylor & Francis Verlag GmbH, Kaufingerstraße 24, 80331 München, Germany

www.ingramcontent.com/pod-product-compliance
Ingram Content Group UK Ltd.
Pitfield, Milton Keynes, MK11 3LW, UK
UKHW022317250926
475702UK00046B/905

* 9 7 8 1 0 3 2 2 9 1 8 9 5 *